Lincoln Christian College

D1287429

RENDER UNTO CAESAR
THE FLAG-SALUTE CONTROVERSY

RENDER UNTO CAESAR

*THE
FLAG-
SALUTE
CONTRO-
VERSY*

DAVID R. MANWARING

THE UNIVERSITY OF CHICAGO PRESS

Chicago and London

Library of Congress Catalog Card Number: 62-13563

THE UNIVERSITY OF CHICAGO PRESS, CHICAGO 60637
The University of Chicago Press, Ltd., London W.C. 1

© *1962 by The University of Chicago. All rights reserved*
Published 1962. Second Impression 1968. Printed in the
United States of America

TO JANE

47033

PREFACE

On June 3, 1940, the Supreme Court of the United States held that public school authorities constitutionally could expel a child from school for refusing on sincere religious grounds to salute the American flag. On June 14, 1943, the Court over-ruled its previous holding and declared that no civilian, adult or child, could be compelled to salute the flag, nor subjected to disabilities for refusing to do so, whatever his reason for refusing. Behind this dramatic reversal of field lie two and a half decades of sporadic controversy culminating in a bitter eight-year legal struggle by Jehovah's Witnesses, the best or-ganized and most aggressive of America's non-saluting sects.

The legal controversy over the compulsory flag salute is worthy of intensive study from several directions. First, it is a classic example of group involvement in constitutional litiga-tion, differing from other prominent examples—e.g., the re-strictive covenant cases*—in that all of the groups involved were motivated by wholly non-economic considerations. Sec-ond, there is too little general or scholarly recognition of the potentially revolutionary impact of the flag-salute cases on our legal doctrine of religious freedom. Finally, the two sharply opposed decisions, occurring within the space of three years, provide an ideal setting for examination of the complex and *mutual* educational relationship between the Supreme Court and its various "publics."

I take the opportunity here to express my thanks to the many people who have helped me in this research. The United States Department of Justice kindly allowed me to examine a number of departmental materials; special thanks are due Mr. Arthur B. Caldwell, then head of the Civil Rights Section, for assistance and counsel at several stages of my work. The New

* See VOSE, CAUCASIANS ONLY (1959).

York office of the American Civil Liberties Union allowed me to browse about in their official minutes, and gave me invaluable assistance in finding my way through the Union's voluminous archives. School authorities of Minersville, Pennsylvania and the state of West Virginia gave me access to important documents and correspondence on the flag-salute cases, as did John B. McGurl, Jr., of Minersville, and William G. Fennell of New York City. A number of people on both sides of the flag-salute issue granted personal interviews, most noteworthy being the following: Hayden C. Covington of New York City, W. W. Trent, Horace S. Meldahl, Walter Barnett and Lucy, David and Louellan McClure of Charleston, West Virginia, Joseph W. Henderson of Philadelphia, and Walter Gobitas of Minersville. This book began as a doctoral dissertation at the University of Wisconsin. A special vote of thanks is due my mentor, Professor David Fellman, without whose advice, encouragement and supreme patience this project almost certainly would have been stillborn. Several fellowships from the University of Wisconsin and a predoctoral fellowship at the Brookings Institution greatly facilitated my work.

Finally, special mention must be made of my wife, to whom this book is dedicated, who has struggled through four versions of this work with me, and knows about as much about the flag-salute controversy as I do; and Roger, age eleven months, who helped not at all.

DAVID R. MANWARING

GENEVA, NEW YORK
January 1962

CONTENTS

PATRIOTISM IN THE SCHOOLS: THE FLAG-SALUTE CEREMONY   1

    The Schools and Citizenship Training
    The Flag-Salute Ceremony
    The Salute as an Educational Device: Pro and Con
    Early Religious Opposition to the Salute Ceremony
    Concluding Remarks

JEHOVAH'S WITNESSES: THE CHURCH MILITANT   17

    Doctrines
    God's Visible Organization: Organization and Resources
    Jehovah's Witnesses and Their Public
    Jehovah's Witnesses and the State

CONSTITUTIONAL SETTING: THE BACKGROUND OF PRECEDENT   35

    Substantive Due Process of Law
    Religious Freedom
    Free Speech: "Clear and Present Danger"
    Concluding Remarks

EARLY FLAG-SALUTE LITIGATION: 1935–1940   56

    Massachusetts
    Georgia
    New Jersey
    California
    Texas
    New York
    Florida
    Hinterland: States without Major Litigation
    Pennsylvania
    Concluding Remarks

THE *GOBITIS* CASE: IN THE LOWER COURTS   81

    Early Stages
    In the District Court: On Motion To Dismiss

In the District Court: Trial and Decision
In the Circuit Court of Appeals

THE *GOBITIS* CASE: IN THE SUPREME COURT   118
Briefs and Argument
Entr'acte: *Cantwell v. Connecticut*
The Decision
Concluding Remarks

INTERIM, 1940–1943: PRESS REACTION TO THE *GOBITIS* DECISION   148
Law Reviews and Related Scholarly Writings
Magazines
Newspapers
Concluding Remarks

INTERIM, 1940–1943: THE PERSECUTION OF JEHOVAH'S WITNESSES   163
The General Picture
Persecution Statistics: An Analysis
Organized Forces Involved
Jehovah's Witnesses in Court
Concluding Remarks

LEGAL DEVELOPMENTS ON THE FLAG-SALUTE ISSUE:
THE DECLINE OF *GOBITIS*   187
Further Spread of the Compulsory Flag Salute
Public Law 623
Attempts at Further Punishment: State Court Application
of the *Gobitis* Rule
Judicial Defiance of the *Gobitis* Precedent
Turning Point: The License Tax Cases

***GOBITIS* OVERRULED: THE *BARNETTE* CASE**   208
Beginning Stages: In the District Court
In the Supreme Court: Briefs and Argument
The Decision: *Gobitis* Overruled
Concluding Remarks

AFTER *BARNETTE*: THE FLAG-SALUTE CONTROVERSY IN RETROSPECT   236
Epilogue: Public Reception of the *Barnette* Decision
Later Years: *Barnette* as a Precedent
Looking Back

NOTES   255

INDEX   315

PATRIOTISM IN THE SCHOOLS
THE FLAG-SALUTE CEREMONY

A. *The Schools and Citizenship Training*

The adult character, it is generally agreed, is in large part determined by the training and experiences of childhood. Thus
the proper upbringing of its youth is of vital interest in any
society. Along with parents and the church, the school is expected to play its part in inducing those qualities—honesty,
sexual morality, industry, courtesy, etc.—which go to make
one a desirable and useful member of the group. In the United
States, the rise of compulsory education and the public school
has focused increasing interest on the school as a major pur-
veyor of those values which society (or the politically articulate portion thereof) considers important. Of particular concern to government is that bundle of civic virtues falling under the general appellation "good citizenship." On the one
hand, this implies a level of information: the good citizen is
well informed regarding national and local history, governmental structure, political issues, etc. On the other hand, it
implies a set of values: the good citizen is "loyal" and "patriotic." Strong and continuing legislative concern with both
these phases of citizenship training is evidenced by a stream
of legislation stretching over almost a century and including
every one of the forty-eight states.[1] As of 1940, every state required the public schools to give some sort of instruction in
the social studies—civics, American history, principles embodied in the United States Constitution, or some combination of
these.[2] Almost as many states had statutory provisions calling
for the inculcation of patriotism by the public schools.[3] There
was considerable variety among states. Some called for regular patriotic exercises;[4] some required specific periods of patriotic instruction;[5] some made the inculcation of patriotism

one of the general objectives of the teacher;[6] some imbedded
the requirement in teacher loyalty oaths;[7] some expressed it in
terms of flag respect.[8]

B. *The Flag-Salute Ceremony*

1. ORIGINS

It was logical that many attempts to inculcate patriotism in
school children should focus on the American flag. Flags ever
have been powerful patriotic symbols. The international incidents which have been touched off by discourtesy to a national
flag, or settled in part by a formal act of deference thereto,
need no documentation here. Further evidence of Americans'
attachment to the national emblem is the wide prevalence of
state laws penalizing "flag desecration" or the use of the flag
in advertising.[9]

For over a century there appears to have been no generally
accepted ceremony by which civilians might show their respect for the American flag. The modern ceremony originated
in 1892 as part of a campaign by the magazine *Youth's Companion* to stimulate patriotism in the schools. Two *Companion*
writers, Francis Bellamy and James B. Upham, hit upon the
idea of celebrating the quadricentennial of Columbus' discov-
ery of America with a mass tribute to the flag. Eventually,
Congress was prevailed upon to authorize, and President Harrison to issue, a proclamation declaring October 12, 1892, a
national holiday and calling for suitable observances in the
public schools.[10]

The original flag-salute ceremony proceeded as follows.
Those participating stood facing the flag and recited the following pledge: "I pledge allegiance to my flag and the Republic for which it stands, one nation indivisible, with liberty and
justice for all." At the words "to my flag," the right hand was
extended, palm up and slightly raised, toward the flag. This
position was held till the end of the pledge, after which the
arm was dropped to the side. Amendments approved at the
National Flag Conferences of 1923 and 1924 produced the
pledge familiar until recently: "I pledge allegiance to the
Flag of the United States of America and to the Republic for
which it stands; one nation, indivisible, with liberty and jus-

2

tice for all."[11] The similarity of the "stiff-arm" form of the salute to the hated Nazi salute led Congress in 1942 to provide that the salute should be rendered by placing the right hand over the heart.[12]

2. FLAG SALUTING IN SCHOOL: STATUTORY BASIS AND ACTUAL INCIDENCE

a) *Flag-salute statutes.*—The first "flag salute" statute was passed in 1898—on the day after the United States declared war on Spain—by the legislature of New York, and provided that

... It shall be the duty of the state superintendent of public instruction to prepare, for the use of the public schools of the state, a program providing for a salute to the flag at the opening of each day of school, and such other patriotic exercises as may be deemed by him to be expedient, under such regulations and instructions as may best meet the varied needs of the different grades in such schools.[13]

Similar statutes were passed by Rhode Island in 1901,[14] Arizona in 1903,[15] Kansas in 1907,[16] and Maryland in 1918.[17] It is not at all clear whether these laws were intended or interpreted to require local school authorities to use the program prepared by the state superintendent.[18]

After 1918, a quite different type of flag-salute law appeared. In 1919, apparently in reaction to the IWW disorders at Centralia,[19] the Washington state legislature decreed:

Every board of directors ... shall cause appropriate flag exercises to be held in every school at least once in each week at which exercises the pupils shall recite the following salute to the flag: "I pledge allegiance to my flag and the republic for which it stands, one nation indivisible, with liberty and justice for all."[20]

Failure of a school officer or teacher to carry out this provision was declared adequate ground for dismissal, and a punishable misdemeanor as well. Roughly similar laws were enacted by Delaware in 1925,[21] New Jersey in 1932,[22] and Massachusetts in 1935.[23] The changed temper reflected in these later laws is striking. Unlike the early statutes, which represented nothing more than benevolent meddling with the curriculum, they evidence strong legislative fears that without the stringent application of rewards and punishments, many teachers would not seek to inculcate loyalty and patriotism in their charges at all. This was a period of great concern over the dangers of "red" infiltration and subversion. The same legislative session that passed the Massachusetts flag-salute law also produced a statute exacting a special loyalty oath from all teachers.[24]

None of the flag-salute laws explicitly made the ceremony compulsory for the individual pupils. In view of the realities of educational procedure, however, a specific statement hardly was necessary. The state requirement that the local schools give such "instruction" gave them full authority to make it compulsory on the students. Furthermore, during the numbered grades, at least, there seldom is such a thing as an optional course or routine; the whole grade or "room" does everything together. At the high-school level, such exercises would take place in general school assembly, itself never an optional item. It is safe to assume that the legislators expected that all children would participate in the flag-salute ceremony, and that any refusals—and these undoubtedly were hard to imagine—would be dealt with as for any other rebellion against school routine.

b) General flag "instruction."—As of 1940, eighteen states had statutory provisions calling for some sort of *teaching* regarding the flag. Five of these seem pretty clearly to have contemplated regular use of the flag-salute ceremony; three called for instruction in flag saluting,[25] while two more called in varying language for instruction in flag respect through "appropriate ceremonial."[26] Most provided more generally for instruction in flag "use," "display," "respect," or "etiquette."[27] Six states merely required prospective teachers to swear that they would teach flag respect "by precept and example."[28] Finally, three states had legislation or legislative resolutions *encouraging* school authorities to make some use of the flag-salute ceremony.[29]

c) Incidence of the flag-salute ceremony.—As far as legal authority is concerned, the flag-salute ceremony certainly was an allowable part of the local school routine. Barring constitutional objections, it could be made compulsory in any state having some statutory provision respecting patriotism or the flag to which such a requirement might be related; absent this, it would depend on the particular state's education laws. School boards, standing temporarily in the place of the parents, have very broad discretionary power over the local school programs, channeled only in part by state law.

As to the actual incidence of the ceremony from state to state, the data are scarce and unsatisfactory; generally, documentation is available only in cases when somebody objected to participating in the salute. It seems safe to assume that the salute ceremony was used state-wide in the nine states having flag-salute statutes and in most of those requiring flag "instruction." The salute and pledge probably were in at least sporadic local use in every state. This writer was able to turn up some documentary evidence of local use of the ritual before 1940 in twenty-four states: California, Colorado, Connecticut, Delaware, Florida, Georgia, Idaho, Maryland, Massachusetts, New Hampshire, New Jersey, New York, Ohio, Oklahoma, Oregon, Pennsylvania, Texas, Vermont, Washington, Kansas, Minnesota, Nebraska, Virginia, and Wyoming.[30] In all but the last five of these states, the ceremony had been made compulsory at least in some localities. The results of a questionnaire circulated under the auspices of the American Civil Liberties Union seem to indicate that the flag-salute ceremony also was in use and compulsory in Arizona, Illinois, Iowa, Rhode Island, South Dakota, and West Virginia.[31]

That the thirty-state list set forth above is probably quite conservative is indicated by the meager statutory basis on which some localities had adopted the flag-salute ceremony. The ceremony was used locally in New Jersey, Ohio, and Pennsylvania long before those states had any relevant supporting legislation.[32]

C. The Salute as an Educational Device: Pro and Con

1. PRO: PATRIOTIC ORGANIZATIONS

Support for the flag-salute ceremony as a part of the school program, particularly after World War I, came mainly from the many and various citizens' organizations taking an active interest in overt displays of patriotism, or "Americanism." These groups left their marks on many aspects of the school curriculum. The activities of a few of the more noticeable of them are noted in the following paragraphs.[33]

a) The American Legion.—The American Legion (motto: "For God and Country") was founded in 1919 and remains the leading veterans' organization in the United States. One of its avowed purposes is to "foster and perpetuate a one hundred per cent Americanism."[34] At its first convention, the Legion set up a National Americanism Commission, among whose purposes was to "foster the teaching of Americanism in all schools."[35] The Legion has been especially active on the subject of flag respect. The first convention passed a resolution calling for state laws requiring that the flag be displayed at all public gatherings and during school hours over school buildings, and that at least ten minutes per day be allotted to patriotic exercises in all public and private schools.[36] The National Flag Conferences of 1923 and 1924 were held under the auspices of the National Americanism Commission,[37] and it was the Legion that proposed the first amendment to the original pledge of allegiance.[38] By 1924, an estimated six and a half million leaflet copies of the 1923 flag code already had been distributed free to school children, three million by the Legion itself.[39] The sixth national convention urged state legislatures to incorporate the amended flag code into public school curriculums.[40] In 1934, the sixteenth annual Legion convention passed a resolution urging state legislation to require daily flag-salute exercises in all public schools.[41] The Legion is given much credit for the passage of the Massachusetts flag-salute law.[42] Much of the organization's strength as a pressure group stems from the diligence and effectiveness with which local Legion posts push the national program.[43]

b) The Veterans of Foreign Wars.—The Veterans of Foreign Wars were organized on a national scale in 1913. In 1921, the VFW established a National Americanism Committee, one of whose purposes was "to educate posterity in the principles of true Americanism through publications and work in public schools and institutions." The VFW has shown continuing interest in modes of flag respect. The group claims primary credit for the adoption of "The Star-Spangled Banner" as the American national anthem. The VFW was represented at the National Flag Conferences, and had distributed some four million copies of the flag code to school children by 1931.[44] At the same time, the VFW motto, "One flag, one language, one country," seems to have been the basis of an alternative pledge of allegiance: "I give my hands and my heart and my head to God and my country; one country, one language, one flag."[45]

c) *The Ku Klux Klan.*—The modern version of the Ku Klux Klan was founded in 1915, "to keep eternally ablaze the sacred fire of a fervent devotion to a pure Americanism." While specializing mainly in white supremacy and xenophobia, the Klan found time for the sort of patriotic endeavor favored by the other citizens' groups. It was very active in attempts to secure legislation requiring display of the flag over school buildings. In 1925, the Klan specifically indorsed the 1923 flag code. Members of the Klan subsidiary, the Junior Order, received extensive instruction in flag etiquette.[46]

d) *DAR and other patriotic women's groups.*—The Daughters of the American Revolution organized officially in 1890. While their chief interest still lies in Revolutionary history and genealogy, they have shown an active interest in promoting present-day patriotism, especially through their Patriotic Education Committee.[47] The group's interest in flag respect has manifested itself in a number of ways. The DAR manual for new immigrants contains full instruction regarding flag etiquette and the pledge of allegiance.[48] Youthful members of a DAR subsidiary, the Children of the American Revolution, are instructed in the rules of flag respect and encouraged to promote respect for the flag and national anthem in their local communities.[49] The Daughters are reported to have been active in promoting the passage of the Massachusetts flag-salute statute.[50]

In 1927, the DAR and the American Legion Auxiliary joined to call a "Women's Patriotic Conference of National Defense." Among the actions of the conference were resolutions indorsing the 1923 flag code, urging Congress to adopt a resolution to the same effect and urging Congress to "declare and protect 'The Star-Spangled Banner' as the national anthem for all time."[51] Aside from the two sponsors, the composition of this conference is not clear. Reportedly, it was attended by representatives of thirty-three womens' organizations representing some two million women.[52]

e) *Other organizations.*—The Sons of the American Revolution have shown a lively interest in patriotic instruction. The group's National Committee on Patriotic Education claims credit for starting the movement to inaugurate June 14 as "Flag Day," as well as for the passage of laws in many states punishing improper use of the flag in advertising. The thirty-seventh SAR congress in 1926 advocated a "movement to standardize patriotic exercises in the schools of the country."[53] The Junior Order United American Mechanics, one of whose avowed purposes is to "teach . . . devotion to our country's flag," claims credit for the passage of state laws protecting the flag and requiring that it be displayed over school buildings.[54] The Order of DeMolay, a Mason subsidiary, in 1923 sharply criticized the parents of a Kansas youth who had refused for religious reasons to salute the flag.[55] The Massachusetts Elks Association claims to have been "largely responsible" for the passage of the Massachusetts flag-salute law.[56]

Not all of the groups listed above actively promoted use of the flag-salute ceremony in the public schools. Some taught children flag respect on their own, and others became interested only in reaction to attacks on the ceremony. Some organizations not listed here first entered the picture only after the acceleration of the flag-salute controversy in 1935. What all these groups had in common was that all were satisfied that the ceremony was a fine idea in itself, and were predisposed to take unkindly any opposition to the ritual, whatever the source or reason.

It is hard to evaluate the total influence of the patriotic organizations. According to one authority, only the American Legion exercised substantial and continuing influence over public school curriculums.[57] Still, much smaller and weaker groups have been effective on occasions; a glance at the growing list of special "days" in the schools will illustrate the point.[58] Most of the groups listed above probably were influential in some states, weak in others. Certainly their cumulative effect was considerable.

2. CON: THE TEACHING PROFESSION

Early opposition to flag-salute laws and parallel statutory provisions seems to have been generally weak and sporadic. The ceremony itself was clearly a desirable one, and most people suffered no direct injury from its mandatory inclusion in the school program. The flag-salute statutes acted primarily as restrictions on the freedom of action of the teachers, and were resented as such. Aside from the implied insult which it carried, the requirement of regular flag ceremonies was viewed as just one more item on a long list of harassments which included a flood of special holiday observances (Arbor Day, General Pulaski Day, etc.), required instruction in temperance and kindness to animals, mandatory Bible reading, and so on.[59] Objections were few and cautious, however; there were many more serious grievances about which its was relatively safer (because less easily misconstrued) to complain. It is not surprising that very little of the criticism that did appear in print came from mere teachers, and that it focused entirely on the ceremony's pedagogical effectiveness, eschewing any objection to flag saluting as such.

Aside from a few side comments,[60] discussion of the educational merits of the flag-salute ceremony was concentrated in a half-dozen articles, five at least impliedly criticizing the ceremony, one defending it. Three articles asserted that rote repetition of the pledge of allegiance by the whole class was leaving pupils with highly distorted impressions of the pledge itself. Two of these, appearing in 1936 and 1937, rested their case on a roster of horrible examples produced when pupils were asked to write down what they had been saying every day, including such gems as "I pledge a legion . . . ," "connation, invisible . . . ," "one nation in the visible [vestibule] . . . ," "with liberty and jesta straw."[61] A more sophisticated approach was taken in 1941 by Professor Herbert T. Olander of the University of Pittsburgh.[62] By having pupils write both their version of the pledge and an interpretation in their own words of what the pledge meant, he was able to establish a positive correlation between comprehension of the pledge and the ability to write it correctly. His survey of some 2,883 pupils confirmed the bleak conclusion of the earlier articles.

"Apparently," he commented, "the method of having children merely repeat orally the vow of allegiance to their country has decided limitations."[63]

A fourth article, while readily conceding the validity of the findings of these surveys, sharply criticized the conclusions drawn therefrom. "If it is jargon to the child," wrote Gary Cleveland Myers, "the teacher is to blame." "How often in university classes," he complained, "or at teachers' institutes one hears an 'educator' make fun of the flag salute. He might as well make fun of the flag."[64]

A more cogent objection to the "jargon" criticism would have been that it was based on the mistaken assumption that the purpose of the pledge of allegiance was to communicate to the intellect. Actually the flag ceremony, with its solemn trappings, unmistakable symbolism and mass participation, was designed to produce a purely *emotional* response. In this objective it probably was quite successful.

The other two articles attacked regular flag saluting on a more fundamental level. W. C. Ruediger of George Washington University argued that constant repetition of the pledge in school could only impair its emotional value by producing plain *boredom*. "This routine repetition makes the flag-saluting ceremony perfunctory and so devoid of feeling; . . . Furthermore, needless compulsory routine tends to set up in some minds an antagonistic attitude. . . ."[65] The other article, by Harold Benjamin, argued that the preoccupation of teachers and parents with the flag salute tended to distract attention from the real business of inculcating patriotism. "As parents and teachers let us not make the pitiful error of thinking we can produce that quality of citizenship by a flag-waving magic. To teach patriotism is a hard and complex job. . . ."[66]

It should be noted that only Ruediger's article actually opposed regular flag saluting; the others claimed or admitted only that such repetition was inadequate by itself to produce patriotism. These articles did make it clear, however, that the flag ceremony, as administered in most schools, was in fact a perfunctory and hence ineffective routine. Furthermore, whatever the disclaimers of the authors, their demonstration of the ineffectiveness of the flag salute standing alone was a tacit refutation of the case for making this exercise a required part of the school program. Finally, the Myers article seems to indicate that this implied refutation enjoyed wide, if unpublicized, currency among professional educators.

D. *Early Religious Opposition to the Salute Ceremony*

Religious opposition to the flag-salute ceremony probably is as old as the ceremony itself. Such opposition does not appear to have led to an open clash with school authorities until 1918. By 1929 there had been at least ten such instances in eight states, involving at least four religious sects. One of the most important results of these clashes was the appearance of the American Civil Liberties Union as a declared opponent of the compulsory flag salute, ready to offer legal aid to any religious objector to the ceremony.

1. THE MENNONITES

The Mennonites comprise a small, extremely fragmented sect, conservative in social standards and uncompromisingly pacifist.[67] Their opposition to war was at the root of their unwillingness to participate in the flag-salute ceremony. In the words of one spokesman,

> We love peace, we desire to be true to the entire New Testament which we feel teaches nonresistance, also that we shall love our enemies, which makes it impossible for us to take any part in promoting war. Pledging allegiance to a flag as we see it, though we honor and respect it, at least implies a pledge to defend it against all its enemies, which would mean to resort to arms and to take human life.[68]

The Mennonites' first recorded brush with the flag salute came in 1918 when Ora Troyer was prosecuted in West Liberty, Ohio, for failing to keep his nine-year-old foster daughter in school. The girl had been sent home repeatedly for refusing, on his instructions, to participate in the regular flag-salute ceremony. Convicted and fined in the local mayor's court, Troyer appealed to the Logan County Court of Common Pleas. He raised no constitutional objections, alleging only that he had complied with the school laws by sending his child to school each morning. The court overruled this plea, noting that Troyer had, by his instructions, made it impossible for her to attend in compliance with the rules. The judge went on to denounce Troyer's position in strong terms:

. . . The child was told by defendant below not to salute . . . in the time of war. . . . Such conduct on the part of our citizens is not conscionable, for conscience would lead to respect for government and to its defense, especially in time of war, but rather it is the forerunner of disloyalty and treason. . . .[69]

In 1926, a Mennonite boy refused to participate in the flag ceremony of a school in Oklahoma. After some controversy, he appears to have been allowed to come to school *after* the opening flag exercises.[70]

On February 15, 1928, the Delaware State Board of Education ruled that under that state's flag-salute law all public school children must participate in the regular flag exercises.[71] Shortly thereafter, the Greenwood public schools expelled thirty-eight Mennonite children for their refusal to comply. The Mennonites opened private classes in the church basement, meanwhile making futile attempts to persuade the local school board to reverse its decision.[72] The American Civil Liberties Union was eager to bring a court action on behalf of the expelled children, challenging the constitutionality of the state flag-salute law.[73] The idea had to be abandoned, however, since the Mennonites' doctrine of non-resistance would not allow them to act as plaintiffs in a court of law.[74]

2. THE JEHOVITES

The Jehovites, or "children of Israel," were a small sect of about five or six hundred members, concentrated in the area around Denver, Colorado, and apparently held together only by the magnetic personality of their leader, one "Joshua Jehovah." Considering themselves descendants of ten of the twelve tribes of Israel,[75] members of the sect all took the surname of *Jehovah* or *Jahveh*, and computed their ages from the dates of their conversions. The Jehovites viewed the flag salute and all other ceremonies as idolatrous. Their religious tenets forbade them to serve as parties plaintiff in any earthly court.[76]

Up to 1926, the flag-salute ceremony had been used only sporadically in the Denver public schools. Early in that year, however, the Jehovites formally announced that their children would refuse to give the salute. An aroused school board then told at least twelve Jehovite pupils to salute or stay home.[77] Expulsions continued apace until April, 1926, when some fifty Jehovite children were out of school.[78] Appeals to the county superintendent and the State Board of Education proved fruitless.[79]

It was this conflict which first led to the involvement of the American Civil Liberties Union in the flag-salute controversy. In late April, 1926, the ACLU retained the Denver firm of Whitehead and Vogl to seek a court test of the Denver rule and the resulting expulsions.[80] The proposed test was blocked, however, by the Jehovites' conscientious inability to serve as plaintiffs. The next few months were occupied with futile attempts either to work out a mutually satisfactory compromise or to find a way into court without Jehovite plaintiffs.[81]

The stalemate ended abruptly in the fall of 1926 when, simultaneously, the dominant figure on the local school board moved away[82] and the Jehovites quietly agreed to furnish plaintiffs if necessary.[83] When school reopened in September, the Jehovite children enrolled without incident.[84] The ACLU celebrated this "victory" with a bristling press release which put the Union on record as ready to fight any attempt to exact the flag salute against religious objections.[85]

3. THE ELIJAH VOICE SOCIETY: THE TREMAIN COMMITMENT

The Elijah Voice Society was a small group of followers of Charles Taze Russell which broke away from the main Russellite movement in 1918 in protest against the changes instituted by Russell's successor, Joseph F. Rutherford.[86] Members of the society based their unwillingness to salute the flag mainly on their absolute refusal to recognize the authority of any earthly government.[87] A second ground was the alleged militaristic tendency of the ceremony: "[N]ational patriotism tends toward militarism and war...."[88]

On September 8, 1925, Mr. and Mrs. J. W. Tremain, members of the Elijah Voice Society, withdrew their nine-year-old son, Russell, from school after school authorities refused to excuse him from participation in the flag exercises.[89] On September 16, Tremain was arrested on a charge of contributing to the delinquency of his son. At his trial, he refused to recognize the court's jurisdiction and made no defense.[90] He was convicted and served eight days in jail in lieu of a twenty-five dollar fine.[91] While Tremain was still in jail, Russell was taken from his home and placed in a detention home;[92] later he was transferred to the State Children's Home.[93] On June 4, 1926, Judge Brown of the juvenile court awarded permanent custody of the boy to the state institution, with full authority to put him up for adoption. Referring to the parents' anti-salute teachings, he commented, "If such an act on the part of the parents is not placing the child in danger of growing up to lead an idle, dissolute or immoral life, then I am unable to understand what would be."[94]

The American Civil Liberties Union entered the field in July, 1926, with dire threats of immediate litigation,[95] but found itself unable to get into court. The Tremains refused even to defend themselves in court, to say nothing of suing; and there simply was no form of legal action which could be pursued without their co-operation.[96] The ensuing stalemate was punctuated only by the persistent efforts of Dr. Sidney Strong, a Seattle minister, to secure a compromise which would return Russell to his parents. It proved impossible to find any public school in Bellingham, nearby Seattle, or elsewhere in the area, which would allow Russell to attend without saluting the flag.[97] For reasons which are unclear, the Tremains balked at a compromise, approved by Judge Brown, which would have restored Russell to their custody on condition that they place him in a public or private school (private schools in the area did not require the salute).[98]

Finally, on November 28, 1927, the Bellingham juvenile court ordered Russell returned to his parents on condition that they place him in a public or private school.[99] Obviously, something in the situation must have changed to make this compromise possible after all. It is not recorded whether Russell then enrolled at a private or public school.

4. THE CHURCH OF GOD

Two flag-salute incidents involved members of the Church of God. Little is known about this group; indeed, it is not entirely clear that the same Church of God was involved in the

CHAPTER TWO

JEHOVAH'S WITNESSES
THE CHURCH MILITANT

The sect now known as Jehovah's Witnesses[1] originated in 1870 in Pittsburgh, Pennsylvania, as a small Bible class under the lead of "Pastor" Charles Taze Russell.[2] Today the Witnesses constitute a multi-corporate, tightly run army of missionaries, with over 700,000 members proselytizing in almost every country of the world.[3] The sect has had three leaders, each of whom has left his mark on the movement. Russell (1870–1916), the founder, established what has remained the basic theology of the movement and set the precedent for its heavy reliance on the printed word for missionary purposes. "Judge" Joseph Franklin Rutherford (1916–42), previously Russell's legal aid,[4] instituted several major revisions in Russell's theology which led to a complete revamping of the sect's orientation, organization, and methods. Under his leadership the Witnesses became militant, defiant, and non-saluting. It is with the Witnesses under Rutherford that the balance of this chapter will deal. The present leader, Nathan Homer Knorr, has worked to prepare the Witnesses for a more or less permanent existence in the world. Under his leadership, they have become less combative, mellower in their outlook on the world—in a word, more "respectable."

A. *Doctrines*

Jehovah's Witnesses, probably more than any other denomination, base *all* their actions on their religious beliefs. Their creed is an all-encompassing affair, purporting to explain all human history, to predict the certain course of the future, and to point out to the individual exactly how he must conduct his life to achieve salvation. The Witnesses consider God's whole plan for mankind to be revealed in the Bible, which, properly read, is true and consistent throughout.[5] God caused the Scriptures to be written in cryptic, metaphorical language, different passages of which are relevant to different historical periods and addressed to different generations.[6] The guidance necessary to understand the Bible, and hence God's current intentions, is available only from God Himself, speaking through His chosen agents, the Witness leadership.[7]

Witness theology centers around the imminent violent end of this evil world, largely as forecast in the book of Revelation. In tempting Adam and Eve, Satan challenged Jehovah's supremacy, claiming that He could not place anyone on earth who would remain faithful in the face of Satanic opposition. Jehovah refrained from destroying Satan immediately, and even left him in full charge of earthly affairs, so that this boast might be put to a fair test.[8] The crux of the Witness message is that Satan's time—and ours—is running out. Many examples of human integrity—e.g., Abel, Noah, and the current Witnesses—have amply refuted Satan's main claim.[9] By dying on the cross, Christ won back mankind's lost right to physical immortality, thus setting the stage for the restoration of the original divine scheme.[10] The signs predicted in Matthew 24:5–14 have all come to pass in the last several decades.[11] At the great battle of Armageddon, to be fought in this generation, the heavenly forces led by Christ will take Satan prisoner and utterly destroy all his works, his demon cohorts and the vast majority of mankind who will have given him their allegiance. None will be spared but the faithful—i.e., Jehovah's Witnesses. The earth will be restored to its Edenic splendor, and a substantial portion of those who died in earlier ages will be resurrected and made physically perfect and immortal. After a thousand years of peace under Christ's rule, Satan will be released for a short time to tempt the people once more; then he and all who follow him will be destroyed. Those remaining faithful will live on forever under the direct rule of Jehovah.[12] Such is the Witnesses' hope.

While this general world view has remained unchanged, the Witnesses' picture of their own role has altered radically and decisively since World War I. Russell pictured the sect as comprising the last remnant of the 144,000 saints chosen from birth to rule with Christ in Heaven after Armageddon. Members of this small group were distinguished by their saintly character and their ability to comprehend and accept Russell's message.[13] Widespread proselytization would be pointless; most of humanity, virtuous or evil, must die at Armageddon and be resurrected for a second chance during the millennium.[14] Russell did virtually all the preaching, as he sought to call out all the "elect" before the onset of Armageddon, which, by a variety of calculations, he had placed sometime in 1914.[15] The failure of Christ's legions to put in an appearance in 1914 left Russell's successor with a bit of explaining to do if the movement was to hold together.[16] "Judge" Rutherford met the crisis with a major doctrinal innovation, the concept of the "Jonadab" class.[17] The elect are saints from birth, but there is a much larger group of people who have sinned much, not through evil intent but through ignorance and wrong training. These too can be saved from the horrors of Armageddon, if they will foresake their evil ways and join God's organization (Jehovah's Witnesses) before the onset, after which repentance is cheap. They must remain in this "city of refuge" and abide by all the rules therein until after the battle, when they will go, not to Heaven with the elect, but to the newly restored earth, to begin repopulating it prior to the general resurrection of the dead.[18] The Jonadab concept revolutionized Witness values and practices. The great task remaining before the end is to call out the Jonadabs. Every human being in the world must have a chance to choose sides, either for or against God's organization.[19] This means personal ministry. Each Witness, elect or Jonadab, is expected to devote every bit of time, money and effort he can spare from making a decent living to the spreading of the "good news" of the coming kingdom.[20] Every Witness is an ordained minister with a duty to preach;[21] his congregation is the whole non-Witness world. The Witnesses' organization, worship and morality revolve closely about the "witness work."

The Jonadab concept also is central to the extreme narrowing and stiffening of the Witness standards of behavior. While the truth was considered receivable only by a chosen few, unbelievers bore no more fault than their equally ignorant ancestors, and Russell could speak of a general resurrection of all the dead.[22] But if the truth is receivable by anyone not actually evil at heart, then those who reject the Witness message affirmatively cast their lot with Satan. These will perish at Armageddon and can expect no resurrection; they have had their chance.[23] In effect, then, the Witness preachers are performing more than a mission of mercy; they are the instruments through which Christ carries out the last judgment. The same rigid, "one chance" rule applies to the Witnesses themselves. A Witness who backslides in any substantial matter of doctrine or conduct is doomed beyond hope of redemption. Both elect and Jonadabs are pictured as being in a *covenant* with Jehovah, with specified duties and rewards; non-performance in any respect nullifies the contract.[24]

This view of salvation is noteworthy for its simplicity, certainty, and relative absence of spiritual content. Obedient Witnesses in good standing are automatically saved; everyone else is doomed. The non-spiritual aspect is heightened by the nature of the Witnesses' hope: the vast majority are Jonadabs, who joined the movement for reasons of physical safety and expect a purely physical reward—eternal life on earth.

B. *God's Visible Organization: Organization and Resources*

1. MEMBERSHIP: NUMBERS AND CHARACTERISTICS

Information on the numbers, distribution and characteristics of Jehovah's Witnesses is very sketchy, largely because of the extreme secretiveness of the Witnesses themselves, especially under Rutherford.[25] In recent years there have been published reports on the average numbers actually engaged in preaching. On the basis of these figures, the *active* Witness membership in 1938 numbered at least 28,400 in the United States, and more than 72,000 world-wide.[26] In 1943, the respective figures were in excess of 72,200 and 137,000.[27] At the end of 1955, the figures were 187,120 and 642,929.[28] This by no means exhausts the number of people who consider themselves Witnesses; convention attendance often doubles or trebles the estimated active membership.[29] There is a much wider circle of "fellow travelers" who subscribe to the sect's doctrinal magazine but take no active part in the movement.[30]

Only subjective estimates are possible as to the types of

people who become Jehovah's Witnesses. On the whole, they seem to include a fairly faithful cross section of the general population. The typical Witness, however, is likely to be somewhat below average in wealth, education and talent.[31] Witness membership also has an unusually high percentage of men and old people.[32] The educational level was especially low under Rutherford, who was openly skeptical of the value of secular education beyond the bare essentials of literacy.[33] Those who join and remain in the movement are fired with a zeal that is incredible to the outsider.[34] Their heretofore dull, tangled lives have become meaningful and challenging. They are soldiers of the Lord in a great struggle and have only to give unflinching obedience to be absolutely certain of sharing in the great victory. They expect and welcome persecution as a divinely permitted test of their faith.[35]

2. ORGANIZATION

Jehovah's Witnesses carry out their mundane affairs through a series of corporations, only two of which—both based in Brooklyn, New York—need concern us here. The Watch Tower Bible and Tract Society, founded in Pittsburgh in 1884,[36] is the "principal" corporation of the movement, referred to reverently as "the Society" by rank-and-file Witnesses. During the period under study it had a genuinely "grass roots" basis, and its president was elected annually by the whole membership.[37] Less conspicuous but more important is the Watchtower Bible and Tract Society, Inc., established in New York in 1909 to handle the sect's expanding business affairs.[38] Rutherford, who handled the details, thoughtfully gave this corporation a self-perpetuating membership of about forty loyal supporters[39] and gave its president a life term and untrammeled control of corporation affairs.[40] This corporation owns all the sect's physical properties in the United States.[41] During Russell's life, such formal details were irrelevant. His personality dominated the general course of the movement; details were left to the democratically run local chapters.

Lacking Russell's personal force, and envisaging a great expansion of the movement and its activities, "Judge" Rutherford took strong steps to convert this loose organization into a centralized, disciplined machine completely responsive to the head man, whoever he might be. With his absolute control over the New York corporation, and hence over the all-important publishing establishment, he quite easily reduced the more democratic Pennsylvania corporation to a sort of satellite status;[42] elections in the latter body have been meaningless at least since 1930.[43] In the meantime, nationally appointed representatives made steady encroachments on the prerogatives of the democratically chosen local leaders. Witnesses were encouraged to see the great struggle as being between God's and Satan's *organizations*.[44] Rutherford legitimized an accomplished fact in 1938 by publishing scriptural proofs showing that Christ was personally directing God's organization and that all officers properly should be appointed by him through his chosen agents in the national office.[45] The vast majority of Witnesses—who have never shown much interest in running their own affairs—accepted this final loss of local automony with great enthusiasm.[46]

In the "theocratic" reorganization of 1938, Rutherford set up a smoothly functioning, quasi-military organization. The United States was divided into six regions, each under a "regional servant." Below these there were 154 zones, under "zone servants." Each congregation, or "company," was run by a "company servant," who was responsible to his respective zone servant. The zone servants wielded very broad discretionary powers over the local companies and were key figures in maintaining discipline and pushing forward with the witness work.[47] With the tighter organization came greater stress on individual discipline and conformity. The national office has an extremely efficient surveillance network capable of quickly seeking out and punishing any Witness lagging in his work or his faith.[48]

3. THE WITNESS WORK

Jehovah's Witnesses proselytize almost entirely through the medium of the printed word. Other media—radio, sound truck, individual Witness persuasiveness—are utilized for the sole purpose of getting into the hands of prospective converts books or magazines setting forth the sect's biblical interpretations. The Witnesses' own printing plant turns out large numbers of books and pamphlets and two semi-monthly magazines:

the *Watchtower*, the theological organ, and *The Golden Age* (renamed *Consolation* in 1937),[49] a sort of newsletter. Witness literature is generally *sold*, although individual Witnesses often will give away smaller items for the sake of making a placement, especially with a new prospect.[50] The alleged profitableness of the witness work is a matter of dispute.[51] The Society's claim that it takes a loss on its literature[52] is weakened by its use of low-cost Witness labor,[53] its seven-figure annual turnover,[54] and the total secrecy surrounding its finances.[55] The point is a moot one; the Society's money resources are limited only by the total resources of all the members, who have never failed to come to its aid in time of financial need.[56]

From the beginning, Jehovah's Witnesses have spread their message primarily by going from door to door with their literature, and trying to persuade the householder to accept some.[57] Since 1928, this form of witnessing has been concentrated on Sunday, the only day open to Witnesses holding full-time jobs.[58] In February, 1940, the Witnesses inaugurated the practice of street-corner witnessing; on weekends and assorted evenings, one or two workers would station themselves on each street corner of a downtown section, bearing specially designed magazine bags, sometimes calling out their message or carrying placards.[59]

Other attempts to attract the attention of the masses centered around "Judge" Rutherford's great oratorical talents. Fifteen-minute transcribed Bible lectures went out over a radio network of several hundred stations until a widespread Catholic boycott campaign—provoked by Rutherford's virulent anti-Catholicism—forced abandonment of the venture in 1937. From about 1935 through the mid-1940's, standard equipment of every Witness missionary was a portable phonograph with a set of recorded lectures. The sound truck also has seen use.[60]

Special mention must be made of the annual convention, attended diligently by the great majority of Witnesses.[61] Besides furnishing the occasions for major doctrinal revelations, these gatherings directly promote the witness work; the thousands of conventioners spend all their spare time distributing new publications just made available, thus saturating the large convention city to a degree otherwise impossible.[62] During most of the period under study, the Witnesses held their national convention on a multi-city basis, with speeches at the key city reaching subsidiary conventions by radio-telephone.[63]

C. *Jehovah's Witnesses and Their Public*

1. THE WITNESSES: ATTITUDE AND BEHAVIOR

The outstanding characteristic of the Witnesses under Rutherford was their total alienation from the world about them. More than either Russell or Knorr, Rutherford pushed the social implications of Witness theology to their full bitter extent.[64] This world has been ruled by Satan ever since the Fall; all its institutions are under his control and are wholly evil.[65] Rutherford listed God's enemies under the headings of religion (specially defined as the worship of powers other than Jehovah), commerce and politics, the first of these being dominant. Every wielder of governmental, economic or ecclesiastical power is either an agent or a dupe of the archfiend.[66] Therefore, there is no hope of improving man's lot through merely human efforts at charity or political reform; men of good will can better devote their energy to preparing for and announcing the coming of the new kingdom.[67]

The primary target of Witness enmity is the Roman Catholic Church, described by Rutherford as "the chief visible enemy of God, and therefore the greatest and worst public enemy."[68] As the dominant religious force during most of what the Witnesses regard as nineteen centuries of apostasy, the Church is the obvious candidate to serve as the tangible earthly villain essential to this sort of movement. Jehovah's Witnesses see the hierarchy as the center of a vast conspiracy to silence the message of the coming kingdom by "getting" Jehovah's Witnesses;[69] every hostile gesture from whatever source is by definition Catholic-inspired.[70] It must be said that the Church did or condoned much to strengthen the Witnesses' devil theories. The great effectiveness of the radio boycott campaign and the active participation of priests and bishops[71] were highly suggestive to the suggestible. A stronger case in point was the activity of a group calling itself the "Defenders of the Faith," in Pilot Grove, Missouri, whose main occupation seems to have been a systematic campaign of personal villification aimed at Russell and Rutherford.[72]

Witness attacks on the outside world, especially during Rutherford's last decade, proceeded on two levels. Rutherford himself, in his books and the *Watchtower* (written entirely by him),[73] kept his attacks on a general, almost pedantic level. Quite a different tone was set by *The Golden Age*, almost entirely written by C. W. Woodworth and restrained only sporadically by the Witness legal office.[74] Woodworth pitched his appeal at the lowest possible intellectual level, lashing out at a wide variety of pet grievances, ranging from aluminum cookware[75] and soft drinks[76] to NRA[77] and interest on loans.[78] While he struck out at all religious denominations,[79] Woodworth naturally reserved his choicest venom for the Catholic church. He made most effective use of straight ridicule aimed at the Church's alleged preoccupation with money—with much deadpan quoting of price lists for masses, prayers, medals, etc.[80]—and the alleged femininity of clerical garb—referring to "the girls" and their "lingerie" and "petticoats."[81] Woodworth could not stop with ridicule, however; *The Golden Age* was filled with lurid charges of clerical immorality and criminality.[82] Finally there was a constant stream of personal vituperation directed by name at all who incurred the Witnesses' bad favor.[83]

While Witnesses have always been admonished to be meek and law-abiding, it was understandably difficult for them to act civilly toward such despicable people as those described in the oracular literature they were distributing. Any potential conflict was dispelled, however, by a series of revelations by Rutherford in the 1930's. The witness work has two purposes: to call forth those who can and will be saved, *and* to serve notice on the rest of evil mankind of Jehovah's intentions toward them.[84]

God permits the religionists to exist in their practice for a short time . . . to the end that they might receive torment, and this they receive by having their "religious susceptibilities shocked."[85]

This dual task, moreover, was to be carried out regardless of any obstruction from public or private sources. As early as 1929, Rutherford had revealed that the admonition in Romans

13:1–7 regarding submission to the "higher powers," and parallel references in Hebrews 13:17 and I Peter 13, 14, refer not to any earthly government, but to Jehovah, Christ and their representatives in the Brooklyn offices of the Watchtower Society.[86] Matthew 10:23 ("when they persecute you in one town, flee to the next") later was pronounced irrelevant now that Satan had been cast out of Heaven.[87] Finally, in 1940, Rutherford rejected pacifism as a rule of conduct for his Witnesses. While not volunteering violence, they might resist as violently as necessary when threatened with personal injury or destruction of witnessing materials.[88]

Hardly spectacular in themselves, these pronouncements had an explosive effect on Witness behavior. The Witnesses believe firmly that nothing is revealed to them without a definite purpose. They readily became convinced that their divinely sanctioned work was properly subject to no restraints of time, place or propriety whatever; to make any concessions to public convenience and order would be an affront to Jehovah. Anyway, objections could come only from the very "opposers" marked out for "torment."[89] The resulting abuses are easy to document: hyperaggressive doorstep witnessing which often bordered on housebreaking,[90] single-file parades on a busy main street,[91] offensively loud sound trucks,[92] etc. In short, during the period under study, the offensive character of the Witnesses' message was fully matched by the irritating manner in which it was disseminated.

2. LEGAL OBSTRUCTION: 1928–39

Local hostility to the witness work manifested itself soon after the decision to concentrate door-to-door canvassing on Sunday; the first arrests took place in 1928, in South Amboy, New Jersey.[93] Before 1940, the Witnesses' growing quarrel with local government centered mainly along the eastern seaboard, with the chief battlefield being the state of New Jersey.[94] The main charges brought against the Witnesses were selling or peddling without a license, carrying on worldly business on the Sabbath and disturbing the peace. In the late 1930's, they also ran afoul of early versions of the now famous "group libel" statutes. The permit ordinances were especially troublesome to the Witnesses. Some were bona fide attempts to identify canvassers and regulate time, place and manner of canvassing. Others made a virtual censor of the licensing authority. This was all beside the point to the Witnesses, who refused to apply for *any* permit; such submission would be an insult to the Almighty.[95]

The growing flood of arrests led in 1935 to the re-establishment of the legal department, which had lain dormant since Rutherford's accession to the presidency.[96] Olin R. Moyle, himself a Witness, who already had won several permit cases, was brought in from Wisconsin to serve as full-time legal counsel.[97] The legal department was and is decentralized, consisting of the chief counsel, several assistants and clerical help in Brooklyn, and a large number of attorneys—all Witnesses—scattered about the country.[98]

While the legal department handled some especially important trials, Witness defendants generally were expected to conduct their own defenses at the trial level, following a standard set of instructions issued by the Society.[99] If convicted, they uniformly refused to pay fines, going to jail in preference.[100] At least by 1933, the Society adopted the policy of appealing all adverse court decisions.[101] All appeals were handled by attorneys in the legal department; representatives from Brooklyn took personal charge of especially important cases.

In their early appeals, Witness lawyers relied exclusively on freedom of religion in their briefs, arguing that the various antipeddling ordinances could not constitutionally be applied against the distribution of religious tracts.[102] For reasons that will be developed in the next chapter, this argument got nowhere during the 1930's. Once the Witnesses managed to push it as far as the United States Supreme Court, only to lose out in a *per curiam* memorandum decision.[103]

The turning point came in the 1938 case of *Lovell v. Griffin*,[104] when the Witnesses first invoked freedom of the press. The issue was first raised in the *amicus curiae* brief of the Workers' Defense League, and found its way from there into Moyle's brief.[105] The Supreme Court held unanimously that a permit ordinance vesting virtually untrammeled discretion in the licensing authority could not constitutionally be applied to the distribution of literature. A year later, in *Schneider v.*

Irvington,[106] the Court struck down four more local ordinances as violative of freedom of the press. Three of these prohibited all leaflet distribution on the public streets, ostensibly to prevent littering. This was held to be too insubstantial a public interest to justify such a stringent restraint.

Litigation aside, Jehovah's Witnesses developed a number of practical devices for discouraging or side-stepping official harassment. Most spectacular of these was the "locust" technique, whereby Witnesses would descend upon a hostile town in numbers large enough to canvass the whole population before the police could get into action. Seventy-eight fully motorized battalions, consisting of some 12,600 specially trained volunteers, were held in readiness to deal with recalcitrant communities anywhere in the United States.[107] After 1937, the Witnesses also turned to evasive tactics—e.g., offering literature for "no fixed contribution," or dispensing with literature altogether on first contacts (the most dangerous phase) in favor of phonograph lectures.[108] Observing the rough and ready character of much local justice, Witnesses also took stenographic records of all trials and gave wide publicity to any abuses.[109]

By 1939, the Witnesses' local troubles seemed definitely to be on the decline. They suffered only 471 arrests in 1938, as contrasted to a peak of 1,149 in 1936.[110] Moreover, aside from Connecticut, which still was plying its "group libel" law,[111] the seaboard states were abandoning the struggle.[112] The largest factor in the decline seems to have been sheer exhaustion engendered by the "locust" technique and the volume and increasing success of Witness litigation in the state courts.[113] The *Lovell* and *Schneider* decisions came more as climaxes than causes of the trend; they put the anti-Witness forces once and for all on the defensive. While the Witnesses remained as irritating as ever, overt public hostility might have died out in time, had no new stimuli appeared. When Jehovah's Witnesses' feud with the world exploded into violence in 1940, the igniting sparks were the tension attending the onset of World War II[114] and the resurgence of the controversy over the Witnesses' refusal to salute and pledge allegiance to the American flag.

D. *Jehovah's Witnesses and the State*

1. GENERAL

Jehovah's Witnesses reject as hopelessly evil all governments now in existence, as well as any others that human efforts may create.[115] At Armageddon, Jehovah will destroy all existing states and establish his kingdom—the only possible "good" government.[116] While comparatively the best in the world, the United States government is still completely under Satan's thumb and must be destroyed with the rest.[117] This proposition has proved hard for many American Witnesses to accept; in 1941, Rutherford found it necessary again to insist that both the Axis powers and the United States must be swept away at Armageddon—then expected momentarily.[118]

Jehovah's Witnesses can be said to be loyal to the extent that the state rightfully can demand, and no further. They are scrupulously law-abiding within the limitations of conscience, and have no competing loyalties except to the wholly nonpolitical Watchtower Society. *Patriotism,* insofar as the term implies a more active devotion than mere loyalty, would seem to be incompatible with the responsibilities of a faithful Witness; the secular state is an evil to be tolerated, not helped. Yet, for all the official theology, many members have retained a strong attachment to their homelands; children in particular were able to testify with every evidence of sincerity that they loved their country and were eager (within the limits of divine law) to be "good Americans."[119]

The only major quarrel between the American Witnesses and their national government concerns the issue of military service. During World War I, Rutherford and the whole Witness editorial committee were prosecuted under the Espionage Act and spent some time in prison for publishing material sharply criticizing our entry into the war and strongly encouraging all Witnesses to claim exemption as conscientious objectors.[120] Witness objections to military service are based on two grounds. While by no means pacifists, Jehovah's Witnesses oppose the taking of any life, human or otherwise, except in accordance with God's rules—e.g., the biblical wars and slaughtering for food; modern wars, fought for secular ends, violate God's law.[121] The second ground, which assumed importance in World War II, centers about the new missionary character of the movement. Every Witness is an ordained minister, an ambassador of Jehovah, with the single job of spreading the kingdom message; he can have no interest in and take no part in the petty quarrels of earthly princes.[122] During World War II, Jehovah's Witnesses consistently demanded total exemption from service as ministers. If denied this classification, they refused to be inducted or, in most cases, even to submit to the discipline of the conscientious objector camps.[123] Over 4,300 served prison sentences for violation of the draft laws during World War II.[124]

2. THE FLAG-SALUTE ISSUE

Official Witness history describes the flag-salute ceremony as an imitation of the Nazi "Heil Hitler," imported into the United States in 1935 for the specific purpose of "framing" Jehovah's Witnesses.[125] Actually, as has been indicated, Jehovah's Witnesses entered the flag-salute controversy very late; when they did so, it seems to have been at least partly by accident.

In 1935, Massachusetts enacted a "strong" flag-salute law requiring teachers to lead their pupils in the salute and pledge at stated intervals. Long before this, however, the Lynn public schools had a set of daily opening exercises which included the salute, pledge and a prayer. In the fall of 1935, Carleton B. Nicholls, Jr., was enrolled in the third grade at the Breed school in Lynn. In the first and second grades, he had saluted and given the pledge without objection.[126]

Meanwhile, Jehovah's Witnesses were having their troubles in Nazi Germany. Hitler banned the movement in 1933. The Witnesses responded with open defiance, refusing to give the Nazi salute and vigorously denouncing Hitler's policies. Eventually, some 10,000 Witnesses wound up in concentration camps.[127] At the Witnesses' 1935 American national convention, Rutherford delivered a spirited defense of the German Witnesses, saying in part:

The Devil deceives the people and turns them away from God, and puts forth his agents who claim that the salvation of the people comes by reason of his agents. A striking example of this is the exaltation of one Hitler in Germany. He issues the command that all persons shall "Heil Hitler," which in the English language means "Salvation is by Hitler." But all people who have faith in God know that neither Hitler, Mussolini, the NRA scheme nor any other scheme nor any other creature can bring salvation to the people. . . . Thus all such "Heil Jehovah and Christ Jesus." They do not "Heil Hitler" nor any other creature. . . .[128]

That this line of reasoning could apply equally well to the American flag salute seems obvious, when viewed in retrospect. At the time, however, it does not appear to have occurred to the leaders of the Watchtower Society until forced upon their attention by extraordinary zeal among the rank and file.[129]

At the 1935 graduation exercises at Lynn Classical High School, a student successfully refused to lead the flag-salute ceremony.[130] This incident, together with Rutherford's convention speech, must have occasioned considerable discussion in the Nicholls household, the upshot of which was that Carleton "decided in his own mind that it would be wrong to salute the United States flag. . . ."[131] On September 20, 1935, it was noticed that Carleton stood quietly during the ceremony, but took no further part. When questioned, Carleton stated that, as a Witness, he could not pay homage to "the Devil's emblem."[132] Carleton Nicholls, Sr., backed his son's stand unreservedly:

The Scriptures prove the truth of my assertion that this world, this country, the entire worldly kingdom, is not possessed by any government or any country, but by the Devil. . . . Why, then, should I, or my son, pledge allegiance to the Devil's kingdom?[133]

On September 30, the elder Nicholls and a friend accompanied Carleton to school. During the opening exercises all three remained seated, despite a demand by the principal that they participate. The two adults were arrested after allegedly refusing to leave, and were subsequently fined for disturbing a public meeting.[134]

On October 6, Rutherford delivered his famous radio address on "Saluting a Flag," throwing the full support of the Witness organization behind Carleton's refusal to salute.

The Nichols [sic] lad . . . has made a wise choice, declaring himself for Jehovah God and his kingdom. . . . All who act wisely will do the same thing.[135]

Legal counsel Moyle was sent to Lynn to argue Carleton's position. At a special meeting on October 8, despite arguments by Moyle and Nicholls, Sr., the Lynn school committee voted to exclude Carleton from school until he agreed "of his own free will" to participate in the flag ceremony.[136] On October 25, 1935, Moyle filed a petition before state supreme court Justice Henry T. Lummus, requesting a writ of mandamus to compel the Lynn school committee to reinstate Carleton in the public schools.[137]

Jehovah's Witnesses justify their refusal to salute the flag on two grounds, both stemming from Exodus 20:3–5:

> You shall have no other gods before me.
> You shall not make yourself a graven image, or any likeness of anything . . . you shall not bow down to them or serve them. . . .

The key assumption is that saluting a flag constitutes an act of religious devotion. "To salute a flag means, in effect, that the person saluting ascribes salvation to what the flag represents. . . ."[138] This view, while odd, is not entirely without biblical support.[139] Given such significance, the flag salute takes on a sinister character in the light of the Witnesses' attitude toward the state.

> . . . [T]he nations of the world are under the control of Satan the Devil. . . .[140]

> . . . Flags of the various nations represent the government and what the government stands for. The law of the nation or government that compels the child of God to salute the national flag *compels that person to salute the Devil as the invisible god of the nation*. The Christian, therefore, must choose to yield to God's enemy or to remain true to Almighty God. . . .[141]

In short, to salute the flag of any earthly nation is to align oneself squarely on the side of Satan. This argument was especially stressed in the 1930's; it certainly is the one most in accord with the temper of the movement during that period.

But it is not necessary to take such an extreme position; nor did the Witnesses always do so. If saluting is a religious act, then it is forbidden by God's law *however worthy the object of respect*. In other words, refusal to salute need imply no disrespect for flag or country; it is the particular mode of showing respect which is objectionable.[142] This rather mild argument was invoked occasionally in the 1930's when the Witnesses sought to influence outsiders;[143] it became the *only* admitted ground for refusal as the Witnesses' troubles deepened in the 1940's.[144]

Much stress was laid on the unequal responsibilities of Witnesses and non-Witnesses. For an outsider to salute the flag is sinful, but no more so than the rest of his behavior; he still can be saved if he will. For a Witness to salute, under any pressure, is to violate his covenant and earn certain destruction at Armageddon.

> . . . The act of saluting the flag is not an offense; but the one who has made a covenant to do God's will, commits a wrong leading him into destruction. Those who desire to salute flags should do so, but those who have agreed to serve Jehovah God must obey him if they would live at all. . . .[145]

The primary focus of the Witnesses' objections, therefore, has been not to compulsory flag-salute regulations as such, but to their application to Jehovah's Witnesses, whose covenant obligations prevent compliance.[146]

3. THE WITNESSES AS LITIGANTS: STRENGTH AND WEAKNESS

With the entry of Jehovah's Witnesses, the flag-salute controversy soon was transferred completely to the judicial arena. Both the strengths and weaknesses of the sect pointed toward a resort to the courts.

Unlike any of their predecessors in the controversy, Jehovah's Witnesses were willing and able to sue, repeatedly if necessary. While litigation among Witnesses was discouraged, outsiders (including expelled brethren) might be sued in the outsiders' (earthly) courts.[147] One factor in this favorable attitude undoubtedly was the legalistic bent of Rutherford, an attorney for twenty-six years before he assumed the presidency.

Another consideration impelling the Witnesses to litigation was their total helplessness in any other arena. Their numbers, and hence their political weight, were negligible. Further impairing any appeal to the legislature or public opinion was the Witnesses' extreme unpopularity. Their offensive literature, their aggressive missionary methods, their doubtful patriotism, and their inability to advance the most reasonable argument without dragging in the iniquities of the Catholic Church,[148] all tended to convince a large segment of the population that any Witness misfortunes were well deserved.

The Witnesses were quite well equipped to carry on a long, hard court fight. They had a small but competent legal department backed by substantial financial resources. The tight hierarchical organization assured Witness lawyers of a ready supply of plaintiffs who would sue when, how, *and if* directed—in sharp contrast to the ACLU's unsuccessful efforts to come up with a plaintiff of record in the 1920's.

One very mixed blessing was the fanatical zeal of the individual Witnesses. Faithful to the death, they were prepared to go to any length demanded by their superiors. Their absolute belief in all teachings of the Watchtower Society made them reliable and sincere courtroom witnesses. On the other hand, their enthusiasm often led them into trouble too deep for the legal department to get them out of. The very intensity of their beliefs had a serious effect on communication within the sect. With no intent to deceive, Witnesses tended to interpret everything in terms of their doctrines, seeing what they expected to see. This distortion of vision seems to have been present at all levels of the organization; it was to be a constant disrupting influence in the sect's briefs and arguments in court.

CHAPTER THREE

CONSTITUTIONAL SETTING
THE BACKGROUND OF PRECEDENT

Before dealing at greater length with Jehovah's Witnesses' many days in court on the flag-salute issue, it is necessary to review the general state of the constitutional law to which they were appealing. The compulsory flag salute, enforced by suspension or expulsion of refusers, was alleged to violate the due process clause of the Fourteenth Amendment on three major counts: (*a*) that it was an arbitrary and capricious restriction upon the personal liberty of parents and children; (*b*) that it violated the religious freedom of both parents and children; and (*c*) that the forced recitation of particular pledges, as well as the communication implied in the compulsory salute, denied the children freedom of speech. Certain other arguments and counterarguments bordering on the frivolous will be dealt with as they arise in the chapters on the actual litigation—e.g., the Witnesses' appeal to the equal protection clause of the Fourteenth Amendment, and repeated arguments by the school authorities that public education is a privilege withdrawal of which does not raise a constitutional question.

A. *Substantive Due Process of Law*

1. GENERAL

When a state or local legislative enactment is challenged as a violation of substantive due process of law, the assertion is that the enactment is unreasonable or arbitrary. Under such a vague test, much depends on who is to bear the burden of proof. The general rule, which has received at least lip service at all times, was succinctly stated as early as 1827:

It is but a decent respect due to the wisdom, the integrity, and the patriotism of the legislative body, by which any law is passed, to presume in favor of its validity, until its violation of the Constitution is proved beyond all reasonable doubt.[1]

This "presumption of constitutionality" has varied sharply in weight from case to case, sometimes approaching the absolute nature of the criminal defendant's "presumption of innocence," sometimes approaching zero. In the early twentieth century, the Supreme Court came very close to reversing the presumption in regard to state regulation of economic affairs, particularly where "freedom of contract" was involved.[2] The onus was on the state authorities in such cases to prove the existence of exceptional circumstances justifying such interference. It is unnecessary to consider whether Jehovah's Witnesses could have profited from this property-oriented body of precedent. By the time the flag-salute controversy reached the Supreme Court, the law had shifted again; an almost impossible burden of proof was now placed upon the party challenging the validity of an enactment.

The most complete formulation of the new presumption of constitutionality, exposing both its strength and its potential limits, is contained in Justice Stone's opinion in *United States v. Carolene Products Co.*:[3]

... [T]he existence of facts supporting the legislative judgment is to be presumed, for regulatory legislation affecting *ordinary commercial transactions* is not to be pronounced unconstitutional unless ... it is of such a nature as to preclude the assumption that it rests upon some rational basis within the knowledge and experience of the legislators. ... [Italics supplied.][4]

In short, anyone challenging legislation under either of the due process clauses must prove that no possible state of facts could support the regulation in question. Furthermore, the rule is the same whether the statute is challenged on its face or as applied.[5] The limitation implied in the italicized phrase was expanded upon in a footnote:

It is unnecessary to consider now whether legislation which restricts those political processes which can ordinarily be expected to bring about repeal of undesirable legislation, is to be subjected to more exacting judicial scrutiny. ...

Nor need we inquire whether similar considerations enter into the review of statutes directed at particular religions ... or national ... or racial minorities ... whether prejudice against discrete and insular minorities may be a special condition, which tends seriously to curtail the operation of those political processes ordinarily to be relied upon to protect minorities. ...[6]

This method of leaving questions unanswered naturally invited their being raised for direct decision later.

2. PARENTAL CONTROL

That a parent's control over the upbringing of his children is to some extent protected by the Constitution was recognized in *Pierce v. Society of Sisters*,[7] in which the Supreme Court unanimously struck down Oregon's attempt to compel all school-age children to attend *public* schools. That decision could be of only very limited benefit to the Witnesses for two reasons. First, the opinion was highly property-oriented, showing most solicitude for the investors and proprietors of the private schools. Second, Justice McReynolds' opinion rather clearly sanctioned the power of the state to require even of private schools

. . . that teachers shall be of good moral character and patriotic disposition, *that certain studies plainly essential to good citizenship must be taught,* and that nothing be taught which is manifestly inimical to the public welfare. [Italics supplied.][8]

The right, if any, of a parent to have his child excused from one or more of the courses in the public school curriculum has been litigated in thirteen states. The courts of eight states have made it quite clear that no such right exists;[9] it "would be a power of disorganizing the school. . . ."[10] Five states have decisions upholding the right of the parent. However, in three, the rule was limited to courses *not required by law to be taught;*[11] in these states, the power of the legislature to make the prescribed curriculum compulsory on pupils as well as teachers would seem beyond question. Only the Nebraska and Colorado courts appear to have viewed the parent's right as a constitutional one, and the opinions written in these courts were less than distinguished. The Nebraska Supreme Court contented itself with the cryptic remark that a contrary rule would be "arbitrary and unreasonable."[12] The Supreme Court of Colorado interpreted the *Pierce* ruling as sanctioning the right of the parent to withdraw his child from specific subjects in the public schools. Indeed, in the case at hand, the court held this "right of choice" to extend not only to subjects, but to individual textbooks.[13]

On the whole, the general right of parental control over the child's education was a very weak ground on which to rest a constitutional challenge to any particular school regulation. The *Pierce* case, properly construed, is hostile to such interference, as are the great majority of the state precedents. The only state court opinion seriously arguing for such a constitutional "right of choice" was badly defective in its reliance on the *Pierce* case. Finally, the disruptive effects to be expected from such unrestrained individualism in a modern public school system went far to discredit the whole notion.

B. *Religious Freedom*

Stripped of the Witnesses' theological embellishments, the religious freedom argument against the compulsory flag salute ran as follows: even assuming that the ceremony is a purely secular requirement, it has religious significance for the Witnesses; they consider it a mortal sin to perform the salute; in overriding these sincere religious scruples the state, through its agents, abridges freedom of religion.

The age-old conflict between conscientious scruples and the demands of secular society has been the subject of a great volume of jurisprudence in both state and federal courts. The great bulk of the case law comes from the former; by comparison, the federal precedents are few, scattered and recent. This disparity is readily understood: the states are responsible for the detailed, day-to-day sort of regulation most likely to collide with the activities of religious non-conformists. Until recently, these collisions remained the exclusive province of the state tribunals; the First Amendment, aimed at the national government, was inapplicable.

This situation changed radically during the 1930's as the Supreme Court took an ever more liberal view of the scope of the Fourteenth Amendment. As early as 1923, the Court had hinted that religious freedom might to some extent be included in the "liberty" protected by the due process clause.[14] In 1934 the hint was expanded into a holding.[15] Finally, in 1940, the Court held in *Cantwell v. Connecticut*[16] that the due process clause applied the full force of the religious freedom guaranty against the states: "The Fourteenth Amendment has rendered the legislatures of the states as incompetent as Congress to enact such laws."[17]

The significance of this development is twofold. First, the First Amendment, as interpreted by the Supreme Court, became a minimum standard for all law, state or federal; much state jurisprudence was or was soon to be superseded. Second, the federal courts, which hitherto had handled a few rather simple questions arising out of federal statutes, now were faced with the full range of problems with which the state courts had been dealing. All religious freedom questions became "federal" questions.

The old state holdings are by no means irrelevant to this study, however. By virtue of their number, variety, antiquity and continuity, they must necessarily have had a profound influence on legal thinking at all governmental levels. Also, almost all the early adjudications of the flag-salute issue took place in state courts.

1. THE CONSTITUTIONAL PROVISIONS

The United States Constitution and that of every state have provisions guaranteeing freedom of religion. The First Amendment to the federal Constitution provides simply that "Congress shall make no law respecting an establishment of religion, or prohibiting the free exercise thereof. . . ." While there is great variety of language among the state provisions, their guaranties, like those of the federal provision, fall into a few well-defined categories: a general clause recognizing freedom of worship, prohibitory clauses aimed at particular manifestations of church establishment (preferential status, tithing, etc.), hedges against various devices long used to penalize dissident beliefs (diminished civil rights, religous tests for office, etc.) and, less frequently, some reference to "the rights of conscience" and a limiting clause excluding some practices from constitutional protection. The following are fairly typical combinations of these elements:

All men have a natural and indefeasible right to worship Almighty God according to the dictates of their own consciences; no man can of right be compelled to attend, erect or support any place of worship, or to maintain any ministry against his consent; no human authority can, in any case whatever, control or interfere with the rights of conscience and no preference shall ever be given by law to any religious establishments or modes of worship.[18]

No inhabitant of this State shall be molested in person or property, or prohibited from holding any public office, or trust, on account of his religious opinions; but the right of liberty of conscience shall not be so construed as to excuse acts of licentiousness, or justify practices inconsistent with the peace and safety of the State.[19]

No person shall be deprived of the inestimable privilege of worshipping Almighty God in a manner agreeable to the dictates of his own conscience; nor under any pretense whatever be compelled to attend any place of worship contrary to his faith and judgment. . . .
There shall be no establishment of one religious sect in preference to another; no religious test shall be required as a qualification for any office of public trust, and no person shall be denied the enjoyment of any civil right merely on account of his religious principles.[20]

Particularly to be noted in the foregoing is the heavy emphasis on freedom of religious profession and worship, and on the prevention of religious establishments. Everything seems to be aimed at *religious* oppressions. This is understandable; the evils against which the various framers sought to defend were recent in memory: an established monopoly-church like the Church of England, and the religious strife which had racked England and continental Europe as various sects fought for establishment. The principle aim seems to have been to take the state out of religion.[21] It seems quite improbable that the framers were at all solicitous for the rights of minorities with religious objections to the everyday demands of Caesar. The major sects of the time were pretty well agreed on what matters had religious significance, and our early history is replete with examples of their scant regard for the views of "outside" groups.[22]

Still, neither history nor language is conclusive, especially in those states whose constitutions refer to the "rights of conscience." Again, it may be significant that a number of states saw fit specifically to limit their guaranties to proscribe religiously based acts contrary to public order. Oklahoma, for example, felt called upon to include a special clause excluding polygamy from the protection of its religious freedom grant.[23] The decisive resolution of this ambiguity must come from the constructions which state and federal courts have placed on the various guaranties in a century and a half of application.

2. THE PRECEDENTS: HOLDINGS

a) State cases: Illegal actions.—Many of the state precedents involving religiously based law violations are blurred either by side issues of statutory construction or by serious doubts regarding the good faith of the religious claim asserted. Some of the most clear-cut resolutions of the conflict between religious scruple and secular regulation grew out of the troubles of the newly formed "Salvation Army" in the late nineteenth century. Members of this sect believed it to be their religious duty to attract prospective converts by parading on the public streets with bass drum, tambourines, etc. State courts considering the issue were unanimous in upholding local power to prohibit this rather distracting practice altogether or to subject it to reasonable license requirements.[24]

Many states prohibit the commercial telling of fortunes via palmistry, tea reading and the like. Occasionally, a practitioner of this art has claimed that in reading palms he was merely indulging in religious worship. While accepting such protestations at face value, state courts, with but one exception, have held that the law may be enforced against such "rituals."[25] In *State v. DeLaney*,[26] a New Jersey appellate court held that such laws could not be enforced against a practicing member of the Spiritualist Church.

State laws licensing and otherwise regulating the practice of medicine have borne heavily on faith-healing cults such as Christian Science. These same laws have led a variety of less savory "doctors" to take up religion as a possible means of staying in business. The decisions are unanimous, however, that the medical codes can constitutionally be applied to all healers, religious or secular, regardless of the particular mode of treatment utilized.[27]

Pennsylvania law prohibits public school teachers from wearing religious garb or insignia in the classroom. This law, which works an obvious hardship on those religious devotees—e.g., Roman Catholic nuns—whose religion requires such special dress, was upheld as a reasonable school regulation by a unanimous state supreme court.[28]

On occasion, ministers have been prosecuted for offenses committed in the pulpit itself. It has been held that a minister can be punished for obscene language, even if this is an integral part of the sermon.[29] Nor does religious freedom bar prosecution of a minister for excessive shouting in the course of his sermon.[30]

Every state has legislation of some sort restricting commercial activity on Sunday. Originally, these laws were passed as strictly religious exactions, and were upheld as such in the courts.[31] Since late in the nineteenth century, however, Sunday laws have come to be defended as purely secular regulations designed to protect the health of the workingman. Under this rationalization, they have almost invariably been upheld against challenges based on religious freedom.[32] Here, however, the record is not unanimous. In two decisions, it was suggested that a *real* religious scruple might well prevail against the law.[33] Both cases involved defendants who observed a Saturday sabbath and advanced the implausible claim that their religion required them to work the other six days. In a third case, a religious scruple did prevail. In *State v. Morris*,[34] the Idaho Supreme Court refused to interpret that state's Sunday law so as to punish the display of a religious movie during a church service. So construed, the court held, the statute would violate the state's religious freedom guaranty.

b) State cases: Refusal to act.—The precedents regarding conscientious refusal to perform a legal duty go all the way back to 1793; in that year a Jew refused on religious grounds to be sworn as a witness on Saturday, and was fined.[35] In the 1828 case of *Commonwealth v. Lesher*,[36] the Pennsylvania Supreme Court held that the trial judge in a murder case had acted properly in excusing from service a juror with religious objections to capital punishment; such an exemption was considered most consistent with the spirit of the religious freedom guaranty. This mild invocation of religious liberty, however, provoked Chief Justice Gibson to a long and classic dissent.

The other cases in this category all deal in one way or another with the state's great concern for the welfare of its children. A universal item in state statute books is a provision firmly establishing the duty of parents to furnish the necessities—food, clothing, education, medical care—to their children, and setting penalties for willful failure in this obligation. On the other hand, many parents belong to religious sects recognizing only *spiritual* healing, and will see their children die before they will submit them to the ministrations of a physician. In all court cases dealing with this conflict, the constitutional issue has been resolved in favor of the state's protective power.[37]

As early as 1905, both state and federal courts upheld compulsory vaccination statutes as applied to adult citizens.[38] While no religious issue was involved in that case, it has always been assumed that religious objections would be equally unavailing.[39] State courts have consistently upheld the power of the state to require that all children attending the public schools be vaccinated, or to authorize similar regulations by local school boards.[40] In a majority of cases, they have further upheld the school law convictions of parents whose children were sent home for failure to fulfil the vaccination requirement.[41] While very few of the cases in either category involved properly presented religious freedom claims,[42] these claims have been flatly rejected where raised.[43]

The widespread practice of opening each session of a public school with readings from the King James version of the Holy Bible, or some similar religious observance, has led to a large number of court tests. Most of these are irrelevant here. Such practices are hardly secular in nature; indeed, the concept in dispute in most of these cases was not religious freedom, but separation of church and state.[44] Still, the cases have some relevance here. The first of the Bible-reading cases turned on the school authorities' odd contention that the Bible was used, not as a religious book, but simply as a book of readings in the teaching of English. The Maine Supreme Court unanimously upheld this "secular" requirement as a reasonable exercise of administrative discretion, religious objections notwithstanding.[45] Of nineteen regulations calling for Bible-reading as a concededly religious observance, thirteen were upheld wholly, and another in part,[46] by state courts. It bears emphasis, however, that ten of these rules expressly exempted conscientious objectors from participation in the exercises.[47] Some favorable decisions laid considerable stress on this feature.[48] Of five regulations clearly demanding participation by all pupils, four were invalidated on some ground.[49]

The 1876 case of *Ferriter v. Tyler*[50] involved an unusual church-state controversy. A Catholic priest requested the local school committee to excuse Catholic pupils from classes for special religious services on Corpus Christi Day. The circumstances of this request seemed to indicate that he was interested less in the holiday—which does not bulk large on the Catholic calendar—than in setting a precedent. When the school committee denied the request, the children stayed away anyway, and were subsequently suspended from school. The offended parents' invocation of religious freedom was rejected by the Vermont Supreme Court. Even granting the good faith of the asserted religious obligation, the court held, it must give way before the controlling discretion of the school committee.

Important because of its uniqueness is the decision in *Hardwicke v. Board of School Trustees*.[51] A local school board required coeducational social dancing exercises as part of the physical education course. C. C. Hardwicke and his two children entertained religious and moral scruples against social dancing. Eventually, the children were expelled for their continued refusal to participate in the exercises. Hardwicke then sued for mandamus to compel their readmission, asserting that his and their religious freedom was being violated. The trial court dismissed the complaint, but the Third District Court of Appeals reversed and was upheld in this in a summary disposition by the California Supreme Court. The opinion in the District Court of Appeals, the only opinion filed in the case, held specifically that the dancing requirement, as applied to the Hardwickes, violated California's religious freedom guaranty. The precedential value of this decision is limited in two respects, however. First, the school board had virtually conceded the essential issue in its pleadings. Its demurrer attacked only certain technical lapses in Hardwicke's complaint—notably, his failure to specify the sect whose teachings he espoused. Second, the court closed its opinion with a passionate dictum distinguishing the compulsory flag salute from the situation at bar. The court could "conceive of no more appropriate act or practice . . ." and asserted that "no just or reasonable interpretation of the Bible" could support a religious objection thereto.[52]

c) *Federal cases: Illegal actions.*—The first federal religious freedom litigation involving actual law violations dealt with the "peculiar institution" of the early Mormons—plural marriage. Shortly after Utah became an incorporated territory, Congress passed legislation making polygamy a crime. This statute was upheld by the United States Supreme Court in *Reynolds v. United States,*[53] despite defendants' pleas that their religion made the practice not only permissible but, where possible, obligatory. In 1890 the Court upheld another statute which, in effect, disenfranchised all practicing members of the Church of Jesus Christ of Latter Day Saints.[54] Later in the same year, the Court sanctioned a climactic law which dissolved the church corporation and confiscated most of its property.[55] Soon thereafter, the Mormon leaders bowed to *force majeure,* and officially renounced polygamy as a church practice.[56]

Under the Eighteenth Amendment and the National Prohibition Act, the Treasury Department strictly regulated the few legally permitted uses of alcoholic beverages. In particular, the use of wine for Jewish sacramental purposes was limited to five gallons per family per year. When the Department moved to cut off the supply of a rabbi for violations of the regulations, he sued for an injunction. The District Court for the Western District of Washington dismissed the action, holding that the regulation was legal and constitutional as applied, religious objections notwithstanding.[57]

Federal statutes long have provided for the exclusion of obscene matter from the mails, and have made it a crime to attempt to mail such material. It has been held that religious motivation constitutes no defense to a prosecution under this legislation.[58]

There are two decisions upholding federal power to prosecute mail fraud carried on in the guise of religion.[59] In both instances the issue before the jury was limited to the alleged bad faith of the defendants; the validity or invalidity of their "religion" was excluded from consideration.

Finally, there remains the case of *Holy Trinity Church v. United States.*[60] Trinity Church had hired its minister from England, thus violating the literal terms of a federal statute regulating the importation of foreign labor. The Supreme Court ruled unanimously that the law had not been intended to apply to such a situation, and held further that "no purpose of action against religion can be imputed to any legislation . . . because this is a religious people."[61]

d) Federal cases: Refusals to act.—All of the federal precedents dealing with the religious refusal of individuals to perform a required act are somehow tied to the problem of military service. There seems to be no court case on record involving a direct religious challenge to compulsory military service. While conscientious objectors long have been exempted from the draft, there never has been any doubt that they could be compelled to serve if Congress so chose. Litigation has arisen only concerning requirements themselves rather remote from the war power of Congress.

The Naturalization Act of 1906 requires an applicant, among other things, to swear "that he will support and defend the Constitution and laws of the United States against all enemies, foreign and domestic, and bear true faith and allegiance to the same."[62] The twenty-second question on a preliminary form in use in and after 1929, to be filled out by applicants, read, "If necessary, are you willing to take up arms in defense of this country?"[63] The United States district courts were inclined to treat this commitment as an integral part of the required oath, and a necessary prerequisite to naturalization. The United States Supreme Court upheld this interpretation by a vote of six to three, in the 1929 case of *United States v. Schwimmer.*[64] Two years later, this rule was applied to a religious objector in the case of *United States v. Macintosh.*[65] Macintosh was a Canadian citizen, a Baptist minister and professor of theology at Yale University. He was willing to take the statutory oath of allegiance, but would not give an unqualifiedly affirmative answer to question 22. By a vote of five to four, the Supreme Court held that Macintosh was not entitled to naturalization since he was, in effect, qualifying his oath of allegiance. The Court was unanimous in holding that no constitutional right of Macintosh's was being violated. The four dissenting justices did not doubt Congress' power to exact a promise of military service from would-be citizens, even in the face of religious objections; they did deny that Congress had made any such demand.

In the Morrill Act of 1862, Congress made substantial land grants to the states on the condition that the proceeds of the sale of such lands be devoted to the maintenance in each state of at least one college teaching agricultural science and other standard branches of instruction, "including military tactics." Although the statute did not expressly require that the military instruction be compulsory on the students, every state so provided in accepting the grants. In 1932, the General Conference of the Methodist Episcopal Church reasserted that denomination's firm opposition to war, called on Congress to exempt from military service any conscientious member of the Methodist Episcopal Church, called on all educational institutions with compulsory ROTC to grant a like exemption, and requested the federal government to withdraw its financial support of college military training.[66] In the following year a member of the Church was suspended from the University of Maryland for refusal to receive the required military training. He went to court and secured an injunction directing his reinstatement. The Maryland Supreme Court reversed, holding that compulsory ROTC violated no constitutional right, and that the student's religious objection was not advanced in good faith, but was merely part of an organized campaign by the Methodist Episcopal Church and the Epworth League.[67] The United States Supreme Court dismissed the ensuing appeal for want of a substantial federal question.[68]

The Supreme Court did recognize the existence of a substantial federal question in *Hamilton v. Regents*.[69] Two members of the Methodist Episcopal Church were suspended from the University of California for religious refusal to take the prescribed courses in military science. From the California Supreme Court's dismissal of their mandamus action, they appealed to the United States Supreme Court. The Court affirmed unanimously in two opinions. Both opinions made clear for the first time that freedom of religion was protected by the due process clause of the Fourteenth Amendment. Justice Butler's prevailing opinion rejected Hamilton's religious freedom argument, holding that attendance at a state university was not a right but a privilege which could be subjected to reasonable conditions, and that the reasonableness of military training as a condition was settled by the *Macintosh* case. Justice Cardozo, speaking also for Justices Brandeis and Stone, carefully avoided reliance on the distasteful *Macintosh* holding. He based his concurrence on the historical fact that even the statutory grace given conscientious objectors had never been stretched to free them from requirements so indirectly related to military service.

3. THE PRECEDENTS: RATIONALE: THE "SECULAR REGULATION" RULE

It bears re-emphasis that the precise question at issue is the extent and nature of the rights of a person entertaining sincere religious objections to a regulation regarded by the rest of society as intrinsically secular. Obviously, the regulation must prevail in at least some cases. On the face of it, the most plausible solution would be for the reviewing court to weigh the particular circumstances and determine whether the social need for conformity with this regulation was great enough to override the individual's religious claim. Indeed, a respectable school of thought reads the precedents as establishing this approach to religious freedom cases.[70] This view is supported by two famous dicta. One of these occurred in the 1872 case of *Watson v. Jones*.[71] In this case the Supreme Court held that secular courts must take as final decisions by a church governing body on intrachurch affairs. Contrary British practice was rejected as a by-product of that country's church establishment:

> In this country the full and free right to entertain any religious beliefs, to practice any religious principle, and to teach any religious doctrine which does not violate the laws of morality and property, and which does not infringe personal rights, is conceded to all. The law knows no heresy and is committed to the support of no dogma, the establishment of no sect. . . .[72]

The other appears in Chief Justice Gibson's classic dissent in *Commonwealth v. Lesher:*

. . . But what are these rights? Simply a right to worship the Supreme Being according to the dictates of the heart, to adopt any creed or hold any opinion whatever on the subject of religion; and to do, or forbear to do, any act, for conscience' sake, the doing or forbearing of which, *is not prejudicial to the public weal. . . .*[73]

While neither dictum is free from ambiguity, either would furnish a convenient standard for the application of an interest-weighing approach to religious freedom cases.

Actually, however, this approach is a relative stranger in religious freedom litigation. As of 1935, American courts, both state and federal, were committed to a quite different rule. It is significant that aside from the Bible-reading cases, which are irrelevant here, there are only three decisions on record in which a religious scruple was held to prevail on constitutional grounds against a legal prohibition or requirement. There was no discussion beyond the bare holding in *DeLaney, Morris* or *Hardwicke*, and the special circumstances surrounding the decisions greatly weaken their precedential value. In every other case in which religious freedom was invoked, the constitutional issue was resolved against the conscientious objector. True, most of these cases would have gone the same way under any reasonable standard; the public interest in the regulation was obviously imperative. Still, it is next to impossible to reconcile decisions such as those in *Macintosh* and in the Sunday-law cases with any sort of interest-weighing approach.

The conclusion suggested by the pattern of the decisions is made manifest by the reasoning employed therein. Invariably, the decisive point was not the importance of the regulation, but the lack of weight assigned the religious objection. Chief Justice Gibson, in the opinion quoted above, went on to say

. . . But *salus populi suprema lex,* is a maxim of universal application; and where liberty of conscience would impinge on the paramount right of the public, it ought to be restrained. . . . [W]ere the laws dispensed with, wherever they happen to be in collision with some supposed religious obligation, government would be perpetually falling short of the exigence. There are few things, however simple, that stand indifferent in the view of all the sects into which the Christian world is divided.[74]

The other decisions bristle with language such as this. For example, in the street parade cases, it was said:

. . . It is not competent to make any exceptions either for or against the body of which petitioner is a member. . . . In law it has the same right, and is subject to the same restrictions, in its public demonstrations, as any secular body or society. . . .[75]

The fact that the defendant represents a religious association has nothing to do with the case. . . .[76]

Similar is the reasoning in a child-care case:

The proposition that religious belief constitutes no defense for violation of a penal statute has been repeatedly announced by the courts. . . .[77]

The one relevant Bible-reading case:

. . . A law is not unconstitutional, because it may prohibit what a citizen may conscientiously think right, or require what he may conscientiously think wrong. . . .[78]

A classic formulation in *Ferriter v. Tyler:*

. . . [T]hat article in the constitution . . . was not designed to exempt any persons from the same subjection that others are under to the laws and their administration on the score that such subjection at times would interfere with the performance of religious rites, and the observance of religious ordinances, which they would deem it their duty to perform . . . but for such subjection. While all stand on equal footing under the laws . . . no one's rights of conscience are violated in a *legal* sense. . . .[79]

The first polygamy case:

. . . Laws are made for the government of actions, and while they cannot interfere with mere religious belief and opinions, they may with practices. . . .[80]

. . . Can a man excuse his practices to the contrary because of his religious belief? To permit this would be to make the professed doctrines of religious belief superior to the law of the land. . . .[81]

Chief Justice Hughes' *Macintosh* dissent:

. . . [G]overnment may enforce obedience to laws regardless of scruples. When one's belief collides with the power of the state, the latter is supreme within its sphere and submission or punishment follows. . . .[82]

Such passages could be multiplied further.[83] These will suffice to show the theme which recurs through all the opinions. This can be summed up in what will be referred to henceforth as the *"secular regulation" rule: There is no constitutional right to exemption on religious grounds from the compulsion of a general regulation dealing with non-religious matters.* This rule applies with equal force to legal requirements and legal prohibitions; cases in one category cite those in the other, without discrimination.[84] The regulation, however, must be truly secular in bent. The converse situation is illustrated by the Bible-reading cases, which show a clear bias in favor of conscientious objectors. Similarly, even the "secularized" Sunday laws produced several dicta suggesting that a real religious objection might be upheld.

An obvious logical corollary of the "secular regulation" rule is that courts will not consider the validity of the asserted religious scruple; there would be no point in it. Moreover, such scrutiny would involve the very official meddling in religious doctrine sought to be avoided by the framers of the religious freedom guaranties. Still, a few decisions have proceeded on the alleged invalidity of the scruple advanced, while a few others treated the matter gratuitously. The California court in the *Hardwicke* case felt free to deny the validity of any religious scruple against flag saluting, and the majority opinion in *Macintosh* leans toward the same approach.[85] Akin are occasional judicial suggestions that certain matters cannot possibly be the subjects of religious beliefs. Examples of this dubious tack are to be found in the polygamy cases.[86] Certain other tests are in better repute. Courts on occasion will consider whether a scruple is asserted in good faith, and whether it is held by the individual as a *religious* belief. Sometimes this issue is central, as in draft exemption proceedings, or in the mail-fraud cases. Even this limited inquiry is somewhat suspect, however; inquiry into the good faith of a religious belief seldom can be uninfluenced by one's views as to its truth.[87]

The "secular regulation" rule itself is touched by this logical difficulty. The question of which matters are religious and which secular is itself a religious question. What if the objector believes—as did Jehovah's Witnesses in the flag-salute controversy—that the obnoxious regulation requires a religious observance? In such a case, the court must rely on the religious presuppositions of the majority.

Whatever its flaws, the "secular regulation" rule is supported by several weighty considerations of logic and expediency. First, this construction of the constitutional guaranties of religious freedom seems to conform most faithfully to their historic purpose: to protect freedom of worship against the sort of religious establishment familiar in England and colonial America. Second, a strong argument can be made that this approach is most consistent with the American doctrine of a "wall of separation" between church and state.[88] Under the rule, the secular courts ignore religion entirely. The atheist, the Catholic and the Jew come before the courts on equal terms. Third, this rule raised fewer practical problems than did alternative approaches. It was obviously impracticable to extend absolute protection to all religious scruples; the result would be chaos. The intermediate, interest-weighing approach would place an onerous burden on the courts, and would necessarily involve them in consideration of the validity and good faith of particular scruples. Furthermore, such a particularistic view did not appeal readily to judges of the nineteenth and early twentieth century, who were more accustomed to seeking differences of kind than of degree.[89] In the absence of doubtful cases (in the eyes of the judges) the rule continued to be applied out of habit and convenience. Only where different approaches meant different results could there be a meaningful challenge to the "secular regulation" rule.

So the "secular regulation" rule remained in 1935, a seemingly impregnable bar to religious pleas for special treatment. Pressure for a shift in theory, when it arose, came not from within this area, but from the cognate field of freedom of speech.

C. *Free Speech: "Clear and Present Danger"*

The rise of the "clear and present danger" test in free speech and press cases should require only cursory summary here. The phrase first was employed by Justice Holmes in *Schenck v. United States:*[90]

The question in every case is whether the words are used in such circumstances and are of such a nature as to create a clear and present danger that they will bring about the substantive evils that Congress has a right to prevent. It is a question of proximity and degree. . . .[91]

In later cases, a majority of the Supreme Court held that that question could be foreclosed by legislative declaration. Thus it was held in *Gitlow v. New York*[92] that:

By enacting the present statute the state has determined . . . that utterances advocating the overthrow of organized government by force . . . are so inimical to the general welfare, and involve such danger of substantive evil, that they may be penalized in the exercise of its police power. . . .[93]

In these cases, Justices Holmes and Brandeis clarified and refined the *Schenck* version of the test:

. . . [I]t must remain open to a defendant to present the issue whether there actually did exist at the time a clear danger; whether the danger, if any was imminent; and whether the evil apprehended was one so substantial as to justify the stringent restriction interposed by the legislature. The legislative declaration . . . creates merely a rebuttable presumption. . . .[94]

During the 1930's, the Supreme Court showed increasing impatience with blanket legislative "findings," striking down a variety of state laws as applied to particular circumstances.[95] By 1937 the Court was clearly leaning toward the Holmes-Brandeis version of the "clear and present danger" test.[96] The Court's increasing resistance to infringements in this area is well illustrated in the 1939 case of *Schneider v. Irvington*.[97] Most of the local ordinances invalidated in this decision prohibited all literature distribution on the public streets, with the ostensible purpose of preventing littering. Eight justices held this purpose too insubstantial to justify the severe restraint imposed. In discussing the standard to be applied, Justice Roberts wrote:

In every case . . . where legislative abridgment of the rights [free speech and press] is asserted, the courts should be astute to examine the effect of the challenged legislation. Mere legislative preferences or beliefs respecting matters of public convenience may well support regulation directed at other personal activities, but be insufficient to justify such as diminishes the exercise of rights so vital to the maintenance of democratic institutions. And so, as cases arise, the delicate and difficult task falls upon the courts to weigh the circumstances and to appraise the substantiality of the reasons advanced in support of the regulation of the free enjoyment of the rights.[98]

The "clear and present danger" test, as formulated by Holmes and Brandeis, was explicitly endorsed by the Supreme Court in 1940,[99] and stiffened still further in 1941.[100]

Worthy of special mention here is *Stromberg v. California*.[101] Here, a unanimous Supreme Court reversed the conviction, under California's "red flag" law, of a Communist youth camp director who had led her charges in pledging allegiance to a red flag. A provision making it a misdemeanor to display the red flag "as a symbol of opposition to organized government" was held unconstitutionally vague.

The significance of this line of decisions is twofold. In the first place, the reasoning of these decisions exerted a strong pressure against the "secular regulation" doctrine laid down in the religion cases. The language of the *Schneider* case is hardly that of judicial deference; the usual presumption of constitutionality is virtually reversed. Throughout, the focus is on the particular *circumstances*. The courts' refusal to consider the circumstances of a given conscientious objection contrasts sharply with the close scrutiny in the free speech cases. Freedom of speech, press, assembly and religion are all protected in the same terms ("Congress shall make no law . . ."); why should they not all receive the same circumstantial application? Sooner or later this apparent contradiction would have to be resolved or justified.

The free speech precedents also have considerable significance for this study in their own right. The great unanswered question in this regard was the extent to which the First Amendment protection of free speech could be held to imply a right of *silence*. If the Constitution protects the right of a man to speak his mind, does it also protect him from compulsion to express views repugnant to him? There was no precedent at all upon the question, which had not been raised in the naturalization cases. If it could be maintained successfully that the two freedoms were related parts of a sort of political "freedom of conscience," then the full force of the "clear and present danger" test could be brought to bear against such coerced expression.

D. *Concluding Remarks*

On the whole, then, the precedents as of 1935 were decidedly inhospitable to the contentions of Jehovah's Witnesses. The prospects can be summarized briefly: As far as ordinary substantive due process was concerned, the case was hopeless. The salute ceremony had at least a plausible relation to citizenship training; Witness objections went only to its wisdom. The *Pierce* decision's protection of parental rights could not be stretched this far, and the favorable state decisions were obsolete. Second, the Witnesses' claim to a religious exemption from participation in the salute ceremony was absolutely barred by the unchallenged "secular regulation" rule. Nor were they in a likely situation to secure a reconsideration of the rule, as their scruple was widely considered both fantastic and immoral. Finally, the free speech cases furnished the leading challenge to the judicial status quo, the full extent of which had not yet been explored.

Thus it would seem that the Witnesses' best prospects were (*a*) to try to utilize the free speech cases in favor of a "right of silence," or (*b*) to combine them with Stone's *Carolene Products* footnote in a direct assault upon the "secular regulation" rule.

CHAPTER FOUR

EARLY FLAG-SALUTE LITIGATION

"Judge" Rutherford's radio speech indorsing Carleton Nicholls' refusal to salute the flag was the signal for similar refusals by Jehovah's Witnesses all over the United States and abroad. This in turn gave rise to an ever growing number of expulsions of such children from school. In mid-1936, 120 Jehovah's Witness children were estimated to have been excluded from school for this reason.[1] By 1939, the figure had passed two hundred.[2] Leading the way was Pennsylvania, with over a hundred expulsions.[3]

Where substantial numbers of children were out of school, and where qualified teachers could be found among the faithful, the Witnesses set up "Kingdom Schools." These schools served the dual purpose of satisfying the compulsory education laws and further instructing Witness children in the true faith. During the late 1930's, such schools were established in Lynn[4] and North Sudbury,[5] Massachusetts; Gates, Monessen and Andreas, Pennsylvania;[6] Paterson, New Jersey;[7] and Ohio, California and Georgia.[8]

The flag-salute issue led to major litigation in seven states before finally receiving a full hearing in the United States Supreme Court in a case arising in Minersville, Pennsylvania. In this chapter we will deal with these early skirmishes, turning in the next chapter to the landmark case of *Minersville School District v. Gobitis.*

A. *Massachusetts*

1. THE GENERAL PICTURE

The events leading to the expulsion of Carleton Nicholls, Jr., from the Lynn public schools have already been related. On the day following the expulsion, Massachusetts Attorney General Paul A. Dever handed down an official opinion strongly backing the Lynn position. Pupils refusing to salute the flag when properly required to do so, he held, were subject to the usual disciplinary measures (including expulsion) which applied to other infractions of school discipline.[9] With the well publicized furor in Lynn, other communities suddenly became apprehensive about possible un-Americanism in their own ranks; officials began to take note of who was not saluting. By early 1939, at least twenty-one Witness children had been flushed out of the state's school system:[10] seven in Saugus,[11] one in Boston, six in Sudbury,[12] one in Cambridge,[13] three in Belchertown[14] and three in Deerfield.[15] Nor were teachers immune. One was fired in Lynn in 1935,[16] another in Quincy in early 1940.[17]

Public opinion in Massachusetts seems to have been almost unanimously, often violently, hostile to the Witnesses' flag-salute stand. Still, the lines did not harden completely on either side for a while. Needham schools were excusing objectors from the ceremony as late as 1937.[18] The Cambridge boy had been excused for two years before he was finally expelled. On the other hand, his sister still was saluting in 1937.[19] In Weymouth, a Witness told her child to salute after being threatened with revocation of her eighty-dollar monthly pension.[20]

2. NICHOLLS V. LYNN

On October 4, 1935, Roger N. Baldwin, executive director of the American Civil Liberties Union, wrote to assure Carleton Nicholls, Sr., of that organization's help in any legal fight.[21] The Union board of directors voted on October 28 to co-operate with the Witnesses in this and other "typical" flag-salute cases.[22] After it became obvious that there was no chance that the Lynn school committee would reverse its position, Union and Witness leaders moved to set up their court action. James P. Roberts of Dedham volunteered his services, and handled the ensuing litigation with only sporadic liaison with Witness counsel Olin R. Moyle and A. Frank Reel, secretary-counsel of the Massachusetts Civil Liberties Committee.[23]

Carleton Nicholls, Jr.'s suit for a writ of mandamus against the mayor and school committee of Lynn came before Massachusetts Supreme Court Justice Henry T. Lummus on October 25, 1935. There was no dispute as to the facts. The petition alleged that the flag-salute rule and Carleton's expulsion thereunder were unauthorized by law and violated both the state and federal constitutions. The answer filed by City Solicitor Patrick Shanahan emphasized the broad discretion vested in local school boards, stressed the school committee's good faith determination that Carleton's conduct had a bad effect on school discipline, and denied that Carleton's religious beliefs had anything to do with the case. At the request of both parties, Justice Lummus referred the case directly to the whole Massachusetts Supreme Court for a final decision on the pleadings.[24] Thus, the first legal test of the compulsory salute reached the high court of Massachusetts in what amounted to an original suit.

Because of the press of business, the hearing in the state Supreme Court was put off at least until December, 1935.[25] In the meantime, the Witnesses' case was badly damaged by their own allies. Operating pretty much on his own,[26] Roberts produced and filed with the Supreme Court a disastrous brief which did not mention the United States Constitution and only mentioned in passing that of Massachusetts. Most of the brief simply poked literate fun at the "moral strabismus" of the Lynn school committee members and decried the "serio-comic recrudescence" of religious persecution in Massachusetts. In all, it was a document well calculated to irritate almost any court.[27] After one horrified look at the Roberts brief, Reel and his associates rushed through a supplemental brief which also was filed with the court.[28] While this brief did mention the United States Constitution, it was only a partial improvement. Carleton Nicholls' religious position was presented only in support of a general contention that the Lynn rule was *unreasonable*, under the doctrine of *Pierce v. Society of Sisters*. Unfortunately, though it could hardly have been anticipated in 1935, the "due process" thinking that went into the *Pierce* case was to be quite out of fashion by the time the *Nicholls* case was ready for a possible appeal. The attractiveness of the supplementary brief probably was not enhanced by the addition as an appendix of a pamphlet copy of Rutherford's radio address of October 6.

Apparently because of calendar congestion, the Massachusetts Supreme Court did not hand down its decision in *Nicholls v. Lynn*[29] until April 4, 1937. The unanimous decision, with the opinion by Chief Justice Rugg, was a complete defeat for the Witnesses and their allies. Rugg made short shrift of the attack on the reasonableness of the ceremony, observing that it was "clearly designed to inculcate patriotism and to instill a recognition of the blessings conferred by orderly government under the Constitutions of the state and nation."[30] His disposition of the religious issue was more ambiguous:

> The pledge of allegiance to the Flag . . . is an acknowledgment of sovereignty, a promise of obedience. . . . It has nothing to do with religion.
> . . . There is nothing in the salute or the pledge of allegiance which constitutes an act of idolatry, or which approaches to any religious observance. It does not in any reasonable sense hurt, molest, or restrain a human being in respect to "worshipping God" within the meaning of the words in the Constitution. . . .[31]

Read carefully, Rugg's opinion did little more than invoke the standard "secular regulation" rule. Yet he seemed continually forced to the point of arguing religion with the plaintiffs. This aspect of the opinion set an unfortunate precedent for other state courts in dealing with the issue.

Both the Witnesses and the ACLU were anxious to get the flag-salute issue before the United States Supreme Court; the question was whether *Nicholls v. Lynn* was the right case for the purpose. The initiative lay with the ACLU, which had offered to pay the expenses of such an appeal.[32] The final decision was put up to Richard W. Hale of Boston, whom Baldwin hoped to interest in handling the case in the Supreme Court.[33] Hale advised against appealing the *Nicholls* decision. "I think it is foreclosed by the Macintosh case. And to get the Court to distinguish it from the Macintosh case I would want to wait for a more appealing record."[34] In view of the handling of the federal issues in the Roberts and Reel briefs, Hale's decision is not surprising. ACLU lawyers decided to await the results of a potentially more appealing case arising in western Massachusetts.

3. THE OPIELOWSKI COMMITMENT

In early February, 1936, the Belchertown public schools expelled the three children of Ignace Opielowski for refusal to salute the flag.[35] Public feeling ran high against the Opielowskis. On April 17, Opielowski was fined forty dollars on two counts of school law violation. On the same day, all three children were found delinquent and committed to the Hampden County Training School,[36] a state institution for "mildly bad but corrigible children."[37] The commitment was stayed pending appeal to the county superior court.[38] Public opinion split badly on the merits of the commitment. Amherst students and faculty rallied to the side of the Opielowskis;[39] the local chapter of the DAR demanded that Opielowski, an alien, be deported.[40] The ACLU officially entered the dispute on April 23, planning to make this its Supreme Court test case.[41] On May 19, 1937, however, the district attorney abandoned the case, allowing the appeal to go through by default. He promised instead to bring new actions against Opielowski, whom he considered the true villain of the piece.[42]

4. *JOHNSON V. DEERFIELD* AND ITS AFTERMATH

The most complex set of cases arose in Deerfield, a tiny community just north of Springfield. The three children of William Johnson started refusing to salute the flag on September 21, 1938.[43] After a confused interlude during which the children apparently were in and out of school,[44] they were sent home indefinitely on October 21 and formally suspended on November 17.[45]

Both Moyle and the ACLU had been eying the possibility of an original action in the federal courts at least since 1936, when they commissioned James Lipsig to prepare a memorandum—completed in mid-1937—on possible federal court jurisdiction of flag-salute litigation.[46] A district court suit against enforcement of the Massachusetts flag-salute law offered special advantages: such a suit would require a three-judge court, whose decisions would be appealable directly to the Supreme Court.[47]

On November 29, 1938,[48] an action was brought in the United States District Court for the district of Massachusetts in the name of William Johnson, for himself and his three children. Plaintiffs requested a declaratory judgment that the Massachusetts statute and the Deerfield application thereof were violative of the Fourteenth Amendment, and an injunction against continued enforcement of the flag-salute requirement against the Johnson children. Considerable stress was laid on Johnson's inability to pay for private instruction, and the resulting danger of legal proceedings brought against him or the children themselves. The religious freedom argument was well presented here, with particular emphasis being placed on the good faith of the children's religious scruples.[49]

On January 4, 1939, the three-judge tribunal denied the requested relief and dismissed the case of *Johnson v. Deerfield*[50] on the merits. The court considered the federal constitutional issue foreclosed by the Supreme Court's dismissal of flag-salute appeals from other states. Any appeal to the state constitution was equally foredoomed by *Nicholls v. Lynn*. Dealing specifically with the merits, the court dismissed the religious argument with a short reference to the "secular regulation" precedents. As a matter of bare due process, the flag-salute rule was clearly reasonable as an educational device.

The Johnsons appealed directly to the Supreme Court. William G. Fennell, one of the ACLU's more active lawyers, joined Moyle on brief. The Bill of Rights Committee of the American Bar Association, entering the controversy for the first time, filed an *amicus curiae* brief in support of the appeal. On April 17, 1939, without having heard oral argument, the Supreme Court handed down a *per curiam* order summarily affirming the decision below on the basis of several earlier *per curiam* dispositions of the issue.[51]

The Johnsons' troubles multiplied after the District Court decision. A few days afterward, local authorities brought a school law prosecution against Johnson for failing to keep his children in school. He was acquitted on February 2, after testifying that he had not and would not *instruct* his children either to salute or not salute.[52] The children were then readmitted to school, pending the appeal of the District Court decision.[53] On April 24 and 25, on direct instructions from their superiors, Deerfield teachers demanded the flag salute and reported the Johnson children's refusal.[54] They were expelled again on April 26,[55] and proceedings were instituted to have them committed to the Hampden County Training School as "habitual school offenders." The action was sucessful, but the commitment was stayed pending appeal.[56] On June 21, 1939, after a trial *de novo*, the county superior court upheld the commitment. Judge John E. Swift offered to place the children on probation on condition that they receive proper instruction in the public schools or elsewhere. Johnson refused the offer, which would have precluded any further appeal. The commitment again was stayed pending appeal.[57] *Commonwealth v. Johnson* was pending in the Massachusetts Supreme Court in 1940, when the flag-salute issue finally reached a hearing on the merits in the United States Supreme Court. The outcome of this appeal can best be presented in later discussion of the aftermath of the decision there.

An interested—and scandalized—spectator at the trial of the Johnson children was Professor George K. Gardner of the Harvard Law School. After a short conference, he and Moyle agreed to pool their talents in the appeals of the case.[58]

5. THE LEGISLATIVE FRONT

In the meantime, almost continuous efforts were under way by those sympathetic to the Witnesses' situation to secure an amendment to the Massachusetts statute expressly exempting religious objectors. One such bill was introduced but later withdrawn in the Massachusetts legislature in 1937.[59] Open committee hearings were held on another exemption bill in early 1938. Appearing for the bill were the Malden superintendent of schools and representatives of the Congregational Churches, the Society of Friends, the Socialist Party, the State Teachers' Union, the Massachusetts Federation of Teachers, the Massachusetts Parent-Teachers Association and the Boston University School of Social Work. Appearing in opposition were the Mayor of Lynn and representatives of the Elks, the Massachusetts Civic Alliance and the Massachusetts Civic League.[60] Again, nothing seems to have come of the attempt. In early 1939, an exemption bill was reported unfavorably to the floor of the Massachusetts Senate by the Committee on Education. A proposed substitute bill by Senator Curtis, directed to the same end, was subjected to sharp criticism and killed by a quick voice vote.[61]

B. *Georgia*

The Atlanta public schools had a regular flag-salute ceremony pursuant to the statutory admonition to offer instruction in "American institutions and ideals."[62] At the start of the 1936 term, Dorothy Leoles, a sixth grader at the Crew Street School refused to participate and was backed up by her father, George Leoles, a naturalized citizen of Greek birth.[63] On or about October 12, 1936, the Atlanta school board voted unanimously to expel Dorothy for insubordination.[64] On November 8, a second girl was expelled for the same offense.[65]

Public reaction in and around Atlanta was violently hostile. Denunciatory resolutions flooded in from local chapters of the American Legion, VFW,[66] Ku Klux Klan, many Greek-American organizations, and a variety of other groups.[67] Sustained picketing by veterans and the Klan eventually destroyed Leoles' hat-cleaning business.[68]

Early in 1937, George Leoles brought suit on behalf of his daughter in Fulton County Superior Court, seeking a writ of mandamus to compel her readmission to public school. He alleged in due form that the flag-salute rule and the expulsion thereunder violated his and his daughter's religious freedom under the state and federal constitutions. The school board filed a demurrer, alleging that, even granting the facts in the petition, there was no proper cause for issuing the writ. The superior court upheld the demurrer and dismissed the action.[69] Leoles appealed to the Georgia Supreme Court.

On May 13, 1937, the Georgia Supreme Court handed down its decision in *Leoles v. Landers*,[70] unanimously affirming the decisions below. Chief Justice Russell's opinion proceeded on two points. First, he argued that public education was a privilege, not a right, and could be conditioned on "reasonable" requirements like the flag salute. Second, he enlarged on the rationale of *Nicholls v. Lynn*, at the same time further obscuring the orthodox "secular regulation" bent of that opinion:

. . . The act of saluting the flag of the United States is by no stretch of reasonable imagination "a religious rite." It is only an act showing one's respect for the government. . . . So for a pupil to salute the flag in this country is just part of a patriotic ceremony . . . and is not a bowing down in worship of an image in the place of God. . . .[71]

Again, the judges seemed to be arguing religion with the Witnesses.

Leoles appealed his case to the United States Supreme Court. This was the first flag-salute appeal to reach the high tribunal. On December 13, 1937, the Supreme Court, acting *per curiam*, dismissed the appeal for want of a substantial federal question, relying on *Hamilton v. Regents*.[72] It is not clear whether the Court was relying on the "privilege" argument or the "secular regulation" rule, both of which had been invoked in *Hamilton*; the justices may simply have thought that case to be generally controlling on these facts.

C. *New Jersey*

In late 1935, there was a small flurry of expulsions in New Jersey. Three Witness pupils were ousted in Woodbine,[73] one in Lakewood,[74] three in Union City,[75] and two in Secaucus.[76] Another girl was suspended in Camden in early 1940.[77] On the other hand, two boys were excused from participating in the ceremony in Bayonne.[78]

In Secaucus, Vivien and Alma Hering began refusing early in October, 1935. Partly at the urging of the American Legion, they were formally expelled on November 1.[79] Alternative education was not secured until January, 1936; in the meantime, Mr. and Mrs. Hering were fined five dollars apiece for failure to keep their children in some school.[80]

On November 11, 1935, the ACLU Board of Directors authorized Abraham Isserman, a member of the board and head of the Newark law firm of Isserman and Isserman, to bring a court action on behalf of the Hering children.[81] It was first necessary to exhaust the series of administrative appeals afforded by New Jersey law: to the State Commissioner of Education, then to the State Board of Education and *then* to the Supreme Court—then New Jersey's second highest appellate court. Moyle and Isserman co-operated on the administrative appeals, but Isserman took full charge of the court proceedings.

Under the urgings of Rutherford, Moyle wrote a highly theological brief on the appeal to the Commissioner, contending that the compulsory salute was a form of imposed religion and void as a violation of divine law.[82] Isserman added a careful attempt to distinguish away *Hamilton v. Regents* on the bases of the relatively slight state interest involved here and the fact that grade-school education in some school, unlike university education, was required by law.[83]

On May 21, 1936, the State Commissioner of Education rejected the Herings' petition for reinstatement of their children.[84] On August 11, the State Board of Education dismissed an appeal from this ruling.[85] The case then went to the New Jersey Supreme Court on a writ of certiorari.

On February 5, 1937, the Supreme Court unanimously dismissed the appeal in *Hering v. Board of Education*.[86] Judge Bodine's opinion was short and wholly unfavorable:

. . . The pledge of allegiance is, by no stretch of the imagination, a religious rite. . . . Those who do not desire to conform with the demands of the statute can seek their schooling elsewhere.[87]

The case then went on certiorari to the New Jersey Court of Errors and Appeals.

Isserman's brief in the Court of Errors and Appeals was the strongest effort yet and was reworked into a "model brief" for flag-salute litigation.[88] It pretty well exhausted all plausible legal resources. First, Isserman made a determined attempt to demonstrate that the Constitution allowed religious scruples to be overridden only in cases of pressing need. Second, he advanced the new argument that freedom of speech included a right *not* to utter unfelt sentiments. Primary reliance was placed on *Stromberg v. California;* if people had a right to salute a *hostile* flag, surely they had an equal right merely to abstain from saluting that of the United States. Third, Isserman repeated his attempt to distinguish *Hamilton v. Regents,* and added a list of authorities for the proposition that even a privilege cannot be withheld for an unconstitutional reason. Fourth, he invoked *Pierce v. Society of Sisters* and the favorable curriculum cases in support of the Herings' alleged constitutional right to control their children's education. Finally, he advanced the weird argument that the state had arbitrarily discriminated against public school children in not demanding the flag salute in private schools as well.

At the same time, William G. Fennell prepared an *amicus curiae* brief on behalf of the American Civil Liberties Union. This brief was intended to secure extra publicity for the Union and to show the Court that others besides the Witnesses opposed the compulsory salute. To this end, four prominent New Jersey lawyers and judges were persuaded to add their signatures to the brief.[89]

On September 22, 1937, the New Jersey Court of Errors and Appeals affirmed the decision below without opinion.[90] On March 14, 1938, the United States Supreme Court dismissed an appeal from this ruling, for want of a substantial federal question.[91] Cited were *Hamilton* and *Leoles v. Landers*.

The sporadic nature of the conflict between Jehovah's Witnesses and the school authorities during this early period is well illustrated by the Morgan incident in 1939—the first documented incident after the 1935 expulsions. The two sons of Daniel Morgan, of Fort Lee, first refused to salute in 1937. Action was postponed until April 13, 1939—thirty days before the older boy was to graduate—when the school board expelled both boys at a closed meeting. The following day, Morgan was notified of his dismissal as a state motor vehicle inspector—admittedly in retaliation for his support of his sons' stand.[92]

On May 24, 1939, the New Jersey legislature passed a new statute, obviously aimed at Jehovah's Witnesses, making it a misdemeanor for any person or organization to "influence or attempt to influence any school pupil in this state against the salute to the flag of the United States. . . ."[93]

D. *California*

California had virtually nothing on the statute books regarding the flag salute or patriotic instruction. Still, various localities exercised their discretion to require the salute in school. Enforcement was quite sporadic, however. As late as 1937, the Oakland schools were allowing religious objectors to leave the room during the flag ceremony.[94] The San Francisco school superintendent was on record against the compulsory salute.[95] In Los Angeles, a Witness child was excused from singing the National Anthem.[96] On the other hand, there were individual expulsions in San Leandro,[97] Rosemeade[98] and Sacramento. The oddest controversy arose in McFarland. In late 1935, four children from two families stopped saluting. The parents, while influenced by Witness literature, were not themselves members of the sect. At last notice, no official action had been taken on the refusals; school authorities hoped the affair would blow over. The situation reached public notice when five Witnesses were arrested for playing anti-salute records over a loud-speaker adjacent to the school grounds.[99]

In the fall of 1935, Charlotte Gabrielli was expelled from the Sacramento public schools for her conscientious refusal to participate in the regular flag-salute ceremony.[100] The Sacramento Witnesses were eager to go to court. Moyle, however, flatly opposed litigation in this case. There were promising cases in progress elsewhere. Furthermore, this case was unlikely to get into the Supreme Court since, in the absence of a questionable state statute, there would be no jurisdiction by appeal. The California group went over Moyle's head to Rutherford, who approved the suit,[101] and secured local counsel from the Northern California Civil Liberties Union.

Charlotte's suit for a writ of mandamus to compel her reinstatement came before Superior Court Judge Peter J. Shields. Shields granted the writ, holding that her religious liberty had been unconstitutionally infringed.[102] He argued that a close reading of the precedents indicated that a religious eccentricity might be suppressed only where (a) the deviation was positively harmful to society, and (b) the suppression would have the direct effect of remedying the ill effect of the deviation (e.g., as in the arrest of a nudist). On November 30, 1937, the Third District Court of Appeals unanimously affirmed Judge Shields' decision, but without reaching the constitutional issue.[103] Justice Plummer's opinion relied entirely on a variety of procedural defects in the original expulsion.

On August 31, 1938, the California Supreme Court unanimously reversed the decisions below in *Gabrielli v. Knickerbocker*.[104] Justice Seawell, writing for the court, ignored the procedural niceties of the appellate decision below, but dealt at length with the religious issue. Any issue under the Fourteenth Amendment was held foreclosed by the *per curiam* dismissals of the *Hering* and *Leoles* appeals. In regard to the California religious freedom guaranty, Seawell invoked the "secular regulation" rule, in probably the soundest piece of reasoning to come out of the state courts on this issue:

. . . [T]he exaction by the state of social and patriotic duties of the citizens and such other civic duties as may have reasonable relations to the maintenance of good order, safety, and the public welfare of the nation, may not be interpreted as infringements of the religious freedom clauses of either the state or federal organic law. . . .

. . . [The flag ceremony], in the judgment of the proper governing body, tend[s] to stimulate in the minds of youth in the formative period of life sentiments of lasting affection and respect for and unfaltering loyalty to our government and its institutions.[105]

A petition for rehearing was later denied with one justice dissenting.

Now it was the Witnesses' turn to appeal to the United States Supreme Court. But Moyle's misgivings were justified. On April 17, 1939, the Supreme Court dismissed the appeal for want of jurisdiction; treating the appeal papers as a petition for certiorari, the Court denied certiorari.[106]

Also in 1939, Governor Olson of California vetoed a more explicit flag-salute bill.[107]

E. *Texas*

The flag-salute issue in Texas led to two court cases, neither of which produced any holding on the constitutional issues involved. Between February and April, 1936, the public schools of Brazoria, Texas, a small town south of Houston, suspended five Witness pupils from attendance, including the two children of L. D. Shinn.[108] The American Civil Liberties Union immediately offered its assistance, and secured the services of the Houston law firm of Mandell and Combs.[109] All attempts by Combs to secure a reconciliation fell through; the local principal seems to have believed that he would be violating state law if he granted any exemption from the salute requirement.[110]

In February, 1937, Combs brought a mandamus action on behalf of the Shinns against Principal Barrow and the school board in the Brazoria County District Court. In this procedure, only the constitutional issue was available. An alternative appeal, to the State Board of Education, would have allowed the raising of other points, such as procedural defects in the suspension orders; this course was rejected because it would be virtually impossible to appeal to the courts from an adverse State Board ruling.[111] The District Court handed down an adverse decision almost immediately, and by early May, an appeal was pending in the Texas Court of Civil Appeals for the First District, at Galveston.[112]

The crowded condition of the appellate court's docket gave rise to a question of strategy: to seek an early hearing or to stall. The *Hering* case was on its way up through the state courts; a favorable decision there or in the United States Supreme Court might make all the difference here. On the other hand, there was a very real danger that *Shinn v. Barrow* would become moot in the meantime; under Texas law, a suspension could only extend to the end of the current school year.[113] Ultimately, at Moyle's urging, Combs and the ACLU decided to stall, pending the outcome of the *Hering* case.[114]

On March 14, 1938, the United States Supreme Court dismissed the *Hering* appeal. Shortly thereafter, the *Shinn* case came up for final hearing. On October 27, 1938, the Court of Civil Appeals, two justices sitting, dismissed the case of *Shinn v. Barrow*[115] as moot. There was some indication that the Court might have been divided had the case come to decision on the merits.[116] There could be no Supreme Court appeal, of course, since the decision rested on a point of state procedure.

Shortly before the final failure of the *Shinn* appeal, the Seventh District Court of Civil Appeals, at Amarillo, had to deal with *Reynolds v. Rayborn*,[117] a flag-salute case involving not parents versus school board, but parent versus parent. Early in 1934, R. A. Reynolds divorced his wife, who resumed her maiden name of Rayborn. By oral agreement, Reynolds retained custody of the couple's two children; while the record was carefully vague, it was plain that the wife had no hope of securing a favorable custody decree. On February 9, 1937, Miss Rayborn brought an action seeking to have the daughter, then twelve, transferred to the custody of a state institution. She contended that Reynolds was an unfit father, in that, as a

Witness, he refused to salute the flag and had inculcated the same attitude in the girl. On February 19, the Tarrant County District Court found Alathia Reynolds to be a "neglected and dependent child" by reason of the unfitness of both parents, and ordered her committed to the absolute custody of a children's home in Fort Worth.[118] On April 25, 1938, the Court of Civil Appeals unanimously reversed that part of the judgment depriving Reynolds of custody.

Does the admitted refusal of the father and daughter to salute the flag . . . furnish convincing proof of the unfitness of appellant to have custody of his daughter?

History is replete with the bigotry, intolerance, and dogmatism of religious sects, and the pages thereof are strewn with martyrs who died for their faith. . . .

. . . Beyond my comprehension are the vagaries of people who claim and accept the protection of their government . . . but refuse to salute their country's flag. . . . Yet, however reprehensible to us such conduct may be, their constitutional right must be held sacred; when this ceases, religious freedom ceases.[119]

F. New York

The case of *People ex rel. Fish v. Sandstrom*[120] arose in the little Long Island town of Lake Ronkonkoma. On September 30, 1937, thirteen-year-old Grace Sandstrom refused to salute. From October 7 through October 25, she came to school only to be sent home after refusing to salute. There were two exceptions to this practice. On October 18, she was excused from the ceremony. On October 22, after a very difficult session with the local superintendent, Grace gave the salute while mumbling part of the twentieth psalm. Attempts to enrol Grace in a more sympathetic school in the area fell through because of excessive publicity. Eventually, she enrolled in a Kingdom School in New Jersey.[121]

On October 25, 1937, the attendance officer brought a prosecution against Mr. and Mrs. Sandstrom for failing to keep their daughter in some school—i.e., by making it impossible for her to attend in accordance with the school rules.[122] Arthur Garfield Hays, chief counsel of the ACLU, took personal charge of the case,[123] and put up a bitter contest at the trial held in Brookhaven Justice Court at Centereach, on November 5, 1937.[124] Grace made a very effective witness, setting out her religious position and making clear that she herself reached the decision not to salute.[125] Nevertheless, the jury convicted; the Sandstroms were fined ten dollars each and the sentences were suspended.[126] On December 3, Charles A. Brind, chief of the Law Division of the State Department of Education, handed down an official opinion explicitly reaffirming the 1926 ruling and backing the Lake Ronkonkoma school authorities.[127] On May 10, 1938, the Suffolk County Court affirmed the conviction and sentence.[128] Hays and Moyle joined forces on the appeal to the New York Court of Appeals, while "Judge" Rutherford filed an *amicus curiae* brief on behalf of Jehovah's Witnesses.

On January 17, 1939, the New York Court of Appeals unanimously reversed the convictions; a majority, however, upheld the constitutionality of the flag-salute requirement.[129] Chief Judge Crane, for a six-judge majority, held that no violation had been proved against the parents, who obviously were anxious to keep her in school. Only Grace's personal decision not to salute precluded her attendance; thus any further proceeding must be against her, not the parents. Crane strongly argued against any further legal proceedings expressing considerable distaste for the heavy-handed approach already taken by the Lake Ronkonkoma school authorities. On the constitutional issue, however, he had no doubts:

> Saluting the flag in no sense is an act of worship or a species of idolatry. . . . The flag has nothing to do with religion. . . .[130]

> . . . Many a nation has succumbed to the breakdown of the morale of its people. The State, therefore, is justified in taking such measures as will engender and maintain patriotism in the young.[131]

Judge Lehman concurred in the reversal, but contended that the flag-salute rule and the expulsion were both illegal and unconstitutional. The 1898 statute, he argued, was designed to coerce nobody, except possibly the Commissioner of Public Instruction. At any rate, such a compulsion in these circumstances would be a clear violation of religious liberty.

Episcopalians and Methodists and Presbyterians and Baptists, Catholics and Jews, may all agree that a salute to the flag cannot be disobedience to the will of the Creator; all the judges of the State may agree . . . but this little child has been taught otherwise.[132]

. . . She does not insist upon doing an act which might harm herself or others; she does not refuse to do an act which might promote the peace, safety, strength or welfare of her country. . . . She asks only that she not be compelled to incur the wrath of her God. . . .
. . . The flag is dishonored by a salute by a child in reluctant and terrified obedience to a command of a secular authority which clashes with the dictates of conscience. The flag "cherished by all our hearts" should not be soiled by the tears of a little child. The Constitution does not permit, and the Legislature never intended that the flag should be so soiled and dishonored.[133]

Since the Sandstroms technically had won their case, there could be no appeal to the United States Supreme Court. New York had been sustained in its right to expel non-saluters, but was balked in its first attempt to impose further penalties.

G. *Florida*

On April 13, 1937, Florida Attorney General Cary D. Landis held that local school officials had the legal power to suspend pupils who refused to salute the flag as required by school rules. The opinion did not deal with the constitutional issue.[134] In the fall of 1937, the three children of J. P. Greer, a city employee, were expelled from the Jacksonville public schools for refusal to salute the flag.[135] In November, the city commission passed a resolution ostensibly aimed at Communists, requiring all city employees to sign a pledge promising to give the flag salute on demand.[136] On November 26, Greer and another employee were suspended for refusing to sign the pledge.[137] In December, after a federal District Court in Pennsylvania held a compulsory salute unconstitutional,[138] the city commissioners voted to reinstate the two employees,[139] and the public schools moved to readmit the Greer children.[140]

Other Florida school districts were not so obliging. The six children of Fred Bleich were among eight suspended in November, 1937, from the public schools of Lutz, a village just north of Tampa.[141] After efforts to secure a compromise failed,[142] Moyle and the ACLU moved to bring a mandamus suit on behalf of the Bleichs in the Hillsborough County Circuit Court. The court dismissed the action, and an appeal was taken to the Florida Supreme Court.

On June 27, 1939, the Florida Supreme Court unanimously affirmed the decision below. If the *Gabrielli* opinion was the strongest of the state court opinions, that of Judge Terrell in *State ex rel. Bleich v. Board of Public Instruction*[143] was by far the weakest. What started out as an orthodox appeal to the "secular regulation" rule was buried under an avalanche of theological rhetoric:

> . . . Like all law . . . this command [Exodus 20:4–6] grew out of the exigencies of the times and we cannot see that it has any relation whatever to the present situation. It would be as pertinent to rely on some requirement of the Assyrian, the Hittite, or the code of Hammurabi.
>
> . . . To symbolize the Flag as a graven image and to ascribe to the act of saluting it a species of idolatry is too vague and far fetched to be even tinctured with the flavor of reason. . . .
>
> If an objection as remote from religious grounds as the one involved here may be successfully interposed . . . then there is no limit to the reasons that conscientious objectors may advance as grounds for avoiding patriotic duties. Individual judgment in matters of religion no less than in civic controversies must give way to that of the instrumentality set up by the State to direct it.[144]

On August 1, 1939, a petition for rehearing filed by the state attorney general was denied. This time, Justices Buford and Brown dissented. Buford quickly disposed of Terrell's religious arguments: "The most profound Bible students the world has ever known have disagreed among themselves."[145]

> . . . [W]e should not by law require one to affirmatively engage in an act, not essential to the public welfare or the support of the government, which he or she conscientiously believes to be contrary to his or her religious tenets, and thereby make of such a person a martyr. . . .[146]

No attempt was made to appeal this decision. The Witnesses already were assured of a hearing in the United States Supreme Court by a pair of federal court victories in Pennsylvania.

H. *Hinterland: States without Major Litigation*

Before moving on to Pennsylvania, the scene of our first principal case, let us survey briefly the other states in which the flag-salute issue arose during this early period. In January, 1936, a Witness girl was expelled from school for refusal to salute in Montpelier, Vermont.[147] The American Civil Liberties Union quickly moved to offer legal assistance, but was stymied by inability to secure local counsel.[148] Public opinion was running against the expulsion, however, and the ACLU entertained good hopes of securing a reconciliation.[149] In the fall of 1935, four children were expelled from school in East Liverpool, Ohio. Reinforced by an official opinion from State Attorney General John W. Bricker,[150] school authorities were preparing in January, 1936, to bring school law prosecutions against the Witness parents.[151]

In September, 1936, the public schools of Oxon Hill, Maryland, expelled the six children of August Ludke for refusal to salute the flag. Ludke appealed to the State Board of Education, which in turn requested an opinion from State Attorney General Herbert O'Connor on its authority to rule on the appeal. On September 15, O'Connor ruled that Ludke's complaint raised a matter of constitutional law, and could be dealt with only by the courts.[152] Later in 1936, Ludke secured counsel and sued for a writ of mandamus.[153] The local court dismissed the suit, and he did not appeal. As of 1938, the Ludke children were being tutored privately, and had little hope of getting back into school.[154]

In October, 1935, four Witness children were expelled from school in Malone, Washington, for refusing to salute the flag.[155] After attempts at compromise failed,[156] school authorities took legal steps to have the children adjudged "dependent" and "delinquent" and committed to a state institution. On February 24, 1936, Juvenile Judge William Campbell indignantly threw the action out of court.[157] Soon after, the school board took steps to readmit the children and excuse them from the flag-salute requirement.[158] In April, 1936, twins were expelled in Spokane by a reluctant but dutiful school superintendent.[159] Again, the ACLU offered legal aid, but the parents eventually decided not to sue.[160] Three children were expelled from the Everett public schools in September 1936.[161] Attempts at a court test were balked by the ACLU's inability to secure local counsel. Finally, however, a majority of the school board relented and expressed willingness to readmit the children if the ACLU could "prepare" local public opinion, which was running strongly against the Witnesses.[162]

On February 18, 1938, Oklahoma Attorney General J. Harry Johnson, in response to an inquiry from Le Flore County, ruled that teachers had authority to suspend pupils who refused to salute the flag on demand, but advised that the matter be left to the school board, where the refusal was religiously based.[163] It is assumed that the original inquiry was prompted by something more than idle curiosity. On February 9, 1939, the Arizona attorney general gave the state superintendent of public instruction a ruling that pupils who refused to salute the flag might be expelled.[164] A month later, two Witness children were expelled from schools in rural Arizona.[165]

In the fall of 1935, a junior high school girl in Kansas—the report is no more specific—was allowed to refrain from participating in the flag ceremony after she explained her religious reasons.[166] In the fall of 1938, Mrs. Mildred Nagle, of Holliday, in Johnson County, requested that her two daughters be excused from the school flag exercises.[167] This problem was passed up the line to the state superintendent, who ruled on September 14 that children in public school must salute the flag when called upon by the teacher to do so.[168] There is no record of the final outcome of this episode.

On October 31, 1935, the Chicago school board ordered that pupils be required to salute the flag and give the pledge of allegiance daily. No sanctions were specified.[169] Chicago was also the scene of a peculiar incident in 1936. An irate municipal judge sentenced a woman to six months' imprisonment when she refused his demand that she salute the flag on display in the courtroom.[170] The sentence was reversed on appeal.[171]

In 1939 a bill was introduced unsuccessfully in the Michigan Senate to require the flag salute daily in all public schools.[172] In 1935, a twelve-year-old Witness in St. Paul, Minnesota, was held to be within his rights in refusing to salute the flag.[173] About the same time, four non-saluting Witness children were allowed to remain in the schools of Norwalk, Connecticut,[174] although one of them was excluded from school assembly (where the salute ceremony was held), apparently as a punishment.[175]

I. *Pennsylvania*

1. THE GENERAL PICTURE

Pennsylvania law requires that every child within the state receive public school instruction or its equivalent up to the age of eighteen.[176] Failure of a parent to keep his child in school is punishable by fine, each day constituting a separate offense.[177] Where a child is unable to attend school because of his own misconduct or insubordination, he may be proceeded against as a juvenile delinquent.[178]

Pennsylvania maintains a public school system open to all children over six years of age, and administered in each school district by an elected board of school directors.[179] Within the framework set by the requirements of state law, these local boards have very wide discretion in organizing the curriculums and regulating the conduct of the individual pupils.[180] Like all states, Pennsylvania requires the public schools to offer instruction in certain subjects. Since 1919, one of these has been "civics, including loyalty to the State and National Government."[181] Exercising their discretion under this provision, many Pennsylvania localities had long-standing flag-salute rules as of 1935.

Pennsylvania ran far ahead of other states, with over a hundred pre-1940 expulsions of Jehovah's Witness children.[182] At least eighty-four of these were enrolled in three Kingdom Schools: twenty-eight in Andreas,[183] eighteen in Monessen,[184] and thirty-eight in Gates.[185] School authorities in eastern Pennsylvania seem generally to have taken a mild view, being content to stop with expelling the non-saluting children. There is only one report of any overt display of hostility by teachers or administrators.[186] School officials in Philadelphia,[187] Reading, Berks County[188] and Chester County[189] were reluctant even to resort to expulsion, preferring to seek some form of amicable compromise.

The situation was more serious in southwestern Pennsylvania, where both teachers and administrators reacted violently against non-saluters. There were reports of beatings in school in Grindstone, Nemacolin and Canonsburg. School law prosecutions against parents of expellees were very common, and there were some attempts to bring delinquency actions against individual children.[190] It was next to impossible to find local counsel for legal actions.[191] The outstanding trouble spots in this area were Canonsburg and Monessen.

2. CANONSBURG

Canonsburg had long had a *customary* flag ceremony, centering around three alternative flag pledges—the orthodox one, and two based on the VFW motto.[192] Faced with a number of refusals to participate, the local school board passed a formal resolution demanding the salute from both pupils and teachers,[193] and sought an official opinion as to its power from State Attorney General Charles J. Margiotti.

On October 26, 1935, Margiotti ruled that:

> Regardless of one's religious views, there can be no justification for any refusal to respect the standard of our nation. . . . When disloyalty to our country is part of any creed, it constitutes a defiance to the Constitution which guarantees that creed's existence. . . . Not only can boards of school directors require their teachers to take the oath of allegiance to the United States and administer it to their pupils, but it is the duty of such boards to require this manifestation of loyalty to our country. . . .
>
> Refusal by any pupil . . . to participate . . . would be considered an act of insubordination. . . .[194]

On November 7, 1935, the Canonsburg school board expelled seven Witness children from school, including thirteen-year-old Murray Estep, whose sister Grace was fired from her teaching job on the same day.[195]

Around the end of 1935, an action was brought on behalf of Murray Estep in the Washington County Court of Common Pleas, requesting a writ of mandamus to compel the Canonsburg school authorities to reinstate him. The Canonsburg school board filed a demurrer to the petition. At the hearing of the case on January 14, 1936,[196] the local American Legion post appeared through an attorney to support the Canonsburg stand.[197]

Estep v. Borough of Canonsburg[198] finally came to a decision on April 24, 1937. The Court of Common Pleas voted two to one to dismiss the action. One judge rested his decision wholly on the "secular regulation" rule, while the other relied exclusively on the "privilege" argument. The dissenting judge was not ready to rule for the plaintiff, but thought he had made out a good enough case to justify compelling the school board to file an answer and proceeding to a trial of the facts. There was no appeal; by this time, Moyle was busy with federal court litigation in eastern Pennsylvania.

3. MONESSEN

Jehovah's Witnesses set up a Kingdom School in Monessen to accommodate expelled children from the area, including those from Canonsburg. Classes were taught in a rented building by Ira Bird, who had been fired in a flag-salute dispute at Markleysburg.[199] Monessen officials, led by Mayor James Gold, objected strongly to the venture, which they considered communist in character.[200] On April 17, 1936, Monessen police padlocked the school, seized all literature used therein and jailed Bird incommunicado for two days.[201] Bird reopened the school on his release, only to have it padlocked again after only two days' operation. On May 24, 146 Witnesses appeared in Monessen with petitions denouncing Gold's "Hitleristic and unlawful" actions. After jailing all 146 overnight, Gold fined them five dollars apiece in a summary proceeding which hardly qualified as a trial.[202]

In the meantime, Jehovah's Witnesses brought action in the Westmoreland County Court of Common Pleas seeking an injunction restraining Gold and his police chief from further interference with the school's operation.[203] At the same time, Bird brought a $25,000 damage suit against the same parties for his arbitrary imprisonment. At the preliminary hearing on the former suit, a temporary injunction was issued, pending a hearing before the full three-judge court. Apparently by tacit agreement, both sides avoided any attempt to bring the case to a final hearing—thus leaving the temporary order in force—and Bird dropped his damage suit.[204] As of the beginning of 1937, the Kingdom School in Monessen was operating without interference, aside from three separate rocks hurled through the front window.[205]

J. Concluding Remarks

In the period from September, 1935, to June, 1940, the public school flag-salute ceremony became an issue in at least twenty states, leading to actual or imminent expulsions in sixteen. Most immediately striking about this early period is the relatively small total number of expulsions. The flag ceremony and the Witnesses' objections thereto were both nationwide in incidence; yet, less than half the states reported conflicts, and only in two did the number of expellees exceed ten.[206] This statistic seems to reflect the still tentative nature of the flag-salute controversy during this five-year interval. The initial reaction of the Witnesses themselves to the new rule of conduct was very spotty. Many children began their refusal very tardily, or not at all. The usual mode of refusal was to stand mute; but in at least two instances, children refused to rise at all for the ceremony.[207] Such variation largely disappeared after the "theocratic" reorganization of the sect in 1938.

Even more important as a moderating factor was the ambiguous attitude of many school authorities. Of nine states with specific flag-salute statutes, two—Delaware and Rhode Island—had no reported incidents; individual schools in four others—Kansas, Massachusetts, New Jersey and Washington—had shown a disposition to compromise the matter. It must be remembered that a non-saluter generally was safe unless the teacher chose to report his refusal or otherwise make an issue of it; and teachers were generally quite lukewarm toward the ceremony. School boards, while less tolerant, were not yet sufficiently aroused to search out non-saluters on their own. Unpopular as the adult Witnesses may have been, public sentiment had not yet hardened against their children.

The strategy of litigation of the Witnesses and their allies was a bit unclear and seems to have been the subject of some disagreement. The ACLU, with the apparent concurrence of Rutherford, was eager to bring as many test cases as possible, thus magnifying the importance of the flag salute as a civil liberties issue.[208] As time went on, Moyle became more and more reluctant to bring suits in the state courts,[209] especially after the federal courts began to show promise. He feared an accumulation of adverse precedents which might make change more difficult. Co-operation between Moyle and the Union's attorneys, while real and amicable, was tenuous in its details. In the early cases, Moyle was content to rely on the superior experience of the ACLU in deciding on proper strategy. Later, as in the *Shinn* case, he seems to have taken over the planning function. Finally, it is to be noted that of all the cases discussed in this chapter, Moyle took personal charge only of *Commonwealth v. Johnson;* ACLU representatives or associated attorneys handled the others.

CHAPTER FIVE

THE *GOBITIS* CASE
IN THE LOWER COURTS

A. *Early Stages*

1. THE SETTING

Minersville is a small community (1940 population: 8,686) four miles northwest of Pottsville, in Schuylkill County, Pennsylvania. The area is very hilly, forcing even the larger towns to adopt a sort of "ribbon development" form, concentrating along one main street following the line of a valley. Since the late nineteenth century, the economy of the county has been almost entirely dependent on the anthracite coal industry;[1] as a result, Schuylkill County has been a depression center at least since 1930. The population is heavily Catholic, the proportion in towns like Minersville running as high as 80 per cent. During the period under study, the Irish inhabitants formed a sort of economic and social elite, while the more recent arrivals from Eastern Europe, mostly Poles and Lithuanians, played the role of downtrodden proletariat. Irish dominance extended even to the churches. Each nationality attended its own church; but the hierarchy was Irish, and the parochial schools were attached to the Irish churches.[2]

2. THE PRINCIPALS

Walter Gobitis had lived in Minersville all his life, aside from one year in his childhood.[3] He had attended the Minersville schools and had himself saluted the flag without objection.[4] During the whole period under study here, he ran a prosperous self-service grocery store, and seems to have been generally well liked and respected as a businessman.[5] Mr. and Mrs. Gobitis became Jehovah's Witnesses in 1931, thus terminating the disrupting effects of a mixed Catholic-Protestant marriage.[6] At the time of the original controversy—late 1935

—the Gobitis family had two children in school—Lillian, born November 2, 1923, and William, born September 17, 1925—and three younger children. Lillian and William were enrolled respectively in the seventh and fifth grades in the Minersville public schools.[7]

The Minersville public schools are administered by a superintendent and an elected seven-man school board. The former post was occupied at this time by Charles E. Roudabush, a professional educator, who came to the Minersville school system in 1914.[8] Aside from Roudabush, only two members of the board—both physicians—had any advanced professional training. Probably the most influential member was Dr. Thomas J. McGurl, an Irish Catholic (one of two Catholics on the board)[9] whose brother, John B. McGurl, was board solicitor.

3. OPENING OF THE DISPUTE

The flag-salute ceremony was a well-established *custom* in the Minersville public schools as early as 1914.[10] While there was no formal rule requiring participation, there had been no case of a pupil refusing during Superintendent Roudabush's tenure of office.[11] Shortly after "Judge" Rutherford's October 6, 1935, radio talk on the flag-salute issue, however, Lillian and William Gobitis stopped saluting.[12] Roudabush tried first to thrash the matter out personally with Gobitis, with very bad results. The two men seem to have detested each other from the very start.[13] Roudabush's outrage that *anyone* should refuse the salute was not mellowed by Gobitis' testy rejoinder that he was a citizen not of the United States but of Heaven.[14] Gobitis, for his part, considered Roudabush an out-and-out atheist because of the latter's adherence to the theory of evolution.[15] The upshot was predictable: the children continued their refusal, while Roudabush sought an official opinion from the State Department of Public Instruction as to his legal power to compel the salute.

On October 16, the Department of Public Instruction advised Roudabush that a pupil's disobedience of a *formal* flag-salute requirement might be punished as insubordination.[16] On October 21, a sixth grader, Edmund Wasliewski, refused to salute.[17] The Minersville school board met specially the same evening, but decided to postpone any action until its regular November 6 meeting.[18] On October 26, Attorney General Margiotti handed down his opinion upholding the compulsory salute as applied to both teachers and pupils.

Thus fortified with two state rulings, the Minersville school board met on November 6 to settle the matter. Roudabush reported at length on the refusals.[19] Walter Gobitis and Mrs. Wasliewski presented the standard Witness position on the flag salute, which interested the board not at all.[20] The board members also heard read letters from Lillian and William Gobitis explaining their religious reasons for refusing the salute.[21] Then, by unanimous vote, the board resolved

That the Superintendent of the Minersville Public Schools be required to demand that all teachers and pupils of the said schools be required to salute the flag of our Country as a part of the daily exercises. That refusal to salute the flag shall be regarded as an act of insubordination and shall be dealt with accordingly.[22]

Immediately following this vote, Roudabush rose and announced:

I hereby expel from the Minersville schools Lillian Gobitis, William Gobitis and Edmund Wasliewski for this act of insubordination, to wit, failure to salute the flag in our school exercises.[23]

Such were the events leading up to the expulsion of the Gobitis children. In retrospect, Gobitis regards the whole episode as another instance of Catholic persecution, engineered by the McGurls, with Roudabush serving as a "willing tool."[24] This is dubious history. Gobitis remains on good terms with Dr. McGurl and the other board members. The only real bitterness, then or after, was between Gobitis and Roudabush, whose extreme emotional commitment on this issue was further highlighted by the almost indecent haste with which he moved to expel the Witness children. The school board members, while either friendly or at least indifferent toward Gobitis, did not understand and were impatient with his religious arguments against the flag salute. They undoubtedly thought that they were "settling" the matter, and that things would return to normal once Gobitis had cooled down and gotten his children readmitted on the board's terms.[25]

The population of Minersville seems to have taken the dispute very calmly. The expulsions received no notice in the local press.[26] Most people seem to have approved, or at least accepted, the board's action.[27] On the other hand, there seems to have been very little public resentment directed either at Gobitis or at his children. A rumored lynch mob failed to materialize,[28] and a proposed boycott of Gobitis' grocery fizzled after one day. The local American Legion post was badly split, and took no definite action during at least the first two years of the dispute.[29]

The compulsory flag-salute regulation and the expulsions thereunder did not settle the issue, of course; Gobitis remained adamant and the children stayed out of school. After failing to get Lillian and William admitted to the Pottsville schools—which also demanded the salute—Gobitis enrolled both children in the Kingdom School in Andreas, Pennsylvania, about thirty miles from Minersville. Administered by Verna S. Jones and taught by Erma Metzger, both Witnesses, this school was financed entirely by apportioned levies on the parents of the thirty-odd Witness children enrolled therein.[30] After Lillian finished the eighth grade, the highest offered in the Jones school, she enrolled in Pottsville Business College, the only non-religious private school within reasonable traveling distance.[31]

4. RESORT TO THE COURTS

Walter Gobitis was eager to take his troubles to court, but had much difficulty securing counsel.[32] He wrote for help to the Witnesses' national headquarters, but none was forthcoming at first. Olin R. Moyle, national legal counsel, was beset by limited resources and an overabundance of willing plaintiffs. As it happened, the *Nicholls, Leoles* and *Hering* cases were first in line. With these pending, Moyle was very reluctant to commence any more litigation in the state courts. When Moyle turned his attention to the federal courts, he had Pennsylvania very much in mind for his first litigation; but his first choice in plaintiffs probably was the Esteps in Canonsburg. While Moyle was busy elsewhere, however, the Esteps found local counsel, sued and eventually lost in the Washington County Court of Common Pleas. With the Esteps no longer attractive subjects for a federal suit, Moyle turned his attention to Minersville. On May 3, 1937, he filed a bill of complaint in the United States District Court for the Eastern District of Pennsylvania at Philadelphia, denouncing the Minersville regulation and the expulsions thereunder as violative of the Eighth and Fourteenth Amendments and requesting an injunction against their continued enforcement against the Gobitis children.[33] Harry M. McCaughey, a Philadelphia lawyer who had handled some Witness cases before, was retained as local counsel of record (Moyle not being a member of the Pennsylvania state or federal bars).

The American Civil Liberties Union, already co-operating closely with Moyle, took an active interest in the Gobitis suit, and wrote to two affiliated Philadelphia lawyers with a view to having one of them work with Moyle and McCaughey.[34] One of these, Alexander H. Frey of the University of Pennsylvania Law School, may have done so.[35] If so, his contact was almost entirely through McCaughey, who himself took a very minor part in the actual litigation. Moyle was in very firm command of the action throughout.[36]

On May 12, 1937, the Minersville school board met to consider Gobitis' action. The board voted unanimously to fight the case and granted John B. McGurl's request for authority to retain Philadelphia counsel to cope with the unfamiliar procedure of the District Court there.[37] McGurl subsequently retained the firm of Rawle and Henderson. This firm, particularly its head, Joseph W. Henderson, took complete charge of the litigation, McGurl serving mainly as liaison between Henderson and the Minersville authorities.[38] On May 27, 1937, Henderson filed with the District Court a motion to dismiss the bill of complaint with reasonable costs to be awarded to the defendant school authorities.[39]

B. *In the District Court: On Motion To Dismiss*

1. THE BILL OF COMPLAINT AND MOTION TO DISMISS[40]

Technically, this suit was brought by Walter Gobitis personally and as next friend of his two minor children against the Minersville School District, the Minersville school board, and the individual board members plus Roudabush. The bill of complaint had twenty-two paragraphs, sixteen of which (I–

IV, VI–XVII) were devoted to the factual background of the suit: the legal setting, the identity of the parties, the events leading up to the expulsions, the religious views of the plaintiffs and the financial burden placed on the elder Gobitis by the expulsion of his children from the free public schools. Paragraph V asserted in the language of the relevant statutes that the District Court had jurisdiction under sections 24(14) and 24(1) of the Judicial Code.[41] In other words, it was asserted that the suit was one to redress deprivation under color of state law of rights secured by the United States Constitution, and that it arose under the Constitution and involved a property right worth more than $3,000. The last five paragraphs contained the constitutional attack on the compulsory flag salute. Paragraph XVIII asserted that the Minersville regulation was invalid on its face under the Fourteenth Amendment. Paragraph XIX urged that the regulation, as applied to the Gobitis children, denied them freedom of speech and religion and the equal protection of the laws. Paragraph XX argued that expulsion from public school, with its attendant hardships and dangers, was a cruel and unusual punishment for mere nonsaluting and violative of the Eighth Amendment. Paragraph XXI alleged that the regulation and the expulsions thereunder violated in various ways the federal due process rights of Walter Gobitis. Paragraph XXII was crucial:

Complainants further allege that the acts, conduct and decisions of said defendants aforesaid cannot be justified under the police power in that the failure and refusal to salute the flag on the part of the said minor complainants does not and cannot affect the public interest or safety or the rights and welfare of others.[42]

The District Court was requested to enjoin the school authorities from continuing to enforce against the Gobitis children either the flag-salute requirement or the expulsion order, and "from in anywise hindering or molesting or interfering with the right of said minor complainants to enjoy full religious freedom in the manner dictated by conscience."[43]

The defendants' motion to dismiss the complaint was short but complete. The first four paragraphs contended that the District Court had no jurisdiction, because the jurisdictional amount was inadequately urged, the controversy was not one arising under the Constitution or laws of the United States, and there was no federally secured right at issue. As to the merits, it was urged that the challenged regulation was both legal and constitutional, and that the "alleged right" of public education was not properly enforceable by injunctive procedure.

2. DEFENDANTS' PAPER BOOK IN SUPPORT OF THE MOTION TO DISMISS[44]

The paper book in support of the motion to dismiss was written by Henderson and signed by him, John B. McGurl and another member of the firm, George M. Brodhead. The argument was divided into two sections, the first denying District Court jurisdiction, the second denying that the facts alleged in the complaint, if true, entitled plaintiffs to any relief.

a) Jurisdiction.—Section 24(1) of the Judicial Code gave federal District Courts original jurisdiction over civil suits in law or equity arising under the Constitution or laws of the United States and involving more than $3,000. Henderson denied that either prerequisite was present. The mere assertion that the jurisdictional amount was present, without supporting allegations of specific fact, would not suffice, he argued, where the stated money figure was clearly inflated. "We fail to see how the plaintiffs can reasonably spend $3,000 in educating their two children in an adjoining public school or in a local private day school."[45] Nor did the case "arise" under the federal Constitution in Henderson's view. The Minersville school board, he pointed out, was only authorized to make "reasonable" regulations.

... The plaintiffs have averred that the regulation was contrary to the provisions of the Constitution. By so contending, it follows that the plaintiffs are in fact maintaining that the regulation itself is unreasonable. ...

If the plaintiffs in effect contend that the regulation of the school board is not a reasonable one, they must likewise contend that the regulation was made without authority and not under the powers granted to the school board. ... Such a controversy is not one arising under the Constitution.[46]

Henderson relied on several cases in which the illegality under state law of challenged official actions was a necessary element in the claim under the Fourteenth Amendment.[47] The argument was thin, but worth trying.

Section 24(14) of the Judicial Code gave the District Courts original jurisdiction of suits to redress deprivations "under color of any law, . . . of any right, privilege, or immunity, secured by the Constitution. . . ." At the time of this suit, there was considerable confusion as to just which constitutional rights were actually *secured* by the Constituiton within the meaning of this statute. Henderson strongly advanced what was then the prevailing view: that the "secured" rights were those arising out of national citizenship, such as freedom of movement, freedom to petition Congress, etc.; freedom of speech and religion were only "protected" against state infringement, and must be vindicated in the first instance through the state courts.[48]

b) The merits.—Henderson began his argument on the merits with strong emphasis on the wide discretion which obviously must be left to local school boards in matters like this.

. . . [A] regulation requiring pupils to salute the American flag for the purpose of inculcating patriotism . . . seems just as reasonable . . . a part of a pupil's education as a requirement to study history or any other of the subjects enumerated in the School Code.[49]

In rebuttal of the Witnesses' religious objections, Henderson summoned up and quoted from *Hamilton v. Regents, United States v. Macintosh* and a host of other "secular regulation" precedents. He went on to argue that the Witnesses simply were wrong in ascribing religious significance to the flag ceremony:

. . . [T]o attempt to affix the label "religion" to the exercise of saluting the flag does not affect the intrinsic nature of the proceeding.
. . . Not one religious word is uttered in the recitation of the usual Pledge of Allegiance and not one religious tremor can move throughout the human body by its recitation.[50]

Finally, Henderson called attention to and quoted liberally from the various state decisions upholding the compulsory salute, with particular emphasis on the *Estep* case.

3. COMPLAINANTS' BRIEF ON THE MOTION TO DISMISS[51]

The brief opposing the motion to dismiss was written by Moyle and signed by him and McCaughey. It is quite clear that Moyle had not seen Henderson's brief in support of the motion; he dwelled almost entirely on the merits, giving only cursory and rather weak treatment to the jurisdictional issue.

a) *Jurisdiction.*—Moyle failed to anticipate the particular grounds of Henderson's jurisdictional challenge from the meager clues furnished by the motion to dismiss. Thus, he argued that Henderson's challenge to the stated jurisdictional amount came too early, since factual allegations must be admitted as true for purposes of the motion to dismiss. As to whether the case "arose" under the Constitution, Moyle simply reviewed all the constitutional issues that had been raised in the bill of complaint, again missing Henderson's point. As to jurisdiction under Section 24(14), Moyle did about as well as he could, in view of the hostile state of the precedents, arguing flatly that *all* Fourteenth Amendment rights were within the reach of that provision.

b) *The merits.*—Moyle's main point, of course, was that the Minersville regulation invaded freedom of religion in violation of the due process clause of the Fourteenth Amendment. Citing a variety of dubiously relevant cases—notably *Reynolds v. United States* and *Hardwicke*—he argued that

> . . . [A]ny such interference or infringement is only permissible in the interests of public safety, morality, and to preserve personal rights and the rights of property. . . .
> . . . [T]he Bill in Equity shows a clear cut violation of the constitutional right of freedom of worship and freedom of religion. The Defendants must then prove that the infringement is justified. . . .[52]

He went on to contend that no justification *could* be given, since it was against common sense that the children's refusal to salute could in any way harm the public interest. At any rate, the compulsory salute could do no good, tending to breed more hypocrisy than patriotism in the pupils compelled.

Drawing directly from Isserman's model brief, Moyle claimed also that the compulsory flag salute constituted a violation of freedom of speech. Primary reliance again was placed upon *Stromberg v. California;* the conduct at issue here clearly was less harmful than that condoned in that case. "Compelling words, or a gesture equivalent to words, under penalty, is quite as clear an invasion of a right to free speech as is a prohibition against words or symbols."[53]

Moyle also advanced several peripheral constitutional arguments. In rebuttal to the common privilege argument, he invoked the respectable, if hardly logical, judicial doctrine that the grant of a privilege might not be conditioned on the surrender of a constitutional right.[54] He also asserted that the compulsory salute violated Walter Gobitis' constitutional right to control the education of his children. This point might have been at least tenable under the *Pierce* precedent, but for the weird content given the argument here. Since the state could not interfere with parents' decision to send their children to private schools, Moyle argued, it could not interfere with a decision to send them to *public* schools. The weakness of this logic need not be labored. Equally weak was Moyle's appeal to the equal protection clause of the Fourteenth Amendment. Again drawing from Isserman's brief, he claimed that the Minersville regulation set up an arbitrary classification in that it required the salute only from school children, and only from those in the public schools. It was suggested that this case was a mirror image of the *Pierce* situation; here it was the parents of public school children who were victimized. It need only be commented that the equal protection clause demands equal treatment only for those similarly situated, and that the *Pierce* case in essence upheld the right of parents to have their children educated *differently* than in the public schools.

In a final section, Moyle sought to deal with the adverse precedents. *Hamilton v. Regents* was distinguished on the grounds set forth in Isserman's model brief: the comparative triviality of the state interest involved here; and the fact that grade-school education, unlike university attendance, was required by law. Moyle freely admitted that the state courts generally had held against the Witnesses on the flag-salute issue, but emphasized the common reliance of these decisions on the contention that the flag ceremony was "not a religious rite." The complaint did not claim that it was, he noted; the decisive fact was that the Gobitis children *believed* that it was. Simply in overruling this religious scruple, the state was violating religious freedom. Moyle conceded, however, that an objection completely remote from religion might be unjustified. He therefore sought to demonstrate that flag saluting had assumed many of the attributes of a religion. "We are told that it [the flag] requires not only our service but our reverence, devotion and love."[55] He quoted in full the glowing tributes to the flag contained in the *Encyclopedia Americana* and the DAR manual for new citizens. "One of the earmarks of a national religion is the force and brutality used in making all people conform to its tenets."[56] Moyle saw modern day counterparts of the religious oppressions under Nebuchadnezzar and Caesar in the harassments visited on Witnesses in Pennsylvania and elsewhere, as well as the severe persecution directed at them in Nazi Germany.

4. THE DECISION ON THE MOTION TO DISMISS

On December 1, 1937, Judge Albert Branson Maris denied the motion to dismiss and ordered the case to trial.[57] A Quaker and a veteran of World War I, Judge Maris had been appointed as District Judge by President Roosevelt on June 22, 1936.[58] Moyle denies having "selected" Judge Maris' court;[59] he could hardly have chosen better if he had. While Maris conducted himself with scrupulous fairness throughout, he displayed a breadth of tolerance which had eluded many previous judges on this issue. Judge Maris' opinion dealt first and mainly with the merits of the dispute; then, on the basis of his findings there, he considered his jurisdiction to dispose of the case.

a) The merits.—Judge Maris assumed implicitly that the religious freedom guaranteed by the Fourteenth Amendment was coterminous with that protected by article I, section 3 of the Pennsylvania Constitution, and, by implication, by the First Amendment—a holding the Supreme Court was to reach only three years later. As to the scope of this liberty, Maris quoted very selectively from Judge Gibson's dissent in *Commonwealth v. Lesher,* stressing the right "to do or forbear to do, any act for conscience' sake, the doing or forbearing of which is not prejudicial to the public weal." In applying this principle, Maris rejected both the "secular regulation" rule and the general ruling in the state decisions that the flag salute had nothing to do with religion.

. . . If an individual sincerely bases his acts or refusals to act on religious grounds they must be accepted as such and may only be interfered with if it becomes necessary to do so in connection with the exercise of the police power. . . .

. . . [N]o man, even though he be a school director or a judge, is empowered to censor another's religious convictions *or set bounds to the areas of human conduct in which those convictions should be permitted to control his actions,* unless compelled to do so by an overriding public necessity. . . . [Italics supplied.] [60]

Judge Maris' opinion broke much new ground: (*a*) it rejected the sharp distinction between enactments dealing with secular matters and those touching matters specifically religious; (*b*) it demanded that this particular application of the rule be justified; and (*c*) it tacitly placed the burden of proof on the authorities. Maris readily adopted the Moyle-Isserman argument distinguishing *Hamilton v. Regents.*

While frankly doubting that refusal to salute the flag could in any way prejudice the public good, Judge Maris held this to be a matter of fact to be fought out at the trial. Assuming the absence of such justification for purposes of the motion to dismiss, he held that the Minersville regulation, as applied to the Gobitis children, violated the religious freedom guaranties of the Pennsylvania and United States constitutions.

b) *Jurisdiction.*—Judge Maris agreed with Henderson and the current weight of authority that he had no jurisdiction under Section 24(14) of the Judicial Code. Section 24(1) was a different matter. Maris flatly rejected Henderson's argument that the Minersville regulation, if unconstitutional, was also illegal and therefore raised no federal constitutional question. The regulation, he pointed out, was perfectly reasonable *on its face;* it was the application that was challenged. This sort of abuse of legally vested authority was clearly within the prohibition of the Fourteenth Amendment and Section 24(1). [61] Maris held the existence of a jurisdictional amount in controversy to be a matter for proof or disproof at the trial; he was not prepared to hold the plaintiffs' allegation on this score to be unreasonable on its face.

Judge Maris' rejection of the "secular regulation" rule destroyed any chance for the Minersville authorities to win a verdict on the law alone. Short of an appeal, their only hope was to win out on at least one of the two remaining factual issues: (*a*) Was Walter Gobitis damaged in excess of $3,000 by the exclusion of his children from public school? (*b*) Did the refusal of the Gobitis children to salute the flag in school do or threaten some harm to the public welfare sufficiently serious to call for the remedial action of the police power?

5. AFTERMATH: BETWEEN RULING AND TRIAL

Judge Maris' ruling attracted fairly wide attention. Both Pottsville newspapers reported the decision, but avoided any editorial comment at this point. Two Philadelphia papers, the *Record* and the *Evening Bulletin,* carried strongly favorable editorials.[62] Educators reacted similarly. Joy Elmer Morgan, editor of the *National Education Association Journal* came out against compelling the salute.[63] State Superintendent Lester K. Ade denounced the compulsory salute as "fine for Hitler and Mussolini, but not for the American public." "Forcing children to salute the flag," he argued, "doesn't get at the fundamental attitude of respect. . . . It ought to come from the heart. . . ."[64] The superintendents of Berks and Reading Counties and Easton also went on record against compelling the salute at this time.[65] The Philadelphia superintendent was indifferent; schools there had no trouble and he seemed to expect none.[66]

On the other hand, this rebuff in court seems only to have hardened the resolve of the Minersville authorities to fight to the finish. Roudabush stated publicly and emphatically that he would not readmit the Gobitis children without the flag salute unless and until a final court order was placed in his hands.[67] He was backed strongly in this position by local patriotic organizations. In the month following Maris' decision, letters of support came from the Improved Order of Red Men,[68] the GAR Federation[69] and the American Legion.[70] More substantial were the communications from the Patriotic Order of the Sons of America[71] and the Order of Independent Americans,[72] both of which offered financial aid, if such should be needed. This was important; the Minersville school district was in no financial condition to pay for an appeal.[73]

Little information is available as to the preparations for trial by the two sides. Moyle delegated Gobitis to obtain itemized receipts for any expenses not yet so documented which he had incurred on account of the expulsions.[74] Aside from that, he kept his own counsel. Henderson's correspondence with the Minersville authorities reflected a preoccupation with the necessity of securing expert testimony in support of two propositions: that the flag salute was in no way religious; and "that the refusal of a pupil to salute the flag would affect the public welfare and safety of the citizens by reason of the disrespect shown to the government and its laws, which such refusal would engender."[75] Nothing seems to have been done regarding the first, rather novel, point; as to the second, it was eventually decided that Roudabush himself should testify from his own expert knowledge as a veteran educator.[76]

6. THE JOINT AND SEVERAL ANSWERS[77]

Defendants' answer, filed on December 30, 1937, was written by Henderson, and signed by him, McGurl and all the individual defendants. This document was in the usual form, answering the complaint paragraph by paragraph, carefully avoiding any unnecessary or accidental concessions and sharply delineating the disputed areas of fact for purposes of the subsequent trial. The factual allegations identifying the parties and relating the history of the controversy up to the bringing of suit were admitted with only minor quibbles. To the paragraphs dealing with the Gobitis family's religious beliefs Henderson opposed a formal denial, pleading ignorance of the matter and demanding strict proof at the trial. Henderson flatly denied the allegations of paragraphs X—that the plaintiffs were loyal, law abiding citizens—and V—that the District Court had jurisdiction. He formally refused to admit or deny the constitutional contentions of the last five paragraphs of the complaint—proper form, since these were not questions of fact—but went on to deny them in essentially the same language in which they had been advanced.

In addition to these formal responses, Henderson got in several counterclaims which previewed the tack he was to take at the trial. He alleged in sufficient form that Walter Gobitis could have found alternative education for his children more cheaply than he had.[78] He further reiterated his contention that public education was not a property right enforceable at equity. He strongly denied that the flag salute was in any way religious. He repeatedly asserted the legality and constitutionality of the Minersville regulation. In response to the crucial twenty-second paragraph of the complaint, Henderson stressed the good faith of the school board in determining that the compulsory salute was "a necessary and reasonable method of teaching loyalty," as required by Pennsylvania law.

. . . [T]he failure or refusal of any pupil or group of pupils to salute the national flag would be disrespectful to the government of which the flag is a symbol and would tend to promote disrespect for that government and its laws, with the result that the public welfare and safety and wellbeing of the citizens of the United States would be ultimately harmed and seriously affected thereby.[79]

Again, the District Court was requested to dismiss the action with costs.

C. *In the District Court: Trial and Decision*

1. THE TRIAL

The trial of the case was held on February 15, 1938. At the outset, Henderson, for the defendants, objected to the taking of evidence and filed a new motion to dismiss. Judge Maris denied the motion on the basis of his previous opinion; an exception was noted for defendants.[80] Moyle then read into the record those paragraphs of the bill of complaint which had been admitted in whole or in part by the defendants.

a) Complainants' evidence.—Moyle's first and principal witness was *Walter Gobitis*. He testified in great detail about the factual background of the case, provoking many objections by Henderson and a judicial admonition to Moyle against cluttering up the record. Gobitis testified fully regarding his religious beliefs, and—in standard Witness fashion—avoided any hint that he had told the children not to salute: "Well, I have taught them to believe and study the Bible for a long time . . . and as we were talking things over at home, no doubt, they got a lot of knowledge in that respect concerning idolatry, we have talked about that."[81]

The balance of Gobitis' testimony dealt with the crucial issue of the monetary amount in controversy. This part of the trial was marked by much confusion and a great deal of bickering; it need only be summarized here. Moyle lumped together the expenses incurred by both William and Lillian Gobitis, and extrapolated from there to reach the further expenses that would be incurred by the time both children reached the maximum school age of eighteen. Bills showing the tuition and winter room and board expenses for the children at Andreas were admitted without objection; they were a minor item, totalling only $440.56.[82] Gobitis' expenses in driving the children to and from Andreas were the subject of much trouble. In the absence of any itemized records, Gobitis was allowed—over passionate objections by Henderson—to estimate his costs at about four cents per mile—yielding an extrapolated grand total of $1,180.80.[83] Finally, evidence was admitted regarding the past and probable future costs of sending the children to Pottsville Business College, an item totalling $1,640.00,[84] over Henderson's objection that Gobitis had had cheaper alternatives. Gobitis testified that other private schools in the area were prohibitively expensive and that none of the neighboring public schools would accept the children without the flag salute. Cross-examined by Henderson on the costs of nearby parochial schools, Gobitis replied curtly that the cost of such education would be "very high."[85] Judge Maris excluded several peripheral items of expense from consideration: Gobitis' school taxes for the period of the dispute; assorted legal expenses incurred before the beginning of the suit; and possible additional expenses should his four younger children also be expelled for not saluting.

At the conclusion of Gobitis' testimony, Henderson again moved that the case be dismissed for want of the required jurisdictional amount in controversy. Judge Maris denied the motion "for the present."[86]

William Gobitis made a strong and appealing witness, despite his relatively brief time on the stand. After being led through some redundant preliminaries, he testified cogently and convincingly about his religious beliefs and his conscientious objection to the flag salute. Under questioning by Judge Maris, he testified that he loved his country and wanted to do everything he could to be a good citizen. There was no cross-examination.

Lillian Gobitis testified very briefly. She readily identified the biblical passages justifying her refusal to salute, adding I John 21:5 to those already mentioned. She further testified that she believed in being loyal to her country and had obeyed all school rules except the flag-salute regulation. There were no further questions.

Frederick William Franz, a leading figure in the Witness editorial department, testified regarding Jehovah's Witnesses' doctrines touching on the flag salute. Henderson's objection that the testimony was immaterial was overruled, since it might have some bearing on the question of the Gobitises' sincerity. Franz stated flatly that performance of the flag salute by one of Jehovah's Witnesses would lead to that person's absolute destruction at the hand of God. He supported this assertion with biblical passages equating "bowing down" with all gestures of adoration, pointed to the refusal of the ancient Israelites to salute the banners they carried in battle, and noted the quasi-religious expressions of reverence often directed at the American flag. At the close of his testimony, Henderson renewed his objection and was again overruled.

b) Defendants' evidence.—Superintendent Roudabush was the only witness called for the defense. Over Moyle's objection, he was allowed to testify that there were several good parochial schools near Minersville that admitted non-Catholics, often at little or no expense. Under questioning from the bench, he confessed ignorance as to whether those schools demanded the flag salute. Roudabush's testimony about the desirability of the salute and the dangers of non-conformity led to a series of very damaging exchanges with Judge Maris:

By Mr. Henderson:

Q. . . . Doctor, in your opinion, what is the effect when a few children do not salute the flag and others do, so far as your school system is concerned?

A. It would be demoralizing on the whole group.

Q. Why?

A. The tendency would be to spread. In our mixed population where we have foreigners of every variety, it would be no time until they would form a dislike, a disregard for our flag and country. May I say that the thing that goes hard with us when some one refuses to salute the flag is to refuse to pledge allegiance to the country for which it stands.

Now, I believe when we make a citizen out of an alien the first thing that we require is they have to denounce their allegiance to the foreign country, and it would seem reasonable to suppose that they would be required to pledge allegiance to the country in which they want to become citizens.

BY THE COURT:

Q. Just a minute. Is there any arrangement, Doctor, for any children who explain that they refuse to salute the flag because of religious reasons, to pledge allegiance separate from the salute?

A. No, we have never made any provisions; we feel it is not a religious exercise in any way and has nothing to do with anybody's religion.

Q. Do you feel that these views to the contrary here held by these two pupils are not sincerely held?

A. I feel that they were indoctrinated.

Q. Do you feel their parents' views were not sincerely held?

A. I believe they are probably sincerely held, but misled; they are perverted views.

Q. I suppose you would say the same thing about a Mohammedan, wouldn't you, or a Hindu?

A. No, that is a whole—

Q. In other words, anyone who didn't agree with your religious views and mine would be indoctrinated, or hold perverted views, because he doesn't believe with you?

A. As I see it, your Honor, I feel that this is not a matter of religion at all, it has nothing to do with religion, and I think the objection by the Jehovah's Witnesses is uncalled for.[87]

Another exchange was precipitated when Roudabush expressed his opinion that refusal to salute constituted disrespect for the ideals and institutions of the United States.

BY THE COURT:

Q. Without admitting it, admitting that a misguided person sincerely feels that he must weaken his whole religious conscience to do it, would you say that is disrespect to our flag?

A. I would, I feel he should be put right. They should show the proper reverence of the country and the flag.

Q. Do I understand you to mean the public schools should see their religious beliefs are changed?

A. Try to correct the thing that exists and that is wrong.[88]

Roudabush's testimony regarding the importance of the salute in the teaching of loyalty led to a series of exchanges with Maris and Moyle:

BY THE COURT:

Q. Is it your experience or not that this daily exercise repeated every day tends to become somewhat a formalistic matter, a matter of form with a lot of children?

A. I believe it does, just the same as going to church, or anything else. . . . But there comes a time when there will be a thinking back to the lessons that were inculcated in the public schools.[89]

BY MR. MOYLE:

Q. And it is absolutely necessary to salute the flag in order to teach loyalty?

A. Oh, no, one of the means, it is one of the means of teaching loyalty.

Q. Then you admit that loyalty could be taught—

A. It is taught otherwise.

Q. —without saluting the flag?

BY THE COURT:

Q. I would imagine, Doctor, what you really mean, in your opinion, it is an appropriate method?

A. Yes.

Q. But not a necessary method, there are other methods?

A. There are other methods.

Q. You say it is an appropriate method, and you have adopted it?

A. Yes sir.

BY MR. MOYLE:

Q. Then you admit loyalty could be taught without the flag salute, is that right?

A. Yes, sir. I will not admit, though, that we do not have a right to ask—

Q. I understand.[90]

Moyle then elicited the admission that, the flag salute aside, the Gobitis children's conduct in school had been exemplary. The examination ended on a note of bickering, with Moyle trying unsuccessfully to compel Roudabush to admit the possibility of a conscientious objection to the salute.

c) *Rebuttal and surrebuttal.*—In rebuttal to Roudabush's testimony, Moyle offered two new witnesses. One, Charles E. Hessler, was to testify that the general effect of the compulsory salute was to encourage lawlessness and persecution. The other, Erma Metzger, was to testify to the loyalty and exemplary character of the flag-salute expellees attending her class at the Jones Kingdom School. Judge Maris excluded both witnesses after objections by Henderson, holding that their testimony would be immaterial to the issues at hand.

In surrebuttal, Henderson read into the record excerpts from several textbooks in use in the Minersville schools, all stressing the importance of loyalty, patriotism and flag respect. One of these was so glowing in its tribute to the flag that Maris felt called upon to protest that Henderson was providing evidence for the other side. The apparent purpose of these readings was to show that the flag-salute ceremony was so integral a part of the school curriculum that an adverse decision would have disrupting effects subject to no simple boundaries.

At the close of the trial, Henderson renewed his motion to dismiss the bill of complaint on jurisdictional grounds. Judge Maris took the motion under advisement.

2. THE BRIEFS ON FINDINGS OF FACT AND LAW

Each side filed requests for findings of fact and law, and a supporting brief. The plaintiffs also filed a reply brief after receiving a copy of the defendants' brief.

a) *Defendants' brief.*[91]—Henderson again denied emphatically that the District Court had jurisdiction under any federal statute. While he reproduced the main points from his earlier brief, he concentrated here on the question of jurisdictional amount. He sharply attacked Walter Gobitis' testimony, noting his uncertainty as to the exact length of the Andreas school year, the number of trips actually made to Andreas, etc. His estimate of per-mile operating costs of his car was dismissed by Henderson as a mere guess by an interested party. On the basis of the judicial rule that plaintiffs are under a duty to minimize damages, Henderson attacked the inclusion of expenses from Pottsville Business College. In fact, he argued, both children probably could have been placed in local parochial schools at a mere fraction of the costs alleged here. Even granting the validity of all the cost figures, Henderson argued that schooling expenses for Lillian and William Gobitis must be computed separately. Since neither child's education had cost as much as $3,000, the cause must be dismissed. Finally, Henderson contended that the Supreme Court's refusal to hear the *Leoles* and *Hering* appeals left no "substantial federal question" to be decided.

Henderson's discussion of the merits of the case was in most respects a somewhat less quotation-laden duplicate of that in his earlier brief on the motion to dismiss. Henderson further stressed the controlling nature of the *per curiam* Supreme Court dispositions of *Leoles* and *Hering*. He went on to cite the trial record with prudent vagueness as demonstrating that the flag salute had nothing to do with religion. Henderson closed with a strong appeal for the public policy underlying the flag-salute ceremony—the promotion of group loyalty. He quoted at length from Roudabush's testimony on the harmful effects to be expected from the refusal of pupils to salute.

b) Plaintiffs' brief.[92]—Moyle's brief for the plaintiffs concentrated on the two points left at issue by Judge Maris' opinion on the motion to dismiss. As to the jurisdictional amount, Moyle insisted that the cost estimates presented at the trial were, if anything, too low. The estimates of future school expenses made no allowance for possible contingencies, he argued, and four cents a mile was an obviously low cost figure for operation of a car over mountain roads. Moyle lashed out sharply at Henderson's suggestion that Gobitis should have tried a local parochial school:

... It is submitted that where the public schools deny the right of education to the children of a taxpayer it is not reasonable that the state require that they secure such education in the school of a religious denomination.[93]

As to the effects of non-saluting on the public welfare, Moyle repeated his assertion that it was incumbent on the defendants to demonstrate some adverse effect. He bitterly attacked Superintendent Roudabush's testimony on this point:

Lincoln Christian College

It is submitted that the record discloses no *competent* evidence of peril to the public safety, health or morals through the position taken by the plaintiffs. The witness Roudabush has shown himself entirely incompetent as an expert on the safety of the state. Speaking glibly of respect, reverence and loyalty to the flag and country, he in the same breath voices sentiments wholly foreign to the principles of freedom, tolerance and justice which have abounded in this country for the greater part of two centuries. He would make religion a state matter. . . .[94]

Citing his previous brief and Maris' opinion on the motion to dismiss, Moyle called for a judgment.

c) Plaintiffs' reply brief.[95]—In his reply brief, Moyle dealt with two points: the claim that the expenses for Lillian and William Gobitis must be treated separately, and the heavy reliance placed by Henderson on the Supreme Court dismissals of *Leoles* and *Hering*. On the first point, Moyle simply pointed out that Walter Gobitis was also a party to this action, and both children's costs came out of his pocket. He emphasized the fact that the Supreme Court, in *Hering* and *Leoles*, had relied on *Hamilton v. Regents*, which was clearly distinguishable from this case. Finally, Moyle made the risky argument that those *per curiam* decisions should be ignored, whatever their relevance:

The doctrine of *stare decisis* is not conclusive. It has much, little or no force according to the nature of the question decided. Here are important questions of personal liberty and freedom. . . .

Defendants make no attempt to answer these or similar questions. They frowardly assert the rule of precedents and exalt it above the inherent rights of individuals. The better rule would be, "Let this decision be right whether other decisions were right or not."[96]

3. THE REQUESTS FOR FINDINGS OF FACT AND LAW

a) Plaintiffs.[97]—Plaintiffs' requests for findings of fact very nearly duplicated the original allegations of the bill of complaint. All these were affirmed by Judge Maris, with two limitations. The proposed finding as to the religious objections to the flag salute was affirmed "as to plaintiffs," and that dealing with the presence of the necessary jurisdictional amount was affirmed "as to plaintiff Walter Gobitis only." Of plaintiffs' six proposed findings of law, two were catch-all attacks on the constitutionality of the Minersville regulation, drawn in the language of the original complaint. Both were refused "as drawn." Maris affirmed the other four proposed findings: that there was jurisdiction under Section 24(1) of the Judicial Code, that the regulation could not be justified under the police power, that plaintiffs lacked adequate remedy at law, and that they were entitled to an injunction.

b) Defendants.[98]—Defendants requested some twenty-seven findings of fact and ten findings of law. Ten proposed fact findings on the history of the dispute substantially duplicated those of plaintiffs and were affirmed. Five more dealt with additional factual details considered important for defendants' case—the alternative education of the children and the traditional nature of the Minersville flag ceremony—and were also affirmed. It is the findings that were refused that are significant. Maris refused "as drawn" a finding that the compulsory flag salute was "reasonable" and four others emphasizing that the ceremony had no religious significance. He affirmed a finding that Gobitis had not tried to enrol his children in local parochial schools, but rejected another implying that he should have. Four proposed findings denied that there was a requisite jurisdictional amount in controversy (*a*) as to William Gobitis, (*b*) as to Lillian, (*c*) as to Walter Gobitis and (*d*) at all. The latter two findings were rejected. Finally, Maris flatly refused the proposed finding that refusal to salute the flag was disrespectful and dangerous.

Judge Maris affirmed proposed findings of law dealing with the statutory power of the Minersville school board, denying jurisdiction under Section 24(14) of the Judicial Code and denying that any right secured by the federal Constitution had been violated. On the other hand, he rejected findings denying jurisdiction under Section 24(1) of the Judicial Code, upholding the reasonableness of the salute requirement, denying any violation of rights secured by the Pennsylvania Constitution, denying that public education was a right enforceable at equity, denying that there was a good cause of action and calling for a dismissal of the case.

4. FINAL OPINION AND DECREE

Judge Maris handed down his final decision in the case of *Gobitis v. Minersville School District*[99] on June 18, 1938. At the outset of his opinion, Maris reviewed the established facts, making several special findings beyond those expressly requested. Most significant was his finding that

The enforcement of defendants' regulation requiring the flag salute by children who are sincerely opposed to it upon conscientious religious grounds is not a reasonable method of teaching civics, including loyalty to the State and Federal Government, but tends to have the contrary effect upon such children.[100]

Regarding Gobitis' expenses, Maris seems to have completely accepted Moyle's evidence. He found Gobitis' expenses in educating Lillian and William to be in excess of $1,200 and $2,000 respectively, a combined total of $3,200.

After summing up the holdings of his earlier opinion, Maris stated, "The facts as I have found them sustain the allegations of the bill."[101] The plaintiffs manifestly were sincere in their beliefs, and "it is not for this court to say that since the act has no religious significance to us it can have no such significance to them."[102] Crucial was his finding on the effect of the children's refusal to salute:

I think it is also clear from the evidence that the refusal of these two earnest Christian children to salute the flag cannot even remotely prejudice or imperil the safety, health, morals, property or personal rights of their fellows. . . . Our country's safety surely does not depend upon the totalitarian idea of forcing all citizens into one common mold of thinking and acting or requiring them to render a lip service of loyalty in a manner which conflicts with their sincere religious convictions. . . .[103]

As to the question of jurisdiction, Maris held that jurisdiction obviously obtained as to Walter Gobitis, since his costs were in excess of $3,000. Since no *separate* objection had been advanced to jurisdiction over the minor plaintiffs, the court retained jurisdiction over all three plaintiffs. Maris' conclusions of law, then, were (*a*) that he had jurisdiction, (*b*) that enforcement of the Minersville regulation had deprived the minor plaintiffs of liberty without due process of law in violation of the Fourteenth Amendment, and (*c*) that plaintiffs were entitled to an injunction.

The decree filed on July 11, 1938, had four sections. The first two set out the District Court's jurisdiction and the unconstitutionality of the Minersville regulation. The third permanently enjoined the various defendants and their agents from

a) continuing in force the order expelling the said minor complainants from the Minersville Public Schools and from prohibiting their attendance at said schools;
b) requiring said minor complainants to salute the national flag as a condition of their right to attend said schools.[104]

The fourth section directed defendants to pay all costs of the action.

Several aspects of the proceedings in the District Court stand out in retrospect. Most striking is the high proportion of the time and energy of both sides which was devoted to the issue of jurisdiction. For financial reasons, the school board was anxious to win without a trial if possible. An added incentive was Judge Maris' first opinion, which made it plain that Gobitis had a won case if he could stay in court.

Also notable was the defendants' continued stress on the alleged invalidity of the Gobitis children's religious beliefs. Henderson went beyond the necessities of the "secular regulation" rule in refusing to concede that the children's views were religious in nature at all—a point both immaterial and difficult to prove. While conceding them to be sincere in their convictions, Henderson persisted in the argument that the children's refusal to salute was disrespectful. The apparent implication is that refusal to salute was considered *intrinsically* disloyal, whatever the motivation.

No summary narrative can convey the atmosphere of bickering and scarcely veiled hostility which pervaded the whole proceeding, manifested in quibbling comments in the answer, well-bred aspersions in the briefs, niggling and impatient objections during the trial and the rough in-fighting which marked the cross-examinations of Gobitis and Roudabush. Any case involving a real contest is likely to be hard fought; but there is a fine line between a hard fight and a bitter one. This case fell in the latter category.

Finally, attention must be directed to the active role played by Judge Maris in the trial. In the frequent absence of meeting of minds between witness and lawyer, it was often necessary for Maris to take over the questioning himself if the facts were to be brought out at all. Maris also went after facts not dealt with by either counsel. His questioning of William Gobitis and his sharp inquisition of Roudabush did more harm to the Minersville cause than all of Moyle's efforts.

D. *In the Circuit Court of Appeals*

1. ON THE WAY TO THE CIRCUIT COURT

Reaction to Judge Maris' decision outside Minersville was generally favorable. Most of the articulate praise came from Philadelphia, where the *Bulletin* and *Inquirer* carried markedly favorable editorials.[105] Philadelphia school officials generally approved the decision; "Any principal with good sense," said one, "would hardly insist that a child salute the flag under such circumstances."[106] The *Pottsville Evening Republican* broke its long editorial silence on the controversy with a cautious but markedly approving editorial which strongly defended the flag ceremony against the Witnesses' criticisms, but came out strongly against compulsion of religious objectors.[107]

The reaction in Minersville was somewhat different. Obviously smarting from his rough treatment in court, Roudabush issued a bristling public statement condemning the decision:

The salute to the flag in the Minersville Public Schools is not, nor ever has been compulsory, but it has always been expected from teachers and pupils. . . .

Boys and girls who do not acknowledge allegiance to their country of birth are aliens, and do not belong in the public schools which are tax supported. . . .

[Teachers have] as much right to teach and require the elements of patriotism as a parent has to indoctrinate the children with false religion. . . .

Some years ago in Pennsylvania a hex-murder was justified by the murderer because he felt that he was doing what his religion required of him to do. Would the Court say that this murderer was entitled to his belief? . . .

Judge Maris is right, there is no idolatry in the flag salute or sin in pledging allegiance to our country.[108]

On June 29, 1938, the Minersville school board voted unanimously to appeal the decision to the Circuit Court of Appeals, also located in Philadelphia.[109] The Board subsequently rebuffed an attempt by Gobitis to put his children back in school:

We have taken an appeal to a higher court. . . . So long as the case is still pending and your children will refuse to salute the flag, the Board has decided to stand by its position.[110]

On August 9, Judge Maris allowed the appeal, and provided that the appeal should operate as a supersedeas, staying the effect of the injunction until a final determination could be had in a higher court. The appeal bond was set at $250.[111]

Immediately after the school board voted for an appeal, Roudabush seems to have sent out urgent appeals for financial aid to the various patriotic organizations which had expressed interest theretofore. The response was immediate and strongly favorable, especially from the POSA and OIA. Ultimately, according to Roudabush, all costs of the litigation were borne by the patriotic groups.[112] As of February 1, 1939, after which there are no available statistics, outside contributions to the board's fight totalled $975.50—$760 from POSA, and $115.50 from OIA.[113] At that time, court and attorney expenses had mounted to $1,207.65.[114] More money must have come in later; some specifically promised funds had not arrived at that date—e.g., from the Improved Order of Red Men.[115]

2. ASSIGNMENTS OF ERROR[116]

Upon the allowance of the appeal, Henderson had only to walk down the hall in the Federal Court Building to file his assignments of error with the Circuit Court of Appeals. In all, there were twenty-five assignments, reflecting every unsuccessful objection made by Henderson at the trial and each rejected contention in the defendants' pleadings. Five assignments objected generally to the whole course of events in the court below. Ten concentrated on the issue of jurisdiction, particularly attacking Walter Gobitis' cost estimates on the operation of his car, his failure to enrol his children in a parochial school, his resort instead to Pottsville Business College, and Maris' decision that expenses for educating the two children could be aggregated for the purpose of determining the amount in controversy.

The remaining ten assignments of error related somehow to

the merits of the case. Three attacked the admission of Fred Franz' testimony. One challenged Maris' holding that the individual must be the judge of his own beliefs and his rejection of the proposed findings of fact regarding the inherently secular nature of the flag ceremony. Another found error in his finding that the compulsory salute was not a reasonable method of teaching patriotism. Two challenged his finding that the children and their father were loyal and well intentioned. Finally, two assignments urged that Maris had erred in finding that the Minersville regulation, as applied to the Gobitis children, violated the due process clause of the Fourteenth Amendment.[117]

Viewed in retrospect, appellants' whole case seems to have turned on the assignment reasserting the "secular regulation" rule. Most of Henderson's jurisdictional arguments were patently weak. Gobitis could hardly be criticized for sending his children to Pottsville Business College, for example, if the only alternative was a parochial school. The weakest jurisdictional link—Gobitis' car expenses—was the sort of trial detail on which the initial determination of the trial judge would carry much weight. On the religious freedom issue, on the other hand, Henderson had good ground for hope. In jettisoning the "secular regulation" rule, Judge Maris had been able to buttress his position with nothing better than the misleading quotation from *Commonwealth v. Lesher,* and had flouted a whole host of state and federal precedents—including the recent *Leoles* and *Hering* dispositions.

3. THE BRIEFS

a) *Appellants.*[118]—Henderson's jurisdictional argument was in large part a duplicate of that in his District Court briefs, denying that the action arose under the federal Constitution or involved $3,000 in controversy, and attacking at length Walter Gobitis' testimony regarding his expenses. Henderson omitted as no longer necessary his argument against jurisdiction under Section 24(14) of the Judicial Code.

In his discussion of the merits, Henderson expanded his treatment of previous flag-salute decisions. He pointed out that the Supreme Court had dismissed the *Hering* and *Leoles* appeals on the basis of *Hamilton v. Regents, after* (and, presumably, with knowledge of) Judge Maris' opinion on the motion to dismiss. To his quotations from state flag-salute opinions, Henderson now could add excerpts from the final decision in *Gabrielli v. Knickerbocker*. He also strengthened and streamlined his argument regarding the possible ill effects of pupil non-saluting. Apparently in an attempt to blunt Moyle's attacks, Henderson added the statement that "Dr. Roudabush, as superintendent of schools, is familiar with conditions surrounding the youth of today and was particularly qualified to testify as to pupils' reactions to such a situation."[119] Henderson's argument on the crucial religious freedom issue—denying that the flag salute had anything to do with religion and invoking the "secular regulation" rule—was substantially identical with that in his earlier briefs.

b) *Appellees.*[120]—In his section on jurisdiction, Moyle quoted from Judge Maris' opinion in support of the proposition that the case arose under the Constitution. His defense of the cost figures establishing the necessary jurisdictional amount largely duplicated that in his two briefs below in support of findings of fact and law.

Most of Moyle's discussion of the merits centered on the religious freedom issue. His argument on this point was considerably revamped, both for better and worse. He greatly strengthened his earlier argument that the overriding of a religious scruple was itself a violation of religious freedom in the constitutional sense, lashing out strongly at the oft-used argument that the flag ceremony was "not a religious rite":

. . . Their attendance at school is conditioned upon their stifling conscience and doing an act which they believe to be morally wrong. This is an interference with their worship of Almighty God. . . .[121]

. . . [T]o say that the act is not a religious rite is an evasion of the issue. One may have conscientious reasons or religious reasons for refusing to commit an act, without such being considered a religious rite. Some people believe that dancing is forbidden. . . .

The real issue is: Do the plaintiffs believe it wrong for them to salute the flag? . . .[122]

The second stage in Moyle's argument was that

. . . When a person assailing a law or regulation on constitutional grounds has shown a prima facie violation of a constitutional right, the State must then prove that the infringement is justified. . . .[123]

For this crucial and dubious proposition, however, he was able to cite only the dictum in *Watson v. Jones*. Moyle's third point was that no such justification had been shown in evidence by the defendants. Here he repeated his bitter attack on Roudabush's testimony and quoted from Judge Maris' favorable finding on this point. In support of a general assertion that "school boards are not omnipotent," he listed all the favorable Bible-reading and school-curriculum decisions,[124] with emphasis on the *Hardwicke* case. The miscellaneous authorities cited by Moyle, in his brief below on the motion to dismiss, in support of the plausibility of the Gobitis children's scruple appeared again in his Circuit Court brief, but in a new and potentially disastrous format. The heading of this section now read, "The flag salute regulation is invalid because it may not be assumed that it was within the intention of the legislature to empower school authorities to enact regulations contravening the law of Almighty God."[125] Thrown in for extra effect were quotations from the *Trinity Church* case and Blackstone's *Commentaries*.[126] While the hand was Moyle's, the voice obviously was that of "Judge" Rutherford, who could hardly be satisfied with a religious argument cast otherwise than as an eternal verity.[127] This maladroit phrasing of the point made it irrelevant to the constitutional issue, and lent support to Henderson's plea that the matter was one for the Pennsylvania courts.

Moyle reproduced from his first District Court brief the contentions that the Minersville regulation denied the minor plaintiffs the equal protection of the laws and conditioned the privilege of public education on the surrender of a constitutional right. Perhaps by inadvertence, the potentially strong invocation of freedom of speech was omitted.

Moyle reproduced his argument from his first District Court brief distinguishing *Hamilton v. Regents*. He took a different tack on the adverse flag-salute precedents, however, carefully omitting any mention of the Supreme Court *per curiam* dispositions. He bitterly denounced the state court opinions in *Hering* and *Leoles* for their persistent second-guessing of the Witnesses' religious beliefs. The strong, thoroughly non-theological *Gabrielli* opinion presented a tougher problem. Here Moyle resorted to table-thumping:

. . . Follow the doctrine to its logical conclusion and it means that any liberty can be muzzled. . . . All that is necessary is the claim that the measure is designed to promote public safety, although the actual result may be the destruction thereof.[128]

Finally, Moyle again asserted that the real product of the compulsory flag salute was lawlessness and intolerance. In an appendix, he repeated in expanded form his catalog of the Witnesses' troubles over the flag salute at home and abroad.

    c) *The American Civil Liberties Union.*[129]—On November 9, 1938, with Court permission,[130] the American Civil Liberties Union filed a very short brief *amicus curiae*, written by William G. Fennell and signed by Arthur Garfield Hays and Jerome M. Britchey, of the New York office. The primary purpose of this brief seems simply to have been to get the Union on record in support of the appellees. The argument therein was based mainly on a leading note on the controversy published in the *Harvard Law Review*.[131] Fennell first argued that the deprivation of religious liberty was too obvious to merit extended argument; the children had been expelled for religious refusal to salute. Regarding the alleged intrinsic secularity of the salute, Fennell noted the well-established provision of an alternative to the formal oath—itself not a religious act—taken by jurors and public officers. He went on to distinguish *Hamilton v. Regents* on the same grounds used by Moyle and Maris. He concluded with a strongly worded denial that the Minersville regulation constituted a reasonable method of inculcating patriotism, likening it to the compulsory salutes then in vogue in Germany and Italy.

4. THE DECISION

The case was argued on November 9, 1938, before Judges Clark, Biggs and Kalodner. A few words seem in order about these men. William Clark, a native of Newark, New Jersey, took three degrees from Harvard and served overseas in World War I. A Presbyterian and a Republican, he was appointed by President Coolidge as judge of the District Court for the District of New Jersey in 1925. He gained national attention in 1930, when he tried unsuccessfully to hold the Eighteenth Amendment unconstitutional,[132] and in 1938 when he issued the original injunction in *Committee for Industrial Organization v. Hague.*[133] President Roosevelt elevated him to the Circuit Court of Appeals on July 5, 1938.[134] John Biggs, Jr., a native of Wilmington, Delaware, took his law degree at Harvard, and served in World War I. Also a Presbyterian, he is a member of the Sons of the American Revolution and the American Legion. President Roosevelt appointed him to the Circuit Court on February 16, 1937.[135] Harry E. Kalodner, a native of Philadelphia, took his law degree at Pennsylvania. Jewish and a Democrat, he is a member of the Elks and the American Legion. He was appointed in 1938 as judge of the District Court for the Eastern District of Pennsylvania to replace Judge Maris, who had just been elevated to the Circuit Court of Appeals.[136] Since Maris could not sit on the appeal from his own decision, Kalodner was called on to substitute for him.

After oral argument, the case hung fire for a full year, to the intense frustration of Roudabush and his colleagues. "[T]he judge [*sic*] in the case is a friend of Judge Maris . . . and does not wish to reverse his decision," wrote Roudabush, "I would write the judge a letter but I know just what would happen, I would be put in the pen for contempt of court, but the courts of this country seem to be getting by with about anything."[137]

Finally, on November 10, 1939, the Circuit Court of Appeals unanimously affirmed the decision below.[138] Judge Clark's opinion was long and discursive, and was full of contempt for the illiberal stand taken by the Minersville authorities. At the same time, it contributed a thoughtful analysis of the precedents and placed Judge Maris' reasoning on a sounder legal basis.

For Judge Clark, the merits of the case expressed themselves in two questions: (*a*) Did the Witnesses' beliefs fall within the scope of the constitutional guaranties of *religious* freedom? (*b*) If so, did the conflict here at issue fall into one of those categories in which religion historically has had to yield to the needs of society? In considering the first question, Clark took Henderson's religious argument at its face value. "Appellant suggests that religion is an objective rather than a subjective matter. . . . In other words, he applies some sort of average reasonable man standard."[139] Arguing from the "minimum" definition of "religion" in *Davis v. Beason*—". . . one's views of his relations to his Creator, and to the obligations they impose . . ."[140]—Clark concluded that "the definition excludes any theory of sensible choice. If the requirement is present, the doctrinal views of the average man or the average official are wholly irrelevant."[141] Clark finally held that the Witnesses' beliefs fell within the "minimum" definition.

Obviously, the constitutional protection afforded religious beliefs was limited by circumstances. Where were the limits to be drawn? In an elaborate survey of the precedents, Clark concluded that American society had overruled religious objections in three types of situation:

. . . (a) wherever its mental or physical health is affected; (b) wherever a violation of its sense of reverence makes a breach of the peace reasonably forseeable, and (c) wherever the "defense of the realm" is imperiled.[142]

However, he continued, almost all these instances had involved anti-social *actions* by religiously motivated individuals.

. . . In most of them, the religious objector is prohibited from propitiating the Deity in a certain way; *he is not forced to commit a sacrilege.* For instance, a Mormon is not damned for monogamy, the astrologist or spiritualist for personally consulting the stars or the spirits, or the Salvationists for using the soft pedal. . . . [Italics supplied.][143]

The state, Clark noted, had penalized religiously motivated refusals to act only in cases involving military service and vaccination. The first was obviously a special case; what of the other? Clark then proceeded rather ironically to weigh the compulsory flag salute as a "vaccination" against the "disease" of non-patriotism, from the point of view of the seriousness of the disease and the efficacy of the remedy. As to the first, he commented:

. . . After all, even mercenary troops used to win wars. . . . We conclude that patriotism is an added advantage rather than an essential whose absence is dangerous in the clear and present sense.[144]

What of the efficacy of the compulsory salute? Clark conceded that children could be forced to learn Latin or eat spinach, but

. . . [T]his pedagogical victory has more often than not been won at the expense of the disciplinarian. In our particular circumstance, then, that resentment clashes with and cancels the very affection sought to be instilled. . . .[145]

In short, he concluded, "We do not find the essential relationship between infant patriotism and the martial spirit."[146]

Noting that William Penn had been expelled from Oxford for offenses not too dissimilar to the Gobitis children's, Clark quoted from a letter of George Washington assuring the Quakers that he favored treating "the conscientious scruples of all men . . . with great delicacy and tenderness. . . ."[147] "The appellant School Board," he concluded, "has failed to 'treat the conscientious scruples' of all children with that 'great delicacy and tenderness.' We agree with the father of our country that they should and we concur with the learned District Court in saying that they must."[148]

In a short appendix, Judge Clark dealt with some of the more technical legal problems. He settled the jurisdictional question in one sentence: "In this connection we observe that the jurisdictional issue at bar has been settled in favor of exercise, Hague v. Committee for Industrial Organization. . . ."[149] This amounted to a holding that jurisdiction obtained under Section 24(14) of the Judicial Code—thus rendering irrelevant fully half the trial in the court below. *Hamilton v. Regents* was distinguished from the present case on the first of the two grounds advanced by Moyle and Maris. The *per curiam* dispositions of *Leoles, Hering* and *Johnson v. Deerfield* were distinguished on the ground that they dealt with flag-salute regulations which had been sanctioned by state statute and upheld by the state supreme courts, thus making "the connection between an omission to salute the flag and the commission of an injury to the public weal . . . legally and factually closer."[150] Clark also cited the heavy criticism which the state court decisions had received in the law reviews.

Clark closed his appendix with an attempt to soften the fact that he and the court below were substituting their judgment for that of the local authorities on a highly debatable matter of policy.

The record before us sheds but little light upon the problems of educational psychology here discussed. . . . To decide questions of reasonableness in the absence of undisputed factual proof or knowledge is of course open to criticism. . . . We feel, however, that this criticism cannot reach the instant case. The matter here can hardly be reduced to statistics. It is rather one of logical conjecure and comparison with the pattern of decided cases, based, furthermore, upon the learned trial judge's special finding of unreasonableness.[151]

The most important aspect of Judge Clark's opinion for our purposes is the manner in which he dealt with the "secular regulation" rule. The gist of this rule, it will be recalled, is that, constitutional guaranties notwithstanding, religious scruples will not excuse one from the operation of a general law dealing with purely secular matters. Judge Maris had rejected this rule as unreasonable, but had not been able to find any convincing supporting authority. Judge Clark handled this problem by limiting the "secular regulation" precedents to their actual fact situations and holdings—without the accompanying dicta. When the present situation was placed beside the circumstances in those cases, they became readily distinguishable. The flag-salute regulation could benefit from the precedents only as long as they were embodied in a general, "automatically" functioning formula like the "secular regulation" rule.

Also significant was Clark's importation of the "clear and present danger" test into the religious freedom area. This phrase showed up repeatedly in the opinion,[152] and not by accident. "That essence of the 'essential relationship' to the desired end we have borrowed from the settled law of another and cognate part of this same provision of the Bill of Rights."[153] In making the free speech cases relevant here, Clark furnished a strong rationale to support Moyle's argument that the burden of proof must be upon the school authorities to support their infringement on religious scruples.

A less happy aspect of Clark's opinion was his assumption that the efficacy of the compulsory salute must be measured by its effect on the persons compelled. For most children, the ceremony was not compulsory in any real sense; they liked it. What of the effect of the ceremony—and the refusal of some to participate—on them? This distortion of the issue was to recur constantly in subsequent flag-salute litigation.

5. ON THE WAY TO THE SUPREME COURT

The decision of the Circuit Court of Appeals aroused little general attention. Almost two years had elapsed since the impact of Judge Maris' first opinion; now it was clear that any settlement of the issue must await a Supreme Court test. The decision came as a blow to Minersville authorities. Roudabush denounced Clark's opinion as "a hodge-podge of perverted quotations . . . based . . . on the assumption that little children have the right and ability to formulate religious beliefs and conscientious objections."[154]

Henderson immediately recommended that a petition for a writ of certiorari be filed with the Supreme Court.[155] On December 4, 1939, the Minersville school board considered the matter but declined to authorize further action.[156] The members were worried by a strange suggestion from the State Department of Public Instruction that the board might be liable for the Gobitis children's educational expenses even if it had been correct in expelling them. If such actually would be the case, they wished to forego the added expense of still another appeal; they were willing to stand considerable outlays, however, if a victory in the Supreme Court would relieve them of such liability.[157] On January 8, 1940, the Minersville board finally authorized Henderson to proceed after he assured them strongly that they could not possibly be held financially liable no matter which way the decision went in the Supreme Court.[158]

On January 7, 1940, the delegates at a meeting of the Association of Patriotic Societies of Schuylkill County pledged to enlist their respective organizations in support of the Supreme Court appeal.[159] On January 10, the members of the 13th District of the American Legion voted unanimously to seek the aid of the Pennsylvania Department of the Legion.[160] While the record of financial assistance peters out at this point, it appears that the move to the Supreme Court was in no danger of foundering for lack of funds.

After the delay by the school board, Henderson had to scramble to get his petition for certiorari filed in time, finally getting in just under the deadline, on January 30, 1940.[161] The accompanying brief was typically short, simply asserting (*a*) that the decisions below conflicted with the Supreme Court's disposition of the *Leoles, Hering, Johnson* and *Gabrielli* appeals; (*b*) that they conflicted with the state court decisions in these cases and in *Nicholls, Sandstrom* and *Estep;* and (*c*) that the flag-salute regulation and the expulsions thereunder in no way violated either the United States or Pennsylvania Constitution.[162]

On March 4, 1940, the United States Supreme Court granted a writ of certiorari.[163]

CHAPTER SIX

THE *GOBITIS* CASE

IN THE SUPREME COURT

A. *Briefs and Argument*

In all, four briefs were filed with the Supreme Court. Rawle and Henderson, along with Solicitor McGurl, filed the brief for petitioners, the Minersville school authorities. The legal office of the Watchtower Bible and Tract Society filed the brief for respondents, Walter, Lillian and William Gobitis. With the consent of both sides, the American Civil Liberties Union and the Bill of Rights Committee of the American Bar Association filed briefs *amici curiae*, both in support of the Witnesses.

1. THE MINERSVILLE BRIEF

The brief for the Minersville School District *et al.* was written by Henderson and signed by him, McGurl, Brodhead, and still a third member of the firm, Thomas F. Mount. Of the twenty-five assignments of error urged in the Circuit Court, eleven were retained, all bearing on two questions:

1. Was the expulsion of the minor respondents for the refusal to salute the flag in violation of any of their rights under the Constitutions of the United States of America and of the Commonwealth of Pennsylvania?

2. Is the refusal of said pupils to salute the national flag at a daily exercise of a public school founded on a religious belief?[1]

Henderson prudently abandoned all challenges to the jurisdiction of the District Court or the alleged procedural errors committed therein. The jurisdictional issue clearly was dead in view of *Hague v. CIO*,[2] and the other issues were rendered virtually hopeless by the loss in the Circuit Court.

Henderson opened his brief with a detailed summary of the background of the litigation: the legal authority of the school board, the statutory requirement of patriotic instruction, the regulation, the refusals, the expulsions. The object seems to have been to emphasize the ordinary and *regular* manner in which everything had happened. Of no constitutional significance in itself, this picture furnished a propitious setting for the invocation of the "secular regulation" rule.

a) The Fourteenth Amendment.—At the outset of his discussion of the Fourteenth Amendment, Henderson reminded the Court that it had four times disposed of similar attacks on flag-salute regulations in the *Hering, Johnson, Leoles* and *Gabrielli* cases. These, he emphasized, were binding dispositions of the *merits* of the controversy. He heaped scorn on the attempts by the courts below to avoid these precedents. It was irrelevant which legislative body of a state had demanded the salute, or whether the state courts had had an opportunity to uphold the action, or whether the Supreme Court had accompanied its decisions with full opinions, or whether the law review comment was favorable. A precedent was a precedent.

Henderson appealed strongly to the "secular regulation" rule, quoting liberally from *Reynolds v. United States, Hamilton v. Regents,* and *United States v. Macintosh* and citing the other available federal court precedents. He recognized, however, that his case had a serious potential weakness—the apparent harshness of the measures taken by the Minersville authorities. Why should children be thrown out of school for their objections to a *ritual?* Who cared if they saluted or not? Wasn't this pushing the "secular regulation" rule to an absurd extreme? To refute the notion that the compulsory flag salute was somehow different from other regulations under the police power, Henderson carefully built up an appealing case for the public policy involved here. First, the end, public morale, was clearly good:

... Any breakdown in the *esprit de corps* or morale of this country may conceivably have a more devastating effect upon the nation than a catastrophe resulting from disease, breach of peace, or even an invasion of the realm. ... [A]ny effort by educational authorities to strengthen the morale should be fostered and encouraged.[3]

Second, the method was a reasonable one, and not different in kind from a variety of other compulsory items in the public school program; all capitalized on the fact that children's minds are still pliable.

The youth of today will be the adult citizens of tomorrow and the public schools should be permitted through patriotic exercises to inculcate in them a love of country. . . .[4]

Students at the public schools are instructed in patriotism and love of country in many ways. . . . [T]he exercise of saluting the flag is as reasonable a method of teaching loyalty as any of the other studies and activities. . . .[5]

The argument was rounded out with a gloomy forecast of the results which would follow an adverse decision here, based on Roudabush's "expert" testimony:

The morale of each community group affects the morale of other groups and in due course that of the state and of the nation. The decision in this case is of nationwide significance and will effect [sic] not merely the Minersville School District but countless other school districts throughout this country. . . . If the contention of respondents is sustained . . . a large number of children, who are members of Jehovah's Witnesses and possibly many who are not, will refuse to salute the national flag at daily school exercises. Such demonstration of disrespect to our government will influence and affect other pupils in the schools, and the morale of their respective communities, and ultimately that of the nation itself, will be shaken and demoralized.[6]

b) *Other contentions.*—The remaining sections of Henderson's brief were rather anticlimactic. First, he argued at some length that the Minersville regulation was not violative of the religious freedom guaranty of the Pennsylvania Constitution, citing all the "secular regulation" precedents arising in that state, plus the recent *Estep* decision. Henderson probably advanced this contention simply to get some more state precedents into the brief. Judge Maris' incidental holding on this issue could hardly serve as the basis either of an injunction or an appeal.[7]

The last section of Henderson's brief was the hardest to take seriously. Here, he attempted to show, not only that the children's belief was incorrect, but that it was not *religious*. After quoting liberally from the state flag-salute cases, he concluded,

The act of saluting the national flag at daily school exercises can not be made a religious rite by the respondents' mistaken interpretation of the Bible. The ceremony is in no way referable to the religious beliefs of any of the participants and *it therefore follows that a pupil's refusal to salute the flag cannot be based on a religious belief.* [Italics supplied.][8]

Not content with this, Henderson went on to claim that the Bible actually approves of flag saluting, citing a half-dozen scriptural passages, only one of which was relevant.[9] He closed with a rather open appeal to anti-Witness feeling:

. . . [W]hile members of Jehovah's Witnesses endeavor to extend religious implications to a ceremony purely patriotic in design, they do not accord to others the religious freedom which they demand for themselves, claiming that there is no limit to which they may go when they think they are worshipping God. . . .[10]

Henderson's brief made maximum, if not optimum, use of the favorable precedents at hand. The main section on the Fourteenth Amendment was much improved over his previous efforts, and posed a real problem for the Witnesses and their allies. The argument based on the Pennsylvania Constitution was superfluous but harmless. The only real wrong step was the weird collection of religious arguments at the end. This tended to impair Henderson's carefully nurtured impression of even-handed regularity, by suggesting a current of malice— and religious malice, at that—underlying the Minersville expulsions.

2. THE JEHOVAH'S WITNESSES BRIEF

While the *Gobitis* case was still pending in the Circuit Court of Appeals, legal counsel Olin R. Moyle became involved in a dispute with "Judge" Rutherford, and was fired from his position and expelled from the movement. Rutherford took over the legal office himself, bringing in Hayden Covington, a young Texas attorney and a devout Witness, to assist him.[11] The departure of Moyle inevitably led to a general deterioration of the cordial working relations he had maintained with sympathetic outside groups. Rutherford rebuffed all efforts to co-ordinate the various briefs.

The brief filed for respondents was written by Rutherford and signed by him, Covington and McCaughey. Rutherford threw out most of Moyle's brief, retaining only those parts which probably had been furnished by him in the first place.

The brief suffered greatly from Rutherford's discursiveness and his penchant for theological polemics; the strong points of the Moyle brief were made haphazardly and badly, if at all.

Most of Rutherford's brief was devoted to the proposition that the Minersville regulation violated the religious freedom guaranty of the Pennsylvania Constitution—the first time this provision had received direct mention by a Witness brief in this litigation, and hardly an improvement. This section actually was headed as follows:

> The vital question in the instant case is this: Shall the creature man be free to exercise his conscientious belief in God and his obedience to the law of Almighty God, the Creator, or shall the creature man be compelled to obey the law or rule of the State, which law of the State, as the creature conscientiously believes, is in direct conflict with the law of Almighty God?
>
> In brief the issue may be stated thus:
>
> The arbitrary totalitarian rule of the State versus full devotion and obedience to the THEOCRATIC GOVERNMENT or Kingdom of Jehovah God under Christ Jesus His anointed King.[12]

This tone was maintained throughout the brief. Rutherford sought to show (a) that any state law contrary to God's law was void under the Pennsylvania Constitution, and (b) that the flag salute was, in fact, forbidden by God's law. To the first end, he again cited Blackstone, the *Trinity Church* dictum, etc. As to the latter point, Rutherford insisted that "Enforcing such a rule against pupils or children is thereby compelling them to adopt and practice a religion."[13] He defined religion as "a formal ceremony or reverence . . . bestowed upon, a higher power, real or supposed, thereby attributing to such higher power sovereignty, protection and salvation. . . ."[14] To show that the flag salute fitted this definition, Rutherford resorted to dictionary definitions of *salute, image,* and certain key terms in the *Encyclopedia Americana*'s panegyric on the flag:

> The flag, like the cross, is *sacred.* . . . The rules and regulations relative to human attitude toward national standards use strong, expressive words, as "Service to the Flag," . . . "*Reverence* for the Flag," "*Devotion* to the Flag." [Italics supplied.][15]

Such a religious observance, Rutherford went on, was strictly forbidden by Exodus 20:3–5. He stressed the concept of the covenant; no Witness of Jehovah dared salute the flag, whatever the pressure, on pain of total destruction. An adverse decision, then, would not "settle" the controversy; it would merely drive all Witness children out of the public schools.

Rutherford's treatment of the Fourteenth Amendment was very perfunctory. He cited *Pierce v. Society of Sisters* as invalidating the compulsory flag salute. He followed this with a short attack on the reasonableness of the Minersville regulation. If the flag salute was so desirable, why not require it of all school children, or even from all citizens? The first part of this rhetorical question is answered by what was said previously in regard to Moyle's appeal to the equal protection clause. The latter part ignored the obvious differences between the legal status of adults and that of children. The whole rationale of the compulsory salute was based on this difference.

Throughout his brief, Rutherford tried to link the Minersville regulation to the bogey of totalitarianism, noting the ceremony's physical similarity to the Nazi salute and relating the Witnesses' troubles in Germany. More or less in support of this point, he retained Moyle's appendix on the evil effects produced in the United States by the compulsory flag salute.

On the whole, this was a discouragingly bad brief. It ignored all the most crucial constitutional issues, and seemed calculated to produce a negative emotional effect with its repeated recourse to argument *ad hominem*. The heavy load of presenting the Witnesses' legal case fell on the *amicus curiae* briefs.

3. THE AMERICAN CIVIL LIBERTIES UNION BRIEF

The brief filed by the American Civil Liberties Union as friends of the Court was written and signed by Professor George K. Gardner and also signed by Arthur Garfield Hays, Osmond K. Fraenkel, Jerome M. Britchey and William G. Fennell of the New York office of the ACLU, and Alexander H. Frey of Philadelphia. Gardner had become very interested in the flag-salute issue through his involvement in *Commonwealth v. Johnson*. At the suggestion of Grenville Clark, chairman of the ABA Committee on the Bill of Rights,[16] he offered to brief and argue the case for the ACLU, which offer was gladly accepted.[17] He and Moyle agreed to split the allotted oral argument time between themselves, which agreement was honored, though grudgingly, by Rutherford.[18]

Almost all of Gardner's brief was devoted to the religious freedom issue. He began by arguing that the respondents' right to hold and act on their belief regarding flag-saluting was protected by the Fourteenth Amendment. Gardner heaped scorn on Henderson's denial of the religious nature of the children's beliefs:

... It would be a novel doctrine to assert that the first two commandments ... do not affirm something about the believer's relations with his Creator and the obligations which they impose of reverence for his Being and character.[19]

To concede the children's sincerity was to concede the whole issue. That religious freedom was protected by the Fourteenth Amendment was considered settled by *Hamilton v. Regents*. "[W]e assume as already established beyond question," Gardner wrote, "that ... America secures to each individual *the right to refrain from expressions which do violence to his beliefs*."[20] Gardner considered it clear beyond argument that this freedom had been violated. The Minersville regulation did much more than force the Gobitis children out of school; "it threatened them with prosecution and commitment as 'delinquent children' which would, in all probability, have been the actual consequence had not their father purchased them private instruction by paying the practical equivalent of a substantial fine."[21]

In contending that the deprivation of liberty here was without due process of law, Gardner sought in effect to limit the application of the "secular regulation" rule by marking off the limits of the "police power" itself. He stressed the doctrine of the Virginia Statute of Religious Freedom—later adopted in *Reynolds v. United States*—that beliefs should be suppressed only when they erupted in "overt acts against peace and good order."

... [T]o hold that opinions and beliefs about God and the flag of the United States may be made the subject of rewards and punishments—before the fruits of these beliefs have been made manifest in action—seems to us to be contrary to the sound doctrine of *Reynolds v. United States.* ... .[22]

What bothered Gardner, in other words, was the fact that the Minersville regulation reached out to penalize beliefs which would otherwise have remained innocuous, if not unnoticed.

The remainder of Gardner's religious freedom argument centered on the fact that the flag-salute issue could lead—and had led in Massachusetts—to delinquency prosecutions. This part of the brief was framed as an argument that the compulsory salute could not be effective in inculcating patriotism. It was obvious enough that such compulsion would produce no patriotism in the children compelled. What of their classmates? If the objecting children were expelled, and allowed simply to remain at large, other pupils would be tempted to emulate this easy way out of school. If, as was almost inevitable, the school authorities moved to have the expellees incarcerated, they would undoubtedly produce obedience in the remaining pupils; but the dominant emotion would be fear, not love of country.

This logical consequence of the position taken by the petitioners but illustrates the dilemma in which authority inevitably involves itself when it attempts to command, rather than inspire respect. If the commanded forms of respect be not forthcoming, authority must then either acknowledge its impotence . . . or else enter upon the enterprise of persecuting its subjects for their beliefs.[23]

This part of Gardner's argument suffered from a double weakness. First, his prediction of the probable reactions of non-Witness pupils was highly debatable and probably incorrect. Second, his heaviest emphasis was on the prospect of delinquency proceedings, a matter quite irrelevant to *this* case. The one argument that would have been germane—that upholding the compulsory salute would be tantamount to upholding in advance such further punishment—was never clearly advanced.

Finally, Gardner contended that Minersville was meddling in a matter of primary federal concern:

. . . It is not competent for Pennsylvania to involve the flag of the United States in a controversy with its citizens over the forms of respect which loyalty to the flag and Government of the United States demand.[24]

Halter v. Nebraska[25] notwithstanding, it was argued, the silence of Congress did not constitute indorsement of anything the state might wish to perpetrate in the name of "loyalty."

The American Civil Liberties Union brief made a substantial contribution to the attack on the compulsory flag salute. Particularly strong was the argument that the regulation unconstitutionally reached out to molest mere beliefs. This worthy attempt to circumvent the "secular regulation" rule was largely obscured by the dubious argumentation in the second half of the brief. Gardner obviously was deeply stirred by the delinquency proceedings in Massachusetts, and allowed his emotional commitment to lead him into irrelevancies.

4. THE AMERICAN BAR ASSOCIATION BRIEF

The American Bar Association's Committee on the Bill of Rights also filed a brief *amicus curiae*. This was the third such appearance made by the Committee, and the second in a flag-salute case. It had filed similar briefs in *Hague v. CIO* and in support of the appeal in *Johnson v. Deerfield*. The propriety of the Committee filing briefs "in the name of" the Association had been the subject of considerable dispute,[26] and the necessary permission to file a brief here had been granted by a narrow 53 to 51 vote in the House of Delegates.[27] The brief was signed by eight of the nine members of the committee.[28] Most of the actual writing seems to have been done by the Chairman, Grenville Clark.[29] Much spadework on the brief was done by Louis Lusky, a former law clerk to Justice Stone.[30] It was at Clark's initiative that any attempts were made to co-ordinate the briefs.[31] As has been noted, he got no co-operation from Rutherford. Co-operation between Clark and Gardner seems to have consisted less in actual "dividing up" of issues than in simple avoidance of duplication, through the regular exchange of information.

In an introductory note, Clark emphasized that the Committee's primary interest was in clarifying the law of civil liberties:

The Committee has no interest in this litigation save as its outcome (*a*) will affect the integrity of the basic right to freedom of conscience, and (*b*) will bear upon the extent of governmental power affirmatively to *force* our people to express themselves in a particular manner. . . .[32]

Freedom, it was suggested, is heavily dependent on public understanding, which had been badly obscured by the erroneous state flag-salute decisions.

The Committee brief attacked the compulsory flag-salute regulation both as an unjustified infringement of freedom of religion and as an unreasonable and arbitrary restriction of personal liberty. A closing section denied the alleged right of school authorities to exact the flag salute as a condition of the privilege of free public education.

a) *Freedom of religion.*—At the outset of his religious freedom argument, Clark took pains to demolish the blithe assertion of petitioners and many state courts that the Witnesses simply were wrong in ascribing religious significance to the flag salute. In so doing, he struck a damaging blow at the basic assumption underlying the "secular regulation" rule—that various actions could be termed *intrinsically* secular or religious. "So far as the respondent children are concerned," it was argued, "the salute must be regarded as a religious ritual."

> The truth is that the attempt to adjudge whether or not a particular ceremony can have or does in fact have a religious significance is something beyond the competence of legislatures and courts. This is so for the simple reason that whether or not such religious significance exists lies inherently within the mind and heart of the individual man or woman.[33]

Conceding that some asserted beliefs might be so farfetched as to raise real questions of sincerity or sanity, Clark offered historical examples in support of the plausibility of the Witnesses' scruple: the vigorous and successful protests of the Jews when Pilate imported busts of Caesar into Jerusalem; the refusal of a Roman soldier, a Christian, to wear a laurel wreath when appearing before the emperor; and the more recent refusal of the Quakers to doff their hats to civil authority.

The crux of the case was the standard of review to be applied to regulations impinging on religious scruples. Under the old rule, a secular regulation was subject only to ordinary due process scrutiny, with the burden of proof resting on the objecting party to establish the lack of rational justification for the application of the regulation to him. Clark's solution to the problem was to ignore the very existence of the "secular regulation" rule. Following Judge Clark's lead, he limited the "secular regulation" precedents to their factual situations, deriving from them the rule that in each instance the public interest in compliance must be weighed against the public interest in freedom of conscience. In this determination, the burden of proof should be quite different from that involved in ordinary due process cases.

. . . [W]hen legislation undertakes to restrict or override religious beliefs it runs head on against a great affirmative principle expressly declared by the First Amendment. . . . So strong is the policy of safeguarding the basic individual liberties—including religious freedom—that the presumption should be against, rather than for, the validity of any statute abridging those liberties. . . . We respectfully submit that in a case of this kind the Court should *itself* be convinced of the existence of a public need which is sufficiently urgent to override the great principle of religious freedom in the particular case.[34]

For authority, Clark quoted that part of Stone's *Carolene Products* footnote leaving open the question of the standard of review applicable to regulations striking at "discrete and insular minorities"; for the answer to that unanswered question, he cited Justice Roberts' strong language in *Schneider v. Irvington,* particularly that insisting that the legislative interest invoked must be substantial. Further building on the *Schneider* and *Hague* cases, Clark argued that the authorities must demonstrate not only the reasonableness but the *necessity* of the infringement of conscience; if there was some alternative way which would not conflict with religious scruples, this must be tried instead.

. . . [W]hen the fundamental individual liberties are at stake, the Government is *restricted in its choice of methods* and may even be required to adopt a relatively inefficient and inconvenient means to achieve a proper purpose.[35]

In short, Clark was inviting the Court to extend to religious freedom cases the circumstantial approach already in use in cases involving freedom of speech, press and assembly; thus all First Amendment freedoms would be on the same level.

Applying this stringent standard, Clark denied that the Minersville regulation had been or could be justified. He began by pointing to the novelty and insubstantiality of "morale" as a legislative interest. Quoting from the Virginia Statute of Religious Freedom, he insisted that the Gobitis children's refusal to salute could be punished only if tantamount to "overt acts against peace and good order." This situation was contrasted with the old religious freedom precedents, in which the legislative interest was obvious and imperative.[36]

Clark went on to deny that the compulsory flag salute was either a reasonable or necessary means of promoting morale, even should that be accepted as a legitimate legislative end. He drew a sharp distinction between the *voluntary* salute, a spontaneous show of devotion, and a *compulsory ceremony*, engaged in through fear of punishment. The latter could not be expected to produce patriotism in anybody. Roudabush's testimony as to the value of the ceremony was dismissed as mere unsupported expression of opinion. Clark emphasized that this was a question of common sense; "the court cannot depend on experts because there are no experts."[37] "[I]t simply does not make sense," he argued, "that morale is raised by a compulsory salute offending the child's deepest convictions."[38] Especially significant here was Clark's insistence on treating the effect on the objecting children as decisive of the issue; the school authorities must prove that *they* would be made more patriotic through the compulsory salute. What of the effect of the ceremony and the refusals on the other children, those with no objections to saluting? Clark dismissed this question as *irrelevant;* the regimented uniformity contended for by the school board might be appropriate in an army, but not in a schoolroom. "[T]he purpose of American schools is primarily to impart knowledge and to prepare for life under free institutions. The purpose is *not* to turn out a regimented group seasoned to coercive methods."[39]

Finally, whatever the debatable merits of the flag-salute ceremony, by no stretch of the imagination could the actions of the school authorities be called *necessary*. They themselves had conceded that patriotism could be taught in other ways. And, if the ceremony was used, why not exempt conscientious objectors and explain the situation to the other pupils? Why was it necessary to expel such children? Clark concluded that petitioners had not even advanced enough in justification of the compulsory salute to sustain it under the liberal standards of ordinary due process, much less under the exacting rule urged here.

b) Other points.—Clark's appeal to ordinary substantive due process can be briefly stated. Everything said against the compulsory flag salute in the section on religious freedom applied equally here. It had been shown to be unnecessary and of at best dubious value; indeed, it probably did more harm than good. In addition, Clark stressed the logical extensions of such a power. Could the schools require children to salute a picture of Jefferson—or of the incumbent president? What of an attempt to require *everybody* to salute the flag at stated intervals? If such an enactment would be struck down as arbitrary—and this was hardly to be doubted—then the rule could not be saved by restricting its application to school children.[40]

Finally, Clark struck at the oft-made contention that public education was a mere privilege the granting of which could be conditioned on the flag salute. He stressed the very substantial nature of the injury suffered by Gobitis. Citing *Hague v. CIO*, he denied that such an injury could be justified by a state's proprietary interest in its schools; such necessities of life, when furnished by the state, must be dealt out without arbitrary discrimination. Clark invoked the now-familiar Isserman-Moyle-Maris rationale to distinguish *Hamilton v. Regents*.

The Bill of Rights Committee brief was both strong and important. The legal workmanship was the best of that in the four briefs filed. Clark's demolition of the "privilege" and "no religious significance" arguments put in unanswerable form points which had been argued tolerably well elsewhere. Much more important was the religious freedom section, which provided the first fully reasoned and well documented substitute for the "secular regulation" rule, and argued (in effect) for equal preferential treatment for all the freedoms of the First Amendment.

Even the best brief has it weaknesses, though. Clark's substantive due process argument was vulnerable. Reasonableness is an issue turning on specific facts; the long and favorable tradition surrounding the flag salute might well distinguish it from leader worship and *heiling*. The hypothetical extreme case of a flag-salute requirement for the whole population ignored the vital differences between adults and children. Much more serious was Clark's insistence in the otherwise strong religious freedom section that the compulsory salute, to be valid, must produce patriotism in the objecting children. This argument ran directly counter to his main contention that the public interest in compliance must be weighed against the public interest in freedom of conscience. The state very rarely pushes the citizen around for his *own* good; it is the effect on others around him that is important. This distortion was doubly unfortunate, in that it was not necessary to Clark's argument.

5. ORAL ARGUMENT

Oral argument in the *Gobitis* case was heard on April 25, 1940. Henderson argued for the Minersville authorities. As agreed, Rutherford and Gardner shared the argument time alloted to the respondents. No contemporary record seems to have been kept of the argument, and very little is known about it. The natural assumption, reinforced by general impressions from this writer's conversation with Henderson,[41] is that he echoed the main arguments of his brief, with special emphasis on the section dealing with the Fourteenth Amendment. The argument seems to have been well received. Henderson and McGurl were eminently satisfied with their showing.[42]

Rutherford's oral argument emphasized the weakest elements of his brief.[43] He concentrated exclusively on his theological arguments against flag saluting. There were no questions or discussion from the bench during or after Rutherford's argument, to the apparent disappointment of Rutherford, who had finished well within his time limit for the purpose of entertaining questions.[44]

All that is definitely known of Professor Gardner's argument is that he received very rough treatment from the justices, and that most of his trouble came from Associate Justice Felix Frankfurter, himself a former professor at Harvard Law

School. More than a decade later, Gardner still recalls this episode with undisguised disgust.

Probably no historic occasion ever evoked such a thoroughly uninspired and unsatisfactory discussion as occurred at the oral argument of the *Gobitis* case. The proceedings reflected credit on no one in the room—except possibly Mr. Henderson and Mr. Rutherford—and are best forgotten.[45]

No specific information on the Frankfurter-Gardner colloquy was forthcoming from the participants themselves,[46] and none of the other interested parties has any clear recollection as to the subject matter of the dispute.[47] There seems to be no dissent, however, from the proposition that Gardner got much the worst of it.[48]

Actually, the general outlines of the conflict between Frankfurter and Gardner seem fairly clear in retrospect. In 1940 Frankfurter was just beginning to exhibit personal tendencies which now have become legendary. One of these was his propensity for badgering counsel during oral argument, commonly described as "the Felix problem."[49] Another was his special zeal in insisting that the Court confine its consideration of constitutional questions as narrowly as possible.[50] We have already noted Gardner's preoccupation with the not-too-relevant issue of subsequent punishment of flag-salute expellees. It is immaterial who first referred to this point in the argument; the subject could hardly have been avoided. Gardner probably spent his whole time allotment on the defensive.

B. *Entr'acte:* Cantwell v. Connecticut

On May 20, 1940, just two weeks before *Gobitis* was decided, the Supreme Court decided the case of *Cantwell v. Connecticut.*[51] The three Cantwell brothers had been convicted of selling Witness literature from door to door without the permit required by state law. The permit was to issue automatically if the licensing authority was satisfied that the canvassing was for religious or other genuinely charitable purposes. Jesse Cantwell also had been convicted of breach of the peace after he induced unsuspecting Catholic pedestrians to listen to a phonograph record containing one of "Judge" Rutherford's vitriolic attacks on the Catholic Church. The Supreme Court unanimously reversed all the convictions, in an opinion by Justice Roberts. The permit statute was held to be an unconstitutional prior restraint on religious expression; the breach of peace conviction fell under the "clear and present danger" rule. Most important for present purposes were the dicta in which these holdings were couched. First, Roberts' opinion held for the first time that the Fourteenth Amendment extended to freedom of religion exactly the same measure of protection against state action which was secured against federal action by the First Amendment. Second, Roberts reaffirmed the *Schneider* rationale in potentially significant language:

. . . Thus the [First] Amendment embraces two concepts—freedom to believe and freedom to act. The first is absolute but, in the nature of things, the second cannot be. Conduct remains subject to regulation for the protection of society. . . . *In every case the power to regulate must be so exercised as not, in attaining a permissible end, unduly to infringe the protected freedom.* . . . [Italics supplied.][52]

At first glance, this dictum seemed to support the Bill of Rights Committee's interest-weighing approach to religious freedom cases. It should be noted, however, that the permit statute involved here was explicit in its meddling with admittedly religious matters. Also, the opinion laid heavy emphasis on the Cantwells' right to free *expression* of their religious beliefs. In this view, the decision presented no direct challenge to the "secular regulation" rule.

C. *The Decision*

1. THE JUSTICES

The Supreme Court that heard and decided the *Gobitis* case was composed of Chief Justice Charles Evans Hughes and Associate Justices James C. McReynolds, Harlan F. Stone, Owen J. Roberts, Hugo L. Black, Stanley Reed, Felix Frankfurter, William O. Douglas and Frank Murphy. Only Murphy and Douglas were new to the flag-salute issue; six justices had participated in *Leoles, Hering* and *Johnson v. Deerfield*, while Frankfurter had joined in the last of these. The Court might conceivably have reversed the decisions below without argument or opinion, on the basis of these earlier *per curiam* dispositions. The extraordinary persistence of the Witnesses, together with the surprising defiance shown by two federal courts, evidently convinced the justices that a more extended treatment would be necessary, if the issue was to be laid to rest.

But would this extended treatment involve any substantial reconsideration of the issue? This must depend, of course, on the degree to which the various justices considered it already settled. Chief Justice Hughes must be classed among those who probably entertained no doubts at this point. He had strongly indorsed the "secular regulation" rule in his *Macintosh* dissent, and joined the majority opinion in *Hamilton v. Regents.* Also, the *per curiam* flag-salute dispositions probably represented his views more than those of any other Justice.[53] Roberts' votes in *Hamilton* and *Macintosh,* and McReynolds' in these and many other civil liberties cases pretty much eliminated them as possible converts to the anti-salute position. Justice Stone was the only senior Justice whose position remained ambiguous.

Of the five Roosevelt appointees, the most obvious attribute to be noted was their comparative newness to the Court. Justice Black, the senior member, was in his third year, Justice Murphy in his fourth month. Their chief common denominator drawing Roosevelt's favor was their strong support for the Administration's economic policies. Just three years after the "court-packing" fight, they were well qualified to appreciate the virtues of judicial self-restraint. Black and Reed had been in the thick of the fight for Roosevelt's plan to reorganize the Court.[54] On the other hand, Black, Murphy and Frankfurter were prominently on record against various forms of oppression of the poor and helpless.[55] None of the quintet had faced a "hard" civil liberties case; none was really "committed" on the flag-salute issue.

No discussion of the background of the *Gobitis* decision would be complete without some mention of the dominant position of Chief Justice Hughes.[56] Hughes "ran" the Court to a degree probably unparalleled since Marshall; in the general run of cases, his associates seem to have been content so to be "run." Hughes was generally better prepared than his brethren, and pushed the discussion along at a rapid-fire pace. In this context, his powerful personality and persuasive tongue exercised their maximum influence. This influence probably was magnified by the Court's set procedure in conference. Discussion of a given case proceeds in descending order of seniority, with the Chief Justice leading off; voting, on the other hand, begins with the newest Justice, with the Chief voting last. Hughes' opening statement gave his position a momentum that often was decisive; in many cases, his was the only statement. Justices generally were reluctant to disagree with Hughes unless they felt strongly about it. The inverse order of voting placed an extra pressure to conformity on the junior justices, especially in "minor" cases in which there may have been little real discussion. The point is that *Gobitis* seemed to be such a minor case. It was remote from the issues currently dividing the justices, and presented an issue thrice decided by the Court in the previous five years. In such circumstances, the initial presumption must have been against reconsideration.

In the conference room, Hughes converted this presumption into a virtual certainty with a strongly negative opening statement. He stressed the broad powers of a state over its own public schools, denied that there was any infringement on freedom of religion, and termed the issue one of educational policy and inappropriate for judicial meddling. There was no other discussion. It is not clear whether a formal vote was taken; the justices seemed to be unanimously in favor of reversal. Before they left the room, Hughes designated Justice Frankfurter to write the Court's opinion. It was not until he failed to initial Frankfurter's circulated opinion that anyone realized that Justice Stone intended to dissent from the ruling.[57]

The final decision in *Minersville School District v. Gobitis*[58] was handed down on June 3, 1940. At this point Justices Frankfurter and Stone take center stage alone as principal antagonists.[59] The decision itself was quite predictable in the circumstances; the opinions were not. Under no necessity to tailor his opinion to hold wavering votes, Frankfurter enjoyed considerable freedom in the framing of his arguments. The doctrinal forms given the controversy in the majority and minority opinions in *Gobitis* were grounded in the predilections of these two justices and their particular reactions to the arguments advanced by the parties.

2. JUSTICE FRANKFURTER FOR THE MAJORITY

a) *The man.*—When Felix Frankfurter came to the Supreme Court in 1938, he brought with him a wide reputation as a legal scholar, a liberal and a libertarian. A professor of law at Harvard since 1914, he had been active in the formation of the American Civil Liberties Union and the magazine *New Republic*,[60] had fought the excessive use of court injunctions in labor disputes[61] and had labored mightily on behalf of Sacco and Vanzetti.[62] He was an ardent supporter and trusted advisor of Franklin D. Roosevelt, and one of the most famous members of that amorphous entity, the "brain trust."[63] As a libertarian, Frankfurter cannot have been pleased by the heavy-handed approach adopted by the Minersville school authorities; he privately conceded that it was "foolish and perhaps worse."[64] As a legal scholar, on the other hand, he cannot have been unaware of the long line of precedents embodied in the "secular regulation" rule. The decisive question, then, was the extent to which Frankfurter would be willing to strike out consciously in a new direction—perhaps that suggested by the Bill of Rights Committee brief—to bring the legal situation into accord with his libertarian preferences.

Here the evidence is more complete. Several decades' experience with the old Court's obstruction of social welfare legislation had left Frankfurter with a lasting distrust of judicial review as a positive instrument of liberalism. In particular, he had developed a strong aversion to the broad power exercised by the Court under the due process clause of the Fourteenth Amendment. In 1924, he went so far as to suggest that the power be eliminated, presumably by constitutional amendment.[65] Eight months later, commenting on *Pierce v. Society of Sisters,* Frankfurter was unmollified by the libertarian outcome: illiberal statutes would soon be repealed, but there could be no repeal of illiberal Supreme Court edicts. Furthermore, Frankfurter felt that courts—even liberal courts—were not the proper agents of liberalism.

. . . It must never be forgotten that our constant preoccupation with the constitutionality of legislation rather than its wisdom tends to preoccupation of the American mind with a false value. . . . [T]he tendency of focusing attention on constitutionality is to make constitutionality synonymous with propriety. . . . Particularly in legislation affecting freedom of thought and freedom of speech much that is highly illiberal would be clearly constitutional. . . . [T]he real battles of liberalism are not won in the Supreme Court. . . .[66]

Frankfurter's continuing preoccupation with judicial self-restraint was manifest in a note he wrote Justice Stone in an attempt to sway him from his intention to dissent.

What weighs with me strongly in this case is my anxiety that, while we lean in the direction of the libertarian aspect, we do not exercise our judicial power unduly, and as though we ourselves were legislators by holding with too tight a rein the organs of popular government. . . .[67]

For my intention . . . was to use this opinion as a vehicle for preaching the true democratic faith of not relying on the Court for the impossible task of assuring a vigorous, mature, self-respecting and tolerant democracy by bringing the responsibility . . . directly home where it belongs—to the people and their representatives themselves.[68]

Frankfurter drew attention to the troubled times and the clear approach of World War II, suggesting that legislatures should then be given freer rein to seek to promote the national security. He emphasized the degree to which the present decision left the Court free to draw more exact lines in the future (". . . how very little this case authorizes . . .")[69] whereas a contrary decision might commit the Court too far in the wrong direction (". . . a tail of implications as to legislative power that is certainly debatable . . .").[70] One searches Frankfurter's note to Stone in vain for any reference to religious freedom. The implication is strong that he considered the religious freedom issue closed; the only precedents cited in the note related to ordinary substantive due process.

b) *The opinion.*—It is important to examine Justice Frankfurter's *Gobitis* opinion both for what it said and did not say. There were a number of passages—particularly those aimed at specific contentions in the briefs—that were unclear by themselves, and the resulting confusions have infected subsequent judicial opinions as well as professional and lay commentary on the decision.

The form of the opinion was dominated by two major assumptions. First, Frankfurter eschewed any reliance on the "privilege" argument. Second, he considered it "surely not debatable" that the ceremony could be required of school children in general;[71] the only issue at hand was whether the Gobitis children were entitled to be exempted from participation. The opinion itself was divided into two main sections. Freedom of conscience draws support from two related but noncoterminous guaranties implicit in the due process clause of the Fourteenth Amendment. First, it is protected with all the rigor of the incorporated First Amendment *insofar as it falls within the specific scope of the phrase "free exercise of religion."* Quite apart from this special protection, though, freedom of conscience, like freedom of contract, is a part of the general "liberty" of which no person can be deprived without "due process of law." Frankfurter first disposed of the religious freedom issue; the second and longer part of his opinion was devoted to a thorough treatment of the general due process issue. Throughout his argument, Frankfurter developed his philosophy of judicial self-restraint and suggested limited areas in which this philosophy might *not* be controlling.

Religious freedom.—"In the judicial enforcement of religious freedom we are concerned with a historic concept."[72] This proposition was crucial to Frankfurter's reasoning; the religious freedom guaranty of the First Amendment was confined to the very special meaning it had to the framers.[73] Frankfurter's discussion was a model of concise accuracy in stating the law as it then stood. First, he summed up the area protected:

Certainly the affirmative pursuit of one's convictions about the ultimate mystery of the universe and man's relation to it is placed beyond the reach of law. Government may not interfere with organized or individual expression of belief or disbelief. . . . Likewise the Constitution assures generous immunity to the individual from imposition of penalties for offending, in the course of his own religious activities, the religious views of others . . . Cantwell v. Connecticut. . . .[74]

Rutherford to the contrary, however, there must be limits if society was to function, the most important of which was the "secular regulation" rule:

. . . Conscientious scruples have not, in the course of the long struggle for religious toleration, relieved the individual from obedience to a general law not aimed at the promotion or restriction of religious beliefs. The mere possession of religious convictions which contradict the relevant concerns of society does not relieve the citizen from the discharge of political responsibilities. The necessity for this adjustment has again and again been recognized. . . .[75]

There followed the familiar citations to *Reynolds v. United States, Hamilton v. Regents,* etc. Frankfurter refused to acknowledge any qualitative difference between this and other secular requirements that had been upheld against religious objections.

Substantive due process.—Quoting Lincoln's famous dilemma—"Must a government of necessity be too *strong* for the liberties of its people, or too *weak* to maintain its own existence?"[76]—Frankfurter emphasized that, trivial as this controversy might seem, its resolution involved weighty issues of governmental power. "No mere textual reading or logical talisman can solve the dilemma."[77] Frankfurter admitted that "morale" lacked the specificity and immediacy present in other objectives of the police power, but denied that it was therefore illegitimate.

. . . The ultimate foundation of a free society is the binding tie of cohesive sentiment. Such a sentiment is fostered by all those agencies of the mind and spirit which may serve to gather up the traditions of a people. . . . The flag is the symbol of our national unity, transcending all internal differences. . . .[78]

This statement of the public policy behind flag saluting rose far above the petty alarms of Henderson's brief; never has the case for "flag worship" been more appealingly put.

The bulk of Frankfurter's argument was devoted to a particularly strong statement of the presumption of constitutionality, and the application of that principle to the case at hand. He emphasized that the Minersville regulation had the same constitutional dignity as if it had been passed by the Pennsylvania legislature. He properly resolved all doubts in favor of the regulation:

. . . The influences which help toward a common feeling for the common country are manifold. Some may seem harsh and others no doubt are foolish. Surely, however, the end is legitimate. And the effective means for its attainment are still so uncertain . . . as to preclude us from putting the widely prevalent belief in flag-saluting beyond the pale of legislative power. . . .

We are dealing with the formative period in the development of citizenship. Great diversity of psychological and ethical opinion exists among us concerning the best way to train children for their place in society. . . .[79]

Somewhat less clearly, Frankfurter also injected the issue of relative expertise:

. . . To stigmatize legislative judgment in providing for this universal gesture of respect . . . as a lawless inroad on . . . freedom of conscience . . . would amount to no less than the pronouncement of pedagogical and psychological dogma in a field where courts possess no marked and certainly no controlling competence. . . .

. . . [T]he courtroom is not the arena for debating issues of educational policy. . . . So to hold would in effect make us the school board for the country. . . .[80]

In dealing with the specific issue, Frankfurter took at face value Roudabush's expressed fears of the consequences of non-saluting:

. . . [F]or us to insist that, though the ceremony may be required, exceptional immunity must be given to dissidents, is to maintain that there is no basis for a legislative judgment that such an exemption might introduce elements of difficulty into the school discipline, might cast doubts in the minds of the other children which would themselves weaken the effect of the exercise.[81]

Frankfurter's due process discussion seems to have been aimed principally at the arguments advanced in the Bill of Rights Committee brief. In passages already quoted, he had disposed of the Committee's insistence on measuring the effectiveness of the salute by its effect on the objecting child and its hypothetical extreme of a compulsory salute for all citizens. He curtly disposed of the other hypothetical "horror"—a required salute to a leader: "It mocks reason and denies our whole history. . . ."[82] Frankfurter closed this part of his argument—and his opinion—with a general pronouncement against the ready transfer of political controversies to the courts:

Judicial review, itself a limitation on popular government, is a fundamental part of our constitutional scheme. But to the legislature no less than to courts is committed the guardianship of deeply-cherished liberties. . . . To fight out the wise use of legislative authority in the forum of public opinion and before legislative assemblies rather than to transfer such a contest to the judicial arena, serves to vindicate the self-confidence of a free people.[83]

At this point, a brief footnote disposed of Gardner's assertion that flag respect was a national concern with the notation that Congress had not acted upon the subject.

Judicial self-restraint and the political processes.—The arguments already described clearly would have sufficed to dispose of this case. Frankfurter did not stop there, however. He went on to try to circumscribe in final terms the areas within which the Court would second-guess the legislative judgment. These attempts appear at two widely separated points in Frankfurter's opinion, dealing in terms with freedom of speech and the general role of judicial review.

Although free speech had not been invoked in the briefs filed in the Supreme Court, Frankfurter incidentally touched on the issue essentially in the form given it in Moyle's first District Court brief—i.e., the contention that freedom of speech implied a right not to utter repugnant sentiments. Even granting such an implied right—and Frankfurter clearly did not—

. . . the question remains whether school children, like the Gobitis children, must be excused from conduct required of all the other children in the promotion of national cohesion. We are dealing with an interest inferior to none in the hierarchy of legal values. National unity is the basis of national security. . . . Compare Schneider v. Irvington. . . .[84]

In short, the social interest involved here far outweighed that rejected in *Schneider*. But *Schneider* and like cases also scrutinized *means* and *effects*. What of these? Clearly, Frankfurter was satisfied to apply here the ordinary "rational basis" standard used in other substantive due process cases; free speech added nothing to the protection already derived from the due process clause.

Frankfurter resolved the apparent inconsistency of his position near the end of his opinion:

. . . Except where the transgression of constitutional liberty is too plain for argument, personal freedom is best maintained—so long as the remedial channels of the democratic process remain open and unobstructed—when it is ingrained in a people's habits and not enforced against popular policy by the coercion of adjudicated law. . . .[85]

. . . Where all the effective means of inducing political change are left free from interference, education in the abandonment of foolish legislation is itself a training in liberty. . . .[86]

In a footnote, he distinguished the major free speech precedents; there, "the Court was concerned with restrictions cutting off appropriate means through which, in a free society, the processes of popular rule may effectively function."[87] This clearly was a restatement of part of Justice Stone's *Carolene Products* footnote. The Court must exercise great restraint, leaving all doubtful statutes to the test of the political process —except when that process itself was endangered. Then and only then, the Court would weigh for itself the competing interests and the necessity of the means used. Frankfurter was trying to confine within the narrowest possible bounds the "sovereign prerogative of choice"[88] exercised by the Court under the due process clause.

What were the implications of this part of Frankfurter's argument for freedom of conscience? Two general conclusions can be advanced. First, this particular form of conscientious non-compliance, even if included in the "historic" meaning of the First Amendment, could draw no *special* protection from that provision. Refusal to salute the flag was no part of any political process. Furthermore, since such a right could not be absolute, its protection would involve the Court in the very judicial policy-making most abhorrent to Frankfurter. Second, Frankfurter's reasoning left the "secular regulation" rule unimpaired. Even his extreme tolerance excluded laws "aimed at the promotion or restriction of religious beliefs." In its narrow historic meaning, the religious freedom clause was merely a manifestation of the general imperative embodied in the "no-establishment" clause: that government should take no cognizance of religious matters. Violations in these related areas could be expected to be obvious and extremely hard to justify in terms of secular legislative interests; judicial legislation would be at a minimum.[89]

It bears emphasis that these were latent implications. Nothing in this part of Frankfurter's opinion was actually necessary to the decision of the case at hand. It was just this line of argument, however, which introduced a large element of uncertainty into an otherwise clear opinion, leaving even legal commentators uncertain as to just what had actually been decided.

3. JUSTICE STONE DISSENTING

a) The man.—Harlan F. Stone was appointed to the Supreme Court by President Coolidge in 1925. A conservative and a Republican,[90] he nevertheless voted to uphold most New Deal legislation. He was notable throughout his career for his willingness to uphold the legality of statutes he personally considered unwise or downright immoral.[91] Stone was not such an apostle of judicial self-restraint in the field of civil liberties, however. Attention already has been drawn to his pointed *Carolene Products* footnote. Frankfurter's reliance on this footnote, it must be noted, was somewhat misplaced. Stone was arguing for a stricter standard of review "in those cases where there is danger that the ordinary political processes . . . *may not operate. . . .*"[92] In short, the stringency of review should be determined in part by the presence or absence of alternative modes of correction—a principle with respectable antecedents in American constitutional law.[93] Stone's rationale, unlike Frankfurter's, provided protection not only against direct attacks on the political processes, but against indirect impairments thereof by prejudice against minorities.

During World War I, Stone served on a presidential board of inquiry investigating the cases of several thousand conscientious objectors who had run afoul of the draft laws. His experiences went far to shape his thinking on the problem of religious freedom. He was deeply disturbed by the truly religious objectors, and strongly favored lenient treatment. The sharp distinction he drew between these and the "political" objectors—the "glib talkers"—was reflected in his later discordant votes in *Schwimmer* and *Macintosh.*[94] Stone came away from this investigation with a strong acceptance of the act-omission dichotomy in religious freedom matters later developed by Judge Clark's Circuit Court opinion in *Gobitis.*

. . . [C]onscience is violated if [the citizen] is coerced into doing an act which is opposed to his deepest convictions of right and wrong. . . . However vigorous the State may be in repressing the commission of acts which are regarded as injurious to the State, it may well stay its hand before it compels the commission of acts which violate the conscience.[95]

Justice Stone had joined in the three *per curiam* dispositions of the flag-salute issue, whether from conviction or merely from reticence it is unclear. It is not known just when he decided to dissent in *Gobitis,* but he seems to have made up his mind before the case came up in conference.[96] Originally he planned simply to note his dissent, but, under the urging of his law clerk, finally decided to write an opinion. As a result of this hesitation, his opinion circulated only after most of the justices already had initialed Frankfurter's.[97] Once resolved to write an opinion, Stone became increasingly worked up emotionally. When the decision was announced, he read his dissenting opinion in full and with great emotion.[98]

b) The opinion.—Justice Stone's dissenting opinion centered entirely on the First Amendment. He invoked two related concepts: freedom of religion and the free thought imperative underlying the whole First Amendment. His argument on both points was dominated by the act-omission dichotomy already alluded to.

The law which is thus sustained is unique in the history of Anglo-American legislation. It does more than suppress freedom of speech and . . . religion. . . . For by this law the state seeks to coerce these children to express a sentiment which, as they interpret it, they do not entertain, and which violates their deepest religious convictions.[99]

Thus, what for Frankfurter did not touch First Amendment rights at all was for Stone the most flagrant violation possible.

Freedom of religion.—Following the lead of the Bill of Rights Committee, Stone freely recognized the vitality of the "secular regulation" precedents, but limited them to the highly important legislative ends there involved—defense, crime prevention, etc.

... But it is a long step, and one which I am unable to take, to the position that government may, as a supposed educational measure ... compel public affirmations which violate their religious conscience.[100]

Following the same lead, he cited *Hague* and *Schneider* as evidence that even a valid legislative end would not justify means that were unnecessarily restrictive of civil liberty. That the regulation here was necessary could hardly be maintained.

... [T]here are other ways to teach loyalty and patriotism. ... I cannot say that government here is deprived of any interest or function which it is entitled to maintain at the expense of civil liberties by requiring it to resort to the alternatives which do not coerce an affirmation of belief.[101]

Freedom of thought.—Unlike Frankfurter, who relied strictly on the specific prohibitions thereof, Stone appealed directly to the underlying purpose, or theme, of the First Amendment:

The guaranties of civil liberty are but guaranties of freedom of the human mind and spirit and of reasonable freedom and opportunity to express them. They *presuppose* the right of the individual to hold such opinions as he will and to give them reasonably free expression, and his freedom, and that of the state as well, to teach and persuade others by the communication of ideas. The very essence of the liberty which they guarantee is the freedom of the individual from compulsion as to what he shall think and what he shall say, *at least* where the compulsion is to bear false witness to his religion. If these guaranties are to have any meaning they must, I think, be deemed to withhold from the state any authority to compel belief or the expression of it where that expression violates religious convictions, whatever may be the legislative view of the desirability of such compulsion. [Italics supplied.][102]

Stone, then, saw the compulsion to express a state of mind to be no different qualitatively from the compulsion of belief itself. It is significant that he did not—and logically could not—expressly limit this principle to freedom of *religious* thought. Finally, Stone regarded freedom of thought, unlike freedom of expression, as *absolute*, beyond any considerations of competing interests.

Stone sharply rebuked what he considered Frankfurter's misuse of his *Carolene Products* footnote, and laid down his version of the standard to be applied "if ... it is considered that there is some scope for the determination by legislatures. . . ."[103] This rationale was based squarely on the last paragraph of that footnote, suggesting the special duty to protect "discrete and insular minorities." Stone found Jehovah's Witnesses to be precisely the sort of minority he had had in mind:

... Here we have such a small minority entertaining in good faith a religious belief, which is such a departure from the usual course of human conduct, that most persons are disposed to regard it with little toleration or concern. In such circumstances careful scrutiny of legislative efforts to secure conformity of belief . . . is especially needful if civil rights are to receive any protection. Tested by this standard, I am not prepared to say that the right of this small and helpless minority, including children having a strong religious conviction, whether they understand its nature or not, to refrain from an expression obnoxious to their religion, is to be overborne by the interest of the state in maintaining discipline in the schools.[104]

The theoretical difference between Stone and Frankfurter on this point was narrow, but probably irreconcilable. Frankfurter would view suspiciously any regulation *on its face* "aimed" or "directed" at minorities; Stone would extend such scrutiny to "legislation which operates to repress"[105] them.

D. *Concluding Remarks*

It is important to view the *Gobitis* case in its proper perspective. The holding was a narrow one, upholding only the expulsion of non-saluters without any express indorsement of attempts at further punishment of expellees or their parents. The decision did not hold that "national unity" outweighed freedom of religion, or place the latter on a par with ordinary substantive due process.

It is impossible to explain the division in this case by saying that one side was "right" and the other "wrong." This was a case where the Court had to choose a path. For over a decade, the Supreme Court had been taking an increasingly active role in the protection of civil liberties, but this trend had not yet affected the area of religious freedom. Frankfurter's opinion was essentially a conservative one, taking a stand squarely on the existing precedential law and describing the First Amendment as protecting only the rights expressly set forth therein. Besides being the line of least resistance, this approach was congenial to Frankfurter's strong distrust of judicial activism. Stone, on the other hand, tried to push the Court further in the direction in which it already was moving. Rejecting any absolute acceptance of the "secular regulation" rule, he sought to extend to religious freedom litigation the circumstantial approach already in vogue in free speech cases. Beyond this, he tried to establish an absolute immunity for what he considered the underlying imperative of the First Amendment— freedom of thought in a broad sense. A liberal holdover from the "old" Court, he was less chary of judicial review than Frankfurter. A choice between the two positions can be judged only by results and in the light of the values of the beholder.

A word is in order regarding the two justices' use of the briefs. Frankfurter largely followed the Minersville brief regarding the "secular regulation" rule and the value of "morale." He ignored the Rutherford and Gardner briefs almost entirely, but was at pains to rebut every argument advanced by the Bill of Rights Committee. Stone seems to have borrowed heavily from the ABA brief for his religious freedom section; his discussion of freedom of thought seemed to build from the basis laid down in the ACLU brief. It is possible to overestimate the influence of briefs, however. Stone and Frankfurter had formed their major beliefs on this issue long before the brief writers did. Probably, they drew citations and—especially in the case of Stone—style from the briefs for the presentation of views independently formulated and long held.

With this decision, the Witnesses and their allies seemed definitely and finally to have lost their long fight. They had achieved their strategic goal, the Supreme Court, only to have that tribunal, contrary to all their expectations, rule against them. Yet we know from our history that this decision did not settle the flag controversy, which only grew in scope and bitterness. Within three years the issue was back in the Supreme Court. It is to the story of those crucial three years that we turn next.

CHAPTER SEVEN

INTERIM, 1940–1943

PRESS REACTION TO THE *GOBITIS* DECISION

Press reaction to the *Gobitis* decision was voluminous and, on the whole, unfavorable. In this chapter we shall survey this reaction with a view to ascertaining more definitely its direction and vehemence. Attention also will be given the various distortions which crept into the commentaries. Different writers seized upon different parts of Frankfurter's opinion as *the* holding in *Gobitis*. The picture often differed strikingly from the original.

A. *Law Reviews and Related Scholarly Writings*

1. PRELIMINARY: PRE-*GOBITIS* COMMENT

Legal comment was the only area of the press in which it was feasible to explore thoroughly the views expressed on the flag-salute issue before *Gobitis* was decided. In the period from 1935 to June, 1940, there were thirty-two comments in twenty-six law reviews on the growing flag controversy, comprising ten articles,[1] one editorial[2] and twenty-three notes,[3] almost all of the last being written by students. All of these dealt at least incidentally with the state flag-salute decisions or with pending state litigation. Of twenty-seven comments mentioning the lower court decisions in *Gobitis*, five were noncommittal,[4] two disapproved of them,[5] and twenty indorsed them and criticized the state cases.[6] Of the eight comments dealing only with various of the state decisions, five were critical,[7] one favorable[8] and two noncommittal.[9] The dominant theme in the comments favoring the lower court decisions in *Gobitis* was a sharp attack on the assertion made by many of the state courts that the salute ceremony, not being a religious rite, was not properly subject to any religious objection. Fifteen writers heartily indorsed Judge Maris' insistence that the individual must be the judge of his own beliefs.[10] Appearing somewhat less frequently were expressions of doubt as to the value of the compulsory salute as a patriotic stimulus,[11] and denials of any adequate public necessity for such an infringement on religious liberty.[12] The writers supporting the compulsory salute rested heavily on the desirability of the ceremony[13] and the "fact" that the salute was not a religious rite.[14] These lines of argument were quite in order, in view of the rudimentary reasoning of the state court opinions. Frankfurter's *Gobitis* opinion, however, completely reshaped and considerably refined the central issues. The themes described above were either dropped completely or drastically altered in later legal comment.

2. COMMENT ON *GOBITIS*

a) The general division.—Scholarly comment on the *Gobitis* decision overflowed the legal periodicals somewhat. Our discussion here will include passages from four books,[15] two articles in the *American Political Science Review*[16] and one in the *Political Science Quarterly*.[17] Thirty-two law reviews carried thirty-nine comments. Of these, twenty-five articles,[18] fourteen notes[19] and one editorial[20] dealt prominently or exclusively with the *Gobitis* decision, while nineteen—thirteen articles,[21] three notes,[22] one editorial[23] and two reprints of a judicial opinion[24]—dealt only in passing with that case.

Thirty-one of the comments were openly or tacitly critical of the *Gobitis* decision,[25] four were favorable,[26] and eleven were noncommittal.[27] This last figure, it will be noted, included ten incidental comments. Of the four approving comments, two seemed to rely on the great importance of national unity.[28] The other two relied specifically on the "secular regulation" rule.[29] Of the disapproving comments, fourteen concentrated their main criticism on Frankfurter's language regarding the duty of judicial self-restraint.[30] Fourteen, including six of the comments just mentioned, more or less specifically attacked his handling of the religious freedom issue.[31] There were seven comments expressing general distaste for the decision itself or for the policy there upheld,[32] terming the decision "unfortunate,"[33] or "an aberration."[34] Finally, seven of the other unfavorable comments discussed above directed sharp attacks at the *policy* upheld by *Gobitis*.[35] For example:

... All of the eloquence by which the majority extol the ceremony of flag saluting as a free expression of patriotism turns sour when used to describe the brutal compulsion which requires a sensitive and conscientious child to stultify himself in public. . . .[36]

The most impressive assault on the *Gobitis* precedent from a policy viewpoint was an article by Victor Rotnem, head of the Justice Department's Civil Rights Section, and F. G. Folsom, also of the Department. Commenting on the wave of anti-Witness persecution apparently resulting from that decision, they wrote:

This ugly picture of the two years following the Gobitis decision is an eloquent argument in support of the minority contention of Mr. Justice Stone. The placing of symbolic exercises on a higher plane than freedom of conscience has made this symbol an instrument of oppression of a religious minority. . . .

It seems probable that a reversal of that ruling would profoundly enhance respect for the flag. . . .[37]

b) Analysis: Some misconceptions.—It is important to remember that the key to Frankfurter's *Gobitis* opinion lay in the "secular regulation" rule. Religious freedom, as protected by the incorporated First Amendment, was excluded from the case at the outset. The operative language in Frankfurter's argument for judicial self-restraint and his panegyrics on national unity were directed to the narrow issue of the *reasonableness* of the salute requirement under the due process clause. Read closely, the *Gobitis* case did *not* hold (*a*) that national unity was more important than religious freedom, or (*b*) that religious freedom could be violated with impunity as long as the political channels were kept open. It is in the light of this analysis that we must consider the treatment of *Gobitis* in the law review comments.

The fourteen comments specifically attacking Frankfurter's position on judicial self-restraint seem to reflect the second of the misconceptions noted above. This is certainly true of William G. Fennell's bitter criticism:

... It seems to imply that the popular majority may with immunity from court interference impose legislation which violates the constitutional rights of the minority—except in the limited sphere where freedom of expression, by the press, speech, or assembly are involved. It ignores the fact that the Constitution has heretofore been considered a limitation on majority will. . . .[38]

While the point is less certain, the same defect seems present in the brief notation that "the opinion itself seems to indicate that the Supreme Court will no longer serve as the arbitrator of the legality of acts of local school boards."[39] On the other hand, some of the criticism may have been directed at Frankfurter's rhetoric, with no intention of equating the rhetoric with the holding. This is probably the proper interpretation of Professor Corwin's caustic comment:

. . . But even more distasteful than the ruling itself is Justice Frankfurter's smug assumption that the Court is the happy possessor of a potent formula which enables it in cases like this to dispense with exercising its own judgment. . . .[40]

Twenty-three comments dealt more or less specifically with the immediate issue—the conflict between religious scruples and the pursuit of national unity.[41] This number includes all of the favorable comments, five of the non-committal comments, and the fourteen comments which attacked Frankfurter's opinion on this point. Here, the other misconception described above was prevalent. The only wholly satisfactory account of this issue—and of the whole case—was an unsigned, completely noncommittal article in the *International Juridical Association Monthly Bulletin*.[42] There, the relevant passage read as follows:

. . . Thus the religious guarantee cannot be invoked where, as here, the challenged legislation is not "directed against loyalties of particular sects" but is a general measure enacted in furtherance of an important public purpose, even though the legislation happens to work special hardship on certain persons because of their religious beliefs. This eliminates the religious aspect of the case and leaves only the question whether the salute . . . is a reasonable way to promote the interest of national unity. . . .[43]

The author of the twice-reprinted judicial opinion touched only briefly on *Gobitis*, but seemed also to grasp the essential point. Judge Miner quoted Frankfurter's "secular regulation" argument, saying, "The Flag Salute decision . . . has served to re-emphasize the determination to subject alleged religious practices to reasonable regulations."[44]

Five comments occupied an ambiguous middle position between right and wrong, defying any definite classification. One may have had the idea, but was too vague for certainty. General reference was made to "the orthodox doctrine that the police power . . . supersedes personal liberties where the public interest requires it."[45] This sentence was followed by citations of both religious freedom cases and ordinary due process cases. Two articles in the *California State Bar Journal* repeated the approximate language of the "secular regulation" rule, but the context showed no recognition of its significance. One of these held the Court to have relied on the doctrine that "religious freedom, when the exercise of religious doctrines is contrary to good morals, can be prohibited."[46] The other quoted without comment Frankfurter's "secular regulation" argument, then concluded that the decision was irreconcilable with *Cantwell.*[47] Finally, the Fennell article[48] and the comment in *Jurist*[49] seemed to recognize Frankfurter's "secular regulation" argument for what it was, but insisted that this was a *new departure* from the usual rule that religious scruples need yield only to urgent public necessities.

Finally, fifteen comments more or less clearly fell into the first distortion mentioned above. Eight of these stated in various language that the Court had weighed the Gobitis children's religious freedom against the public interest in national unity and had decided in favor of the latter.[50] "The necessity for cohesive patriotic sentiments was felt to be more important than the non-conformist religious views of the Witnesses."[51] "The social interest here held paramount to religious liberty is the 'cohesive sentiment' of nationalism. . . ."[52] Another comment referred to "this determination that a state's interest in fostering patriotism transcends one's concern for his religious rights."[53] Seven comments were less clear.[54] These concentrated on the Court's supposed reliance on the overriding importance of national unity, without specifically relating this to the religious freedom question. The necessary implication of such an interpretation would seem to be the same as the explicit statements of the comments discussed immediately above. Consider the following statements, for example: "The opinion of Justice Frankfurter . . . seems based on the supposed fact that the necessity of fostering national unity through inculcating loyalty for the flag transcends all other considerations."[55] "The principal reason upon which the court seemed to base its decision—that such a regulation will cement national unity, which end is of sufficient importance to justify an invasion of personal liberty—seems questionable."[56]

B. *Magazines*

1. GENERAL CIRCULATION PERIODICALS

Comment on *Gobitis* was generally scarce in the general circulation magazines; most did not mention the case at all. *Life* mentioned the decision in passing, but that was all.[57] Beulah Amidon, in *Survey Graphic*, described the misuse of the *Gobitis* decision as an excuse for persecution of Jehovah's Witnesses, but expressed no opinion on the merits of the case.[58] H. R. Southworth, in the *Nation*, noted that the decision had aggravated the Witnesses' precarious situation in 1940, but likewise was silent on the merits.[59] *Newsweek* mentioned the decision soon after it was handed down, commenting ambiguously that the Court was "adjourning on a patriotic note."[60] Of all the brief comments, *Time*'s was closest to being unfavorable.[61] Describing in a faintly sardonic tone the "fifth column" hysteria beginning to sweep the country, the article continued:

Not part of the undercurrent but a ripple on the stream was a decision of the Supreme Court which held that the regulation of the Minersville, Pa. school board requiring school children to salute the flag was constitutional. . . .[62]

Only the *New Republic*, the magazine Frankfurter had helped found, dealt with the *Gobitis* decision at length, repeatedly, and unfavorably. In an editorial devoted specially to that case,[63] the editors assumed, as did many of the law reviews, that the case should be decided by balancing the opposing interests in religious freedom and national unity. Proceeding on this assumption, they concluded that there was no emergency requiring such an infringement, and that there were ample alternative means of securing the desired end. The editorial closed:

. . . This country is now in the grip of a war hysteria; we are in great danger of adopting Hitler's philosophy in the effort to oppose Hitler's legions. When the Supreme Court says in effect that we must sacrifice religious liberty in the interest of the American state, which is worth preserving because it guarantees religious liberty, it comes dangerously close to being a victim of that hysteria.[64]

Shortly thereafter, the *New Republic* carried an article by Walton Hamilton and George Braden, discussing the current Supreme Court at length and, on the whole, favorably.[65] In the course of this survey, the authors noted caustically that

. . . Already Mr. Justice Frankfurter has been heroically saving America from a couple of school children whose devotion to Jehovah would have been compromised by a salute to the flag. In the process, he discovered, though he piled up words to hide it, that religious liberty is a local question. . . .[66]

In the same issue, an editorial commented on a recent German court decision punishing Jehovah's Witnesses for their refusal to "heil" Hitler.[67] The editorial concluded:

The United States Supreme Court and a Nazi court might come to different conclusions—or to the same conclusion—for different reasons, which might be admirable in one case and not in the other. Yet we are sure that the majority members of our Court who concurred in the Frankfurter decision would be embarrassed to know that their attitude was in substance the same as that of the German tribunal.[68]

As far as this writer could find there was no article in a general circulation magazine *approving* the *Gobitis* decision.

2. RELIGIOUS MAGAZINES

A complete survey of the multitude of religious journals operating in the United States would be the work of another, equally long study. We have been content here to sample the reaction at both ends of the spectrum of opinion, as regards attitudes toward Jehovah's Witnesses. On the one hand, *Christian Century* has been generally sympathetic toward the Witnesses and their troubles. As might be expected, it reacted strongly and adversely to the *Gobitis* decision. An editorial soon after, dealing particularly with *Gobitis*, urged that the general rule was "that there shall be complete freedom of conscience in all matters that do not manifestly and adversely affect the social order. . . ."[69] The rest of the editorial was devoted to a strong denial of the necessity or wisdom of a compulsory salute ceremony. Attention was called to Charles II's wisdom in allowing William Penn to keep his hat on in the royal presence.

. . . Willingness to salute the flag is no criterion of loyalty. To make this particular ceremony a test is to make the flag mean something quite different from what Justice Frankfurter says it means.
. . . It is bitterly ironical that a free government should inflict a penalty for refusal to salute a symbol of freedom. . . .[70]

Two weeks later, *Christian Century* returned to the attack with new bitterness. For the first time, criticism was leveled against Frankfurter's opinion, particularly the passages on judicial self-restraint:

. . . If the legislative branch, or any other administrative body acting under legislative sanction, enacts laws which encroach upon the liberties of the people, whose business is it, if not that of the courts, to render the prevailing decision as to what a wise adjustment requires? . . .[71]
Well, a question of educational policy may also be a question of fundamental rights, and the courts have not always considered such questions to be beyond their jurisdiction. . . .
. . . Courts that will not protect even Jehovah's Witnesses will not long protect anybody.[72]

In the next issue, an article by John Haynes Holmes regarding the persecution of Jehovah's Witnesses blamed the increase in anti-Witness violence on the "unfortunate" *Gobitis* decision.[73] Barbed remarks about that case continued to appear from time to time.[74]

At the other end of the spectrum was the Catholic Church, which had little reason to love the Witnesses. The Catholic law reviews—*Fordham Law Review, Georgetown Law Journal, Jurist, Notre Dame Lawyer, St. Johns Law Review* and *University of Detroit Law Journal*[75]—were unanimously hostile to the *Gobitis* decision. As was noted in the preceding section, three of these concentrated their disapproval on Frankfurter's judicial self-restraint argument, and four dealt specifically and badly with the religious freedom issue. The *Gobitis* decision came in for sharp criticism in an article in *Catholic Education Review*[76] and in several items in *America*.[77] Representative of both the tenor and content of the criticism was an article by Paul L. Blakely, S.J., in *America*.[78] Blakely made the usual points against the efficacy and wisdom of the compulsory salute as an instrument of patriotic instruction. Second, he indulged in the misconception so common in the law review articles:

. . . It follows, therefore, as I read the Court's decision, that to bolster up a school exercise, which, while "allowable" and even useful, is certainly not essential in the teaching of patriotism, one of the most precious rights under the Federal and our State Constitutions, can be, and must be, destroyed.

. . . The Court balances a non-essential school exercise against the fundamental constitutional right of religious freedom and decides against the right (and duty) of every man to worship Almighty God according to the dictates of his conscience.[79]

Finally, Blakely turned to the issue which seems especially to have bothered the Catholic writers:

. . . *"The court room is not the arena for debating issues of educational policy."* . . .

Had that been in the mind of the Court in the October term of 1924, when the Oregon case was argued, today there would not be a single private school in Oregon. . . .

Lillian and William Gobitis are inconsiderable persons. But their case is the case of every man who holds that freedom in education and religion are our most precious rights.

Yet, "The court room is not the arena for debating issues of educational policy," writes Mr. Justice Frankfurter. If that be true, where is our protection when the next campaign to close our schools through the Oregon method begins?[80]

It is suspected that Blakely's last point probably bulked quite large in Catholic thinking. As has been said, the Church had no reason to love Jehovah's Witnesses; nor had it previously shown any marked sympathy for their flag-salute troubles.[81] The anti-Witness fulminations of Father Felix's "Defenders of the Faith" had received a blanket indorsement from *America* less than a year before the *Gobitis* decision.[82] As interpreted by Blakely, the *Gobitis* opinion contained much bad law; but it is to be doubted that the decision would have provoked such angry denunciation, but for the doubts it raised as to the continued vitality of *Pierce v. Society of Sisters.*

3. EDUCATIONAL JOURNALS

Attention has been directed in an earlier chapter to the educational journals' comments dealing with the merits of the flag-salute ceremony as an educational device. None of these expressed any view on the constitutional issue. One pre-*Gobitis* comment and three later articles did deal with the legal merits. One of these was an excellent article in *Business Education World*, defending the *Gabrielli* decision.[83] The author made a persuasive case, marshalling the "secular regulation" rule, the presumption of constitutionality and the historic discretion of school boards. The anti-*Gobitis* stand of *Catholic Education Review* has already been mentioned. A long article on *Gobitis* in the *Harvard Educational Review* remarked morosely that "[T]he decision goes quite as far toward the subordination of the civil liberties of minorities to the will of the majority as any other decision of the Supreme Court. . . ."[84] The author distinguished the old "secular regulation" precedents from the present situation and criticized the Court for not following the libertarian line of *Cantwell* and *Schneider*. Finally, there was a short article by Henry Steele Commager in *Scholastic*, approving the *Gobitis* decision.[85] One of the misconceptions noted in many comments was the argument that the court in *Gobitis* had refused to interfere with majority rule as long as the political channels remained open. In line with his own predilections,[86] Commager turned this misconception to the credit of the *Gobitis* ruling. Describing the compulsory salute as a borderline case of constitutionality, he argued for the right of legislatures to experiment, to make mistakes.

. . . But what is the proper remedy for a mistaken experiment? Is it to rush to the Court and ask the Court to nullify the misguided law? Or is it to allow public opinion to come around to the point where it recognizes the mistake and asks the legislature to repeal the law?

Has not the majority . . . the right to make mistakes? And can we not trust our legislature to correct their mistakes? Is there, indeed, any hope for democracy if it is to depend, always, on correction from the judiciary? . . .[87]

C. *Newspapers*

Of the forty newspapers surveyed for purposes of this study,* fourteen had no immediate editorial reaction to the *Gobitis* decision.[88] Of the twenty-seven comments appearing in twenty-six newspapers,[89] eight were definitely favorable,[90] seven were definitely unfavorable,[91] two were too ambiguous to be classified,[92] and ten *accepted* the decision with misgivings about the flag salute *policy*.[93]

Of the favorable decisions, the editorial in the *Washington Post* was intellectually the best.[94] It advanced the "privilege" argument, insisted that the salute had no religious significance and invoked the "secular regulation" rule. Two papers rested mainly on hostility to anyone who would refuse to salute.

. . . Nor is there an inherent right of any group to be given free education by a people to whom that group refuses its allegiance and cooperation. . . .[95]

. . . Any who cannot say so much as that, with heartfelt sincerity, do not belong in America.[96]

The remaining five papers pointed to the great desirability of the flag ceremony as an educational policy.[97] Of these, most persuasive were the editorials in the two Detroit papers emphasizing the distinction between adults—as to whom a compulsory salute would be absurd—and children, for whom the salute was one of many compulsory routines designed to mold them into useful adults.[98]

Of the seven unfavorable comments on the *Gobitis* decision, four denounced the decision in general terms.[99] A common theme in these denunciations was that the decision simply abetted the persecution of a helpless religious minority. The

* The discussion in this survey is based on a survey of forty newspapers, selected in large part on the basis of availability. Most, therefore, are big-city, large-circulation papers. To this group were added several high-quality, low-circulation papers such as the *Christian Science Monitor*, and local papers from areas of special interest to this study—Schuylkill County, Pennsylvania, and Charleston, West Virginia. For practical reasons, the search was limited to a period of a month or so after the *Gobitis* decision. This survey, then, is of immediate editorial reactions, not afterthoughts.

other three papers came to some grips with Frankfurter's constitutional arguments. The *Los Angeles Times* sharply attacked Frankfurter's judicial self-restraint argument, and noted caustically that if Congress could exempt conscientious objectors from military service without ill effects, school discipline had nothing to fear from the exemption of a few non-saluting children.[100] The *St. Louis Post-Dispatch* reiterated the main points made in the religious freedom section of the Bill of Rights Committee's *Gobitis* brief. "But this argument was cast aside by the Supreme Court, and now by judicial fiat Lillian and William Gobitis will be compelled to perform an action which, in their creed, is a sin against God."[101] Probably the most perceptive critique was contained in the short editorial comment in the *Christian Science Monitor:*

> The wish of the Supreme Court to avoid being made "the school board for the country" is understandable. Yet there is a question whether in this case dealing with the scruples of a religious sect it has not taken a step toward abdicating its position as a constitutional guarantor of freedom of worship.
>
> Every liberty, of course, has its limits. But if freedom of conscience can be encroached upon by "legislation of a general scope" so long as this does not aim at particular sects, then in excited times a great deal may be done under the name of general welfare which leads in the direction of State religion, or State irreligion as in Nazi Germany or Soviet Russia.
>
> ... A voluntary unity of 99 per cent makes the flag a more impressive symbol than an artificial "unity" of 100 per cent.[102]

This comment included the best of most of the other attacks. Furthermore, it was the only unfavorable editorial to comprehend the significance of Frankfurter's "secular regulation" argument and the threat contained therein in times of unrest.

Of the two ambiguous comments, one, in the *Cleveland Plain Dealer*, concluded:

> After all, patriotism is a matter of the heart and cannot be defined or curtailed by statute. We doubt if anyone can be made patriotic by compelling him to salute the flag. We are quite sure no one will ever be harmed by such compulsion.[103]

The other, in the *New York Sun*, noted the apparent conflict between this decision and that in *Cantwell*, but conceded that the decisions dealt with different circumstances. It was suggested that the pair of cases furnished "much on which to ponder."[104]

Most interesting were the ten editorials accepting the decision but opposing the policy. These generally expressed no opinion on the constitutional merits, but took the decision as a *fact*. In general, they emphasized the fact that the Court had not indorsed the compulsory salute as a policy. Characteristic are the following passages:

> The Court's function here was to declare the law, not to say whether the law is wise or foolish. . . .
>
> . . . For their obedience to their parents the youngsters can be lawfully barred from an education in the public schools. In the eyes of such laws it is better that these children be condemned to ignorance and illiteracy. Does that make them better citizens?
>
> This is lawful, for the Court says it does not contravene the Constitution, but that does not make it any the less silly.[105]

> This ends the legal resources of the sect known as Jehovah's Witnesses in seeking to protect its youthful members from this exercise of forced patriotism. But it ought not to end common sense among the school teachers and administrative officers of the nation. After all, the Supreme Court has not ruled that a teacher *must* ignore the consciences of her pupils or that a school board . . . must forsake the dictates of common sense. . . .[106]

> The greatest sufferers seem to be the children. . . . In such a situation much can be done by the school authorities, through tact, kindness and the avoidance of the appearance of coercion, to mitigate the conflict between parental and public authority and the shock to youthful feelings and youthful consciences.[107]

D. *Concluding Remarks*

Several generalizations can be made about the press comment surveyed here. First, the predominance of adverse criticism was striking. The judgment of the legal periodicals was overwhelming. Similarly one-sided was the response of the other magazines studied. Notable here was the almost total absence of comment by the general circulation magazines. The news magazines generally were disinterested in the subject. The monthly magazines were ill-equipped to editorialize, and were further hampered by the unfortunate timing of the decision. The only area in which the *Gobitis* decision broke even was among the educational journals dealing specifically with the constitutional merits. But the sample was very small, especially in view of the larger number of journals either studiedly non-committal or critical of the flag ceremony itself. The apparently even division among the newspaper editorials was, it is submitted, illusory. The largest single category of comment was that *accepting* the decision. Most of the editorials in this group carried a definite air of embarrassment. It should be recalled that both of the Philadelphia papers and the *Pottsville Evening Republican* had given at least qualified approval to the district court decision in *Gobitis*.[108] Several others were outspokenly favorable when *Gobitis* was finally overruled.[109] The editorial writers' diligent attempts to minimize the importance and effects of the decision seem more representative of their true attitude. When these comments are viewed in their true light, the articulate newspaper response is seen to divide about two to one against the *Gobitis* decision.

Second, the adverse comment on the flag-salute issue cannot be viewed as beginning with the *Gobitis* decision. The great volume of law review comment before June, 1940, is the best evidence for that. While the content of these criticisms of the compulsory salute was different, the tenor and general division was the same. Similarly, the issue vexed the teaching profession's magazines as early as 1936. The significant point is that the *Gobitis* decision in no way halted or even discouraged press opposition to the compulsory salute. The only appreciable effect was to reduce a number of newspaper editorial writers to a sort of embarrassed ambiguity.

Third, the great majority of the comments combined to build up a highly distorted image of the *Gobitis* holding. The general gist of most of the criticisms—and of much of the praise—was that the Court had invoked the values of national unity and judicial self-restraint against an otherwise perfectly valid religious freedom claim. This interpretation led naturally to the fear that under that decision no freedom was safe—aside from the so-called "political" freedoms—in the coming years of crisis. The essentially conservative holding in *Gobitis* was transformed in the press comments into a radical and dangerous innovation hatched by Justice Frankfurter.

This was the intellectual response to the *Gobitis* decision. "The opposite reaction was less intellectual but more emphatic."[110] The next chapter will deal with the wave of anti-Witness persecution which swept the country in the summer of 1940, and was generally attributed to the *Gobitis* decision.

CHAPTER EIGHT

INTERIM, 1940–1943
THE PERSECUTION OF JEHOVAH'S WITNESSES

A. *The General Picture*

The wave of anti-Witness persecution which swept the country after the *Gobitis* decision is legendary. It is generally assumed that this outburst was caused in large part by that decision.[1] This must be considered only partly true. It seems pretty clear in view of all the circumstances that the Witnesses were in for a difficult summer whichever way the decision went. While it is a hard point to document precisely, the persecution probably was more widespread and vigorous because of the Supreme Court's apparent indorsement. But the events after June 3, 1940, must be evaluated in the light of certain background details.

First, it must be emphasized that the public and private persecution of Jehovah's Witnesses did not *begin* in June, 1940. Their troubles with local authorities over their proselytizing methods dated back to 1928. The large and continuing volume of arrests during the 1930's under various local ordinances has been treated in an earlier chapter. Their increasingly aggressive behavior led to sharp clashes with authority, especially in Pennsylvania. Private violence, actual and threatened, had been on the upswing throughout the spring of 1940. On June 8, the Witness central office sent the ACLU and the Justice Department a list of some thirty incidents in twenty states for the period ending June 2, 1940.[2] A few instances will indicate the rising tension. On May 22, three Witnesses, mistaken for Nazi agents, were run out of Del Rio, Texas.[3] On June 1, another group was chased from Auburn, California. Between those dates, Witnesses were run out of Brownwood, San Antonio and Harlingen, Texas.[4] A group just escaped mob violence in Glenwood, Arkansas, on May 25.[5] Incidents on and after May 29 were rougher. On that date, two Witnesses were badly beaten by a mob in Sanford, Maine.[6] On June 1, ninety Witnesses were arrested after a wave of minor assaults in Waxahachie, Texas.[7] On June 3, they were still being held "for investigation."[8] On June 1, seventy Witnesses were "rescued" from a mob in Odessa, Texas. They were jailed and grilled through the night regarding their unwillingness to salute the flag. On June 2, all seventy were turned over to a mob of over a thousand who chased and stoned them five miles down the railroad right of way.[9] Also on June 2, four Witnesses were badly beaten by a mob in Little Rock, Arkansas.[10]

Second, certain behavior of the Witnesses themselves undoubtedly contributed to the increase in violence committed against them. It has been noted that "street witnessing"—the practice of stationing oneself on a downtown street corner with a shoulder-bag of magazines, pamphlets and even books to be offered the passing crowd—was not initiated in its modern form until February, 1940. It is likely that the system did not really get going until the comfortable weather of late spring. Needless to say, a Witness on a downtown street corner was much more likely to collect a crowd than if he were going from door to door in a quiet residential neighborhood. Furthermore, the violent turn in the incidents on May 29 coincided nicely with the appearance of the May 29 issue of *Consolation*, which was devoted entirely to the flag-salute issue. It must also be remembered that public apprehension was growing steadily with the German march through the lowlands, the evacuation of Dunkirk and the invasion of Norway, closely followed by the shocking collapse of France in early June.

Still, the outburst that followed June 3 was impressive. Incidents in June and after were worse and much more numerous. The most spectacular early outbreak occurred in York County, Maine. Two Witnesses were beaten in Sanford on June 8, when they refused to salute. The following day, in Kennebunk, a carload of men conveniently equipped with throwing-size rocks "just happened to stop" in front of the Jehovah's Witness Kingdom Hall which doubled as the home of the company servant. The Witnesses, already jittery from a fortnight of tension, greeted the visitors with shotgun fire, seriously wounding one. Six Witnesses were arrested for attempted murder. In the meantime, an enraged mob of 2,500, failing to reach the prisoners, sacked and burned the Kingdom Hall, then drifted over to Biddeford to attack houses suspected of containing Witnesses.[11] On June 10, shortly after the arraignment of the six Witnesses, substantially the same mob besieged the home of an elderly Witness who had been jostled at the hearing. He also responded with buckshot, wounding one.[12] The violence finally died down after Governor Barrows threatened to send the National Guard to York County.[13] The well-publicized outburst in Maine may well have had as much to do with triggering persecution elsewhere as the *Gobitis* decision itself. Considerable publicity was given the absurd claim of mob members to have found pictures of Hitler and Stalin on the walls of the Kingdom Hall, as well as maps of the military installations and defense plants.[14]

Other violence followed thick and fast. On June 16, the whole adult population of Litchfield, Illinois, turned out to attack sixty Jehovah's Witnesses. Litchfield police, unable to control the mob, put the Witnesses in jail, then called in the state police to protect the jail.[15] Of the Witnesses' nineteen cars, sixteen were overturned and three driven into the city reservoir.[16] On June 18, five Witnesses—three men and two women—were mauled by mobs in Rawlins, Wyoming, and two of their cars were burned.[17] On June 22, a Witness was tarred and feathered in Parco, Wyoming.[18] On June 27, a crowd led by the American Legion descended on a Jehovah's Witness trailer camp that had been set up near Jackson, Mississippi, in preparation for a regional convention. The Witnesses and their trailers were escorted across the state line and turned over to Louisiana Legionnaires. The Witnesses were passed from county to county, finally winding up in the vicinity of Dallas, Texas.[19]

Events after June, 1940, settled into a rather steady pattern of less flagrant violations. A few cases stood out however. In August, 1940, a Nebraska Witness was lured from his house, abducted and castrated.[20] September, 1942, saw two major outbreaks. On September 19, the Witnesses' convention ground near Little Rock, Arkansas, was invaded by a group of workers from a federal pipeline project. Armed with guns, pipes and screwdrivers, they mercilessly beat all the Witnesses they could find. Two Witnesses were shot and four others hospitalized.[21] The following day, while sheriff's officers were guarding the convention grounds, another mob attacked a tourist camp where the Witnesses were staying.[22] On September 20, there was a pitched battle in Klammath Falls, Oregon, between a company of Jehovah's Witnesses and a mob of a thousand townspeople who stormed their Kingdom Hall.[23] The most disturbing aspect of the mounting persecution was the frequent involvement of local public officials. Deputy sheriffs took an active part in the Jackson, Mississippi, exodus.[24] On June 19, policemen joined a mob that broke up a Witness meeting in Rockville, Maryland.[25] On June 29, seven Jehovah's Witnesses arrived in Richwood, West Virginia, with a letter for the mayor requesting protection while they distributed a petition in the area. In the mayor's absence, they were detained by Deputy Sheriff William Catlette and Police Chief Bert Stewart, while members of the American Legion were summoned. The Witnesses were then forced to drink large amounts of castor oil, tied together with a police department rope and marched through and out of town.[26] In almost all the other incidents described above, there were charges of lackadaisical or nonexistent police protection. Nor was it always just the police who were involved in persecution incidents. Around June 3, 1940, a number of Jehovah's Witnesses were jailed in Harlan, Kentucky, on a charge of sedition.[27] On June 20, 1940, seven middle-aged women were haled into court in Connersville, Indiana, on charges of flag desecration. The basis of the charge seems to have been their distribution of literature opposing the compulsory salute. Five who pleaded guilty were let off with light sentences. When Grace Trent and Lucy McKee pleaded not guilty, the charge against them was changed to "riotous conspiracy," and they were held for trial.[28] At their trial in September, they were convicted, fined $500 apiece, and sentenced to from two to ten years in prison.[29] At this time, their attorney and a number of Witnesses who had attended the trial were mobbed, beaten and run out of town.[30] Some towns passed ordinances specifically forbidding the distribution of Witness literature.[31] It became fashionable in many places to jail Witnesses on sight, "just in case."

The Witnesses' collisions with local ordinances regulating peddling and door-to-door canvassing continued unabated. Thus the mass literature distribution efforts attending the regional conventions led to thirty-four arrests in Detroit for canvassing without licenses,[32] and twenty-one in Boston for street selling without licenses.[33] Earlier, an unlicensed street parade in Manchester, New Hampshire, led to the arrest of sixty-eight Witnesses.[34]

Data are scarce regarding economic discrimination against Jehovah's Witnesses, but they clearly existed in substantial amount. Jehovah's Witnesses were stricken from the relief rolls of Clarksburg, West Virginia, in July, 1940.[35] Relief was cut off from a Belleville, Illinois, family in October, 1940.[36] Two coal miners in Shenandoah, Pennsylvania, quit their jobs rather than take part in a compulsory flag-salute ceremony.[37] Shortly after Pearl Harbor, union pressure forced employers to fire two Witnesses in Hillside, New Jersey,[38] and one in Shreveport, Louisiana.[39] In a notable case, the Pittsburgh Plate Glass Company plant at Clarksburg, West Virginia, under pressure from both AFL and CIO unions, fired seven Jehovah's Witness glasscutters, on December 14, 1941.[40] This incident produced what may have been a turning point in the Witnesses' economic discrimination problem. In early 1943, after securing assurances from the unions that they would not object, and a promise from the Witnesses not to distribute tracts at the plant, the President's Fair Employment Practices Commission ordered the seven employees reinstated with full seniority.[41]

B. *Persecution Statistics: An Analysis*

1. GENERAL CONSIDERATIONS

There has been no serious attempt heretofore to analyze the geographic and temporal distribution of anti-Witness persecution in the years following the *Gobitis* decision, largely because of the absence of any coherent compilation of persecution incidents. The analysis in this section is based entirely on figures compiled from the case files of the United States Department of

Justice.* The data in those files consist mainly of signed and notarized complaints sent in by individual Witnesses, and, as such, have certain inherent limitations. First the adequacy and specificity of Witness reporting clearly varied drastically from region to region. Reports from the southeastern United States were rarely in such a form as to be usable at all. Second, the material in the files affords no reliable information as to the level of persecution before *Gobitis*. No complaints were received in 1940 before June 3. Shortly after that date, apparently, somebody—probably the ACLU—advised the Witnesses to report persecution incidents to the Department of Justice.[42] Third, the complaints were not uniformly accurate. People with the Witnesses' outlook tend to see persecution in every untoward occurrence. Also, there was a tendency to try to read official misconduct into every incident, in order to furnish the "state action" necessary to justify federal intervention. No attempt has been made to cope with these weaknesses. The data in the files have been taken at face value. A complaint was omitted only if refuted by its own allegations. Information was not added from other sources; the limited nature of the writer's access to the files precluded much cross-checking.

2. VARIATION THROUGH TIME

Figures 1, 2 and 3 show the variation through time of various forms of alleged persecution from May, 1940,[43] through December, 1943. Some explanation is in order regarding the designation of variables. *Violence* refers to specific acts of physical violence directed against the person, whether by private assailants or public officers. *Official involvement* refers not only to actual participation in violence by public officers, but also to refusal or culpable failure to prevent or punish violence directed at Jehovah's Witnesses. *Arbitrary arrest* refers to incarceration or detention apparently for its own sake. This

* These files comprise 39 bulging folders of completely raw data. The writer was afforded limited access to them for the purpose of making this statistical survey. The figures compiled herein are the work of the writer, using his own system of classification. The Justice Department has not in any way indorsed either the accuracy of these figures or the conclusions drawn from them. Specific information here and in later chapters is drawn from Department sources only to the extent explicitly indicated in text or footnotes.

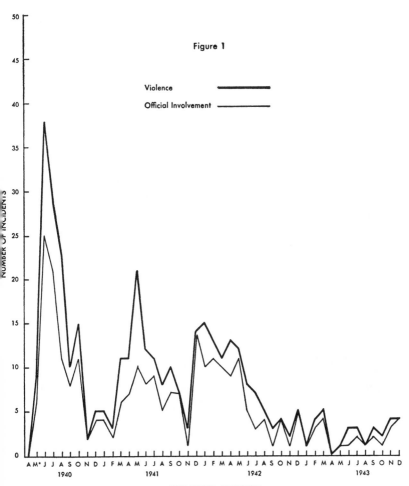

Figure 1

Violence ━━━━━━━
Official Involvement ──────

NUMBER OF INCIDENTS

TIME PERIOD (MONTHS)*

* May 1940 on the graph includes June 1-2.

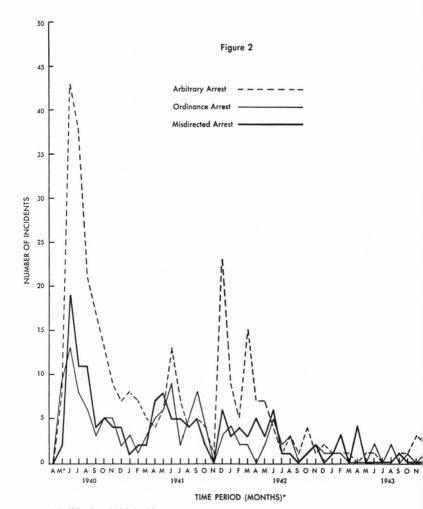

Figure 2

Arbitrary Arrest

Ordinance Arrest

Misdirected Arrest

NUMBER OF INCIDENTS

TIME PERIOD (MONTHS)*

* May 1940 on the graph includes June 1-2.

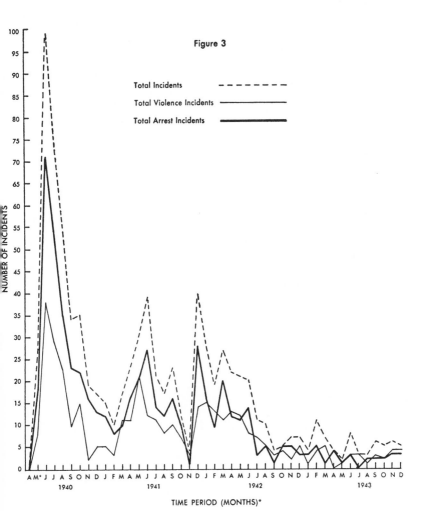

Figure 3

Total Incidents ----------
Total Violence Incidents ——————
Total Arrest Incidents ——————

NUMBER OF INCIDENTS

TIME PERIOD (MONTHS)*

May 1940 on the graph includes June 1-2

includes both arrest without charges and arrest on charges later dropped without trial. *Ordinance arrest* refers to arrest and prosecution under typical ordinances—constitutional or not—impinging on the Witnesses' missionary work. Crucial for this designation are the real intent to prosecute, and the normal, good-faith application of the ordinances. *Misdirected arrest* refers to arrest and prosecution under what appear to be grossly misapplied ordinances or statutes. This includes a variety of circumstances—e.g., sedition prosecutions, prosecution only of the victim of an assault, group libel prosecutions.[44] Finally, *total incidents* refers to the total number of incidents including one or more of the elements listed above.

In terms of total figures, the persecution of Jehovah's Witnesses was definitely a warm weather phenomenon; the totals in all categories tended to dip sharply as winter set in. This is understandable; both Witnesses and potential mob members were likely to spend more of their time indoors during cold weather. The graphs show three marked deviations from the seasonal pattern. The first of these is the abnormally high totals in the summer of 1940. That this deviation was related to the flag-salute litigation is suggested by the sharp increase between May and June. While most categories dropped sharply after June, the absolute totals remained very high until the onset of winter. The second major deviation centers around December, 1941. After reaching a very low nadir in November, all categories rose sharply in December, and remained very high through May, 1942. While not as high as the June, 1940, figure, this peak was very impressive, coming as it did in defiance of the elements. The relevance of the Japanese attack on Pearl Harbor is obvious. Seeing World War II as the first skirmish of Armageddon, the Witnesses redoubled their missionary efforts. A population suddenly catapulted into what looked like a war for survival did not receive these efforts with either tolerance or patience. The third deviation from the seasonal pattern was less obvious but equally significant. After remaining at a high level through winter and spring, all categories of persecution went into a marked decline after May, 1942—again, in defiance of the elements. Most categories reached a low point in September or October and varied randomly just above the zero mark thereafter. Only the violence factor offered any resistance to this trend, showing substantial rises in the spring and fall of 1943.

Different categories fluctuated along different lines. Those most drastically affected by the pressures of mid-1940 were violence and arbitrary arrest. These plus misdirected arrest showed the most definite response to Pearl Harbor. Ordinance arrest, more than any other category, varied strictly as a seasonal phenomenon. Total arrests and total violence tended to vary in unison.

In about 20 per cent of the incidents, the flag-salute issue was specifically named as a factor. This is quite impressive, especially in view of the undoubted fact that it was an unmentioned factor in many more instances. This proportion remained fairly constant throughout the period under study, until mid-1943, when it dropped to zero.

3. GEOGRAPHICAL DISTRIBUTION

Because of the inconsistent quality of Witness reporting, no general attempt has been made here to compare persecution totals in the various states or regions of the United States. Mention should be made, however, of the striking pre-eminence of Texas and Oklahoma in all categories. In terms of total incidents, these two states contributed almost 40 per cent of the national total, with respective figures of 227 and 97.

A more useful classification is attempted in Table 1. It will be noted that larger cities tended to have slightly more total incidents apiece than did smaller units, whether the denominator used is the number of cities involved or the total number of cities of the given population class. On the other hand, the number of incidents per unit population rises sharply as we move down the population scale. The "persecution index"[45] ranges from 1.56 for the biggest cities up to a striking 34.83 for towns of between 2,500 and 10,000 inhabitants. The index for rural areas, on the other hand, is well below the national average. This would tend to demonstrate what one would suspect anyway—that persecution of Jehovah's Witnesses was essentially a small-town affair.[46] This makes considerable sense. Small-town populations are likely to be less tolerant of outsiders, which Witness canvassers are likely to be. Furthermore, the police in such communities generally are non-pro-

TABLE 1

Incidence of Persecution in Various Population Units

Size Unit	Number of Units	Per Cent of Total Population	Number of Incidents Reported	Number of Units Reported	Incidents per Units Reported	Incidents per Total Units	Persecution Index (Incidents per Per Cent of Population)
Over 100,000	92	28.8	45	16	2.81	0.49	1.56
25,000–100,000	320	11.2	84	33	2.55	0.26	7.50
10,000– 25,000	665	7.6	146	63	2.32	0.22	19.21
2,500– 10,000	2,387	8.9	310	146	2.12	0.13	34.83
Total Urban	3,464	56.5	585	258	2.27	0.17	10.35
Total Rural (under 2,500)	13,288	43.5	258	187	1.38	0.02	5.91
Total U.S.	16,752	100.0	843	445	1.89	0.09	8.43

fessional, inadequate in number to handle mobs, and imbued with the same prejudices as their civilian neighbors.[47] The index for rural areas, however, indicates that there is a lower limit. Police, Witnesses and potential assailants all were too scarce and too thinly scattered for trouble to develop on the scale possible in a more urban environment.

C. *Organized Forces Involved*

Other organized forces besides the Witnesses were at work during the period 1940–43, some working to ameliorate the situation, others apparently bent on contrary ends.

1. VETERANS' ORGANIZATIONS

The only veterans' organization to figure prominently in the Witnesses' troubles was the American Legion. The Legion's strong involvement in the flag-salute controversy has been described in previous chapters. To the extent that any single group could qualify for the designation, the American Legion was Jehovah's Witnesses' antagonist on the flag-salute issue. Of 843 incidents of alleged persecution, known members of the American Legion were accused of active participation in 176, or over a fifth of the total. Some Legion posts quite frankly assumed the prerogative of passing in advance on the qualifications of those wishing to distribute literature within the municipality.[48] Involvement of the national organization was not as clear. It was quick to insist that it had no control over the policies of the autonomous local posts.[49] The leadership at all levels disclaimed any responsibility for the violent behavior of many individual legionnaires. On the other hand, it seems clear in retrospect that if the national organization lacked control over its state and local functionaries, it was only because it did not choose to exercise such control.[50] Official pronouncements by Legion notables at all levels seemed well calculated to aggravate the existing situation. On June 30, 1940, when matters already were bad enough, Dr. A. C. Bryan, commander of the Mississippi department of the Legion announced,

We, the American Legion, in co-operation with the police department, are making every effort to round up these "Witnesses."

It is the duty of every citizen to report these persons to the police. The literature being issued by members of this organization is printed chiefly in Germany by German printers and on German paper.[51]

The total falsity of the charge[52] is only incidental here; its inflammatory character is obvious. In July, 1940, National Commander Raymond J. Kelly urged "summary treatment" of "subversives."[53] On March 9, 1942, Homer Chaillaux, chairman of the Legion's Americanism Commission, sharply attacked the Witnesses' "unamerican activities," and suggested the passage of local ordinances to deal with them.[54]

Complaints about other organizations in the Witnesses' persecution reports were negligible. Other evidence, however, indicates that the Veterans of Foreign Wars were not inactive. The Michigan department of the VFW protested strongly against the holding of the Witnesses' 1940 regional convention in Detroit, citing in particular their refusal to salute the flag.[55] Local VFW posts were reported to have instigated the passage of a number of local ordinances conditioning a permit to distribute literature within the municipality on the giving of the flag salute.[56]

2. THE CATHOLIC CHURCH

The Witnesses considered the widespread persecution to be part of a systematic campaign to stamp them out, planned and led by the Roman Catholic element in the American Legion.[57] This was in line with the official line picturing the Church as the fount of all evil, and, in view of the history of unpleasantness between the two sects, had some plausibility. There is no support for the charge in the files, however. They list no instance of participation in or approval of anti-Witness persecution on the part of any clergyman;[58] nor does the number of individual Catholics accused exceed the proportion one would expect to find in any normal cross section of the American population. While certain Catholic writers used the flag-salute issue in rather blatant attempts to inflame public sentiment against the Witnesses,[59] the attitude of the Church at large seems to have been one of strict neutrality.

3. THE AMERICAN CIVIL LIBERTIES UNION

The American Civil Liberties Union, as always, did its best on the Witnesses' behalf. These efforts fell into three main categories. First, the ACLU continued to assist the Witnesses in major litigation, helping them secure local counsel, and filing briefs *amicus curiae*.[60] Second, it took what measures were open to it to check the widespread mob attacks on members of the sect. In all serious cases the Union offered a $500 reward for information leading to the arrest and conviction of the mobsters. Such offers were sent to Erin, Tennessee; Jackson, Mississippi; and Kennebunk, Rawlins, Litchfield, and Connersville, among others.[61] ACLU leaders took pride in the absence of further incidents in localities where such rewards were advertised.[62] In July, 1940, Arthur Garfield Hays, general counsel for the Union, sent telegrams to the mayors of eighteen cities urging them to give full protection to the Witness regional conventions scheduled to take place July 24–28.[63] Some efforts were made to bring damage suits on behalf of assaulted Witnesses against their assailants.[64] None of these devices was very satisfactory. In areas where mob violence thrived, the authorities and juries were likely to be unsympathetic. In many localities, the ACLU was almost as unpopular as the Witnesses. Both the Union and the Witnesses, therefore, were impelled to look elsewhere for help. The third category of activity carried on by the ACLU was a persistent campaign to persuade the Justice Department's Civil Rights Section to take active steps to stem the tide of violence and persecution.[65]

4. THE CIVIL RIGHTS SECTION

The Civil Rights Section of the Department of Justice was established by Attorney General Murphy on February 3, 1939. Its first head was Henry A. Schweinhaut. He was succeeded by Victor W. Rotnem in 1941. The Section was to study and combat, by prosecution if necessary, violations of the constitutional and statutory "civil rights" of individuals, by whomever committed. The flood of Jehovah's Witness complaints naturally flowed directly into the files of the Civil Rights Section. The Section did its limited best to ameliorate the situation. These efforts fell into two categories—prosecution and mediation.

a) Prosecutions.—The Civil Rights Section's chief statutory weapons against civil rights violations were sections 19 and 20 of the Criminal Code.[66] Section 19 made it a felony for two or more persons to conspire to "injure, oppress, threaten, or intimidate any citizen in the free exercise or enjoyment of any right or privilege secured to him by the Constitution or laws of the United States. . . ." This provision, applicable against private individuals, was of very limited usefulness, because it punished only violations of rights arising out of the basic constitutional relationship of the citizen to his national government. It did not reach violations of rights protected only against state action, such as freedom of speech and religion. Under section 20, anyone who "under color of any law . . . willfully subjects, or causes to be subjected, any inhabitant . . . to the deprivation of any rights, privileges, or immunities secured or protected by the Constitution and laws of the United States . . ." was guilty of a misdemeanor.[67] This provision reached violations of Fourteenth Amendment rights, but was applicable only where some sort of official participation could be proved. It clearly was applicable to acts of suppression by local sheriffs, etc., against Jehovah's Witnesses. The great unanswered question was whether section 20 would reach official *inaction*—e.g., denial of protection against mob violence. When the Jehovah's Witness complaints reached the Civil Rights Section, there was very little guiding experience with the use of section 20. The more extensive experience with section 19 was not encouraging.[68]

The Section moved cautiously and infrequently in prosecuting apparent violations of the rights of Jehovah's Witnesses. The complaints had to be sorted carefully. Some were highly biased or inaccurate or both. In many more there was no plausible basis for federal jurisdiction. It was very important to select only the most clear-cut cases for prosecution, since both grand[69] and petit juries had to be drawn from the locality of the offense and thus were likely to reflect local prejudices against the Witnesses—and against federal "meddling."[70] It was felt that the serious repercussions of a lost case should be avoided even at the cost of letting obvious violations go unpunished.[71]

Nor were caution and uncertainty the only factors holding

the Section back. In some districts, the United States attorneys shared the local prejudices and were frankly reluctant to act against local officials or residents on behalf of the Witnesses.[72] Moreover, while Schweinhaut and Rotnem seem to have received good backing from their immediate superior, Assistant Attorney General Wendell Berge, they got less support elsewhere.[73] In particular, Robert H. Jackson, Attorney General until October, 1941, seems to have been less than sympathetic to the Section's work.[74]

It is in the light of these limiting factors that we must view the sparse record of prosecutions brought by the Civil Rights Section. In general, a pragmatic view was taken. No action was taken in cases where (a) adequate remedial action had been initiated by state or local authorities; (b) the Witnesses were testing the legality of their treatment in the courts, either by appealing from convictions or by suing their assailants; or (c) subsequent events in the locality had produced an improved situation which could only be harmed by federal intervention.[75] Still, a number of cases were presented to grand juries. Not one of them produced an indictment. The grand jurors evinced considerable hostility toward Jehovah's Witnesses.[76] After considerable delay, the Civil Rights Section finally secured Department permission to proceed by information against the perpetrators of the most flagrant official violation, the Richwood, West Virginia, "castor oil" incident. In June, 1942, Deputy Sheriff Catlette and Chief of Police Stewart were tried and convicted of violating section 20. Catlette received the maximum sentence, one year's imprisonment and a $1,000 fine, while Stewart was let off with a $250 fine. The conviction was affirmed by the Fourth Circuit Court of Appeals.[77] Soon thereafter, the victims of the assault brought damage suits against Catlette, receiving out-of-court settlements totalling $1,170.[78]

b) Mediation.—From the beginning, the Civil Rights Section's main reliance was on informal mediation with local authorities. Schweinhaut seems personally to have interceded successfully on behalf of several incarcerated Witnesses in Florida, and to have secured the repeal of two restrictive local ordinances.[79] While the Department rejected the ACLU proposal to send federal agents to the Witness conventions,[80] the

United States attorneys in the cities involved were directed to urge the local authorities to furnish adequate protection.[81] It apparently was standard practice for the Civil Rights Section, through Mr. Berge, to ask the local United States attorneys to contact municipal authorities involved in incidents of alleged persecution and bring to their attention the possibility that they might be violating section 20.[82] Special steps were taken in Texas. In late 1940, the United States Attorney for the Western District of Texas made a special tour of Monahans, Odessa and Midland, giving a speech in each town regarding the harmless nature of Jehovah's Witnesses and the extent of their constitutional rights. The tour apparently was a success; there was no more violence in that area.[83] On February 22, 1942, Clyde Eastus, the United States Attorney for the Northern District of Texas, gave a radio talk in which he urged the Witnesses to show more moderation in their behavior and pleaded with the local authorities and the American Legion to respect the Witnesses' constitutional rights. Again, careful mention was made of the possibility of prosecution under section 20.[84] It is reported that persecution fell off sharply in the Northern District after this talk.[85]

The Civil Rights Section early became convinced that it would be desirable to place general instructions in the hands of every United States attorney regarding the handling of Witness complaints of alleged incidents. A circular containing such instructions was drawn up in July, 1940, but Department authorization was withheld.[86] The objection to the circular seems to have been twofold: that the persecution consisted mainly of private assaults raising no federal question, and that the Witnesses did not merit such special treatment. The Civil Rights Section again applied unsuccessfully for authorization of a similar circular in July, 1941. After this, a new approach was adopted. A memorandum dealing with religious freedom in general was prepared and approved, and went out to the United States attorneys on May 4, 1942.[87] It emphasized the constructive role which could be played by local officials and leading citizens in calming public agitations. Cases delineating the Witnesses' constitutional rights were cited. The crucial passages were as follows:

It is pointed out that prosecutive action against such public officials who willfully interfere with constitutional guarantees may be had under Section 52. . . . However . . . it is not the desire of the Department to institute numerous prosecutions against overzealous public officials. . . .

When the United States Attorneys are advised that local authorities are subjecting religious groups to treatment which might amount to a violation of Section 52, they should take steps to secure the cooperation of such state and local officials involved through personal conferences or by letter, to the end that official vigilantism violative of freedom of worship may be avoided. . . . It should be pointed out to these officials that the conscientious objector problem is within the exclusive jurisdiction of the federal government; that the dissemination of seditious doctrines is also a primary concern of the federal authorities; and that in the interest of unified and consistent law enforcement, evidence of subversive activity must be reported to the Department for consideration and appropriate action. . . .

It is, of course, not the desire of the Department to interfere with bona fide enforcement of state and local laws. It is not deemed out of place, however, to caution the local authorities that the application of such regulations as flag laws and peddling ordinances must be tempered in the interest of safeguarding religious freedom. . . .

While this circular did not deal explicitly with Jehovah's Witnesses it did pretty well cover all their troubles. It put the Justice Department firmly on record against local persecution, and conveyed a broad hint that meddling by local authorities might actually *obstruct* the war effort.

On July 18, 1942, the Civil Rights Section prepared another memorandum, which also was sent out to the United States attorneys. This memorandum raised serious doubts as to the legality of any state or local flag-salute regulation. It will be discussed in detail in the following chapter.

D. *Jehovah's Witnesses in Court*

A considerable variety of legal expedients, both old and new, were employed against Jehovah's Witnesses by hostile local authorities. The natural result was a rash of court actions brought by and against Witnesses. These will be treated in terms of the categories developed in section B.

1. ORDINANCE ARRESTS

Two injunction suits brought in federal courts involved the so-called "Green River" ordinances, which prohibited all door-to-door canvassing. Federal District Courts invalidated the ordinances of London, Ohio and Colorado Springs, Colorado, as applied to Jehovah's Witnesses, holding them violative of freedom of speech and press.[88] The remaining cases in this section involved permit ordinances, of which at least two deserve special mention. Moscow, Idaho and Monessen, Pennsylvania had post-*Gobitis* ordinances conditioning a permit to distribute printed matter solely on the applicant's giving of the flag salute and pledge of allegiance. In *Kennedy v. Moscow*,[89] a federal District Court held the former ordinance invalid under *Lovell v. Griffin*. The Monessen regulation fell with three more undistinguished enactments in *Reid v. Brookville*.[90]

Federal court attacks on more ordinary permit ordinances proved somewhat less fruitful. A District Court in Texas enjoined further enforcement against Jehovah's Witnesses of the ordinances of Ranger, Dublin, Coleman and Comanche.[91] The First Circuit Court of Appeals, however, rebuffed Witness injunction suits arising from Haverhill, Massachusetts and Manchester, New Hampshire, finding the challenged permit ordinances to be valid on their faces.[92] Administrative abuses, it was held, could be tested through normal proceedings in the state courts; only the prospect of irreparable injury could justify appeal to federal equity jurisdiction. The Supreme Court denied certiorari in both cases.[93]

Ordinary permit ordinances were held invalid as applied to Jehovah's Witnesses by state courts in Florida,[94] New Jersey[95] and Illinois.[96] Similar regulations were interpreted by the New York courts so as to make them inapplicable to the Witnesses.[97] As applied to Witness placard carriers, the Massachusetts Supreme Court struck down a permit ordinance which restricted the carrying of signs on the public streets,[98] but upheld another which regulated only those "hawkers" who settled themselves in one spot for prolonged periods.[99] The Supreme Court denied certiorari in the latter case.[100]

An important case arose in New Hampshire. A state statute required a municipal permit for any parade or similar public demonstration. The statute laid down no specific standards for the issuance of permits, and conditioned issuance on payment of a flexible fee. Without applying for a permit, sixty-eight Witnesses, including Willis Cox and Walter Chaplinsky, staged a single-file "information march" through the business section of the city of Manchester. All were arrested and convicted of violating the statute. In upholding the convictions, the New Hampshire Supreme Court held that the statute gave the licensing officials discretion only as to time and place, and that the license fee was limited to the amount necessary to reimburse the community for the special expense caused by the parade.[101] In *Cox v. New Hampshire*,[102] the United States Supreme Court unanimously affirmed the decision below, holding that the Witnesses had shown "no interference with religious worship or the practice of religion in any proper sense. . . ."[103] Foreshadowing future disagreement on the Court, the opinion laid considerable emphasis on the extremely limited character of the license fee involved.

2. MISDIRECTED ARRESTS

The most flagrant examples of misdirected arrests, of course, were the Harlan and Connersville prosecutions. In *Beeler v. Smith*,[104] a three-judge District Court permanently enjoined further sedition prosecutions in Harlan based on the Witnesses' stipulated conduct, which, it was held, manifestly did not fall within Kentucky's sedition statute. In *Trent v. Hunt*,[105] however, another three-judge tribunal refused to enjoin further prosecutions in Connersville. While showing considerable anti-Witness bias, the court proceeded mainly on the accepted rule that, absent "special circumstances," a federal court should not interfere with state criminal proceedings. The United States Supreme Court summarily affirmed on that ground.[106] Finally, in December, 1941, the Indiana Supreme Court reversed the convictions of Grace Trent and Lucy McKee, finding nothing in the statutes that could possibly support a felony conviction on the facts charged.[107]

The Witnesses brought several federal actions to stop enforcement against them of local ordinances forbidding distribution of literature reviling any religion where such distribution tended to cause a breach of the peace. They secured an injunction against enforcement of a Muskogee, Oklahoma, ordinance which was enforced against all Witness literature and against nobody else,[108] and got their test of an Oklahoma City ordinance past the demurrer stage.[109] In *Bevins v. Prindable*,[110] however, a three-judge District Court invoked the "special circumstances" rule of *Trent v. Hunt* to refuse an injunction against enforcement of an Illinois regulation. The Supreme Court affirmed summarily.[111]

Most of the state cases in this category involve convictions arising from street fights. In a South Carolina case, both a Witness and his assailant were convicted of breach of peace. The South Carolina Supreme Court reversed the Witness' conviction.[112] The Oklahoma case of *McKee v. State*[113] illustrated an instance in which the Witnesses won the fight. A large group of legionnaires attacked four Witnesses. The latter, who had thoughtfully brought along canes and loaded handbags, did terrible execution before their assailants fled. The Witnesses' conviction for breach of peace was upheld on appeal, but the Court, apparently influenced by the failure of local authorities to prosecute the legionnaires, reduced the sentence from imprisonment to a fine. Finally, we come to the case of Walter Chaplinsky, who was mobbed on the streets of Rochester, New Hampshire. As the police were leading him off to jail, apparently for his own safety, they encountered the city marshal, who had previously warned Chaplinsky to proceed with caution. When Chaplinsky angrily asked why his assailants had not been arrested, the marshal heatedly expressed grave doubt as to Chaplinsky's parentage and ultimate destination.[114] Chaplinsky then called the marshal a "God-damned fascist." Chaplinsky was prosecuted and convicted under a statute forbidding the use of abusive language toward another person in a public place. Provocation was held irrelevant under the statute. In *Chaplinsky v. New Hampshire*,[115] the United States Supreme Court affirmed the conviction, holding unanimously that such "fighting words" could be punished without constitutional objection.

In an Iowa case, it was held that the door-to-door distribution of Witness tracts on Sunday did not constitute Sabbath desecration.[116] The New Hampshire Supreme Court held soon after that tract distribution by Witness children did not violate the child labor laws.[117]

3. MISCELLANEOUS

Several cases defy ready classification. Two of these involve instances in which Jehovah's Witnesses responded to local harassment by invoking the "locust" technique, flooding the community with hundreds of Witnesses. Local authorities retaliated with breach of peace prosecutions against the local Witness ringleaders. A conviction in Hanford, California was reversed for want of any showing of any personal misconduct on the part of the invading Witnesses.[118] The other conviction, arising in Kutztown, Pennsylvania, was supported by ample evidence of misconduct, but was reversed for technical defects in the trial.[119]

Finally, there was the odd case of *Mathews v. West Virginia ex rel. Hamilton*.[120] Mrs. Mathews and Lavon Kelly, a young flag-salute expellee, had been attacked occasionally by strangers while distributing Witness literature on the streets. Seizing on this pretext, the county attorney secured an injunction from the Calhoun County Circuit Court permanently restraining the two women from distributing literature within the county. The West Virginia Supreme Court denied leave to appeal on the ground that the decision below was "plainly right."[121] The case was pending in the United States Supreme Court in 1943.

E. *Concluding Remarks*

The persecution of Jehovah's Witnesses in the early 1940's was both substantial and serious. The record is a reflection of both the temper of the public during that period and that of the Witnesses. The peaks on the graphs would not have been so high, had not the Witnesses leaped forward so eagerly to be persecuted.

The Witnesses' excursions into the federal courts were only partly successful. While they won some cases, the jurisdictional rules and accepted practices of the District Courts rendered them useless against many forms of official persecution. The Witnesses did somewhat better in the state courts; the weakness of many of the ordinance arrests is attested to by the number of ordinances which fell under the elementary standards of *Lovell v. Griffin*. However, against the most prevalent and serious forms of persecution—discriminatory prosecution, arbitrary arrest, violence and police inaction—the courts were almost entirely helpless.

It seems to this writer that the Civil Rights Section of the Department of Justice must receive almost all of the credit for finally putting an end to the rash of anti-Witness activity. The May 4, 1942, memorandum led to a wave of admonitions from United States attorneys to local officials. Such intercession by the federal government served by itself to make the Witnesses a little more respectable. The latent threat of prosecution under section 20 was reinforced by the successful proceeding against Catlette. That the Section's activities were in large part responsible for the declining persecution curves after mid-1942 is further suggested by the fact that it was simple violence, most of it by private parties—which showed the greatest resistance to the downward trend.

Finally, it should be pointed out that persecution did not disappear entirely after 1943. The Department of Justice has a bulging file folder of data on events occurring in 1944 and 1945; sporadic conflicts occur to this day. As long as Jehovah's Witnesses believe as they do and behave as they do, some conflicts are inevitable.

CHAPTER NINE

LEGAL DEVELOPMENTS ON THE FLAG-SALUTE ISSUE

THE DECLINE OF *GOBITIS*

A. *Further Spread of the Compulsory Flag Salute*

As of the beginning of 1940, Jehovah's Witness children had been, or were about to be expelled from school for refusing to salute the flag in fifteen states: Arizona, California, Florida, Kansas, Maryland, Massachusetts, New Jersey, Ohio, Oklahoma, Pennsylvania, Vermont, Washington, Georgia, New York and Texas. After *Gobitis*, the Justice Department received complaints about further expulsions in the first twelve of the above-listed states plus Delaware, Idaho, Illinois, Minnesota, Mississippi, Missouri, Nebraska, North Dakota, South Carolina and Virginia.[1] In six other states—Colorado, New Hampshire, New Mexico, North Carolina, South Dakota and West Virginia—actual or impending expulsions became known through litigation or official pronouncements.[2] In all, then, the flag-salute issue was costing Witness children their right to public education in at least thirty-one states. According to Witness sources, expulsions took place in all forty-eight states and totaled more than 2,000 by 1943.[3]

The flag-salute requirement spread in a variety of ways. Many communities passed new salute regulations in direct response to the *Gobitis* ruling. A prize example was a rule adopted in Raymond, New Hampshire, on June 10, 1940: "Be it resolved that every pupil, regardless of religious persuasion . . . shall salute the . . . Flag whenever the salute is called for. . . . Failure to comply . . . shall immediately exclude any pupil. . . ."[4] Some communities showed their first interest quite late, passing regulations as late as 1941 or 1942.[5] Mississippi passed a new flag-salute law in 1942.[6] In mid-1941, the Oklahoma State Superintendent of Schools interpreted that state's

1921 flag-exercise statute to require the orthodox flag-salute ceremony in all public and private schools, and held that pupils refusing to give the regular salute and pledge might be expelled.[7] In most cases, however, the new rash of expulsions simply represented new firmness in the enforcement of old regulations. A number of Massachusetts communities already requiring the salute announced that they were considering "firmer action" in the light of *Gobitis*.[8] The Washington Attorney General overruled his earlier official opinion advising school authorities to refrain from expelling conscientiously motived non-saluters.[9] Attorneys general in eight other states also issued official opinions upholding the constitutionality of old or new flag-salute regulations.[10]

B. *Public Law 623*

On June 22, 1942, Congress passed a joint resolution codifying the rules of flag respect.[11] One of the official designations of this enactment was "Public Law 623," by which name it became generally known. Public Law 623 was sponsored by the American Legion, and largely duplicated that group's standard dissertation on flag respect.[12] Significant for our purposes is the wording of section 7:

. . . [T]he pledge of allegiance to the flag [shall] . . . be rendered by . . . the standard procedure. . . . However, civilians will always show full respect to the flag when the pledge is being given by merely standing at attention, men removing the headdress. . . .

Read in context (and in view of the source), this passage probably was intended to prescribe the conduct of *spectators* at a flag-salute ceremony. Opponents of the compulsory salute, however, seized on the ambiguous language to contend that Congress had expressed its disapproval of such regulations. On July 18, 1942, Victor Rotnem, head of the Civil Rights Section, submitted a memorandum setting forth this position to Assistant Attorney General Berge:

. . . It is felt that Section 7 of the above mentioned law lays down a Federal standard with regard to a matter which is primarily a concern of the national government and there is, therefore, a very real question whether any local regulation . . . prescribing a dif-

ferent measure of respect can be enforced. For example: flag salute
regulations of local school boards. . . .[13]

It was suggested that United States attorneys call this federal
standard to the attention of local authorities who were enforcing flag regulations against conscientious objectors. This interpretation of section 7 was certainly debatable. The language
in question had been composed many years before *Gobitis* by
an outstanding proponent of the compulsory salute.

Whatever its merits, the argument of the Rotnem memorandum was adopted as the position of the Criminal Division.
The same day it was submitted, the memorandum was sent out
to all the United States attorneys. It was tied to the May 4
memorandum, with its veiled threat of prosecution under section 20 of the Criminal Code. Jehovah's Witnesses took the
cue and came up with an alternative pledge of allegiance in an
effort to show that they sincerely respected the flag once it was
divorced from the obnoxious symbolism of the salute.[14] Witness parents began presenting petitions to local school boards
requesting them to amend the flag-salute regulations to allow
conscientious objectors merely to stand at attention and recite
the alternate pledge.

This two-pronged attack often succeeded. The school boards
of Branford, Connecticut, and Wahoo, Nebraska, amended
their regulations and readmitted Witness children.[15] A 1943
Florida statute incorporated section 7 bodily into its provision
for flag instruction.[16] There is no indication, however, that the
legislature intended to indorse the antisalute interpretation of
that section. The greatest triumph for the Rotnem position
came in *Commonwealth v. Nemchik*.[17] Vera Nemchik, whose
five children had been expelled from the public schools of
Wapwallopen, Pennsylvania, was prosecuted for failing to have
them in some school. In reversing her conviction, Judge Flan-
nery of the Luzerne County Court of Quarter Sessions relied
specifically on Justice Department representations regarding
Public Law 623.

Other state officials were less impressed. Three state attorneys general handed down official opinions explicitly rejecting
Rotnem's interpretation of Public Law 623.[18] The Minersville

school board unanimously and emphatically refused to re-admit the children of Walter Gobitis, in spite of strong urging by the local United States attorney.[19]

C. *Attempts at Further Punishment: State Court Application of the* Gobitis *Rule*

Not content with expelling the non-saluting Witness children, local authorities in some areas sought further to punish them, their parents or their religious teachers. There were attempts to have the children declared delinquent or dependent and removed from their parents. Prosecutions were brought against parents for school law violation or for contributing to the delinquency of their offspring, or for "obstructing" the ceremony. In at least one state, agitation against the compulsory salute was made akin to treason.

1. REMOVAL OF CHILDREN

In the period before June, 1943, there were five appellate decisions dealing with official attempts to deprive Jehovah's Witness parents of their children.[20] *Commonwealth v. Johnson*[21] was pending in the Massachusetts Supreme Court when *Gobitis* was decided. It will be recalled that the Johnson children had been committed to a state training school as "habitual school offenders" after their second expulsion from school for refusal to join in the flag salute. A divided court—the exact vote was not made public—reversed the judgment of committal. Noting the quasi-penal nature of the proceeding, the majority opinion stressed the absence of any element of "misbehaving" in the children's refusal to salute. The New Hampshire Supreme Court reached the same result on similar facts in *State v. Lefebvre*.[22]

... [I]t is impossible for us to attribute to the legislature the intent to authorize the breaking up of family life for no other reason than because some of its members have conscientious religious scruples not shared by the majority of the community. . . .[23]

In *People v. Sandstrom,* the New York Court of Appeals had ruled that any further punitive action would have to be taken against the non-saluting child, not its parents. In *Matter of Reed,*[24] the Appellate Division, in the very teeth of this pronouncement, threw out a delinquency proceeding, suggesting that it was really the parents who were to blame for the child's predicament. Shortly before, a trial court in New York had dismissed a similar proceeding in *In re Jones.*[25]

. . . She has been taught by her parents and the religious society to which she belongs that if she salutes the flag, her God will punish her; the school authorities say if she does not salute the flag, the State will punish her. She chooses to obey her God. Is this delinquency? I say no.[26]

In *Stone v. Stone,*[27] a divorce case, the trial court had awarded all community property and custody of the children to the husband, on the basis of the wife's admitted adherence to Witness teachings regarding the flag salute. The Washington Supreme Court unanimously reversed, holding *Reynolds v. Rayborn* to be controlling.

2. PROSECUTION OF PARENTS

In the period under consideration there were three appellate decisions dealing with prosecution of Witness parents under the delinquency laws. In *People v. Chiafreddo,*[28] the Illinois Supreme Court reversed the conviction of a couple for contributing to their daughter's "dependency" on the grounds that the indictment and evidence were inadequate to support a conviction under the relevant statutes. The state had alleged and proved only that the parents had taught the girl not to salute, and that this had caused her exclusion from public school. This, it was ruled, was not enough.

State v. Davis,[29] involving a similar proceeding, reached a peculiar end result. On certification from the trial court, the Arizona Supreme Court interpreted *Gobitis* to mean that Davis might not be punished under the delinquency laws for *teaching* his children that the salute was wrong, but that he could be punished if he *commanded* them not to salute. Somehow, the jury still managed to convict. Davis received a suspended sentence, which was later revoked for repeated violation. The Arizona Supreme Court now dismissed his appeal on procedural grounds.[30] The United States Supreme Court denied certiorari, holding the state procedural ground to be adequate to support the judgment.[31]

In Oklahoma, a Witness parent was convicted of contributing to the delinquency of his child in that he induced her to refuse to participate in the school flag-salute ceremony. His appeal was pending in the Oklahoma Criminal Court of Appeals in June, 1943.[32]

Of five appellate decisions involving school law prosecutions, only one went against the defendant.[33] *Commonwealth v. Nemchik* already has been discussed. In *Matter of Latrecchia*,[34] the author of the prevailing opinion in *Hering* evinced considerable disgust with the whole patriotic crusade. As in *Sandstrom*, Judge Bodine ruled that the parents were not to blame, since they had tried to send their child to school each morning. Quoting liberally from Judge Lehman's separate opinion in *Sandstrom*, he concluded, "Liberty of conscience is not subject to uncontrolled administrative action. Jones v. Opelika. . . ."[35]

Finally, there were two conflicting opinions in Pennsylvania lower appellate courts. In *Commonwealth v. Merle*,[36] the Cambria County Court of Quarter Sessions reversed a conviction, distinguishing early vaccination precedents on the ground that Merle had not refused to *permit* his child to salute. In *Commonwealth v. Bortlik*,[37] however, the Monroe County Court of Common Pleas upheld a conviction, holding the vaccination cases to be directly in point. It was Bortlik's religion and actions which had made it impossible for his children to attend school in accordance with the rules.

3. PROSECUTION OF THIRD PARTIES

In 1942, Mississippi enacted an emergency statute making it a felony to utter language which advanced the cause of any wartime enemy, encouraged disloyalty or "reasonably tends to create an attitude of stubborn refusal to salute, honor or respect the flag or government of the United States. . . ."[38] Convicted persons were to be imprisoned for the duration of the war. Three Jehovah's Witnesses were convicted under the statute, the gist of the charge being that they had made statements against saluting the flag. The Mississippi Supreme Court divided evenly, leaving the convictions undisturbed. An appeal was pending in the United States Supreme Court in June, 1943.[39] Louisiana had a similar wartime statute,[40] but there is no record of a Witness conviction thereunder reaching an appellate court.

Oklahoma's 1923 statute calling for flag exercises also made it a misdemeanor for any teacher to neglect to carry out the ceremony and for any outside party to "obstruct" the use of the ceremony.[41] This statute, lavishly construed by trial courts, led to a rash of cases in early 1943. Convictions included a teacher of a Witness Kingdom School who had used that sect's new alternative flag pledge, two Witnesses who used their majority position on a school board to reinstate several expelled children, and a Witness parent who taught her child not to salute. Appeals from these convictions were pending in the Oklahoma Criminal Court of Appeals in June, 1943.[42]

D. *Judicial Defiance of the* Gobitis *Precedent*

Three state decisions directly repudiated the *Gobitis* precedent. In *Brown v. Skustad*,[43] a "friendly" injunction suit, the St. Louis County District Court issued an injunction restraining further enforcement of the flag-salute regulation of Virginia, Minnesota. The opinion was not altogether clear as to the *ratio decidendi*, invoking both religious freedom and Public Law 623, and expressing considerable distaste for *Gobitis*.

There was no ambiguity about the unanimous decision of the Kansas Supreme Court in *State v. Smith*.[44] Two Witness couples had been prosecuted for school law violation. Their convictions were reversed on the ground that their children had been illegally expelled from public school. Kansas' flag-salute statute, it was held, had never been intended to make participation compulsory; if it had been so intended, it would be violative of the religious freedom guaranty of the state constitution. The opinion exuded distaste for the *Gobitis* ruling. Whatever the First Amendment might mean to the Supreme Court, Kansas' analogous provision could not be stretched to permit a compulsory flag salute.

Even more emphatic was the decision in January, 1943, by the Washington Supreme Court in *Bolling v. Superior Court*.[45] The children of four Witness families had been adjudged delinquent and committed to a temporary guardian after their expulsion from public school. As their appeal came up, another family sought a writ of prohibition from the state high tribunal against similar action. The Washington Supreme Court issued the writ of prohibition and reversed the other commitment orders. The court refused to accept *Gobitis* as controlling, in view of the extent to which that precedent had been impaired by the United States Supreme Court itself.[46] Tacitly rejecting the "secular regulation" rule, the court emphasized the fact that an apparently innocuous custom might have great religious significance to conscientious persons, citing the religious refusal of early Christians to show their loyalty to the emperor by burning a pinch of incense in front of his statue. As applied to religious objectors like the Witnesses, Washington's flag-salute law was held to violate the religious freedom protected by that state's constitution.

The prosecutions discussed heretofore in this chapter constitute a final section of the report on the persecution of Jehovah's Witnesses. No other designation would be accurate. The sole motivation behind most of them seems to have been punishment for punishment's sake. Particularly disheartening were the frequent attempts to place the children in correctional institutions or in the custody of strangers. Since their religious views evidently were well developed and strongly held, a change of custody at that point could gain nothing but sorrow for all concerned.

The hostile reception given these proceedings by most state courts constitutes another negative reaction to the *Gobitis* decision. If the compulsory flag salute was just like any other secular regulation, as held in *Gobitis*, then refusal to salute was just like any other violation of a legal command, and the prosecutions should have succeeded. Much was made of the children's lack of evil intent; but willfulness, in the meaning of the relevant statutes, connoted deliberate violation of the rule, not any bad motives therein. If the Johnson children had refused to be vaccinated, or if Mrs. Stone had been teaching her children to play hooky and steal fruit, those cases surely would have ended differently.

Most of the reviewing courts seem to have been bothered by these cases without being fully aware of what was troubling them. The mere presence of sincere religious scruples was not the root of the disquiet; that had been ignored in the past. The courts seem to have been impressed particularly by the utter harmlessness of the children's "misconduct" and the evident official malice behind the prosecutions. The sharply hostile opinions in *Bolling* and *Smith* were just the culmination of a growing uneasiness with the *Gobitis* rule. However well the "secular regulation" rule might work ordinarily, its application here led to results the judges could not bring themselves to countenance.

E. *Turning Point: The License Tax Cases*

Even as state courts were casting doubt on the vitality of the *Gobitis* decision, the United States Supreme Court itself administered a mortal blow. In the two years following *Gobitis*, the Witnesses had lost eight cases in the Supreme Court.[47] The contrast between this dismal record and their signal successes in state and lower federal courts is explained mainly by the difference in subject matter. The favorable and unappealed lower court decisions merely enforced the *Lovell* and *Schneider* rules against recalcitrant state and local authorities; the Supreme Court cases involved Witness attempts to *expand* those rules. What is striking is that the Witnesses were unable to attract a single vote on the Court during this period; indeed, six of the eight adverse decisions were rendered without argument or opinion. On June 8, 1942, this unanimity was shattered by the five to four decision in *Jones v. Opelika*.[48] More important, the opinions reflected a drastic, perhaps decisive, vote shift on the flag-salute issue. Within another year, *Opelika* had been overruled and *Gobitis* was manifestly doomed.

1. BACKGROUND

Stated briefly, the issue in these cases was the validity of occupational license taxes as applied to the distribution and sale of religious tracts. All the ordinances involved prohibited the carrying on of certain occupations without a license. The sole condition of this license was registration and payment of a specified tax. The proceeds of the tax went into the general fund, to help defray ordinary city expenses. Within any occupational category, the tax was "flat"—i.e., unrelated to the volume of business transacted. Revenue was not always the only purpose of such ordinances. The license requirement, often combined with the threat of revocation, facilitated the enforcement of other regulations. Occasionally the license fee was fixed so high as to discourage the taxed occupation altogether—as witness certain taxes aimed specifically at itinerant merchants competing undesirably with local tradesmen.[49]

None of these ordinances seems to have been written with Jehovah's Witnesses in mind; nor is it likely that they were intended to cover the sort of pamphleteering carried on by that group. But one beset by foes will reach for the nearest weapon. Local authorities, enraged by the Witnesses' message and methods, found it easy to stretch ordinances aimed at street peddling and door-to-door canvassing to cover this nuisance. Making things all the easier was the Witnesses' absolute refusal to apply for such licenses.

The application of occupational license taxes to pamphleteering raised special and difficult problems under the First Amendment as applied by the Fourteenth. Most troublesome was the tax aspect. *Cox v. New Hampshire* had upheld a license fee, but had stressed the fact that the exaction was limited to the amount necessary to cover the policing of the licensed activity. In *Grosjean v. American Press Company*,[50] the Court struck down a Louisiana gross receipts tax aimed at newspapers of over 20,000 weekly circulation. Bulking large in the Court's rationale were the tax's manifest tendency to curtail circulation, its potential prohibitive effect if the rate were raised, and its close kinship to the hated "taxes on knowledge" which abounded in colonial times. The relevance of this precedent was not altogether clear. The occupational license tax was clearly distinguishable in that it did not penalize increased circulation—quite the contrary. On the other hand, its burdensome tendency was obvious; on groups like Jehovah's Witnesses, the effect was likely to be prohibitive. Shortly after the *Grosjean* case, the Court voted unanimously to uphold a gross receipts tax which applied to a variety of businesses, including all newspapers.[51] Thus, it would appear that the occupational license tax would profit simply by its wide, nondiscriminatory coverage.

Also subject to challenge were the provisions of many ordinances that a license might be revoked at any time. In *Lovell* and *Schneider*, the Court had held that pamphleteers, whether on street or doorsteps, might not be subjected to a license requirement which left discretion in the licensing authority to refuse a permit, and implied a similar judgment on ordinances carrying a discretionary revocation power.

Further confusing the legal picture was the question of the label to be attached to the Witnesses' activities. Were they preaching the gospel or selling books? While this issue bulked large in practice, it was, in point of strict law, irrelevant. The fact that the Witness literature was sold did not detract from their claim to protection under freedom of the press. While commercial advertising is outside the First Amendment's protection, expression is not robbed of all immunity by the mere presence of some commercial material or motive.[52] Nor, under the "secular regulation" rule, could the Witnesses derive any additional immunity from the religious character of their pamphleteering.

The license tax issue was litigated in at least twelve states.[53] In five, the courts interpreted the ordinances so as to make them inapplicable to Jehovah's Witnesses' pamphleteering.[54] The main emphasis was laid on the non-commercial nature of the enterprise. Two courts expressed doubt as to the constitutionality of the ordinance if interpreted otherwise.[55] In four states, license tax ordinances were held unconstitutional as applied to this sort of activity.[56] Reliance was placed generally on *Lovell, Schneider* and *Grosjean*. One Virginia ordinance was particularly bad, covering only periodicals and songbooks, and enforced only against Jehovah's Witnesses.[57] Pennsylvania came down on both sides of the issue, upholding a license tax ordinance applied to door-to-door canvassing,[58] but striking down an identical enactment as applied to street distribution of Witness literature.[59] Arkansas had upheld the application of this sort of ordinance to religious pamphleteering as early as 1929.[60]

2. JONES V. OPELIKA

Involved in this complex of cases were license tax ordinances of Opelika, Alabama, Fort Smith, Arkansas, and Casa

Grande, Arizona.[61] In all three ordinances, a license issued automatically on payment of the stated tax; Opelika licenses were revocable at will and without notice. Opelika's ordinance exacted five dollars a year from transient book distributors, one of many categories covered specially. The Fort Smith tax was $2.50 a day, $10 a week or $25 a month. That of Casa Grande was $25 per quarter. The latter two ordinances applied generally to all transient peddlers. Witnesses were arrested and convicted in all three cities for distributing their literature without applying for the required licenses. Roscoe Jones, of Opelika, had been operating on a street corner; the other arrested Witnesses had been going from door to door. The "selling" that took place was somewhat ambiguous. The "client" was asked for a "contribution" of five cents each for magazines and twenty-five cents for books, but the Witness distributor often left literature for free with those unable or unwilling to pay for it. The Supreme Courts of Alabama, Arkansas and Arizona upheld the convictions.[62] *Jones v. Opelika, Bowden v. Fort Smith*[63] and *Jobin v. Arizona*[64] reached the United States Supreme Court early in 1942, the first two by certiorari,[65] the third on appeal.

On June 8, 1942, the Supreme Court voted five to four to affirm the judgments below in all three cases. Justice Reed wrote the majority opinion. Chief Justice Stone and Justices Black, Douglas and Murphy dissented in three opinions.

a) Justice Reed for the majority.—At the outset, Justice Reed sought to limit as narrowly as possible the issues before the Court.

. . . The sole constitutional question considered is whether a nondiscriminatory license fee, presumably appropriate in amount, may be imposed upon these activities.[66]

Justice Reed emphasized that there was no claim that the particular taxes were excessive, and no showing that they had the practical effect, either individually or cumulatively, of suppressing the Witnesses' proselytizing. Possible future abuses of the tax mechanism were not before the Court; neither was the revocation power in the Opelika ordinance, since Jones had not applied for a license at all.

In dealing with the merits, Reed further stressed the fact

that there was no prohibition or restriction involved here, but only taxation. As far as the Constitution was concerned, Reed saw no distinction between an occupational license tax and any other tax a state might see fit to levy on business activities. Most important, these taxes did not strike directly at religious worship or the dissemination of ideas, but only at an incidental manifestation which they shared with more mundane callings —the selling of commodities.

> . . . To subject any religious or didactic group to a reasonable fee for their money-making activities does not require a finding that the licensed acts are purely commercial. It is enough that money is earned by the sale of articles. . . .[67]
>
> . . . Nothing more is asked from one group than from another which uses similar methods of propagation.[68]

In dealing specifically with the separate religious freedom issue, Reed took a more ambiguous stand:

> . . . If we were to assume, as is here argued, that the licensed activities involve religious rites, a different question would be presented. These are not free will offerings. But it is because we view these sales as partaking more of commercial than religious or educational transactions that we find the ordinances, as here presented, valid. . . .[69]

Read closely, this passage detracted nothing from the "secular regulation" rule, but simply reiterated the position just taken with freedom of the press—that expression itself, unsullied by commercial procedures, might be immune from taxes such as these. In any event, it was not the Witnesses' subjective view of their activities that was controlling, but the objective fact that they fell in an objective category customarily subject to state control and taxation.

 b) Stone and Murphy et al., dissenting.—Chief Justice Stone and Justice Murphy wrote dissenting opinions, each of which was joined by all the dissenting Justices. The two opinions covered much the same ground and will be treated together here.

The dissenters rejected all of Reed's attempts to limit the issues. Stone was insistent that the revocation power rendered the Opelika ordinance void on its face, and hence unenforceable against anybody. Both opinions urged that the oppressive amount of the tax had been presented adequately and was before the Court, and that the Opelika and Casa Grande taxes were clearly prohibitive as applied to the Witnesses. Moreover, the possibility that the taxes might be raised still further was considered fatal to the validity of all three ordinances. The non-discriminatory character of the ordinances was dismissed as irrelevant.

The First Amendment is not confined to safeguarding freedom of speech and freedom of religion against discriminatory attempts to wipe them out. On the contrary the Constitution . . . has put those freedoms in a preferred position. Their commands are not restricted to cases where the protected privilege is sought out for attack. They extend at least to every form of taxation which, because it is a condition of the exercise of the privilege, is capable of being used to control or suppress it.[70]

The main vice of the tax was held to lie in two peculiar characteristics. First, the tax was a prior condition of the exercise of First Amendment rights, and thus ideally adapted to their suppression. Second, the flat rate inevitably operated to burden freedom of expression, and was likely to destroy small scale, low-turnover pamphleteering like the Witnesses'. The burden would be multiplied to intolerable proportions by the proliferation of such license taxes across the country. The only permissible form of license fee, in the view of the dissenters, was one adjusted to demonstrated expenses caused the city by the mode of expression being licensed.

The dissenters' treatment of religious freedom was especially significant. It must be borne in mind that the Witnesses' activities had a dual aspect. On the one hand, it was religious preaching; on the other, it was bookselling. Under the traditional rules, the latter aspect was controlling, as in Reed's opinion. For the dissenters, the former aspect dominated the case.

. . . While perhaps not so orthodox as the oral sermon, the use of religious books is an old, recognized and effective mode of worship and means of proselytizing. . . . The mind rebels at the thought that a minister of any of the old established churches could be made to pay fees to the community before entering the pulpit. . . .[71]

200

In short, the "commercial" side of the proselytization was incidental and *irrelevant*. Crucial was the Witnesses' own belief that they were preaching the gospel. When *Gobitis* was decided, there was only one Justice prepared to junk the "secular regulation" rule; now, it appears, there were four.

c) *Addendum:* Gobitis *reconsidered.*—While the issues here differed considerably from those in *Gobitis*, that precedent was clearly relevant. As the clearest modern statement of the "secular regulation" rule, it was controlling on the issue of religious freedom. Yet Reed did not build on *Gobitis* in his *Opelika* opinion, but *distinguished* it:

> . . . No religious symbolism is involved such as was urged against the flag salute in Minersville School District v. Gobitis. . . . For us there is no occasion to apply here the principles taught by that opinion.[72]

But *Gobitis* was manifestly relevant. Why this avoidance? It is possible that it was intended simply to take some of the sting out of the special Black-Douglas-Murphy dissent discussed below. This seems unlikely, however, in view of the thin and unconvincing nature of the distinction. Rather, Reed's opinion reads at this point much more like that of one who seeks *any* plausible pretext for setting aside an embarrassing precedent. It appears likely, especially by hindsight, that somebody in the majority group—probably the newly appointed Robert H. Jackson—disliked *Gobitis* and opposed any reliance thereon.

Among the dissenters, reconsideration of *Gobitis* was more overt. Justices Black, Douglas and Murphy wrote a special dissenting opinion, dealing with none of the issues in *Opelika*, in which they "apologized" for their *Gobitis* votes.

> The opinion of the Court sanctions a device which in our opinion suppresses or tends to suppress the free exercise of a religion practiced by a minority group. This is but another step in the direction which Minersville School Dist. v. Gobitis . . . took against the same religious minority and is a logical extension of the principles upon which that decision rested. Since we joined in the opinion in the Gobitis Case, we think this is an appropriate occasion to state that we now believe that it was also wrongly decided. . . .[73]

This was unusual procedure. These justices were going out of their way to reject a precedent not relied on by the majority. Evidently, they felt strongly about their change of heart and sought out any "appropriate occasion" for a public announcement.

3. INTERIM: A CHANGE IN PERSONNEL

On October 5, 1942, Justice James F. Byrnes resigned, after just one term on the Court, to become Roosevelt's "assistant president" as head of the Office of War Mobilization. This left the justices split four to four on the issues involved in *Opelika*, and gave the anti-*Gobitis* group at least an even split. The President's choice of a replacement was thus of crucial import.

The doom of the *Opelika* holding, and, for the time, of the "secular regulation" rule, was sounded in early February, 1943, when Roosevelt appointed Wiley Rutledge to the vacant seat. Formerly dean of the Iowa Law School, Rutledge had been appointed to the District of Columbia Court of Appeals in April, 1939.[74] On April 15, 1942, that court decided the case of *Busey v. District of Columbia*,[75] involving a license tax statute similar in most respects to that of *Opelika*. Two judges voted to uphold the statute as applied to Jehovah's Witnesses, on substantially the grounds later invoked by Justice Reed. Rutledge dissented vigorously and at some length, challenging both the interpretation of the statute as applicable to the Witnesses and its constitutionality if so construed. His constitutional argument anticipated most of the points later made by Justices Stone and Murphy—the revocation provision, the special vices of a flag privilege tax, the inherent discrimination against weak and impecunious minority groups. His statement on the religious issue sheds some light on the state of his thinking on the flag-salute issue.

. . . This is no time to wear away *further* the freedoms of conscience and mind by nicely technical or doubtful construction. Everywhere they are fighting for life. . . . They can be lost in time also by *steady legal erosion* wearing down broad principle into thin right. *Jehovah's Witnesses have had to choose between their consciences and public education for their children.* In my judgment, they should not have to give up also the right to disseminate their religious views in an orderly manner on the public streets, exercise it at the whim of public officials or be taxed for doing so without their license. I think the judgment should be reversed. [Italics supplied.][76]

This passage would seem to indicate that Rutledge considered *Busey* and *Gobitis* to be constituent parts of the same distasteful process of "legal erosion."

Justice Rutledge was sworn in on February 15, 1943. The same day, the Supreme Court granted a petition for rehearing in *Opelika* and granted certiorari in a new case raising the same issues.[77]

4. *MURDOCK V. PENNSYLVANIA*[78] AND COMPANION CASES

The cases that led to the actual overthrow of *Opelika* arose in Jeannette, Pennsylvania. Jeanette had a fifty-year old ordinance which required all door-to-door solicitors to secure a license and pay a tax ranging in amount from $1.50 a day to twenty dollars for three weeks. Since early 1939, Jehovah's Witnesses had carried on a running battle against the ordinance, incurring more than fifty arrests by early 1940.[79] *Murdock v. Pennsylvania* stemmed from the arrest and conviction of eight Witnesses in February, 1940. A companion case, *Douglas v. Jeannette*,[80] involved an injunction suit brought around the same time to restrain further enforcement of the ordinance. The District Court issued a permanent injunction on the basis of *Reid v. Brookville*, but the Circuit Court reversed, with obvious reluctance, on the basis of *Opelika*.[81]

The cases were argued on March 10 and March 12. Covington again handled the briefs and oral argument for the Witnesses. Osmond K. Fraenkel filed briefs *amicus curiae* for the ACLU. The American Newspaper Publishers Association[82] and the General Conference of Seventh-Day Adventists filed *amicus curiae* briefs in support of the petition for rehearing in *Opelika*.

On May 3, 1943, the Supreme Court voted five to four to reverse the judgments in *Murdock v. Pennsylvania* and *Jones v. Opelika*.[83] The ruling in *Douglas v. Jeannette* was affirmed; it was assumed that Jeannette officials would comply with *Murdock*. On the same day, in *Martin v. Struthers*,[84] another Jehovah's Witness case, the Court voted six to three to invalidate a straight prohibition of doorbell ringing by literature distributors as an infringement on freedom of speech and press. When the *Busey* appeal reached the Court a month later, it was remanded by unanimous vote for reconsideration in the light of *Murdock*.[85]

The opinions in these cases need not be dwelt on at any length. The central issues in *Struthers* and *Jeannette* are irrelevant here. The various opinions in *Murdock* largely reiterated the arguments previously advanced in *Opelika*. Of interest for present purposes are the statements in several opinions touching on the issue of religious freedom. Justice Douglas' majority opinion in *Murdock* expanded on the religious freedom argument raised in *Opelika*.

. . . [W]e do not intimate that any conduct can be made a religious rite and by the zeal of the practitioners swept into the First Amendment. . . . We only hold that spreading one's religious beliefs or preaching the Gospel through the distribution of religious literature and through personal visitations is an age-old type of evangelism with as high a claim to constitutional protection as the more orthodox types. . . .[86]

. . . [T]he mere fact that the religious literature is "sold" by itinerant preachers rather than "donated" does not transform evangelism into a commercial enterprise. . . .[87]

Again, the "secular regulation" rule was clearly repudiated, this time by a majority. Douglas' substitute standard, however, was more than a little hazy. To make the immunity of a practice from regulation turn entirely on its status as a "religious rite" would be to import theology into every case. Some more "secular" method of drawing the line was needed. Furthermore, Douglas' concentration on this aspect of the case left very unclear the degree of immunity from this sort of tax enjoyed by non-religious segments of the press.

While *Martin v. Struthers* turned entirely on freedom of speech and press, Justices Murphy, Douglas and Rutledge felt called upon to write a separate opinion holding the Struthers ordinance also to be a violation of freedom of religion.

. . . [I]f regulation should be necessary to protect the safety and privacy of the home, an effort should be made at the same time to preserve the substance of religious freedom.

There can be no question but that appellant was engaged in a religious activity. . . .[88]

Prohibition may be more convenient to the law maker, and easier to fashion than a regulatory measure which adequately protects the peace and privacy of the home without suppressing legitimate religious activities. But that does not justify a repressive enactment like the one now before us. . . . Freedom of religion has a higher dignity under the Constitution than municipal or personal convenience. . . .[89]

Here was the most explicit rejection of the "secular regulation" rule yet. Municipalities must frame their ordinances so as to place the least restriction feasible on religious activities; and their resolution of this problem was to be subject to judicial scrutiny unhampered by the usual strong presumption of constitutionality.

Justice Jackson's concurring opinion in *Jeannette*, which embodied dissents from *Murdock* and *Struthers*, deserves special notice, both because of his key role in the resolution of the flag-salute controversy, and because he was the only minority writer[90] in these cases to meet the religious freedom issue squarely. A largely self-educated, highly successful New York lawyer, Jackson had served under President Roosevelt as Solicitor General and Attorney General before being appointed in 1941 to fill the vacancy left by Chief Justice Hughes. His opinions reflected three distinctive traits which made him an impressive, if somewhat exasperating figure on the Court: a brilliant and polemical style, a strong impatience with nice legal distinctions and a tendency to think through constitutional questions *de novo*, often arriving at distinctions and priorities peculiarly his own. The first two proclivities were sharply highlighted in his *Jeannette* opinion; the third became prominent in 1943, when the flag-salute issue returned to the Supreme Court.

Jackson's opinion showed considerable hostility toward the Witnesses' behavior and message. He took the somewhat novel position that, since the Witnesses' pamphleteering was eminently worthy of suppression, the Jeannette authorities should not be thwarted merely because they had chosen the wrong procedure and pretext. "How . . . can the Court today hold it a 'high constitutional privilege' to go to homes, including those of devout Catholics on Palm Sunday morning, and thrust upon them literature calling their church a 'whore' and their faith a 'racket'?"[91] On the religious freedom question itself, he took a much more orthodox position:

... When limits are reached which such [secular] communications must observe, can one go farther under the cloak of religious evangelism? ... I had not supposed that the rights of secular and non-religious communications were more narrow or in any way inferior to those of avowed religious groups.

It may be asked why then does the First Amendment separately mention free exercise of religion? The history of religious persecution gives the answer. ... It was to assure religious teaching as much freedom as secular discussion, rather than to assure it greater license, that led to its separate statement.[92]

... The Court is adding a new privilege to override the rights of others to what has before been regarded as religious liberty. ... .[93]

The license tax cases did not furnish an ideal occasion for disputation over the "secular regulation" rule. The issue commanding major attention was a very tricky point in the law of free speech and press. Most of the religious argument turned on the peripheral question of whether the Witnesses' literature distribution was "commercial." Only Murphy's *Struthers* concurrence and Jackson's *Jeannette* concurrence dealt clearly and sharply with the central religious freedom issue. The other opinions, though, all proceeded in terms clearly indicating acceptance or rejection of the "secular regulation" rule. As of May 3, 1943, the rule was dead, with five votes against it. It was not yet buried, however. There was as yet no clear majority holding rejecting the old standard or indorsing a new one.

The implication of the license tax cases for the flag-salute issue was clear enough. Frankfurter's *Gobitis* opinion had leaned heavily on the "secular regulation" rule. The compulsory salute could never withstand the sort of scrutiny ordinarily involved in First Amendment cases. Once freedom of religion became *relevant* to the flag-salute issue, the outcome was easily predictable.

The reasons for the dramatic shift of opinion by Justices Black, Douglas and Murphy can only be surmised. The main stimulus may have come from the events that have been recited in the foregoing chapters. The three justices seem to have come to view both the flag-salute regulations and later license ordinances as parts of a deliberate campaign to suppress Jehovah's Witnesses. *Kennedy v. Moscow* and *Reid v. Brookville* went far to reinforce this suspicion. While existing law compelled affirmance of *Trent* and *Chaplinsky*, the circumstances of these cases did not reflect credit on municipal authorities. The license tax cases were just the last straw. Justice Murphy in particular showed very accurate knowledge of Jehovah's Witnesses' troubles with local ordinances, and drew repeated analogies between these and the tribulations of dissenting sects in Colonial America. It is also to be noted that Murphy, Rutledge and Douglas automatically saw *Struthers* as a religious freedom case. Clearly, they were thinking of all Witness cases in terms of religious suppression by 1943. In short, Black, Douglas and Murphy began to have doubts about the "secular regulation" rule when they began to doubt the good faith of the local authorities.

The days of the *Gobitis* precedent clearly were numbered. All that remained was to get another case into the Supreme Court, and this detail already had been attended to. On March 11, the same day *Murdock* was argued, the Court also heard oral argument in *West Virginia State Board of Education v. Barnette*, testing West Virginia's state-wide flag-salute regulation.

CHAPTER TEN

GOBITIS OVERRULED

THE BARNETTE CASE

A. *Beginning Stages: In the District Court*

1. THE LEGAL SETTING

During the period under study, West Virginia law required that all children be kept in some school between the ages of seven and fourteen. Failure of a parent to meet this requirement was punishable by fine or imprisonment, each day of violation constituting a separate offense.[1] A child "habitually truant"—i.e., absent by his own fault—might be proceeded against as a juvenile delinquent.[2] These provisions were greatly stiffened by a 1941 amendment which provided that a child expelled or suspended for refusal to comply with school rules might not be readmitted without compliance with those rules, and was in the meantime to be deemed "unlawfully absent," with all the consequences flowing therefrom.[3] While there is no direct evidence that this provision was aimed at Jehovah's Witnesses, it might as well have been. In effect, it forbade school boards to compromise the flag-salute issue after originally committing themselves to a strict position. Furthermore, it seemed designed to assure the success of attempts at additional punishment of flag-salute expellees and their parents.

Since 1923, West Virginia law has required every school, public or private, to give instruction in United States history and civics "for the purpose of teaching, fostering and perpetuating the ideals, principles and spirit of Americanism. . . ."[4] The State Board of Education is given considerable discretion over the courses of study offered pursuant to this requirement. On January 9, 1942, the State Board invoked this statutory discretion to pass a resolution dealing with the flag-salute issue. The long "whereas" clause quoted at enormous length from Frankfurter's *Gobitis* opinion. The flavor of this portion can be gained from the following excerpts:

WHEREAS, the West Virginia State Board of Education recognizes that . . . conscientious scruples have not in the course of the long struggle for religious toleration relieved the individual from obedience to the general law not aimed at the promotion or restriction of religious beliefs . . . that national unity is the basis of national security . . . that the public schools . . . are dealing with the formative period in the development of citizenship. . . .[5]

On this basis, the Board resolved

. . . That the West Virginia State Board of Education does hereby recognize and order that the commonly accepted salute to the Flag of the United States . . . now becomes a regular part of the program of activities in the public schools . . . and that all teachers . . . and pupils in such schools shall be required to participate . . . provided, however, that refusal to salute the Flag be regarded as an act of insubordination, and shall be dealt with accordingly.[6]

Thus the flag ceremony became a state-wide requirement, at least in the public schools.[7] That the regulation was aimed at Jehovah's Witnesses seems beyond question; the introductory passage made this about as clear as legal language could. No other flag-salute regulation was quite so transparent in intent.

2. BEGINNING CONFLICTS

Jehovah's Witnesses appear to be quite numerous in West Virginia; Charleston alone currently has three large congregations. According to Witness sources, Witness children were expelled from school in almost every county of the state during 1942.[8] Documented incidents are rare, however; the only specific reports of expulsions came from Harrison,[9] Hancock, Upshur[10] and Calhoun Counties.[11] The record is equally sparse regarding legal actions against non-saluting children or their parents. In spite of the stringent governing statutes, such actions seem to have been neither numerous nor particularly successful; there were no appellate court decisions at all on the subject. One factor operating was the hostility of many trial judges. In *State v. Mercante*,[12] for example, the Hancock County Circuit Court acquitted a Witness parent on a charge of school law violation. While readily conceding the legality of the expulsion of Mercante's daughter for non-saluting, the judge went on to hold that it would be violative of the West Virginia Constitution's religious freedom guaranty to impose any further legal punishment on parent or child. The Upshur County Circuit Court reached the same conclusion in a similar case.[13]

A substantial number of Jehovah's Witness children were expelled from schools in and around Charleston.[14] Our attention will be confined to three families in whose names flag-salute litigation again reached the Supreme Court. Walter Barnette lived a mile north of Charleston and had two daughters enrolled at Slip Hill Grade School. Mrs. Lucy B. McClure[15] lived seven miles north of Charleston and had three children enrolled in different rural schools in the area. Paul Stull lived on the outskirts of South Charleston and had two stepchildren enrolled in South Charleston Grade School. Mrs. McClure and Mrs. Stull were sisters of Walter Barnette. Stull was brother to the Stulls in Mount Lookout who were involved in the Richwood "castor oil" incident. Both the Barnette and Stull families had strong Witness ties going back at least a generation. All three families were quite poor. Mr. McClure worked in the shipping department of a local hardware store, while Barnette and Stull earned less-than-steady incomes as pipe fitting helpers at the local DuPont plant.

Before 1942, the Charleston area public schools had used the flag-salute ceremony only sporadically and on a non-compulsory basis. Even after the January 9 resolution, local authorities moved slowly. Teachers and principals were sympathetic and reluctant to resort to expulsions. They tried hard to persuade Witness children to make some token show of compliance which would enable them to stay in school.[16] The chief pressure for strict enforcement seems to have come from the truant officers. By the end of January, all seven children of the three families had been expelled. The Stull stepchildren enrolled in a Kingdom School near Mount Lookout, probably boarding with relatives there; the Barnette and McClure children remained at large. In the summer of 1942, Walter Barnette and Lucy McClure were convicted and fined for school law violation; but no attempt was made to collect the fine, and the state abandoned the case on appeal. In the spring of 1942, Horace S. Meldahl, a successful Charleston attorney just beginning a long and fruitful association with the Witness legal office,[17] brought three separate actions in the West Virginia Supreme Court seeking a writ of prohibition against continued enforcement of the State Board's January 9 resolution. All were denied without hearing.[18] On June 8, 1942, the picture was radically altered by *Jones v. Opelika.*

3. SUIT FOR INJUNCTION: IN THE DISTRICT COURT

a) Preliminary stages.—When Hayden Covington heard the opinion and dissents in *Jones v. Opelika*, he realized immediately that it was time to bring another test case on the compulsory flag salute. He quickly contacted Meldahl to lay plans for a new injunction suit to be brought in the federal District Court for the Southern District of West Virginia.[19] West Virginia was an attractive forum strategically. A suit to enjoin the state-wide January 9 regulation could be brought before a special three-judge District Court; the direct appeal possible from such a tribunal would assure Covington of a Supreme Court hearing at the next term of the Court. The court at Charleston probably was selected for its convenience to Meldahl, and the particular plaintiffs for their convenience to Charleston.

In early August, 1942, Meldahl filed the bill of complaint with the District Court. Although brought in the names of Walter Barnette, Paul Stull and Lucy McClure, this was a *class* action on behalf of these plaintiffs and all others similarly situated. Named as defendants were the State Board, its individual members, Superintendent Trent, and all persons acting under their direction. After alleging the essential facts, the complaint went on to allege that the January 9 resolution was unconstitutional as a violation of freedom of speech and religion, an infringement on parental rights and a deprivation of liberty without due process of law. It was further urged that the resolution was fatally inconsistent with Public Law 623. The District Court was asked to issue a permanent injunction forbidding enforcement of the flag-salute rule against children of Jehovah's Witnesses. On August 10, 1942, State Attorney General W. S. Wysong and Assistant Attorney General Ira J. Partlow filed a motion to dismiss the complaint, arguing that the *Gobitis* precedent left no substantial federal question to be decided and that Public Law 623 had not changed the legal situation. On August 27, Meldahl filed a further motion requesting an interlocutory injunction pending trial of the case.

On the same day, District Judge Ben Moore acted to set up the statutory three-judge tribunal, calling to his aid District Judge Harry E. Watkins and Judge John J. Parker of the Fourth Circuit Court of Appeals.[20]

b) *The hearing.*—The hearing on the motion for an interlocutory injunction was held on September 14, 1942. Partlow argued for the State Board, Covington for the Witnesses. Two facts became immediately clear. First, Partlow readily admitted that he disapproved the State Board's position, though he was prepared to defend its legality; he personally would have preferred some sort of compromise.[21] Second, Parker was openly critical. He urged the Board to amend its regulation to excuse conscientious objectors from the ceremony, and recessed the hearing overnight to allow the Board to consider his suggestion.[22] The following morning, the State Board voted against compromising the issue.[23]

On September 15, the decisive hearing was held. Parker received word of the Board's intransigence with open disgust, commenting that it was "unfortunate that a case of its kind should be in court at a time when national unity is paramount. . . ."[24] He flatly rejected Partlow's reliance on the *Gobitis* precedent, curtly remarking that dismissal on that ground "will not easily dispose of this case," and citing the suggestive handling of that case in *Jones v. Opelika.*[25] Partlow continued to make it clear that his exclusive reliance was on *Gobitis.*[26] The motion to dismiss was denied pending further proceedings, and the defendants were allowed two weeks to file an answer.[27]

Apparently, no answer was ever filed. Shortly after the hearing, opposing counsel agreed to submit the case for final decree on the pleadings and briefs already filed.[28] There was no real point in proceeding to a trial, since there was no substantial disagreement as to the facts.

c) *The decision.*—On October 6, 1942, the three-judge court handed down its decree, permanently enjoining all the defendants

. . . from requiring the children of the plaintiffs, or any other children having religious scruples against such action, to salute the flag of the United States, or any other flag, or from expelling such children from school for failure to salute it; and that plaintiffs recover of defendants the costs of suit. . . .[29]

Judge Parker wrote the opinion for a unanimous court.[30] At the outset, he rejected out of hand the appeal to Public Law 623. Then he dealt with the troublesome *Gobitis* precedent. While an unreversed decision of the Supreme Court ordinarily is absolutely binding on lower federal courts, Parker felt that the handling of *Gobitis* in *Jones v. Opelika* warranted an exception here. "[W]e would be recreant to our duty as judges, if through a blind following of a decision which the Supreme Court itself has thus impaired . . . we should deny protection to rights which we regard as among the most sacred. . . ."[31]

In dealing with the crucial religious freedom issue, Parker relied very heavily on the two lower court decisions in *Gobitis.* As in Judge Maris' District Court opinion, he tacitly rejected the "secular regulation" rule, holding that religious freedom was infringed upon when the state overruled sincere religious scruples. Also like Maris, he cited only the ambiguous dictum from *Commonwealth v. Lesher* as authority. Like both lower courts in *Gobitis,* he rejected any inquiry into the reasonableness of the scruples involved. In delineating the proper standard to be applied in the resolution of the conflicting interests, Parker built on the tacit rationale of Judge Clark's Circuit Court opinion in *Gobitis.*

. . . To justify the overriding of religious scruples . . . there must be a clear justification therefor in the necessities of national or community life. Like the right of free speech, it is not to be overborne by the police power, unless its exercise presents a clear and present danger to the community. . . .

Can it be said . . . that the requirement that school children salute the flag has such direct relation to the safety of the state, that the conscientious objections of plaintiffs must give way . . . ?[32]

From this premise, the decision flowed easily; "to ask these questions is to answer them, and to answer them in the negative."[33]

The salute to the flag is an expression of the homage of the soul. To force it upon one who has conscientious scruples against giving it, is petty tyranny unworthy of the spirit of this Republic and forbidden, we think, by the fundamental law. . . .[34]

It is notable that, aside from this rather overstated presentation of the "clear and present danger" doctrine,[35] Parker hewed close to the line laid down in the lower court opinions in *Gobitis*. In particular, he completely ignored the long brief filed by Covington; even when he cited the same cases as Covington, he used different passages in different contexts.[36]

4. ON THE WAY TO THE SUPREME COURT

State school authorities complied with the District Court order fully and immediately, making no attempt to secure a stay of the injunction pending appeal. On October 7, Superintendent Trent informed the public that "children belonging to religious sects whose belief prohibits their participating completely in giving the Flag Salute may attend school and will, pending further court rulings, be considered as fulfilling the regulation . . . by standing at attention. . . ."[37] The Barnette, McClure and Stull children were readmitted almost immediately. Only the Barnette children encountered any hostility on their return; they also missed a promotion because of the lost class time.[38] One county near Charleston showed some recalcitrance, but capitulated after Meldahl heatedly offered to send around a federal marshal.[39] Several Witness families balked at having their children even stand at attention during the ceremony.[40] Fearing new repercussions, Meldahl and Covington categorically informed these extremists that they could expect no support from the Watchtower Society if they got into trouble again.[41]

On October 23, the State Board of Education voted to take an appeal to the United States Supreme Court.[42] Reportedly, Partlow opposed the appeal and refused to argue the case in the Supreme Court.[43] The situation was further confused when Attorney General Wysong was defeated for re-election, and his successor entered the armed forces, leaving Partlow as Acting Attorney General.[44] Rather than withdraw the already instituted appeal, Partlow cast about for somebody in or out of the Attorney General's office sympathetic enough to argue the State Board's case in the Supreme Court.[45] The task finally fell to W. Holt Wooddell, who handled the case from this point on. He does not seem to have been enthusiastic either. The appeal was perfected in the Supreme Court on or about January 4, 1943.[46]

B. *In the Supreme Court: Briefs and Argument*

Five briefs were filed in the Supreme Court in the *Barnette* case. Covington filed a long brief for the appellees, Walter Barnette *et al.*, while Wooddell filed a very short brief for the appellant State Board of Education. There were three *amicus curiae* briefs. The ACLU and the Bill of Rights Committee again filed briefs supporting the Witnesses. The American Legion, formally entering the controversy for the first time, filed a short brief urging that the decision be reversed.

These briefs must be evaluated in the light of the situation confronting the brief writers. Four justices were known to be ready to overrule *Gobitis*. The peculiar majority opinion in *Opelika*, and the appointment of Justice Rutledge to the Court made it extremely likely that the Witnesses could count on five or even six favorable votes. The task of their brief writers, then, was to keep that fifth vote, and to overcome any reluctance which that Justice might have to overrule a precedent after so short a time. Writers for the State Board had a more difficult task. Somehow, they must induce one or more hostile justices to subordinate their distaste for the flag salute to their respect for *stare decisis*, either by weakening the former or strengthening the latter. Working in their favor was the fact that the Court already was under fire for what many considered its excessive willingness to overturn precedents old and new.

1. BRIEFS FOR APPELLANTS[47]

a) The West Virginia brief.[48]—The main claim of the West Virginia brief for the State Board of Education was that the Witnesses' complaint should have been dismissed for want of a *substantial* federal question, in view of the *Gobitis* ruling, which had not been overruled or modified since. Wooddell insisted that nothing new was presented in this case; it was *Gobitis* all over again. The balance of this first section of the brief was devoted to a lengthy quotation from Frankfurter's *Gobitis* opinion, reproducing in full his statement of the "secular regulation" rule.

In a rather odd second section, Wooddell urged that "the regulation of Appellants is not inimical to public safety and good order."[49] This proposition was supported with another quotation from *Gobitis*, the key sentence of which read: "The preciousness of the family relation, the authority and independence which give dignity to parenthood, indeed the enjoyment of all freedom, presuppose the kind of ordered society which is summarized by our flag."[50] If this sally was intended to counteract Covington's emphasis on the various attempts which had been made to punish non-saluters and their parents, it was woefully wide of the mark. By citing *Gobitis* in support of such actions, it actually further damaged the reputation of that crucial precedent.

The concluding section of the brief insisted that Public Law 623 had made no change in the legal situation created by *Gobitis*. Wooddell insisted, with supporting citations, that the enactment in question was not a *law*, but merely an expression of congressional opinion. Furthermore, he pointed out, Congress avowedly was merely codifying existing practices regarding the flag, and had shown no intent to alter existing state law. Finally, he noted that other parts of Public Law 623 not cited by the Witnesses clearly recognized the flag salute as the proper form of respect. In short, *Gobitis* was still the law unless overruled.

In retrospect, it is easy to criticize Wooddell's exclusive reliance on *Gobitis* as determinative of the constitutional issue; that precedent was obviously shaky and in need of new support. Still, it is doubtful that anything substantial could have been added to Frankfurter's *Gobitis* arguments, and to make the attempt would be imprudently to admit that the possibility that *Gobitis* might be overruled was taken seriously. In assuming that case to be automatically controlling, Wooddell appealed tacitly to the fundamental value underlying *stare decisis*; that the Court should be consistent, so that parties might safely order their affairs on the basis of existing decisions. Wooddell's actual motivation in hewing to this line of argument probably was less sophisticated; validity of the regulation under the *Gobitis* rule would seem to have been the only favorable point on which all the parties could agree.

b) *The American Legion brief.*—The American Legion's brief *amicus curiae*, written and signed by Ralph B. Gregg of Indianapolis, contributed little in the way of new argument.

Its *raison d'être* probably was the short section reiterating the contention that Public Law 623 had in no way impaired the legality of state and local flag salute regulations. On the constitutional issue, Gregg duplicated the West Virginia brief's exclusive reliance on *Gobitis*, adding the allegations that the flag salute was not a religious rite and that the objective of the compulsory salute—the promotion of national unity—was so important that the regulation should be upheld out of hand.

2. BRIEFS FOR APPELLEES

a) The Jehovah's Witnesses brief.[51]—Covington's brief for Jehovah's Witnesses was very long, haphazardly organized and only partly original. Covington borrowed liberally and literally from the briefs filed in *Gobitis* by the Bill of Rights Committee and his own predecessors in the Witness legal office, usually without benefit of quotation marks. He began by emphasizing the loyalty and sincerity of the Witness children and parents, and the intolerable situation in which they were placed by the West Virginia regulation and statutes. Against any resurgence of the "privilege" argument, he reproduced in full the "unconstitutional conditions" section of Moyle's Circuit Court brief in *Gobitis*. The body of his brief was devoted to three main contentions: (1) that the flag-salute regulation, as applied to Witness children, violated religious freedom as protected by the Fourteenth Amendment; (2) that the regulation violated the due process clause of the Fourteenth Amendment regardless of the religious character of the objection; and (3) that the *Gobitis* decision was pernicious in both its doctrine and effects and should be overruled.

Religious freedom.—Covington spent three sections of his brief setting forth the Witnesses' religious objections to the salute. The third chapters of the books of Daniel and Esther, Fred Franz' *Gobitis* testimony, and Rutherford's dictionary definitions, all were invoked in support of the contention that the flag salute was in fact an act of idolatry forbidden by Scripture. Covington further strengthened his case here by reproducing in full that section of the Bill of Rights Committee's *Gobitis* brief asserting that the Witnesses' religious belief about the salute was plausible and not legally subject to challenge. He repeated the official—and erroneous—Witness claim that the compulsory flag salute was a 1935 invention aimed at Jehovah's Witnesses. Finally, Covington pointed to the Witness doctrine of the "covenant"; while a non-Witness might salute and later repent, a Witness who thus broke his agreement with God would be doomed irrevocably. Thus, Witness children were forced to choose between persecution and absolute damnation.

Covington preserved at least a remnant of Rutherford's claim of absolute immunity from secular interference, citing Blackstone, the *Trinity Church* dictum, etc., to the effect that enactments contrary to divine law were void. He was too good a lawyer, however, to stop there. Covington reproduced in full those parts of the Bill of Rights Committee's *Gobitis* brief arguing that restrictions on religious freedom were presumptively invalid, that such a restriction could be sustained only if necessary to an important legislative end, and that the compulsory flag salute must be justified by its effect upon the objecting child. To the authorities cited against the usefulness of the ceremony in the *Gobitis* briefs, he added the impressive survey by Professor Olander, actually making it an appendix to his brief.[52]

In another section of his brief, Covington expanded further his discussion of the proper standard to be applied in religious freedom cases. Quoting liberally from recent free speech cases, he argued that freedom of religion could be restricted only where its exercise gave rise to a "clear and present danger" to the community. Here again, the gist of the plea was that the various freedoms of the First Amendment should receive equal preference. In an obvious analogy to *Gitlow v. New York,* Covington acidly noted that the *Gobitis* decision had upheld the compulsory salute because of its possible *tendency* to produce desirable states of mind. He also pointed to the much greater tolerance shown by Congress in dealing with the more serious dangers created by German and Italian "enemy aliens" and conscientious objectors to the draft.

Non-religious constitutional objections.—Covington resurrected the argument in Moyle's Circuit Court brief in *Gobitis* that freedom of speech must include freedom not to utter repugnant expressions of belief. Again, the main reliance was on a comparison of the "crime" of non-saluting with the disloyal conduct given immunity in *Stromberg v. California*. In a related point, Covington likened the compulsory flag salute to the "test oaths" long since invalidated by the Court,[53] and called attention to *Kennedy v. Moscow* and *Reid v. Brookville*.

Covington also argued that the compulsory salute was simply an arbitrary and unreasonable restriction of individual liberty. In support of this position, he reproduced in full the substantive due process section of the Bill of Rights Committee's *Gobitis* brief, including the two hypothetical horrors pictured therein—a salute to some other symbol such as a national hero, and a salute by the whole population. In a related thrust, Covington devoted a whole section of his brief to the "inherent, constitutional and absolute power of the parent to direct the spiritual education of the child, and his power to direct the secular education of the child in public and private schools. . . ."[54] Borrowing directly from Moyle's Circuit Court brief in *Gobitis*, he cited *Pierce v. Society of Sisters* and all the favorable curriculum and Bible-reading cases.

The attack on Gobitis.—Covington devoted three full sections of his brief to a blistering attack on the decision and opinion in *Gobitis*. Equating Frankfurter's great deference to the legislative judgment with a determination that the legislature was the judge of its own powers, he cited *Schneider* and the *Carolene Products* footnote as sufficient refutation. He waxed especially bitter at

. . . the *new rule* that the citizen, regardless of how unpopular, oppressed and persecuted, must trust in the *majority* popular will to correct "foolish legislation" which admittedly violates the constitutional liberties of the people. . . .[55]

Likening Frankfurter's "self-restraint" to that of Pilate in dealing with Jesus, he charged the Court with abdicating its constitutional duty and making local school boards the supreme court of the nation.

The main thrust to Covington's argument was that *Gobitis* was condemned by the effects it had produced. Borrowing heavily from the Rotnem-Folsom article in the *American Political Science Review*, he pointed to the wave of anti-Witness persecution which had swept the country after that decision. Covington also noted the widespread attempts at prosecution of flag-salute expellees and their parents, and cited the many favorable appellate decisions the Witnesses had won in such cases. Also included at this point was a long list of law periodicals and newspapers which had criticized the *Gobitis* decisions.

Finally, Covington directed a short but sharp attack at the American Legion brief. Noting the Legion's apparent involvement in the anti-Witness violence, he charged that "The American Legion is not a non-partisan *amicus curiae*, but in this controversy has an active, un-American, self-serving and biased interest in opposing appellees. . . ."[56]

b) *The Bill of Rights Committee brief.*[57]—The *amicus curiae* brief of the American Bar Association's Committee on the Bill of Rights was filed in the Supreme Court on March 8, 1943,[58] after a considerable scramble. The first suggestion that the committee file a brief came only in January. In two hurried mail votes, the committee secured the approval of most of its members[59] and of the Association's Board of Governors.[60] One member of the committee, George L. Buist of South Carolina, was opposed on states'-rights grounds to the filing of a brief, and filed a lengthy protest with the Association.[61] The brief appears to have been written mainly by Professor Zechariah Chafee, Jr., of the Harvard Law School.[62]

Chafee's brief stressed the committee's exclusive interest in the question of freedom of conscience, explicitly eschewing any reliance on Public Law 623. Also omitted was the committee's previous reliance (in *Gobitis*) on substantive due process of law. The main brief divided into two parts, a restatement of the Committee's *Gobitis* brief, and a sharp attack on *Gobitis* on the basis of the ensuing public reaction thereto.

The Gobitis *argument restated.*—Chafee began by reiterating and strengthening the committee's earlier insistence that religious freedom in the constitutional sense was involved here; the rejection of the "secular regulation" rule here was made explicit: "[T]he compulsion of a child to participate in a ceremony which he considers idolatrous worship cannot be brushed aside as raising no issue of religious liberty."[63] Again, he emphasized the extremely dubious credentials of "morale" as a legislative end. He further pointed out that in general it is a more serious interference to force one to commit what he considers sacrilegious action than merely to prohibit the performance of what he considers his religious duty. He reiterated the committee's contention that the compulsion here at issue could be sustained only if found to be both appropriate and necessary to some end sufficiently urgent to outweigh the strong policy expressed in the First Amendment. Again it was urged that it was the compulsion of these children which must be justified. Chafee avoided the error of the Clark brief, however, asserting that there was no evidence that individual refusals, or some exemption arrangement, could adversely affect the efficacy of the flag ceremony.

In a direct assault on the bases of Frankfurter's *Gobitis* opinion, Chafee made a strong appeal for equal treatment of all First Amendment freedoms. He noted that in *Hague* and *Schneider*, the Court had rejected obviously *effective* devices where the legislative end could have been obtained by less restrictive means. Was the Court prepared to say that religious freedom was less important than freedom of speech? Chafee also slapped at Frankfurter's reliance on the political processes to correct abuses, noting the political helplessness of Jehovah's Witnesses. "Such a small religious group is very unlikely to attain sufficient voting power to overthrow compulsory flag salute laws. It must obtain protection from the Bill of Rights, or nowhere."[64]

The aftermath of Gobitis.—In the final section of his brief, Chafee marshalled various aspects of the public reaction to the *Gobitis* decision which tended to discredit it. First, attention was drawn to the overwhelming weight of law-review comment condemning the decision, the worst reception since *Adkins v. Children's Hospital*.[65] Chafee cited twenty-one law review comments, seventeen critical, two noncommital, and only two favorable to the decision. Also cited were seventeen comments written before *Gobitis*, of which twelve attacked the compulsory salute and only two defended it.

Next, Chafee pointed to the precarious position in which the *Gobitis* decision left the expelled children and their parents by making it "easy for school boards to take the first step in a process which would naturally end in imprisoning somebody unless the board was willing to let the law become a dead-letter."[66] He carefully noted that nothing in *Gobitis* precluded such additional punishment.

Finally, Chafee added detail to his tale of persecution and at the same time showed the treatment given the *Gobitis* precedent by the state courts, citing *Commonwealth v. Johnson, State v. Lefebvre, In re Jones, Matter of Reed, Commonwealth v. Nemchik, State v. Smith, Brown v. Skustad* and *Bolling v. Superior Court.* This sheer massing of materials conveyed the desired point—that the almost universal reaction of the state courts to the *Gobitis* decision had been to quarantine it.

Chafee closed sharply:

> Everybody recognizes that national unity is a great ideal, but the whole question is whether national unity has anything to do with the case. . . . The law does not require national unity and it could not. . . . What the law does require is the salute of the flag by children who regard such saluting as a damnable sin. . . . Everything turns on the question whether there is any *reasonable* connection between the enforced participation of the children in a sinful ceremony and the promotion of national unity. The more one looks squarely at facts and probabilities, the better he can see that there never was a reasonable connection.[67]

c) The American Civil Liberties Union brief.—The *amicus curiae* brief of the American Civil Liberties Union was written by William G. Fennell[68] and signed by him, Osmond K. Fraenkel and Arthur Garfield Hays of the ACLU New York office, and Howard B. Lee of West Virginia. Professor Gardner had flatly refused to sign the brief, contending that his presence would only make it harder for the Court—especially Frankfurter—to reverse its previous decision.[69] Fennell's position vis-à-vis the Witnesses was rather ambiguous at this time. He was a long-standing and bitterly outspoken opponent of the compulsory flag salute.[70] At the time of this litigation, however, he was also acting as legal counsel for Olin R. Moyle in his libel suit against the president and board of directors of the Watchtower Society.[71]

Fennell opened his brief with a strong plea that *Gobitis* be overruled, noting that a majority of the justices still on the Court who had participated in that case agreed with him. He further pointed to the rash of prosecutions brought against flag-salute expellees and their parents as vindicating Professor Gardner's argument on this point in his *Gobitis* brief. The main body of the brief was devoted to argument on the issues of religious freedom and Public Law 623.

Religious freedom.—Fennell began by covering some well-traveled ground, showing that religious freedom was protected by the Fourteenth Amendment, that the appellees' scruple was religious in nature, and that the "privilege" argument was inapplicable to these circumstances. He made three new points as to the standard to be applied. First, he sharply criticized Frankfurter's deference to the legislative judgment, denying that this was a mere issue of educational policy. "The State Board . . . is not trying *to educate* the children . . . in any true sense; it is admittedly trying *to compel* them to perform an act. . . ."[72] Second, he dismissed as unrealistic Frankfurter's reliance on the ballot box, citing as contrary authority Stone's *Carolene Products* footnote. Not only were Jehovah's Witnesses "discrete and insular"; they were the subject of active and widespread persecution. The ACLU pamphlet *Jehovah's Witnesses and the War* was attached to the brief as an appendix. Indeed, flag-salute regulations themselves had multiplied since *Gobitis*. "Pragmatically, this does not commend the doctrine that somehow legislative authorities will themselves abandon 'foolish legislation' if the 'effective means of inducing political changes are left free.' "[73] Finally, Fennell laid down what he considered the proper standard—the "clear and present danger" rule. Again, the Court was urged to give religious freedom the same preferred status as freedom of speech. Under such a standard, the regulation was clearly bad.

. . . If grown men can advocate doctrines tending to the overthrow of the government under the constitutional guaranty of freedom of speech (so long as their advocacy does not present a clear and present danger to society), it is absurd to say that the failure of school children to salute the flag presents any greater danger to public safety.[74]

Public Law 623.—Fennell argued that Public Law 623 had completely altered the legal situation existing at the time of *Gobitis*. In laying down a general federal standard governing flag respect—a topic of primary national concern—Congress had ousted all state power to deal with the subject. Primary reliance was placed on *Hines v. Davidowicz*.[75] Even should the Court hold that there was some room for state regulation, Fennell continued, the West Virginia regulation still was bad, as it was obviously inconsistent with the federal standard. In providing no penalties for non-compliance, Congress had expressed its intention to leave flag respect a voluntary affair. Furthermore, it had showed its willingness to accept standing at attention as "full respect." Finally, Fennell noted that the Civil Rights Section of the Justice Department had taken a similar stand.

3. ORAL ARGUMENT

Oral argument was heard in the *Barnette* case on March 11, 1943. A partial record of the argument has been preserved.[76] Wooddell spoke only briefly for the State Board of Education, pointing out that the flag-salute regulation was a general, non-discriminatory educational device of a sort fully indorsed by the *Gobitis* decision. No question was raised here, he argued, that had not already been answered decisively in *Gobitis*.

Hayden Covington spoke for appellees at some length and with considerable vigor. Universally described as a very eloquent speaker, he was then and still is noted for his natty dress, loud voice, almost calisthenic gestures, a truculent manner and a sublime disregard of consequences.[77] He came to Washington determined, win or lose, to give the Court "what for" for its *Gobitis* decision.[78] Covington described that decision as "one of the greatest mistakes that this Court has ever committed," rivaled in magnitude only by the *Dred Scott* case. He again charged that the Court had abdicated its constitutional duty. Calling it "human to err and divine to forgive," he invited the Court to take this opportunity to rectify its previous mistake. Covington particularly emphasized the "clear and presen danger" argument in his oral argument, noting that not even the appellants contended that the children's refusal to salute created such a danger. Pointing to the widespread anti-Witness persecution, he caustically suggested that the only "clear and present danger" created by non-saluting was that of physical violence directed at the non-saluter.

C. *The Decision:* Gobitis *Overruled*

On June 14, 1943—Flag Day—the Supreme Court handed down its decision in *West Virginia State Board of Education v. Barnette*,[79] affirming the decision below by a vote of six to three, and expressly overruling *Gobitis* and the earlier *per curiam* flag-salute dispositions. Justice Jackson delivered an opinion for the Court which was joined by all six members of the majority. Justices Black, Douglas and Murphy also concurred separately in two opinions. Justices Reed and Roberts briefly noted their dissent, and Justice Frankfurter wrote a long and vigorous dissenting opinion.

1. JUSTICE JACKSON FOR THE COURT

Justice Jackson's appearance as majority spokesman in *Barnette* came as a surprise to some, in view of the hostility manifested in his *Jeannette* concurrence. It is likely, however, that he came to the Court already strongly convinced of the wrongness of the *Gobitis* decision. It seems clear in retrospect that it was his "swing" vote which necessitated the odd treatment of that precedent in Reed's *Opelika* opinion.

Jackson's *Barnette* opinion was a peculiar one. For him, the case turned on a preliminary point *assumed* in the *Gobitis* case; most of Frankfurter's argument there became irrelevant. Yet, Jackson's whole opinion was cast as a point-by-point refutation of Frankfurter's reasoning. Thus, much of Jackson's most quotable language was only remotely relevant to the issues at hand.

Jackson made two preliminary points. First, he stressed a consideration which for him distinguished this case from the license tax cases: "The freedom asserted by these appellees does not bring them into collision with rights asserted by any other individual."[80] Second, he distinguished *Hamilton v. Regents* and brushed aside the "privilege" argument on grounds now familiar—the compulsory school laws and the state's special interest in militia service. The body of the opinion divides roughly into two parts: the attack on Frankfurter's *Gobitis* opinion, and Jackson's treatment of what he considered the central legal issue.[81]

a) The attack on Gobitis.—Jackson believed that Frankfurter's *Gobitis* opinion rested on four main arguments, which he proceeded to refute individually. First, he attacked Frankfurter's use of the Lincoln dilemma as a handy oversimplification which tended to resolve all issues in favor of the government. "Government of limited power need not be anemic government."[82] Second,

... It was also considered ... that functions of educational officers ... were such that to interfere with their authority "would in effect make us the school board for the country." ...
... There are village tyrants as well as village Hampdens, but none who acts under color of law is beyond the reach of the Constitution.[83]

Third, Jackson attacked Frankfurter's caveats regarding the limits of judicial competence in educational matters and the desirability of settling policy conflicts in the political rather than the judicial arena so long as the political channels remained unobstructed. Like Stone, Jackson considered this no more than an apology for judicial abdication. "The very purpose of a Bill of Rights was to withdraw certain subjects from the vicissitudes of political controversy, to place them beyond the reach of majorities. . . ."[84] Nor could the Court avoid constitutional questions simply because of lack of special expertise: "[W]e act in these matters not by authority of our competence but by force of our commissions."[85] In place of Frankfurter's limited relaxation of judicial self-restraint in cases involving the integrity of the political process, Jackson advanced a strong formulation of the new "preferred freedoms" position of the majority of the Court. Restrictions of freedom of speech, press and religion were to be weighed by different standards than restrictions on ordinary economic interests.

... Much of the vagueness of the due process clause disappears when the specific prohibitions of the First [Amendment] become its standard. . . . They are susceptible of restriction only to prevent grave and immediate danger to interests which the state may lawfully protect. It is important to note that while it is the Fourteenth Amendment which bears directly upon the State it is the more specific limiting principles of the First Amendment that finally govern this case.[86]

Jackson's arguments were all good statements of existing law, but their relevance here was remote. Certainly there was no perceptible difference between him and Frankfurter except on the "preferred freedoms" doctrine, which Frankfurter had strongly opposed. The point is this: all the challenged passages from Frankfurter's opinion related to the question of substantive due process, while all of Jackson's "refutations" related to First Amendment freedoms. There was no real joinder of argument.

. . . Lastly, and this is the very heart of the Gobitis opinion, it reasons that "national unity is the basis of national security," [and] that the authorities have "the right to select appropriate means for its attainment." . . .[87]

It was in his response to this last point that Jackson delivered his opinion on the constitutional merits of the *Barnette* case.

b) The constitutional merits.—Jackson explicitly excluded questions of religious freedom from his discussion. "It is not necessary to inquire whether non-conformist beliefs will exempt from the duty to salute unless we first find power to make the salute a legal duty."[88] In short, could West Virginia compel *any* student to salute the flag? This power had been assumed in *Gobitis*. Jackson thus completed the distinction of this case from *Murdock*. It is quite clear that Jackson, unlike the other majority justices here, was unwilling to jettison the "secular regulation" rule. Furthermore, Jackson dismissed as irrelevant the general desirability of the flag-salute ceremony, tacitly accepting the Bill of Rights Committee's assertion that the salute was no different in kind from a salute to a leader. "If official power exists to coerce acceptance of any patriotic creed, what it shall contain cannot be decided by courts. . . ."[89]

Turning to the ceremony itself, Jackson drew a sharp distinction between *educational* devices, such as instruction in American history, and *rituals* such as this one; like Stone, he had no doubt as to the state's power to require pupil attendance on the former. He noted the dubious educational credentials of the ceremony, citing the depressing results of the Olander survey. In short, the flag-salute controversy involved not merely an issue of educational policy, but a compulsory ritual, raising issues transcending the educational sphere.

Jackson's starting point in considering the main issue was the obvious proposition that the salute and pledge involved "a form of utterance,"[90] and embodied an "affirmation of a belief and an attitude of mind."[91] The pledge, in particular, contained assertions which were certainly debatable. "It would seem," he commented, "that involuntary affirmation could be commanded only on even more immediate and urgent grounds than silence."[92]

At this point, Jackson's opinion made a logical jump which greatly impaired its over-all clarity. So far, he had been following essentially the rationale of Stone's *Gobitis* dissent: to compel expression of an obnoxious doctrine was in effect a punishment for belief, and hence indistinguishable *in kind* from direct compulsion of belief. Here, however, Jackson seemed to say that compulsory expression of belief was *the same thing* as compulsion of belief. He referred repeatedly to compulsion as a means of attaining national unity and "struggles to coerce uniformity of sentiment."[93] The fact is, of course, that nobody was asking the Witness children to *believe* anything; if they had been willing to give formal compliance with the flag regulations, this case would not have been in court. The beneficial effects were expected to come not from the particular content of the pledge, but from the total impact of the ceremony.[94] Also, Jackson seems to have ignored the very real distinction between the compulsions properly applicable to children and those applicable to adults. These weaknesses are unfortunate, since they were in no way essential to his main argument.

Whether the compulsory salute be viewed as a punishment of belief, or a compulsion thereof, Jackson was clear that it could not stand; it was alien both in theory and practical implications.

. . . As governmental pressure toward unity becomes greater, so strife becomes more bitter as to whose unity it shall be. Probably no deeper division of our people could proceed from any provocation than from finding it necessary to choose what doctrine and whose program public educational officials shall compel youth to unite in embracing. . . . Those who begin coercive elimination of dissent soon find themselves exterminating dissenters. . . .[95]

Jackson closed with some of the most quotable language in modern judicial literature:

> If there is any fixed star in our constitutional constellation, it is that no official, high or petty, can prescribe what shall be orthodox in politics, nationalism, religion, or other matters of opinion or force citizens to confess by word or act their faith therein. If there are any circumstances which permit an exception, they do not now occur to us.
>
> We think the action of the local authorities in compelling the flag salute and pledge transcends constitutional limitations on their power and invades the sphere of intellect and spirit which it is the purpose of the First Amendment to our Constitution to reserve from all official control.[96]

2. CONCURRING OPINIONS

While Justices Black, Douglas and Murphy explicitly joined in the Jackson opinion, they felt impelled to write two separate opinions as well. Probably more important than the natural self-consciousness of one who has just publicly switched sides was a desire to re-emphasize the new majority opinion on religious freedom, which certainly was applicable here.

a) *Black and Douglas.*—After a brief "explanation" of their *Gobitis* votes, Black and Douglas set forth what they considered the proper rule governing religious freedom cases:

> . . . Religious faiths, honestly held, do not free individuals from responsibility to conduct themselves obediently to laws which are either imperatively necessary to protect society as a whole from grave and pressingly imminent dangers or which . . . merely regulate time, place or manner of religious activity. Decision as to the constitutionality of particular laws which strike at the substance of religious tenets and practices must be made by this Court. . . .[97]

Under this standard, the decision was easy; the children's refusal to salute created no "grave danger to the nation."[98] In the closing passages of their opinion, the two justices gave a clue as to their motivation in switching sides, describing the compulsory ceremony as "a form of test oath,"[99] and "a handy implement for disguised religious persecution."[100]

b) *Murphy.*—Justice Murphy's concurring opinion opened with a strong panegyric on religious freedom. "Reflection has convinced me that as a judge, I have no loftier duty than to uphold that spiritual freedom to its farthest reaches."[101] Perhaps sensing difficulties in the application of the "clear and present danger" test in this area, he came up with another standard, at once broader and more cautious:

The right of freedom of thought and of religion as guaranteed by the Constitution against State action includes both the right to speak freely and the right to refrain from speaking at all, except in so far as essential operations of government may require it for the preservation of an orderly society,—as in the case of compulsion to give evidence in court. . . . I am unable to agree that the benefits that may accrue to society from the compulsory flag salute are sufficiently definite and tangible to justify the invasion of freedom and privacy that is entailed. . . .[102]

3. JUSTICE FRANKFURTER DISSENTING

Justice Frankfurter's lone dissenting opinion in *Barnette* is best described as a prolonged and very personal cry of outrage. Not only had the majority decided wrongly and maligned a Frankfurter opinion; they had violated the proprieties of judging itself. Frankfurter lectured his brethren—the tone of the opinion precludes any other description—on the law and their duty as judges in a manner reminiscent of his classroom days at Harvard. It is hardly surprising that Justices Reed and Roberts were content to indicate their continued adherence to Frankfurter's *Gobitis* opinion.[103] Frankfurter's argument divided into three main categories: limiting the issues, judicial self-restraint and the constitutional merits.[104]

a) Limiting the issues.—Frankfurter was at great pains to point out the limited nature of any infringement on liberty in this case. No attempt at further punishment of expellees or parents was before the Court, he insisted. Furthermore, the West Virginia regulation must be considered in the light of the obvious desirability of the flag salute and pledge. "The significance of a symbol lies in what it represents. To reject the swastika does not imply rejection of the Cross."[105] Abandoning his previous reticence, Frankfurter flatly invoked the "privilege" argument. Ignoring the practical realities he had recognized in his *Gobitis* opinion, he treated as decisive the fact that West Virginia did not and could not require children to attend the public schools; those who objected to the salute could get their education elsewhere.

b) *Judicial self-restraint.*—Justice Frankfurter began his opinion by emphasizing the importance of judicial detachment.

. . . It can never be emphasized too much that one's own opinion about the wisdom or evil of a law should be excluded altogether when one is doing one's duty on the bench. The only opinion of our own even looking in that direction that is material is our opinion whether legislators could in reason have enacted such a law.[106]

. . . Tact, respect, and generosity toward variant views will always commend themselves to those charged with the duties of legislation. . . . But the real question is, who is to make such accommodations, the courts or the legislature?[107]

He then set out at some length the history of the Court's involvement in the flag-salute controversy, stressing the embarrassing fact that every justice except Jackson and Rutledge had voted at least once to uphold what was now struck down.

. . . The Court has no reason for existence if it merely reflects the pressures of the day. . . . We are dealing with matters as to which legislators and voters have conflicting views. . . . [W]hat thirteen Justices found to be within the constitutional authority of a state, legislators cannot be deemed unreasonable in enacting. . . . [S]ome other tests . . . must surely be guiding the Court than the absence of a rational justification for the legislation. But I know of no other test which this Court is authorized to apply in nullifying legislation.[108]

Frankfurter specifically denounced the "preferred freedoms" doctrine. "The Constitution does not give us greater veto power when dealing with one phase of 'liberty' than with another. . . . In no instance is this Court the primary protector of the particular liberty. . . ."[109] For Frankfurter, First Amendment freedoms had no greater intrinsic "importance" than ordinary procedural due process of law or the privilege against unreasonable searches and seizures.[110] "Of course patriotism cannot be enforced by flag salute. But neither can the liberal spirit be enforced by judicial invalidation of illiberal legislation."[111] Frankfurter closed his opinion with a repetition of his 1929 argument against judicial review—that courts are not the proper agents of liberalism, and that excessive concentration on the issue of constitutionality could only lead to the atrophy of the liberal spirit.

c) The constitutional merits.—Frankfurter did not deal at any length with Jackson's freedom of thought argument; his only references thereto were buried in his long argument on religious freedom. Actually, he differed with Jackson only with respect to the application of his principles to the present regulation, which he believed different in kind from any compulsion of belief.

> . . . Compelling belief implies denial of opportunity to combat it and to assert dissident views. Such compulsion is one thing. Quite another matter is submission to conformity of action while denying its wisdom or virtue and with ample opportunity for seeking its change or abrogation.[112]
>
> . . . Saluting the flag suppresses no belief nor curbs it. . . . It is not even remotely suggested that the requirement . . . involves the slightest restriction against the fullest opportunity on the part of both the children and of their parents to disavow as publicly as they choose . . . the meaning that others attach to the gesture of salute. . . .[113]

On the same basis, Frankfurter rejected any analogy with the old religious test oaths. It is suggested that the distinction may have been more apparent than real in practice. The beauty and vice of the old test oaths was that they could be demanded of all alike, yet would automatically select out and punish the desired victims. The spawning of new flag-salute regulations after *Gobitis,* and cases like *Kennedy v. Moscow* tend to make the analogy more persuasive yet.

Frankfurter concentrated most of his fire on the religious freedom standard laid down in the concurring opinions, which he considered much more dangerous, and which probably had majority support on the Court at this time. He began by summarizing the old law on the subject, phrasing and rephrasing the "secular regulation" rule, as if incredulous that his brethren could fail to comprehend:

> The constitutional protection of religious freedom terminated disabilities, it did not create new privileges. . . .
>
> The essence of the religious freedom guaranteed by our Constitution is therefore this: no religion shall either receive the state's

support or incur its hostility. Religion is outside the sphere of political government. . . . Much that is the concern of temporal authority affects the spiritual interests of men. But it is not enough to strike down a non-discriminatory law that it may hurt or offend some dissident view. . . . It is only in a theocratic state that ecclesiastical doctrines measure legal right or wrong.[114]

Second, Frankfurter struck out at the standard which his brethren proposed to substitute for the traditional one, an innovation which would involve the Court in the very "legislative" considerations he was most anxious to shut out.

Conscientious scruples, all would admit, cannot stand against every legislative compulsion to do positive acts in conflict with such scruples. We have been told that such compulsions override religious scruples only as to major concerns of the state. *But the determination of what is major and what is minor itself raises questions of policy.* . . . Judges should be very diffident in setting their judgment against that of a state in determining what is and is not a major concern, what means are appropriate . . . and what is the total social cost. . . . [Italics supplied.][115]

Third, Frankfurter warned the majority that it was opening a veritable Pandora's Box of troubles in jettisoning the "secular regulation" rule. What of parents who objected to all patriotic instruction, the teaching of evolution, Bible reading, etc., in the schools? What of the relation of parochial schools to the public school system? What of Jehovah's Witnesses' new troubles with the child labor laws, soon to come before the Court? Was the Court prepared to handle these cases and others that must come in their train with only the interest-weighing approach for a guide? In short, Frankfurter warned that the majority was asking for trouble in giving constitutional sanction to the particular scruples of each of the more than 250 sects operating in the United States.

D. *Concluding Remarks*

It is interesting to contrast the course of this litigation with that in *Gobitis*. In *Gobitis*, there was a hard-fought trial, with bitter wrangling over every possible legal point the school board could bring to bear. As decisions went against it, the board sought by supersedeas to stave off until the last possible moment the readmission of any Witness children. In *Barnette*, the case proceeded on admitted jurisdiction and facts. Counsel for the State Board relied doggedly on a single defense of doubtful vitality. Finally, the Board complied immediately with the first adverse decision. While there may be a number of explanations for this contrast—e.g., the necessarily more impersonal atmosphere of a class action—one reason stands out. The resounding lack of enthusiasm, sometimes approaching open distaste, shown by almost everybody on the State Board's side of the case, has already been mentioned. Obviously, some people in West Virginia felt strongly about the flag salute, else there would have been no regulation and no expulsions. One is left with the net impression, however, that the West Virginia authorities reached out rather mechanically to take the new opportunities *Gobitis* seemed to offer them. At no time did they display the sort of driving personal conviction that was evident in the Pennsylvania conflicts. When challenged in court, they were willing to play the game out to the end, but with no deep personal involvement in the outcome. Nobody really *cared*.

Also noteworthy was the negligible influence of the briefs and oral argument in this case. It is clear in retrospect that both the Supreme Court and the members of the three-judge tribunal below were ready and eager to overrule *Gobitis*, needing only an opportunity. It is unlikely that a single vote was changed by the arguments in the briefs. Nor were the briefs and arguments much more influential on the rhetoric in which the decisions were couched; they were ignored almost completely. While Jackson did borrow some points from the Bill of Rights Committee's brief, this seems to have been a matter less of conversion than of convenience.

Further accentuating the irrelevance of the briefs and argument is the fact that the final decision in *Barnette* proceeded on a ground that had been neither urged nor argued by the parties.[116] The reason is clear enough. Only five justices were prepared to hold that Jehovah's Witnesses did not have to salute the flag; six were ready to say that *nobody* had to. Jackson obviously had strong and long-matured ideas on the subject of freedom of thought,[117] and was eager for an opportunity to put them into judicial writing. This zeal would explain in part his willingness to cram them willy-nilly into the confining framework of the *Barnette* case.

Finally, notice must be taken of the acrimony pervading the Supreme Court opinions in this case. It is rather unusual for a court in overruling a previous decision to accompany the action with a detailed, vigorous and rather unfair attack on the *opinion* in the case being overturned.[118] Indeed, Jackson's discussion of *Gobitis* was couched in a superior tone that would have been hard to take even aside from the distortions. Frankfurter, as we have seen, replied in kind, dissenting in terms that drove away even his fellow dissenters. The decision to attack the *Gobitis* opinion must be attributed almost entirely to Jackson. While much of his basic argument was based on Stone's *Gobitis* dissent, the arrangement and phrasing seemed to reflect a writer who had read the *Gobitis* opinion repeatedly, been thoroughly irritated by it, and spent long hours composing rebuttals to its more obnoxious points. In spending so much unnecessary effort on the *Gobitis* opinion, Jackson may have been making up for his lack of opportunity to dissent from the original decision. There was little disposition among the majority justices to oppose Jackson's course. All were eager to give *Gobitis* as public and emphatic a burial as possible. Stone, who was not altogether happy with the Jackson opinion,[119] had the compensating satisfaction of seeing his earlier dissenting views adopted and expanded. Nor can the personal factor be ignored; Frankfurter's relations during this period with his colleagues were such that it could not have grieved them to see one of his opinions picked apart.[120]

CHAPTER ELEVEN

AFTER *BARNETTE*

THE FLAG-SALUTE CONTROVERSY IN RETROSPECT

A. *Epilogue: Public Reception of the* Barnette *Decision*

1. PRESS REACTION

a) *Law reviews.*—Of seven law review comments dealing wholly or in part with the District Court decision in *Barnette,* six were tacitly or explicitly favorable as to the merits of the holding,[1] while one was noncommittal.[2] The six comments dealing at length with the decision centered their attention on the question of whether a lower federal court should defy an unreversed but clearly obsolete decision, or follow it until the Supreme Court itself made the change. Four comments concluded that the District Court's action had been proper in the unusual circumstances existing at the time,[3] while two held that that court had acted unwisely.[4]

Of fourteen comments on the Supreme Court decision appearing in twelve law periodicals, nine comments were favorable,[5] two were unfavorable[6] and three expressed no opinion.[7] Both unfavorable comments treated the decision as a religious freedom one. One writer, in the *George Washington Law Review,*[8] interpreted the *Gobitis* opinion as a holding that national security outweighed the religious freedom claim involved. She then construed the *Barnette* opinion to hold that because the Witnesses had religious scruples against the salute, nobody could be required to participate. This unfortunate mixture of doctrines needs no further comment. Similar confusion, in less extreme form, was present in the unfavorable comment in the *Georgia Bar Journal.*[9] The writer quoted Frankfurter's opinion on judical self-restraint and the "secular regulation" rule, but treated the *latter* passage as a complete answer to the majority opinion.

Of the favorable comments, only two gave wholly satisfactory accounts of the Jackson rationale.[10] Outstanding was the outspokenly favorable article by Louis Boudin in the *Lawyers Guild Review*.[11] This article was especially interesting in that Boudin, like Jackson, indorsed the "secular regulation" rule and thought that the *Murdock* case was wrongly decided. Boudin seems to have been the only writer to draw a sharp distinction between the issues in the license tax cases and those in the flag-salute litigation. Two comments concentrated their attention on the debate between Frankfurter and Jackson regarding the "preferred position" of First Amendment freedoms, paying little attention to the central holding.[12] Three, while touching on Jackson's main argument, did not seem fully to grasp the point, tying the freedom of thought theme to the "clear and present danger" test, religious rights, etc.[13] One comment asserted that Jackson had held that religious scruples could not be forced to yield to compulsion in the absence of a clear and present danger.[14] One was generally favorable, with no elaboration on the opinions.[15] Three of these comments interpreted Frankfurter's *Gobitis* opinion as holding that national unity was more important than religious liberty.[16]

b) Magazines.—Comment in general circulation magazines was somewhat more plentiful on *Barnette* than it had been on *Gobitis*. *Time* praised the decision under the heading, "Blot Removed."[17] David Lawrence, in *United States News* called the Jackson opinion "a masterful presentation of the far-reaching implications of the Bill of Rights."[18] Neither article dealt at all clearly with the central issue; *Time* in particular seemed to consider this primarily a religious freedom decision. The *New Republic* again carried the most thorough treatment of the issues, a long article by Thomas Reed Powell.[19] Showing his usual good grasp of the issues—he was the only writer in this category fully to perceive Jackson's point—Powell sharply attacked Frankfurter's insistence that the Court show the same self-restraint in civil liberties as in economic regulation cases. He also had some criticism for the bickering which marked the Jackson and Frankfurter opinions.

As in chapter vii, the survey of religious periodicals has been limited to the two extremes of the spectrum of opinion, as regards attitudes toward Jehovah's Witnesses—Catholic and liberal Protestant journals. *Christian Century* had a strongly favorable editorial characterizing Jackson's freedom of conscience passage as language "which should become part of the 'American Scriptures,' to be memorized and taken to heart by every patriot."[20] The writer seemed to have a fairly clear picture of the basic rationale of the Jackson opinion. A short article in *Catholic Action* was rather vague in its praise of *Barnette*, but sharp in its criticism of Frankfurter's judicial self-restraint argument and his reliance in *Gobitis* on the importance of national unity.[21] An editorial in *America*[22] expressed general approval of the decision, and quoted at length fom the favorable treatment in the *Georgetown Law Journal*.[23] Favorable comment from Catholic legal writers in that journal and *Jurist*[24] has been mentioned in the opening subsection of this chapter.

The *Barnette* decision, effecting as it did a major change in existing school law, attracted considerable comment in education journals. *Nation's Schools* carried a strongly favorable article which showed an excellent understanding of the issues involved.[25] Harry N. Rosenfeld, himself an attorney, took particular pains to attack the judicial self-restraint argument in Frankfurter's *Gobitis* opinion. Two other journals treated the decision in very general terms but with tacit approval.[26] Five other comments were strictly noncommittal.[27] Two of these erroneously pictured the decision as a holding that the compulsory salute violated religious liberty.[28]

c) *Newspapers.*—As in chapter vii, the study of newspaper reaction to *Barnette* has been limited to a survey of *immediate* reactions—within several weeks after the decision. In all, thirty-two papers were checked. Of these, thirteen had no immediate editorial comment on the decision.[29]

Of the nineteen papers having editorial comment on the decision itself, fourteen were favorable,[30] four critical[31] and one ambiguous.[32] The ambiguous item was a column in the *New York Journal-American*[33] criticizing the Court for its vacillation on the flag-salute issue. There was no clear indication which decision the author preferred; it was the inconsistency which bothered him.

All four unfavorable comments seem to have treated the *Barnette* decision as a religious freedom holding. The *Washington Evening Star* relied squarely on the "secular regulation" rule:

. . . [T]here will be grave doubts as to the wisdom of the Court's action in overriding the judgment of the State Legislature to hold that compliance with a reasonable regulation, applied almost universally to promote good citizenship, depends on nothing more than the whim of the individual. By that logic the dissidents become the rule-makers and no regulation is safe.[34]

The other three comments, while making some vague reference to the "secular regulation" rule, rested mainly on expressions of hostility toward non-saluters. For example:

. . . [W]ith difficulty the public will understand why disdain of the United States flag is not a punishable offense. . . . If at any time in our history respect for the flag and all it stands for is indicated, now is the time. . . . It [the salute] is a patriotic routine which anyone who lives under the American flag and receives its protective advantages should be willing to accept. . . .[35]

Fourteen papers carried sixteen favorable comments on the decision; three were in the *New York Times*.[36] The only comment explicitly recognizing the broad, non-religious sweep of the Jackson holding appeared in the *Detroit Free Press*.[37] Five comments treated *Barnette* as a religious freedom decision,[38] and a sixth skirted the very edge of the same error.[39] Four comments rested their approval of the decision on opposition to the compulsory salute as a *policy*;[40] this was a strong secondary theme in four other comments.[41] Three comments emphasized and praised the tolerance displayed by the Court in upholding the rights of such an unpopular minority in wartime.[42] For example:

That a democracy, in time of war, and at a time of intense patriotic emotions, could excuse any resident from saluting its flag is impressive evidence of the high regard in which the Bill of Rights is held in this country. . . .[43]

Two other comments mentioned this aspect of the situation in passing.[44] Finally, three comments expressed general satisfaction with the decision, concentrating their detailed discussion on new denunciations of the *Gobitis* holding.[45] It is worth noting that among the papers commenting favorably on *Barnette*, there was one that had approved *Gobitis*,[46] two which had taken ambiguous editorial stands,[47] and four which had accepted the earlier decision with reservations about the wisdom of the policy involved.[48]

2. PERSECUTION OF JEHOVAH'S WITNESSES

For the variation through time of various forms of anti-Witness persecution up to the end of 1943, the reader is referred to the charts in chapter vii. It will be recalled that the persecution in most categories had greatly subsided by the end of 1942. No category of overt persecution seems to have reflected any impact from the *Barnette* ruling. The contrast with the aftermath of *Gobitis* is obvious and striking. The slight increase in violence at the end of 1943 would seem to belie any beneficial effect, but was too remote in time from the decision to be considered a direct result thereof.

Only one interim persecution situation reached an appellate court after June, 1943. This was the Mathews-Kelly injunction case from West Virginia. On October 18, 1943, the Supreme Court remanded the case of *Mathews v. West Virginia ex rel. Hamilton*[49] to the Calhoun County Circuit Court for reconsideration in the light of *Barnette* and *Taylor v. Mississippi*.[50]

Again it must be emphasized that Jehovah's Witnesses' troubles with mobs and local authorities did not miraculously end in 1943. Sporadic physical violence, often involving American Legionnaires, continues to occur.[51] As late as 1953, the Witnesses' troubles with various local ordinances were showing up on the Supreme Court's docket.[52] But 1943 seems to have seen the last of the special *concentrations* of persecution. Since then, conflicts involving the Witnesses have furnished a sort of casual undertone to the daily witness work.

3. THE PATTERN OF COMPLIANCE: LEGAL DEVELOPMENTS

The *Barnette* decision established once and for all the constitutional invalidity of the compulsory flag salute. Further legal developments were controlled by this threshold fact. The same day *Barnette* was decided, the Court also decided *Taylor v. Mississippi*,[53] unanimously reversing the convictions of several Witnesses under that state's sedition law. If non-saluting was constitutionally protected, its advocacy could hardly be made criminal. In September, 1943, the Oklahoma Criminal Court of Appeals unanimously reversed the various convictions pending under that state's law punishing anyone "hindering" the carrying out of the flag ceremonial.[54] In July, 1943, the South Dakota Supreme Court reversed the school law conviction of a Witness whose child had been expelled for refusal to salute the flag; under *Barnette*, it was ruled, the expulsion had been improper.[55] In January, 1944, the Pennsylvania Superior Court reversed two school law convictions of similar origin, one of which had been handed down in defiance of *Barnette*.[56] Mention was made in chapter iv of Daniel Morgan's dismissal as a state motor vehicle inspector because of his sons' refusal to salute the flag. On April 14, 1944, the New Jersey Supreme Court ruled that the dismissal had violated state civil service regulations. Under *Barnette*, it was held, neither the children's refusal nor his indorsement thereof could serve as legal cause for dismissal.[57] Late in that year, the Colorado Supreme Court unanimously struck down a local flag-salute regulation, and held that the complaining Witnesses were entitled to an injunction against further enforcement thereof.[58] Finally, in 1945, the California Third District Court of Appeals reversed a divorce decree denying a Witness custody of her children because of her views regarding the flag salute.[59] The willingness of the state courts to apply the *Barnette* ruling to the full limit of its logic contrasts sharply with the air of distaste and embarrassment attending many determinations under *Gobitis*.

There was no general rush on the part of states with flag-salute laws to amend or repeal them. Only New Jersey amended its flag-salute statute to allow conscientious objectors merely to stand at attention during the ceremony;[60] other state flag laws remained unchanged in the latest statutory compilations.[61] Actually, there was nothing in the flag-salute laws as they stood which required that they be mandatory on the pupils. Most states, therefore, were content to apply the same laws in a new way. Late in 1943, the Oklahoma State Superintendent of Education rescinded his 1941 order authorizing the expulsion of non-saluters.[62] In later years, the attorneys general of Massachusetts and Colorado issued official opinions holding that the flag salute could not be required of any pupil, whatever his reason for refusing.[63]

Attempts to enforce the salute requirement did not die out altogether immediately after *Barnette*. New Jersey school authorities were openly defiant, denouncing the Supreme Court's ruling and announcing their intention to continue demanding the salute.[64] The Department of Justice received single complaints of continued flag-salute enforcement from Maryland and—for the first time—Oregon. The persistence of the issue in Colorado has already been noted. Undoubtedly trouble continued in scattered localities in many states. On the whole, however, state and local compliance with the *Barnette* ruling was immediate and substantial. Official enthusiasm for the salute seems to have been falling off in many areas long before *Barnette* reached the Supreme Court.[65] The compulsory salute had been dead in West Virginia since the District Court decision. Lillian and William Gobitis were by now beyond the compulsory school age, but the Minersville school board moved promptly, if unenthusiastically, to readmit three other Gobitis children expelled between 1940 and 1943.[66] The dearth of Witness complaints to the Justice Department about flag-salute expulsions, together with the almost total absence of new litigation, strongly suggests that Witness children were being readmitted to school in most localities without incident.

In November, 1943, the Department of Justice sent out a circular to all United States attorneys which has remained the Department's standard pronouncement on religious freedom matters.[67] The immediately relevant portion reads as follows:

... It has been reported to the Department that local school board officials are refusing to follow the clear mandate of the *West Virginia State Board of Education* case ... and are continuing to expel children who have asserted conscientious objections to the participation in flag salute exercises.

The Department does not desire to institute wholesale prosecutions against over-zealous public officials. ... Prosecutive action should be reserved for those cases where that remains the only means of alleviating the situation. When, therefore, complaints of interferences with religious liberty by state officials are called to your attention, you are requested to contact the appropriate, responsible state officials, pointing out to them the possibility that their actions may involve a denial of constitutional guarantees and seek their cooperation. . . .[68]

Thus, it was rendered certain that over the course of time the compulsory flag salute would be eliminated everywhere in the United States by the usual threat of litigation together with the steady application of federal pressure.

B. *Later Years:* Barnette *as a Precedent*

The *Barnette* decision settled the flag-salute controversy, apparently permanently; the issue has not arisen again since 1946.[69] In this aspect, as has been noted, *Barnette* was applied willingly and to the full extent of its logic by the state courts. But a decision is more than a mere holding. What has become of the general doctrines of the *Barnette* case since 1943?

It has been pointed out already that much of Jackson's freedom of thought argument was somewhat out of place in the *Barnette* circumstances. Ironically, when an occasion finally arose in which Jackson's reasoning was directly in point and should have been controlling, it was passed over by an evenly divided Court. In *American Communications Association v. Douds*,[70] the Court upheld by default that part of the Taft-Hartley non-communist oath requiring union officers to swear that they did not believe in or belong to any organization believing in the forcible overthrow of the government. Not since 1943 has Jackson's main *Barnette* holding figured in a majority opinion of the Supreme Court.[71]

The subsequent development of the Supreme Court's standard for religious freedom cases has been more ambiguous and demands somewhat more extended treatment. The "secular regulation" rule may have been dead *de facto* in 1943, but it has never received a formal burial in an explicit majority holding. Justice Douglas' foggy rhetoric in *Murdock* was and remains inadequate to that purpose.[72] At the end of 1943, the "secular regulation" rule still maintained a bare existence, in uneasy propinquity with a variety of standards rejecting the old practice and weighing interests with varying degrees of severity against the state, ranging from Stone's almost neutral approach in *Gobitis* to the extreme "clear and present danger" formulation in the Black-Douglas *Barnette* concurrence. In 1944 and 1945, four colorable religious freedom cases reached the opinion writing stage in the Supreme Court, three of them peripheral to the main doctrinal issue. *Follett v. McCormick*,[73] while decided wholly on religious freedom grounds, merely extended the *Murdock* precedent, adding no new analysis. In *United States v. Ballard*,[74] a mail fraud case, a majority held that the trial judge had acted properly in excluding any inquiry into the verity of Ballard's religious claims but allowing consideration of his alleged bad faith. Three justices dissented from the first holding; Justice Jackson, on the other hand, would have extended his *Barnette* holding to require dismissal of the whole prosecution, on the ground that the good faith of a believer could not practically be considered separately from the validity of the belief. In *Re Summers*,[75] the Court voted five to four to uphold the action of the Illinois bar examiners in excluding a pacifist from the state bar (the underlying theory being that he could not in good faith "support" the state constitution with its references to militia service). The majority opinion contributed nothing new to the discussion of standards, resting entirely on the *Schwimmer* and *Macintosh* precedents.[76] Justices Black, Douglas, Murphy and Rutledge invoked both the majority and concurring opinions in *Barnette* in support of reversal. Finally, in *Prince v. Massachusetts*,[77] the Court upheld the child labor conviction of a Witness who permitted her two young charges—also Witnesses—to sell tracts on the street at night. Justice Rutledge's majority opinion, while considerably less than clear, seemed to apply an interest-weighing standard closely akin to that in Stone's *Gobitis* dissent, emphasizing the especially broad power exercised by the state over its children and concluding that religious rights must yield to the strong public interest expressed under the child labor laws. Justice Murphy would have reversed under the Black-Douglas standard; three concurring justices introduced still another standard—born of the *Murdock* disputation—whether or not a religious activity affected non-members of the sect involved.

Between 1945 and 1961, nothing of consequence happened.[78] Justice Frankfurter's expressed fear of a flood of religious freedom litigation failed to take account of the Supreme Court's power to control its own case-load. In that period, the Court dismissed appeals or denied certiorari in religious freedom cases involving draft resistance,[79] incitement to same,[80] zoning ordinances as applied to churches,[81] compulsory education,[82] polygamy,[83] infant blood transfusion over parents' objection,[84] compulsory vaccination of school children,[85] snake handling,[86] denial of unemployment compensation to an objector to Saturday work,[87] application of minimum wage legislation to a religious corporation,[88] and licensing of solicitors for religious charities.[89]

Thus, for fifteen years, state and lower federal courts were left pretty free to make their own choice of standards. The federal Courts of Appeals, to the extent that they took any clear position, generally chose to stick by the "secular regulation" rule.[90] No decision openly adopted any form of interest-weighing approach, and only one decision even recognized any necessity to distinguish *Barnette* and related decisions.[91] The picture is more complex at the state level. Washington and Kansas, it will be recalled, had committed themselves to some sort of interest-weighing approach during the flag-salute controversy. Washington reaffirmed this commitment in extreme "clear and present danger" terms in 1952,[92] then obscured it in 1960.[93] New York clearly committed itself to straight interest-weighing in the Stone manner;[94] Indiana,[95] Tennessee[96] and Texas[97] (in descending order of clarity) showed leanings in the same direction. Alabama,[98] California,[99] Illinois,[100] Kentucky,[101] Louisiana,[102] Maryland,[103] Ohio,[104] and Virginia[105] placed themselves quite firmly in the "secular regulation" camp, with Massachusetts[106] and Utah[107] leaning the same way. The religious freedom decisions in Florida,[108] Georgia,[109] Missouri[110] and North Carolina[111] were too ambiguous to permit classification as to the standard utilized; those in New Jersey[112] and Pennsylvania[113] leaned simultaneously in contradictory directions. Whatever the standard applied, the way of the religiously motivated law violator remained hard. Aside from zoning conflicts—where the cases were in hopeless confusion[114]—and one discredited lower court holding,[115] all decisions went against the religious objector.

Finally, in 1961, the Supreme Court found it necessary to deal with the constitutionality of the state Sunday laws in *Braunfeld v. Brown*[116] and *Gallagher v. Crown Kosher Super Market;*[117] in the latter case a federal District Court had held the statute unconstitutional as applied. In each case, the challenge came from Orthodox Jews who claimed that the law combined with their religion to compel them to observe two sabbaths, to their severe economic detriment. The Court voted six to three to reject this challenge. Chief Justice Warren's prevailing opinion laid great stress on the indirect and incidental nature of the burden imposed here on the exercise of religion; in these circumstances, he felt free to apply a modified form of the "secular regulation" rule:

. . . [I]f the State regulates conduct by enacting a general law within its power, the purpose and effect of which is to advance the State's secular goals, the statute is valid, despite its indirect burden on religious observances unless the State may achieve its purpose by means which do not impose such a burden. . . .[118]

Warren's single qualification was largely vitiated by the very great benefit of the doubt which he gave the state in determining that other forms of sabbath regulation—e.g., a prohibition exempting those observing some other day of the week— "might well undermine the State's goal of providing a day that, as best possible, eliminates the atmosphere of commercial noise and activity."[119] Warren sharply distinguished, however, previous cases in which "the religious practices themselves conflicted with the public interest,"[120] and "legislation attempts to make a religious practice itself unlawful."[121] "In such cases, to make accommodation between the religious action and an exercise of state authority is a particularly delicate task."[122] Clearly implied here is some sort of interest-weighing, although hardly of the sort envisaged by the Black-Douglas formulation.

Much light was cast upon the present position of the Supreme Court by the separate opinions in the Sunday law cases. Justice Brennan, joined by Justice Stewart, dissented on the basis of a straight interest-weighing approach, finding no satisfactory answer to the determinative question: "What over-balancing need is so weighty in the constitutional scale that it justifies this substantial, though indirect, limitation of appellants' freedom?"[123] Justice Frankfurter's concurring opinion (joined by Justice Harlan) is especially significant, marking a substantial retreat from his position in the flag-salute cases.

. . . If the value to the state of achieving the object of a particular regulation is demonstrably outweighed by the impediment to which the regulation subjects those whose religious practices are curtailed by it, or if the object sought by the regulation could with equal effect be achieved by alternative means which do not substantially impede those practices, the regulation cannot be sustained. . . .[124]

In concluding that the Sunday laws survived this test, even as applied to Orthodox Jews, Frankfurter placed heavy reliance on both the long and unbroken history of public acceptance of such legislation and the indirect character of the burden on religion. Justice Douglas did not reach the religious freedom issue; for him, all Sunday laws were invalid as departures from separation of church and state.

Taken together with the *Prince* case, *Braunfeld* and *Gallagher* point to certain definite conclusions. The "secular regulation" rule is clearly defunct. It was unable to muster majority support even in its modest application to "indirect" burdens on religion; Frankfurter and Harlan treated the direct-indirect distinction as merely one element in a general interest-weighing approach. On the other hand, the Court has beat a fast retreat from the extreme positions set out in the *Barnette* and *Struthers* concurrences; the "clear and present danger" standard has been quietly dropped, as far as religious freedom cases are concerned.[125] Between these two rejected extremes, the Court's position remains unclear. The probable majority approach seems closely akin to that in Stone's *Gobitis* dissent, but rather more favorable to state power. Only Justices Brennan and Stewart seemed to apply any presumption of unconstitutionality, while Frankfurter and Harlan indulged a fairly strong presumption in the other direction. Chief Justice Warren's opinion in *Braunfeld* did not meet this issue squarely, but his treatment was at least as close to Frankfurter as to Brennan. It remains for later cases (if any) to resolve the uncertainty. In the meantime, religious freedom, while still in a "preferred position," appears to be vulnerable to any regulation with a substantial public interest behind it.

It is too early to determine the effect of the rhetoric of the Sunday law decisions on lower court practice, particularly in those jurisdictions still adhering to the "secular regulation" rule. Certainly, there is no automatic or compulsory effect. The *holdings* in those cases dealt with an indirect restraint on religion, and shed little light on the general run of religious freedom cases. The rhetoric itself is hardly compelling in authority, since no single formulation was able to command majority support. Some courts may well choose to overhaul their standards in this area simply from a desire to sail with what appear to be the prevailing winds of doctrine. It remains to be seen whether this will make any difference in their actual holdings.

C. *Looking Back*

1. GENERAL: GROUPS AND CONSTITUTIONAL LITIGATION

Gobitis and *Barnette* were only the twin climaxes of a controversy with its roots in the nineteenth century. Before this conflict had run its full course, it had troubled school districts all over the country, engaged the attention of the courts of some twenty states, led to the at least temporary demise of what for a century and a half had been the unchallenged rule of decision in religious freedom cases, caused the United States Supreme Court to reverse itself twice within three years, and embroiled such dissimilar groups as the American Legion, the American Civil Liberties Union, the American Bar Association and the United States Department of Justice.

In form, a lawsuit is simply a contest between two directly interested parties, be they people or institutions; it is an isolated conflict, legally distinct and insulated from all other disputes. Actually—and it should surprise no one at this late date—constitutional litigation (criminal procedural matters aside) tends to be a continuing struggle dominated largely by organized pressure groups. The flag-salute litigation furnishes a classic illustration. If Walter Gobitis' religious beliefs had been merely his own, he undoubtedly would have had to have all his children educated privately. Indeed, without massive interest group backing, neither side of the *Gobitis* litigation could have stayed in court for long. The Witnesses had a real grievance, in which they eventually were upheld; but it took an eight-year struggle, with six trips to the Supreme Court, to reach that end. Furthermore, a requisite number of justices changed their minds in the course of still other litigation brought before the Court by the indefatigable Witness legal office. Jehovah's Witnesses are rivaled only by the National Association for the Advancement of Colored People in the frequency and success with which they have resorted to the courts.[126]

The legal influence of disinterested but sympathetic groups intervening on the side of the Witnesses was limited both by that sect's marked unco-operativeness and by the accidental circumstance that both flag-salute cases came before a Supreme Court that had made up its mind long in advance. The ACLU proved more helpful to the Witnesses in its out-of-court efforts. Most beneficial of all, of course, was the intervention of the Civil Rights Section, which, aside from *Catlette*, did not enter the judicial arena at all.

2. PUBLIC OPINION AND PUBLIC LAW

The *Gobitis* and *Barnette* decisions, coming within three years of each other, furnish an unusual opportunity to examine the relations of the Court with its public. It is a truism that the Court affects public opinion and is in turn affected by it. Both relationships appear to have been present, though in varying degree, in these cases.

Much discussion already has been devoted to the possible effect of the Gobitis decision in stimulating the shocking outburst of persecution which marred the period 1940–42. All that can be said with any degree of assurance is that *Gobitis* almost certainly helped to touch off what was already an explosive situation. In 1940, people were uneasy. The nation was unmistakably *drifting* into an unwanted war with opponents who had shown every sign of invincibility. Public opinion was ripe for a scapegoat—any scapegoat. Worse, the Witnesses of 1935–40 were spoiling for a fight. Events between May 29 and June 1, 1940, suggest that the well-publicized flag-salute issue would have led to substantial persecution whichever way the Supreme Court decided, although the Court's apparent indorsement of the compulsory salute certainly made matters worse. The outstanding ill effect was the proliferation of new flag-salute rules and other "legal" anti-Witness expedients based on that decision. Why did not the *Barnette* decision set off a new outburst? Two reasons are evident. First, by 1943 the Department of Justice, under the urging of its Civil Rights Section, had mounted a truly impressive offensive against all forms of anti-Witness persecution. Second, and almost equally important, was the simple fact that most people by then were sick and tired of both the Witnesses and the flag-salute issue. The nation was actually in a war, there were clear-cut enemies to hate, and there was much constructive work to be done. In these circumstances, the Justice Department had a good chance to calm things down.

Also very striking was the systematic misinterpretation of *Gobitis* and *Barnette* by both press and public. To the average spectator, of course, the matter was simple: the Court had indorsed the compulsory salute in *Gobitis* and condemned it in *Barnette*. But the commentators, both lay and legal, were hardly more sophisticated in most instances. Seizing on the extraneous rhetoric which unfortunately studded the majority opinions in both cases, they produced stereotyped images of both decisions—especially of *Gobitis*—which must greatly have surprised the original opinion writers. There was also a sort of feedback effect at work. The various state and federal court opinions attacking the *Gobitis* rationale showed little real comprehension of the bases of Frankfurter's argument. Most of the press misconceptions of the *Gobitis* decision were represented in Jackson's windmill-tilting in *Barnette*. One obvious moral is that judges should prune their dicta. To an extent, however, such misunderstandings are inevitable. Commentators will always tend to read a judicial opinion in the light of their conception of the original conflict. This phenomenon is most clearly illustrated by the law review notes treating Jackson's *Barnette* opinion as a religious freedom holding.

The effect of public opinion on the Court is also bound up in the question of just why the justices reversed themselves. It simplifies matters somewhat, if we bear in mind that only Justices Black, Douglas and Murphy actually changed sides; the other justices remained consistent. The adverse public reception of the *Gobitis* decision cannot have been without some influence on their thinking. The plain fact was that that ruling had not settled the flag-salute controversy; if anything, it had made it worse. The press, both lay and legal, had shown outspoken hostility. The case had had small and *decreasing* influence as a legal precedent. Expressions of displeasure came even from the Department of Justice. The only tangible results of the decision appeared to be persecution and violence. *Gobitis* may or may not have "caused" the anti-Witness activity; the important point here is that it *seemed* to have caused it. Few Supreme Court decisions in history have suffered from such abysmal public relations.

It is suggested, however, that the real reason for the three justices' change of mind lies closer to the central issue—i.e., the "secular regulation" rule itself.

3. THE DOCTRINAL ISSUE: SEARCH FOR A STANDARD

Whether courts are policy-making bodies is largely a matter of definition. In one sense, at least, judges undoubtedly make policy. Constitutional provisions like the First Amendment do not interpret themselves. Nor, it is submitted, can we solve our present-day problems by reading more closely the records of the First Congress. In the final analysis, the kind of standard to be applied to religious freedom cases will depend on a personal judgment regarding how much freedom an orderly society can stand. It is only natural and proper that a judge should look about him from time to time to see how his evaluations are working out in practice.

The advantages of the "secular regulation" rule are obvious: it is automatic, simple, and completely divorced from touchy issues of religious disputation. It has a serious weakness, however, in that it leaves the way open for a great deal of disguised religious persecution. A "general" regulation can easily be framed so as to deal with almost any obnoxious group. Justices Black, Douglas and Murphy had ample opportunity to appreciate this fact. The crudity of the expedient in *Kennedy v. Moscow*, the suspicious circumstances of the prosecution in *Chaplinsky*, the sheer proliferation of ordinances aimed at the Witnesses, and, climactically, the license tax cases, all demonstrated, as no lawyer's brief could, the uses to which "general," "secular" regulations might be put. The natural reaction, especially in view of the free speech cases and the recent brief by the Bill of Rights Committee, was to adopt a test which made the asserted scruple rather than the nature of the regulation the key determinant. For the Committee and Stone, the gist of this new standard was interest-weighing—the public interest in compliance against the constitutional imperative for religious freedom—with the usual presumpton of constitutionality absent, or even reversed. In its most extreme form, laid out in the Black-Douglas concurrence in *Barnette*, this standard was greatly tightened by the application of the "clear and present danger" test: religious scruples might be overriden only when their observance would create a clear and present danger of some sort of serious harm to the community.

Such a standard would give adequate protection to religious freedom; but would it adequately protect the community? Free speech involves well-defined activities raising rather predictable problems. Religious scruples, on the other hand, can crop up anywhere, with totally unpredictable results. Furthermore, application of the new standard with full force, especially in its extreme "clear and present danger" form, eventually would require reconsideration of many of the multitudinous "secular regulation" precedents. Could *Ferriter v. Tyler* survive under this rule? What of the indiscriminate application of medical licensing laws to the healing endeavors of Christian Scientists?[127] The Court has shown no sign of willingness to take on such a task. Its assiduous avoidance of cases over the years, and its cautious handling of the Sunday law cases which it could not avoid, suggest that the justices are aware of the precariousness of their position and are trying to minimize the effects of their abandonment of the "secular regulation" rule. Indeed, Stone, Black, Douglas, Murphy and the Bill of Rights Committee all seem originally to have assumed that their new standard (in whatever form) could be adopted without impairing any of the old holdings. Under the rule thus interpreted, only the compulsory flag salute would be unenforceable against religious objectors; alone of the many secular regulations, it would be unable to muster the minimum "necessity" which would sustain the other enactments adopted as "precedents" for the new rule. It seems hardly worthwhile to upset a hundred-year-old rule of decision for the sake of such a modest net result.

It is suggested that Jackson's majority opinion furnishes a more realistic approach to the flag-salute problem, in that it recognizes at the outset the crucial fact that there is something *peculiarly* wrong with the compulsory salute; it simply is not "necessary" in the sense that other laws can be shown to be necessary. The heart of the matter, perceived by both Stone and Jackson, is that the salute requirement demands an expression of belief or state of mind. This sort of oppression can be dealt with without running the risks invited by the *Barnette* concurrences. The writer is of the opinion that the Jackson opinion was right on its own ground. There is no "right" answer, on the other hand, to the religious freedom dilemma; the old rule and the new ones all have serious drawbacks. Which is preferable would seem almost a matter of taste.

NOTES

[1] See PIERCE, PUBLIC OPINION AND THE TEACHING OF HISTORY (1926). Alaska and Hawaii, not having been states within the period under consideration, are ignored throughout this study.

[2] Keesecker, *Teaching of Citizenship in the Schools*, 24 SCHOOL LIFE 112, 113 (1939); FEDERAL SECURITY AGENCY, EDUCATION FOR FREEDOM AS PROVIDED BY STATE LAWS 4–10 (1948). See also KY. STAT. §§ 4369i, 4383 (Carroll, 1930).

[3] FEDERAL SECURITY AGENCY, *op. cit. supra* at 20–38. In addition to the statutes there cited, see COLO. STAT. ANN. § 6767j (Courtright, 1930); KY. STAT. § 4369g (Carroll, 1930); OHIO CODE § 7645 (Page, 1938); OKLA. STAT. tit. 70, §§ 1091, 1092, 1174 (1941); R. I. GEN. LAWS ANN. c. 20 (1938).

[4] MINN. STAT. § 2880 (Mason, 1927); NEB. REV. STAT. § 79–1917 (1943); NEV. COMP. LAWS § 5870 (1929 and Supp. 1941).

[5] *E.g.*, IOWA CODE tit. 12, § 4255 (1939); S.D. REV. STAT. §§ 7631, 7660 (1919).

[6] *E.g.*, MONT. REV. CODES § 1079 (1935); VT. STAT. § 4301 (1947).

[7] *E.g.*, CAL. SCHOOL CODE div. 5, § 5.128 (Deering, 1937); ORE. COMP. LAWS ANN. tit. 111, § 2102 (1940).

[8] States having only this sort of patriotic instruction statutes were Delaware, Florida, Maryland and Rhode Island. See notes 14, 17, 21 and 25 *infra*.

[9] See Halter v. Nebraska, 205 U.S. 34 (1907), and the thirty state laws cited, *id.* at 39 n. 1.

[10] Coutts, *How the Flag Pledge Originated*, 126 JOURNAL OF EDUCATION 225 (1942); *The Flag Salute*, 32 NATIONAL EDUCATION ASSOCIATION JOURNAL 265 (1943).

[11] *The Flag Salute*, 32 NATIONAL EDUCATION ASSOCIATION JOURNAL 265 (1943).

[12] Pub. L. no. 829, c. 806, § 7, 56 STAT. c. 1077 (December 22, 1942). In 1954, the relevant part of the pledge was revised to read "... one nation under God, indivisible..." Pub. L. no. 396, 68 STAT. c. 297 (June 14, 1954).

[13] N.Y. Laws 1898, c. 481, § 3, *amended*, N.Y. Laws 1910, c. 140 § 712, N.Y. EDUCATION LAW § 712 (Thompson, 1939).

[14] R.I. Laws 1901, c. 818, § 4, *amended* R.I. Pub. Laws 1932, c. 1927, at 227, R.I. GEN. LAWS ANN. c. 20, § 1 (1938).

[15] Ariz. Laws 1903, no. 19, § 3, at 25, *re-enacted with minor changes*, Ariz. Laws 1912, c. 77, § 117, at 364, ARIZ. CODE tit. 54, § 808 (1939).

16 Kan. Laws 1907, c. 319, § 3, KAN. GEN. STAT. ANN. tit. 72, § 5308 (1935).

17 Md. Laws 1918, c. 75, at 121, MD. CODE ANN. art. 77, § 234 (1939).

18 See FLANDERS, LEGISLATIVE CONTROL OF THE ELEMENTARY CURRICULUM 13–14 (1925). The specific statutory language seems to cut both ways. Compare the New York statute, quoted *supra,* with KAN. GEN. STAT. ANN. tit. 72, § 5308 (1935).

19 San Diego Independent (Cal.), September 15, 1926.

20 Wash. Laws 1919, at 210, § 4, WASH. REV. STAT. ANN. § 4777 (Remington, 1931 and Supp. 1941).

21 34 Del. Laws (1925), c. 180, at 440, DEL. REV. CODE § 2761 (1935).

22 N.J. Laws 1932, c. 145, § 1, at 260, N.J. REV. STAT. tit. 18, § 14–80c (1937).

23 Mass. Acts 1935, c. 258, MASS. GEN. LAWS c. 71, § 69 (1953).

24 Mass. Laws 1935, c. 370, MASS. GEN. LAWS c. 71, § 30A (1953).

25 Colo. Sess. Laws 1923, c. 164, at 550, COLO. STAT. ANN. § 6782h (Courtright, 1930) ; Fla. Laws 1939, c. 19355, § 509(1), FLA. STAT. § 231.09 (1941) ; Idaho Sess. Laws 1925, c. 47, § 1, IDAHO CODE § 32-2218 (1932).

26 Me. Laws 1915, c. 176, ME. REV. STAT. c. 19, § 59 (1930) ; Okla. Laws 1921, c. 111, at 137, OKLA. STAT. tit. 70, § 1091 (1941).

27 Ark. Laws 1931, act 169, § 173; ARK. STAT. § 11615 (1937); Ill. Laws 1935, at 1345, ILL. REV. STAT. c. 122, § 2989 (1939) ; Miss. Laws Spec. Sess. 1935, c. 59, MISS. STAT. § 6226 (1942) ; Neb. Laws 1927, c. 85, § 1, at 253, NEB. REV. STAT. § 79-2139 (1943) ; N.Y. Laws 1924, c. 525, at 947, N.Y. EDUCATION LAW § 712 (Thompson, 1939) ; N.C. Laws 1923, c. 49, N.C. CODE § 5441 (1939) ; Ore. Laws 1929, c. 327, at 367, ORE. COMP. STAT. § 111-2029 (1940) ; Tenn. Pub. Laws 1929, c. 83, at 185, TENN. CODE ANN. § 2508 (Williams, 1934) ; Va. Laws 1928, c. 471 at 122, VA. STAT. § 717 (1936).

28 Cal. Stat. 1931, at 690, CAL. SCHOOL CODE div. 5, § 5.128 (Deering, 1937) ; Colo. Sess. Laws 1921, c. 213, at 719, COLO. STAT. ANN. § 6767j (Courtright, 1930) ; Ind. Acts 1929, c. 16, § 1, at 33, IND. STAT. ANN. § 28-5112 (Burns, 1948 repl.) ; Mont. Laws 1931, c. 19, § 1, MONT. REV. CODES § 1327.1 (1935) ; Ore. Laws 1921, c. 115, § 1 at 226, ORE. COMP. STAT. § 111-2102 (1940) ; Wash. Laws 1931, c. 103, § 1, WASH. REV. STAT. ANN. § 4966-1 (Remington 1931 and Supp. 1941).

29 Ga. Acts 1935, at 1253; Pa. Laws 1937, no. 194, PA. STAT. ANN. § 15-1511 (Purdon, 1950) ; Tex. Laws 1919, at 370 (Sen. Conc. Res. no. 10).

30 See section D *infra;* chapter iv *infra.*

31 See FENNELL, COMPULSORY FLAG SALUTE IN SCHOOLS (1936, 1938). For the raw data gathered from the questionnaire, see AMERICAN CIVIL LIBERTIES UNION ARCHIVES (bound correspondence on file at Princeton and on microfilm in New York Public Library, cited hereafter as "ACLU Archives"), vol. 872, "Academic Freedom."

32 The earliest relevant legislation in New Jersey was N.J. Laws 1919, c. 35, § 3, at 305; but cf. NEWARK BOARD OF EDUCATION, COURSE OF STUDY: DEMOCRACY AND PATRIOTISM 24 (1918). Ohio's earliest legislation is 108 Ohio Laws I, 542 (1919) ; but cf. Troyer v. State, 21 Ohio N.P. (N.S.) 121 (C.P. 1918). Pennsylvania's first law was Pa. Laws 1919, no. 263, at 544; but

evidence indicates that local use of the ceremony dates back to 1915 or earlier. Record, p. 91, Gobitis v. Minersville School District, 24 F. Supp. 271 (E.D. Pa. 1938).

33 This section will deal only with pre-1935 backers of the ceremony. Other groups appeared after the acceleration of the controversy in that year.

34 PIERCE, CITIZENS' ORGANIZATIONS AND THE CIVIC TRAINING OF YOUTH 33 (1933).

35 1 AMERICAN LEGION NAT'L CONV. PROC. 39 (1919).

36 *Ibid.*

37 6 AMERICAN LEGION WEEKLY 14 (June 13, 1924).

38 *Ibid.*

39 *Ibid.*

40 6 AMERICAN LEGION NAT'L CONV. PROC. 34 (1924).

41 16 AMERICAN LEGION NAT'L CONV. PROC. 78 (1934).

42 Boston Post, April 18, 1939.

43 See, *e.g.*, PIERCE, CITIZENS' ORGANIZATIONS AND THE CIVIC TRAINING OF YOUTH 40–42, 44 (1933).

44 *Id.* at 52–55.

45 See PIERCE, PUBLIC OPINION AND THE TEACHING OF HISTORY 57 (1926). See also the alternative pledges involved in Estep v. Borough of Canonsburg (unreported officially), ACLU Archives, vol. 958, "Pennsylvania."

46 PIERCE, CITIZENS' ORGANIZATIONS AND THE CIVIC TRAINING OF YOUTH 112–25 (1933).

47 *Id.* at 15.

48 *Id.* at 17.

49 *Id.* at 31.

50 Springfield Union (Mass.), April 2, 1937.

51 PIERCE, CITIZENS' ORGANIZATIONS AND THE CIVIC TRAINING OF YOUTH 331 (1933).

52 *Id.* at 24.

53 *Id.* at 24–30.

54 *Id.* at 126–29.

55 *Id.* at 107.

56 Boston Post, June 15, 1943.

57 BEALE, ARE AMERICAN TEACHERS FREE? 527–28 (1936). See also GELLERMAN, THE AMERICAN LEGION AS EDUCATOR 238 (1938). The Legion's legislative influence is further attested to by the spate of state laws requiring instruction on the Constitution, "including the study of and devotion to American institutions and ideals." See *id.* at 215–16.

58 See Flanders, *op. cit. supra* note 18, at 64–112, 129–38, 155–58; Federal Security Agency, *op. cit. supra* note 3, at 16–19.

59 Beale, *op. cit. supra* note 57, at 74–75, 326–27.

60 Bloch, *Education for Citizenship and Commercial Law*, 7 LAW SOC. J. 924 (1937); *Compulsory Flag Salute*, 120 JOURNAL OF EDUCATION 195 (1937); Chambers, *You Can't Come to School*, 20 NATION'S SCHOOLS 33, 34 (December, 1937). Professor Kilpatrick of Teachers College, Columbia, is reported

to have attacked the ceremony in a 1932 speech, but the content of the criticism is not on record. Beale, *op. cit. supra* note 57, at 74.

⁶¹ A former high school teacher, *I Pledge a Legion*, 120 JOURNAL OF EDUCATION 122 (1937); Moser & David, *I Pledge a Legion*, 9 JOURNAL OF EDUCATIONAL SOCIOLOGY 436 (1936). Moser was a principal, while David was a local school superintendent.

⁶² Olander, *Children's Knowledge of the Flag Salute*, 35 JOURNAL OF EDUCATIONAL RESEARCH 300 (1941).

⁶³ *Id.* at 305.

⁶⁴ Myers, *Classroom Clinic: That Flag Ritual*, 124 JOURNAL OF EDUCATION 25 (1941).

⁶⁵ RUEDIGER, *Saluting the Flag*, 49 SCHOOL AND SOCIETY 249 (1939).

⁶⁶ Benjamin, *With Liberty and Justice for All*, 35 NATIONAL PARENT-TEACHER 7, 9 (November, 1940).

⁶⁷ CLARK, THE SMALL SECTS IN AMERICA 224–27 (1939).

⁶⁸ Letter, Nevin Bender (Greenwood, Del.) to Roger N. Baldwin, June 29, 1929, ACLU Archives, vol. 357, "Delaware."

⁶⁹ Troyer v. State, 21 Ohio N.P. (N.S.) 121, 124 (C.P. 1918).

⁷⁰ AMERICAN CIVIL LIBERTIES UNION, THE GAG ON TEACHING 12 (1935). The account was vague, and may conceivably be a garbled account of the incident described in subsection 4 *infra*.

⁷¹ Letter, Forrest Bailey to Edith Spruance (Wilmington, Del.), March 24, 1928, ACLU Archives, vol. 336, "Maryland" (misfiled).

⁷² Letter, Nevin Bender to Roger N. Baldwin, June 29, 1929, ACLU Archives, vol. 357, "Delaware."

⁷³ Letter, Roger N. Baldwin to Nevin Bender, July 1, 1929, ACLU Archives, vol. 357, "Delaware."

⁷⁴ Letters, Nevin Bender to Roger N. Baldwin, August 16, 1929, and Lucille B. Milner to Nevin Bender, August 19, 1929, ACLU Archives, vol. 357, "Delaware." See also Leesville Democrat (La.), August 22, 1929.

⁷⁵ ACLU Press Release, October 14, 1926, ACLU Archives, vol. 299, "Colorado."

⁷⁶ Letter, Albert L. Vogl to Wolcott Pitkin (New York attorney, frequent advisor to ACLU), May 12, 1926, ACLU Archives, vol. 299, "Colorado."

⁷⁷ Albert L. Vogl, statement of facts (undated), ACLU Archives, vol. 299, "Colorado."

⁷⁸ Note 70 *supra*.

⁷⁹ Letters, Alice B. McCormack (county superintendent) to Olive A. Jahveh, February 17, 1926, and Mary C. Bradford (state superintendent) to Olive A. Jahveh, March 20, 1926, ACLU Archives, vol. 299, "Colorado."

⁸⁰ Letter, Roger N. Baldwin to Carl Whitehead, April 22, 1926, ACLU Archives, vol. 299, "Colorado"; Los Angeles Times, April 24, 1926.

⁸¹ Notes 76, 77 *supra*; letter, Carl Whitehead to Roger N. Baldwin, July 30, 1926, ACLU Archives, vol. 299, "Colorado."

⁸² Letter, Carl Whitehead to Roger N. Baldwin, September 25, 1926, ACLU Archives, vol. 299, "Colorado."

83 Letter, Carl Whitehead to Roger N. Baldwin, August 3, 1926, ACLU Archives, vol. 299, "Colorado."

84 Letter, Carl Whitehead to Roger N. Baldwin, October 8, 1926, ACLU Archives, vol. 299, "Colorado."

85 ACLU Press Release, October 14, 1926, ACLU Archives, vol. 299, "Colorado."

86 STROUP, THE JEHOVAH'S WITNESSES 14–15 (1945). The Russellites went on to become Jehovah's Witnesses, discussed in chapter ii *infra*.

87 San Francisco Call, August 23, 1926; Bellingham American, September 23, 1925.

88 Elijah Voice Society (Seattle), *Our American Inquisition: Open Letter to Thoughtful People*, OPEN FORUM June 5, 1926, ACLU Archives, vol. 298, "Washington."

89 *Ibid.* See also Roger N. Baldwin, memorandum for files, August 2, 1926, ACLU Archives, vol. 298, "Washington."

90 Tremain refused to testify and had to be restrained from simply wandering out of the courtroom. Bellingham American, September 23, 1925.

91 St. Louis Post-Dispatch, September 17, 1926.

92 Bellingham American, September 13, 1926.

93 *Ibid.*, December 4, 1925.

94 *Ibid.*, June 4, 1926.

95 San Francisco Call, August 23, 1926. See also letter, Roger N. Baldwin to Lucille B. Milner, July 14, 1926, ACLU Archives, vol. 299, "Washington."

96 Letters, J. W. Tremain to Roger N. Baldwin, August 6, 1926; W. L. Lane (of Lane and Thompson, Seattle) to Roger N. Baldwin, September 17, 1926 (two letters); Wolcott Pitkin to Forrest Bailey (of the New York office), December 1, 1926; Roger N. Baldwin to W. L. Lane, December 6, 1926; all in ACLU Archives, vol. 299, "Washington."

97 Letters, Sidney Strong to Roger N. Baldwin, August 23, September 2, September 11, 1926, ACLU Archives, vol. 299, "Washington."

98 Letter, Sidney Strong to Roger N. Baldwin, September 17, 1926, ACLU Archives, vol. 299, "Washington."

99 Bellingham Times, November 28, 1927.

100 Beale, *op. cit. supra* note 57, at 73.

101 Oklahoma (City) Leader, January 13, 1928; unsigned and undated memorandum appearing in the files immediately after the above cited newspaper item, ACLU Archives, vol. 337, "Oklahoma."

102 Mentioned, Hardwicke v. Board of School Trustees, 54 Cal. App. 696, 711, 205 Pac. 49, 56 (1921).

103 PIERCE, CITIZENS' ORGANIZATIONS AND THE CIVIC TRAINING OF YOUTH 107 (1933).

104 Seattle Intelligencer, October 14, 1925. This and the Solano County incident may have resulted in surrender by the parent. A later report cites two such cases without further description. San Diego Independent (Cal.), September 15, 1926.

[105] Letter, Frank Pierpont Graves to Clarence E. Meleney, February 19, 1926, ACLU Archives, vol. 299, "New York."

[106] Letters, Sidney Strong to Roger N. Baldwin, August 23, September 2, 1926, ACLU Archives, vol. 299, "Washington."

CHAPTER TWO

[1] The name was adopted in 1931. Previously they were known as International Bible Students, or "Russellites." WATCHTOWER SOCIETY, LET GOD BE TRUE 9 (1946) ; 1941 YEAR BOOK OF JEHOVAH'S WITNESSES 30–35.

[2] *Modern History of Jehovah's Witnesses* (Pt. 1), WATCHTOWER 4, 7 (1955) (cited hereafter as *History*).

[3] Milwaukee Journal, July 22, 1957.

[4] *History* (Pt. 6), WATCHTOWER 173, 175–76 (1955).

[5] RUTHERFORD, RELIGION 59 (1940).

[6] RUTHERFORD, CHILDREN 219–20 (1941) ; RUTHERFORD, SALVATION 316 (1939) ; RUTHERFORD, CREATION 315–16 (1927) ; *Understanding Prophecy,* WATCHTOWER 211 (1935) ; STROUP, THE JEHOVAH'S WITNESSES 52 (1945).

[7] RUTHERFORD, RELIGION 333–34 (1940) ; *Understanding Prophecy,* WATCHTOWER 211, 214–15 (1935) ; *The Great Multitude* (Pt. 2), WATCHTOWER 243, 246 (1935) ; Stroup, *op. cit. supra,* at 50–53, 139.

[8] RUTHERFORD, SALVATION 15–19, 22 (1939).

[9] *Id.* at 227.

[10] A few words are in order about the Witness version of the atonement. Adam was created physically perfect and immortal, but became mortal and vulnerable to disease after his sin. The transmission of these imperfections to his blameless descendents created an apparent dilemma, since only the obedience of a perfect man could repurchase Adam's lost life-right. Christ was Jehovah's greatest spirit creature, the Logos, sent down to earth as a perfect human being with a life-right like Adam's. By dying voluntarily on the cross, he preserved this right to transfer to mankind. He was resurrected as a spirit creature, thus leaving the bargain intact. Note the rejection of the trinity involved in this view. RUTHERFORD, CHILDREN 110 (1941) ; RUTHERFORD, SALVATION 171–78 (1939) ; *Unity in Action,* WATCHTOWER 147, 149–50 (1938).

[11] RUTHERFORD, ENEMIES 310, 312–13 (1937) ; Harris, *Reporter at Large: I'd Like to Talk to You for a Minute,* NEW YORKER, June 15, 1956, pp. 72, 87–88. See also Stroup, *op. cit. supra* note 6, at 164–65. The signs referred to include wars, famines, natural disasters—and the persecution of the faithful.

[12] RUTHERFORD, SALVATION 25, 252–53, 326–30 (1939) ; Harris, *supra* note 11, at 72, 90.

[13] RUSSELL, THE DIVINE PLAN OF THE AGES, 193–98 (1888). See also CZATT, THE INTERNATIONAL BIBLE STUDENTS 12–13 (1933).

[14] Russell, *op. cit. supra,* at 193–200, 150–52, 157.

[15] *History* (Pt. 1), WATCHTOWER 4, 8 (1955). For Russell's mathematics, see MACMILLAN, FAITH ON THE MARCH 50–51 (1957).

[16] Rutherford's first explanation, a stop-gap one, was that the world had ended *juridically* in 1914, as Satan was then cast out of Heaven and his con-

trol of earth disputed; 1914 marked the *beginning* of the last days. *History* (Pt. 11), WATCHTOWER 333, 334–35 (1955). Cf. RUTHERFORD, ENEMIES 311–12 (1937). Russell's works were re-edited to agree with this new line. See Czatt, *op. cit. supra* note 13, at 8–9.

[17] After the man taken into Jehu's chariot. 2 Kings 10:15–16. See RUTHERFORD, SALVATION 68–70 (1939).

[18] RUTHERFORD, SALVATION 28, 77–78, 82, 92, 142–43, 326–27 (1939); RUTHERFORD, CHILDREN 254, 308–9 (1941); *The Great Multitude* (Pt. 2), WATCHTOWER 243, 247–48 (1935). The term "city of refuge" refers to Numbers 35: 26–28.

[19] RUTHERFORD, ENEMIES 332–33 (1937); RUTHERFORD, RELIGION 332 (1940); RUTHERFORD, CHILDREN 202 (1941); *The Great Multitude* (Pt. 2), WATCHTOWER 243, 246–47 (1935); Macmillan, *op. cit. supra* note 15, at 147.

[20] RUTHERFORD, CHILDREN 211 (1941); RUTHERFORD, SALVATION 269 (1939); *Prisoners* (Pt. 3), WATCHTOWER 291, 293 (1935).

[21] Harris, *supra* note 11 at 72; COLE, TRIUMPHANT KINGDOM *passim* (1957). As late as the nineteen forties, it would appear that a substantial portion of the membership still did not engage in the "witness work." Compare an "active" (preaching) 1943 world membership of 106,000 (Stroup, *op. cit. supra* note 6, at 60) with a 1942 convention attendance of some 129,000 (COLE, JEHOVAH'S WITNESSES 219 [1955]).

[22] Russell, *op. cit. supra* note 13, at 193–98, 240.

[23] RUTHERFORD, ENEMIES 121, 127 (1937); RUTHERFORD, CHILDREN 104 (1941). As a corollary, Witness doctrine now holds that those who knowingly and wilfully violated God's law in past generations (*e.g.*, Adam) will not be raised up again. RUTHERFORD, SALVATION 224–25 (1939); RUTHERFORD, CHILDREN 121–22, 361 (1941).

[24] RUTHERFORD, SALVATION 125–26, 242–43, 261, 266 (1939); RUTHERFORD, CHILDREN 203–4 (1941).

[25] For the experiences of other researchers, see Stroup, *op. cit. supra* note 6, at 22, 24, 35, 72–75; Czatt, *op. cit. supra* note 13, at 20–21.

[26] These are very rough estimates, based on the average number of ministers ("publishers") for that year. COLE, JEHOVAH'S WITNESSES 222–28 (1955). These figures are adjusted for the fact that the average number consistently runs at least 10 per cent below the *peak* number, which itself must be less than the total number who "witness" at some time. See WATCHTOWER 27–29 (1955); WATCHTOWER 24–26 (1956). The world total was reached by adding in 20,000 Witnesses, for the thriving Witness movement suppressed in Germany between 1933 and 1945. COLE, JEHOVAH'S WITNESSES 223 (1955); *History* (Pt. 17), WATCHTOWER 520, 521 (1955). The final figures are rounded off downward.

[27] See note 26 *supra*. Base figures are from Stroup, *op. cit. supra* note 6, at 60.

[28] WATCHTOWER 24, 26 (1956).

[29] See COLE, JEHOVAH'S WITNESSES 219 (1955).

[30] *Id.* at 229. Cf. WATCHTOWER 27, 29 (1955).

[31] Stroup, *op. cit. supra* note 6, at 77; Czatt, *op. cit. supra* note 13, at 20–22.

Cf. High, *Armageddon, Inc.*, SATURDAY EVENING POST, September 14, 1940, p. 18. A more recent study strongly supports the Stroup-Czatt conclusions. SIBLEY & JACOB, CONSCRIPTION OF CONSCIENCE 355–56 (1952).

[32] Stroup, *op. cit. supra* note 6, at 77–78.

[33] *Id.* at 76, 120; Czatt, *op. cit. supra* note 13, at 20.

[34] Stroup, *op. cit. supra* note 6, at 63.

[35] RUTHERFORD, SALVATION 70–71 (1939); *The Lukewarm Spewed Out*, WATCHTOWER 108, 108–9 (1938).

[36] *History* (Pt. 3), WATCHTOWER 76 (1955).

[37] Stroup, *op. cit. supra* note 6, at 21. The charter was revised in 1944 to provide for a closed membership akin to that of the New York corporation. *History* (Pt. 6), WATCHTOWER 173, 175 (1955); SCHNELL, THIRTY YEARS A WATCH TOWER SLAVE 151, 171–72 (1956). The Schnell book is used with care because of its venomous anti-Witness bias. For brute physical facts and details of Russellite theory, it is probably reliable.

[38] *History* (Pt. 5), WATCHTOWER 140, 140–41 (1955).

[39] Stroup, *op. cit. supra* note 6, at 21.

[40] COLE, JEHOVAH'S WITNESSES 87–88 (1955).

[41] Stroup, *op. cit. supra* note 6, at 121–22.

[42] Crucial points in this process were two occasions on which Rutherford squashed revolts against his editorial policies. The first, in 1917, led to the expulsion of a majority of the Pennsylvania corporation's board of directors who sought to oust Rutherford as president. *History* (Pt. 7), WATCHTOWER 204, 204–5 (1955); Macmillan, *op. cit. supra* note 15, at 80–81. The second, in 1925, led to the demise of the Pennsylvania corporation's editorial committee. *His Organization* (Pt. 2), WATCHTOWER 179, 185 (1938).

[43] Stroup, *op. cit. supra* note 6, at 22–23.

[44] *History* (Pt. 10), WATCHTOWER 298–300 (1955).

[45] *His Organization* (Pt. 1), WATCHTOWER 163 (1938); *id.* (Pt. 2), WATCHTOWER 179 (1938).

[46] *History* (Pt. 11), WATCHTOWER, 333 n. (1955). See also Stroup, *op. cit. supra* note 6, at 23.

[47] Stroup, *op. cit. supra* note 6, at 30–31; Schnell, *op. cit. supra* note 37, at 156–57, 159. The zones were abolished in 1941. Macmillan, *op. cit. supra* note 15, at 193–94. They were reinstated in revised form a year later. *Ibid.*; Harris, *supra* note 11, at 72, 93.

[48] Stroup, *op. cit. supra* note 6, at 35, 125–26; Schnell, *op. cit. supra* note 37, at 126–27, 157–58.

[49] *History* (Pt. 16), WATCHTOWER 489, 491 (1955). The magazine was renamed AWAKE! in 1946. *Id.* (Pt. 27), WATCHTOWER 72–73 (1956).

[50] See Jones v. Opelika, 316 U.S. 584, 589, 591 (1942); State v. Meredith, 197 S.C. 351, 353, 15 S.E. (2d) 678 (1941).

[51] See Stroup, *op. cit. supra* note 6, at 39–40; Logan, *Jehovah's Witnesses Ignore Their Founder*, New York Post, June 18, 1940.

[52] 1938 YEAR BOOK OF JEHOVAH'S WITNESSES 66–67.

[53] Stroup, *op. cit. supra* note 6, at 44–46.

54 See, *e.g.*, 1938 YEAR BOOK OF JEHOVAH'S WITNESSES 34.

55 Stroup, *op. cit. supra* note 6, at 40–42; RUTHERFORD, THE THEOCRACY 59–60 (1941).

56 Macmillan, *op. cit. supra* note 15, at 111–13, 120–21, 208–10. But cf. Stroup, *op. cit. supra* note 6, at 44.

57 COLE, JEHOVAH'S WITNESSES 97–98 (1955); *History* (Pt. 3), WATCHTOWER 76, 78–79 (1955).

58 *History* (Pt. 12), WATCHTOWER 365, 367 (1955).

59 *Id.* (Pt. 16), WATCHTOWER 489, 491 (1955); *id.* (Pt. 23), WATCHTOWER 708–710 (1955).

60 *Id.* (Pt. 13), WATCHTOWER 392–95 (1955). The Witnesses still operate their own station, WBBR. *Id.* (Pt. 12), WATCHTOWER 365, 368 (1955).

61 There is considerable official pressure to this end. Stroup, *op. cit. supra* note 6, at 27. The writer observed continuing emphasis on convention attendance in his recent contacts with Witness congregations.

62 See, *e.g.*, Kansas City Star, September 12, 1938; *Big Week for "Witnesses,"* 18 NEWSWEEK 50 (August 18, 1941); *Witnesses in Detroit*, 36 TIME 39 (August 5, 1940).

63 History (Pt. 27), WATCHTOWER 72, 73 (1956).

64 Mention has already been made of Knorr's mellowing influence. Regarding Russell's vacillation on this point, see Russell, *op. cit. supra* note 13, at 153, 249–51, 268–70; Stroup, *op. cit. supra* note 6, at 37; PIKE, JEHOVAH'S WITNESSES 16 (1954).

65 RUTHERFORD, ENEMIES 35, 309, 327, 337 (1937).

66 *Id.* at 67–68, 108–20, 202, 212, 275, 280–90.

67 *The Great Multitude* (Pt. 1), WATCHTOWER 227, 235 (1935); Stroup, *op. cit. supra* note 6, at 88, 132, 135, 158–59.

68 RUTHERFORD, ENEMIES 328 (1937).

69 *Id.* at 243, 282–83.

70 See, *e.g.*, 17 GOLDEN AGE 375–78; 439, 493–94, 502–3, 534–35 (1936).

71 See 15 GOLDEN AGE 617–33 (1934); 17 *id.* 739–51 (1936).

72 For a prize example, see FELIX, RUTHERFORD UNCOVERED (1937).

73 Stroup, *op. cit. supra* note 6, at 50.

74 Olin R. Moyle, personal interview, August 15, 1957. Stroup's assertion that Rutherford was the real editor of this magazine, Stroup, *op. cit. supra* note 6, at 50, will not stand a comparison of styles.

75 15 GOLDEN AGE 11, 57 (1933); *id.* at 771, 803 (1934).

76 *Id.* at 198–204 (1933).

77 *Id.* at 245, 760 (1934).

78 *Id.* at 168 (1933).

79 *E.g.*, *The Decay of Protestantism*, 17 GOLDEN AGE 515 (1936).

80 15 GOLDEN AGE 24, 125 (1933); 16 *id.* 24 (1934); 17 *id.* 270 (1936).

81 15 GOLDEN AGE 752 (1934); 16 *id.* 761 (1935); 17 *id.* 443, 580 (1936).

82 *E.g.*, 16 GOLDEN AGE 23 (1934); *id.* at 762 (1935); 17 *id.* 312 (1936).

83 *E.g.*, 17 GOLDEN AGE 503, 599, 601, 658–71 (1936).

84 *Coals*, WATCHTOWER 142, 145 (1938).

85 RUTHERFORD, RELIGION 187 (1940).

86 *The Higher Powers* (Pt. 1), WATCHTOWER 163 (1929); *id.* (Pt. 2), WATCHTOWER 179 (1929); RUTHERFORD, SALVATION 256–57 (1939).

87 *Prisoners* (Pt. 3), WATCHTOWER 291, 299 (1935).

88 RUTHERFORD, RELIGION 291–99 (1940).

89 See *id.* at 187–89.

90 This complaint was encountered repeatedly in the writer's conversations with people who had experienced the Witness crusades during the 1930's and 1940's. For a well-documented instance, see Commonwealth v. Palms, 141 Pa. Super. 430, 15 Atl. (2d) 481 (1940).

91 See Cox v. New Hampshire, 312 U.S. 569 (1941).

92 See Salia v. New York, 334 U.S. 558 (1948).

93 *History* (Pt. 12), WATCHTOWER 365, 367 (1955).

94 *Id.* (Pt. 14), WATCHTOWER 425, 426–27 (1955).

95 RUTHERFORD, ENEMIES 323 (1937); ROSSIER, PROTEST AGAINST ENACT-MENT OF ASSEMBLY BILLS NUMBERED 30, 31 AND 32 (1936). This pamphlet, directed to the New Jersey legislature, is reprinted at 17 GOLDEN AGE 483 (1936). See also Lovell v. Griffin 303 U.S. 444, 448 (1938).

96 *History* (Pt. 14), WATCHTOWER 425, 426 (1955).

97 Olin R. Moyle, personal interviews, August 15, 16, 1957.

98 1938 YEAR BOOK OF JEHOVAH'S WITNESSES 63–64.

99 *History* (Pt. 14), WATCHTOWER 425, 426 (1955).

100 See 1939 YEAR BOOK OF JEHOVAH'S WITNESSES 81.

101 *History* (Pt. 14), WATCHTOWER 425, 426 (1955).

102 While this accorded with Moyle's own prejudices, it was at the direction of Rutherford himself. Olin R. Moyle, personal interview, August 15, 1957.

103 Coleman v. Griffin, 302 U.S. 636 (1937).

104 303 U.S. 444 (1938).

105 Olin R. Moyle, personal interview, August 15, 1957.

106 308 U.S. 147 (1939).

107 *History* (Pt. 14), WATCHTOWER 425, 426–27 (1955). See also Douglas v. Jeannette, 130 F(2d) 652, 654–55 (3d Cir. 1942).

108 1938 YEAR BOOK OF JEHOVAH'S WITNESSES 64–65. See also the scheme described in Czatt, *op. cit. supra* note 13, at 32.

109 *History* (Pt. 14), WATCHTOWER 425, 427 (1955). See also the report of a Pennsylvania "trial" reproduced in ACLU Archives, vol. 958, "Pennsylvania."

110 1939 YEAR BOOK OF JEHOVAH'S WITNESSES 80; 1938 YEAR BOOK OF JEHOVAH'S WITNESSES 64.

111 1939 YEAR BOOK OF JEHOVAH'S WITNESSES 83.

112 *History* (Pt. 14), WATCHTOWER 425, 427 (1955).

113 In 1938, the Witnesses won 245 of 246 appeals reaching a final disposition in the state courts, and secured 98 acquittals at the trial level. 1939 YEAR BOOK OF JEHOVAH'S WITNESSES 80.

114 In 1939, arrests exceeded 600. 1940 YEAR BOOK OF JEHOVAH'S WITNESSES 74. This may reflect either increased anxiety over the onset of World War II

or merely an increased geographical scope of operations on the part of the Watchtower Society. For a suggestion that the seaboard states had been singled out for preliminary, exploratory attention, see Schnell, *op. cit. supra* note 37, at 101.

115 Rutherford, *Saluting a Flag*, in Loyalty 19 (1935); *Righteous Judgment for the People*, Watchtower 268, 270 (1935).

116 Rutherford, Enemies 335–36 (1937); Rutherford, Creation 310, 336–37 (1927).

117 *Jehovah's Winepress*, Watchtower 286 (1935); Stroup, *op. cit supra* note 6, at 160–61 (1945).

118 Rutherford, The End of the Axis Powers (1941).

119 See the trial record in State *ex rel.* Fish v. Sandstrom, 279 N.Y. 523, 18 N.E.(2d) 840 (1939), reprinted in ACLU Archives, vol. 958, "New York"; Transcript of Record, p. 82, Minersville School District v. Gobitis, 310 U.S. 586 (1940).

120 As to the nature of the materials published, see Watchtower Society, The Finished Mystery 247–53 (1917); Cole, Jehovah's Witnesses 93–94 (1955). The conviction of Rutherford and his cohorts was overturned on a technicality. Rutherford v. United States, 258 Fed. 855 (2d Cir. 1919). Many lesser members, however, went to jail and served full terms for their part in distributing the obnoxious materials. Shaffer v. United States, 255 Fed. 886 (9th Cir. 1919); Stephens v. United States, 261 Fed. 590 (9th Cir. 1919); Hamm v. United States, 261 Fed. 907 (9th Cir. 1920); Sonnenberg v. United States, 264 Fed. 327 (9th Cir., 1920).

121 Rutherford, Creation 112–13 (1927); Stroup, *op. cit. supra* note 6, at 165–66.

122 Rutherford, Neutrality (1939); Pike, *op. cit. supra* note 64, at 105–6. See also Rutherford, The End of the Axis Powers (1941).

123 Sibley & Jacob, *op. cit. supra* note 31, at 69–71, 357, 506–7. Some four hundred Witnesses did accept C.P.S. service. *Id.* at 168. For an apparent shift in organization attitude regarding the IV-E category, see Cole, Jehovah's Witnesses 127–28, 182–84 (1955); Witmer v. United States, 348 U.S. 375 (1955); Sicurella v. United States, 348 U.S. 385 (1955); Simmons v. United States, 348 U.S. 397 (1955); Gonzales v. United States, 348 U.S. 407 (1955).

124 Sibley & Jacob, *op. cit. supra* note 31, at 506–7.

125 Watchtower Society, Qualified To Be Ministers 323 (1955).

126 Record, p. 7, Nicholls v. Lynn, 297 Mass. 65, 7 N.E.(2d) 577 (1936).

127 Cole, Jehovah's Witnesses 120 (1955); *History* (Pt. 15), Watchtower 461, 461–63 (1955).

128 *The Great Multitude* (Pt. 1), Watchtower 227, 235 (1935).

129 Olin R. Moyle, personal interview, August 15, 1957.

130 *Ibid.* See also the reference by Carleton's father. Boston Post, September 21, 1935.

131 Olin R. Moyle, letter to Boston Post, October 14, 1935, quoted, 17 Golden Age 82–83.

132 Record, p. 7, Nicholls v. Lynn, 297 Mass. 65, 7 N.E. (2d) 577 (1936).

133 Boston Post, September 21, 1935.

134 Record, pp. 4, 7, Nicholls v. Lynn 297 Mass. 65, 7 N.E. (2d) 577 (1936).

135 As reprinted in RUTHERFORD, *Saluting a Flag*, in LOYALTY 16 (1935).

136 Record, pp. 3, 8, Nicholls v. Lynn, 297 MASS. 65, 7 N.E. (2d) 577 (1936).

137 *Id.* at 2.

138 RUTHERFORD, *Saluting a Flag*, in LOYALTY 16, 18 (1935).

139 Daniel 3:1–30.

140 RUTHERFORD, *Saluting a Flag*, in LOYALTY 16, 19 (1935).

141 RUTHERFORD, SALVATION 260 (1939). Again, there is some biblical support. Matt. 4:10; John 12:31; I John 5:19; II Cor. 4.

142 Macmillan, *op. cit. supra* note 15, at 172–73.

143 *E.g.*, Rossier, *op. cit. supra* note 95.

144 *Rutherford's Flock*, 16 NEWSWEEK 42 (August 5, 1940). See also the alternative pledge proposed in 1942, quoted in West Virginia State Board of Education v. Barnette, 319 U.S. 624, 628 n.4 (1943).

145 RUTHERFORD, SALVATION 266 (1939).

146 See *id.* at 260–61. "Jehovah's Witnesses are not instructing anyone to refuse to salute the flag . . . Their business is preaching the Gospel, and they are not telling anyone what they should do." Olin R. Moyle, letter to editor, Boston Post, October 14, 1935. See also Macmillan, *op. cit. supra* note 15, at 173.

147 COLE, JEHOVAH'S WITNESSES 122–23 (1955); *Questions from Readers*, WATCHTOWER 126 (1955).

148 *E.g.*, RUTHERFORD, *Saluting a Flag*, in LOYALTY 16, 24–25 (1935); Rossier, *op. cit. supra* note 95.

CHAPTER THREE

1 Ogden v. Saunders, 12 Wheat. (U.S.) 213, 270 (1827).

2 Adkins v. Children's Hospital, 261 U.S. 525 (1923); Adair v. United States, 208 U.S. 161 (1908).

3 304 U.S. 144 (1938).

4 *Id.* at 152.

5 *Id.* at 153–54.

6 *Id.* at 152 n. 4.

7 268 U.S. 510 (1925).

8 *Id.* at 535.

9 Samuel Benedict Memorial School v. Bradford, 111 Ga. 801, 36 S.E. 920 (1900); State *ex rel.* Andrews v. Webber, 108 Ind. 31, 8 N.E. 708 (1886); Cross v. Board of Trustees, 129 Ky. 35, 110 S.W. 346 (1908); Wulff v. Inhabitants of Wakefield, 221 Mass. 427, 109 N.E. 358 (1915); Kidder v. Chellis, 59 N.H. 473 (1879); Sewell v. Board of Education, 29 Ohio St. 89 (1876). Cf. Donahoe v. Richards, 38 Me. 379 (1854); Guernsey v. Pitkin, 32 Vt. 224 (1859).

10 Kidder v. Chellis, 59 N.H. 473, 476 (1879).

11 Morrow v. Wood, 35 Wis. 59 (1874); School District No. 18 v. Thompson, 24 Okla. 1, 103 Pac. 578 (1909); Rulison v. Post, 79 Ill. 567 (1875); Trustees v. People *ex rel.* Van Allen, 87 Ill. 303 (1877).

[12] State *ex rel.* Sheibley v. School District No. 1, 31 Neb. 552, 557, 48 N.W. 393, 395 (1891). See also State *ex rel.* Kelley v. Ferguson, 95 Neb. 63, 144 N.W. 1039 (1914).

[13] People *ex rel.* Vollmar v. Stanley, 81 Colo. 276, 255 Pac. 610 (1927).

[14] Meyer v. Nebraska, 262 U.S. 390, 399 (1923).

[15] Hamilton v. Regents, 293 U.S. 245, 262 (1934). See also Palko v. Connecticut, 302 U.S. 319 (1937).

[16] 310 U.S. 296 (1940).

[17] *Id.* at 303.

[18] PA. CONST. art. 1, § 3.

[19] GA. CONST. art. XIII.

[20] N.J. CONST. art 1, §§ 3, 4.

[21] See RUTLAND, THE BIRTH OF THE BILL OF RIGHTS: 1776–1791, at 43–91 *passim* (1955) ; PFEFFER, CHURCH, STATE AND FREEDOM 81–114 (1953).

[22] See, *e.g.*, People v. Ruggles, 8 John Rep. 225 (N.Y. 1811) ; City Council of Charleston v. Benjamin, 2 Strob. 508 (S.C. App. 1848).

[23] OKLA. CONST. art. 1, § 2.

[24] City of Wilkes-Barre v. Garabed, 11 Pa. Super. 355 (1899) ; State v. White, 64 N.H. 48, 5 Atl. 828 (1886) ; State *ex rel.* Garrabed v. Dering, 84 Wis. 585, 54 N.W. 1104 (1893) ; Frazee's Case, 63 Mich. 396, 30 N.W. 72 (1886). In the last two cases, the convictions were reversed on other grounds. Cf. Pineville v. Marshall, 222 Ky. 4, 299 S.W. 1072 (1927) ; Cook v. City of Harrison, 180 Ark. 546, 21 S.W.(2d) 966 (1929).

[25] McMasters v. State, 21 Okla. Crim. 318, 207 Pac. 566 (1922) ; City of St. Louis v. Hellscher, 295 Mo. 293, 242 S.W. 652 (1922) ; People v. Ashley, 184 App. Div. 520, 172 N.Y.S. 282 (1918) ; State v. Neitzel, 69 Wash. 567, 125 Pac.(2d) 939 (1912).

[26] 122 Atl. 890 (N.J. Sup. Ct. 1923).

[27] Fealy v. City of Birmingham, 15 Ala. App. 367, 73 So. 296 (1916) ; State v. Marble, 72 Ohio St. 21, 73 N.E. 1063 (1905) ; State v. Verbon, 167 Wash. 140, 8 Pac.(2d) 1083 (1932) ; Smith v. People, 51 Colo. 270, 117 Pac. 612 (1911).

[28] Commonwealth v. Herr, 39 Pa. Super. 454, *aff'd*, 299 Pa. 132 (1910). The lower-court opinion was adopted in full by the Supreme Court.

[29] Delk v. Commonwealth, 166 Ky. 39, 178 S.W. 1129 (1915) ; Holcombe v. State, 5 Ga. App. 47, 62 S.E. 647 (1908).

[30] City of Louisiana v. Bottoms, 300 S.W. 316 (St. Louis Ct. App. 1927).

[31] O'Donnell v. Sweeney, 5 Ala. 467 (1843) ; City Council of Charleston v. Benjamin, 2 Strob. 508 (S.C. App. 1848) ; Shover v. State, 10 Ark. 259 (1850) ; State v. Ambs, 20 Mo. 214 (1854) ; Commonwealth v. Wolf, 3 S. & R. 48 (Pa. 1816) ; Omit v. Commonwealth, 21 Pa. 426 (1853) ; Johnston v. Commonwealth, 22 Pa. 102 (1853) ; Mohney v. Cook, 26 Pa. 342 (1855) ; Commonwealth v. Nesbit, 34 Pa. 398 (1859).

[32] Specht v. Commonwealth, 8 Pa. 312 (1848) ; People v. Hoym, 20 How. Pr. 76 (N.Y. Super. 1860) ; *Ex parte* Andrews 18 Cal. 685 (1861) ; Frohlickstein v. Mayor of Mobile, 40 Ala. 725 (1867) ; Commonwealth v. Has, 122 Mass. 40

(1877) ; Bloom v. Richards, 2 Ohio St. 387 (1854) ; State v. Goode, 5 Ohio N.P. 179 (C.P. 1898) ; State v. Powell, 58 Ohio St. 324, 50 N.E. 900 (1898). *Contra: Ex parte* Newman, 9 Cal. 502 (1858), *overruled, Ex parte* Andrews, *supra.*

[33] Specht v. Commonwealth, 8 Pa. 312 (1848) ; City Council of Charleston v. Benjamin, 2 Strob. 508 (S.C. App. 1848).

[34] 28 Idaho 599, 155 Pac. 296 (1916).

[35] Stansbury v. Marks, 2 Dal. 213 (Pa. 1793). Marks subsequently waived the benefit of this testimony and the fine was revoked.

[36] Commonwealth v. Lesher, 17 S. & R. 155 (Pa. 1828).

[37] People v. Pearson, 176 N.Y. 201, 68 N.E. 243 (1903) ; Owens v. State, 6 Okla. Crim. 110, 116 Pac. 345 (1911). See also Beck v. State, 29 Okla. Crim. 240, 233 Pac. 495 (1925) ; State v. Chenoweth, 163 Ind. 94, 71 N.E. 197 (1904).

[38] Jacobson v. Massachusetts, 197 U.S. 11 (1905).

[39] Prince v. Massachusetts, 321 U.S. 158, 166–67 (1944). See also Pfeffer, *op. cit. supra* note 21, at 572–73.

[40] Matter of Viemeister, 179 N.Y. 235, 72 N.E. 97 (1904) ; City of New Braunfels v. Waldschmidt, 109 Tex. 302, 207 S.W. 303 (1918) ; State *ex rel.* O'Bannon v. Cole, 220 Mo. 697, 119 S.W. 424 (1909) ; Staffel v. San Antonio School Board, 201 S.W. 413 (Tex. Civ. App. 1918) ; Vonnegut v. Baun, 206 Ind. 172, 188 N.E. 677 (1934).

[41] People v. Ekerold, 211 N.Y. 386, 105 N.E. 670 (1914) ; Commonwealth v. Aiken, 64 Pa. Super. 96 (1916) ; Commonwealth v. Green, 268 Mass. 585, 168 N.E. 101 (1929) ; State v. Drew, 89 N.H. 54, 192 Atl. 629 (1937). Cf. *In re* Hargy, 23 Ohio N.P. (N.S.) 129 (C.P. 1920), upholding a dependency proceeding. *Contra:* State v. Turney, 31 Ohio Circ. Ct. Rep. 222 (1909) ; Commonwealth v. Smith, 9 Pa. Dist. Rep. 625 (1900).

[42] For thoroughly bungled religious claims, see Vonnegut v. Baun, 206 Ind. 172, 188 N.E. 677 (1934) ; State v. Drew, 89 N.H. 54, 192 Atl. 629 (1937).

[43] Staffel v. San Antonio School Board, 201 S.W. 413 (Tex. Civ. App. 1918) ; Commonwealth v. Green, 268 Mass. 585, 168 N.E. 101 (1929).

[44] Such cases generally involved suits by taxpayers or parents to prevent *any* Bible reading in the schools. See, for example, Billard v. Board of Education, 69 Kan. 53, 76 Pac. 422 (1904) ; Moore v. Monroe, 64 Iowa 367, 20 N.W. 475 (1884).

[45] Donahoe v. Richards, 38 Me. 379 (1854).

[46] One regulation was upheld as applied to all Christians, but was invalidated insofar as it contemplated authorizing reading from the New Testament in classes including Jewish pupils. Herold v. Parish Board, 136 La. 1034, 68 So. 116 (1915).

[47] Herold v. Parish Board, note 46 *supra;* Billard v. Board of Education, 69 Kan. 53, 76 Pac. 422 (1904) ; Moore v. Monroe, 64 Iowa 367, 20 N.W. 475 (1884) ; Spiller v. Inhabitants of Woburn, 94 Mass. (12 Allen) 127 (1866) ; McCormick v. Burt, 95 Ill. 263 (1880) ; Hart v. School District, 2 Lanc. L. Rep. 346 (Pa. C.P. 1885) ; Pfeiffer v. Board of Education, 118 Mich. 560, 77 N.W. 250 (1898) ; Hackett v. Brooksville Graded School District, 120 Ky. 608, 87

S.W. 792 (1905) ; Wilkerson v. City of Rome, 152 Ga. 762, 110 S.E. 895 (1922) ; Kaplan v. Independent School District, 171 Minn. 142, 214 N.W. 18 (1927). *Contra:* State *ex rel.* Weiss v. District Board, 76 Wis. 177, 44 N.W. 967 (1890).

[48] *E.g.*, Spiller v. Woburn, 94 Mass. (12 Allen) 127, 129 (1866) ; Hart v. School District, 2 Lanc. L. Rep. 346, 352 (Pa. C.P. 1885). But cf. Kaplan v. Independent School District, 171 Minn. 142, 214 N.W. 18, 22 (1927).

[49] State *ex rel.* Freeman v. Scheve, 65 Neb. 853, 91 N.W. 846 (1902) ; People *ex rel.* Ring v. Board of Education, 245 Ill. 334, 92 N.E. 251 (1910) ; People *ex rel.* Vollmar v. Stanley, 81 Colo. 276, 255 Pac. 610 (1927) ; State *ex rel.* Finger v. Weedman, 55 S.D. 343, 226 N.W. 348 (1929). Cf. State *ex rel.* Dearle v. Frazier, 102 Wash. 369, 173 Pac. 35 (1918). *Contra:* Commonwealth *ex rel.* Wall v. Cook, 7 Am. L. Reg. (O.S.) 417 (Boston, Mass., Police Ct. 1859). Three Bible-reading regulations were upheld, the mandatory or voluntary nature of which was never made clear. Nessle v. Hum, 2 Ohio Dec. 60 (1894) ; Stevenson v. Hanyon, 7 Pa. Dist. 585 (C.P. 1895) ; Lewis v. Board of Education, 285 N.Y.S. 164 (Sup. Ct. 1935).

[50] 48 Vt. 444 (1876).

[51] 54 Cal. App. 696, 205 Pac. 49, *aff'd per curiam*, 205 Pac. 56 (1921).

[52] *Id.* at 712, 205 Pac. at 55.

[53] 98 U.S. 145 (1879).

[54] Davis v. Beason, 133 U.S. 333 (1890).

[55] Church of Jesus Christ of Latter Day Saints v. United States, 136 U.S. 1 (1890).

[56] Pfeffer, *op. cit. supra* note 21, at 532–33.

[57] Shapiro v. Lyle, 30 F(2d) 971 (W.D. Wash. 1929).

[58] Knowles v. United States, 170 Fed. 409 (8th Cir. 1909).

[59] United States v. White, 150 Fed. 379 (Md. 1906) ; New v. United States, 245 Fed. 710 (9th Cir. 1917).

[60] 143 U.S. 457 (1892).

[61] *Id.* at 465.

[62] 8 U.S.C. 381, quoted, United States v. Schwimmer, 279 U.S. 644, 646 (1929).

[63] Quoted, United States v. Schwimmer, 279 U.S. 644, 647 (1929).

[64] 279 U.S. 644 (1929).

[65] 283 U.S. 605 (1931).

[66] See Hamilton v. Regents, 293 U.S. 245, 252 (1934).

[67] University of Maryland v. Coale, 165 Md. 224, 167 Atl. 54 (1933).

[68] Coale v. Pearson, 290 U.S. 597 (1933).

[69] 293 U.S. 245 (1934).

[70] See, *e.g.*, Pfeffer, The Liberties of an American 46–57 *passim* (1956) ; Hensley, *The Constitutional Aspects of Compulsory Pledges of Allegiance and Salutes*, 3 Lawyer 5, 9–10 (November, 1939) ; Grinnell, *Children, The Bill of Rights and the American Flag*, 24 Mass. L.Q. 1, 5–6 (April–June, 1939) ; 2 Ga. B.J. 74, 75 (1940) ; 51 Harvard L. Rev. 1418, 1422–23 (1938) ; 18 N.Y.U.L.Q. Rev. 124, 125 (1940). Cf. Spicer, The Supreme Court and Fundamental Freedoms 73–74 (1959).

[71] 80 U.S. (13 Wall.) 679 (1871).

72 *Id.* at 728–29.

73 Commonwealth v. Lesher, 17 S. & R. 155, 160 (Pa. 1828).

74 *Id.* at 160–61.

75 Frazee's Case, 63 Mich. 396, 406, 30 N.W. 72, 75 (1886).

76 City of Wilkes-Barre v. Garabed, 11 Pa. Super. 355, 369 (1899).

77 Owens v. State, 6 Okla. Crim. 110, 115, 116 Pac. 345, 347 (1911).

78 Donahoe v. Richards, 38 Me. 379, 410 (1854).

79 48 Vt. at 465.

80 Reynolds v. United States, 98 U.S. 145, 166 (1879).

81 *Id.* at 166–67.

82 283 U.S. at 633.

83 Davis v. Beason, 133 U.S. 333, 341–42 (1890) ; Shapiro v. Lyle, 30 F(2d) 971, 973 (W.D. Wash. 1929) ; Commonwealth v. Herr, 39 Pa. Super. 454, 464 (1910) ; State v. White, 68 N.H. 48, 50, 5 Atl. 828, 830 (1886) ; McMasters v. State, 21 Okla. Crim. 318, 325, 207 Pac. 566, 569 (1922) ; Fealy v. City of Birmingham, 15 Ala. App. 367, 372–73, 73 So. 296, 299 (1916) ; City of Louisiana v. Bottoms, 300 S.W. 316, 318 (St. Louis Ct. App. 1927).

84 See, *e.g.*, Owens v. State, 6 Okla. Crim. 110, 115, 116 Pac. 345, 347 (1911) ; Commonwealth v. Herr, 39 Pa. Super. 454, 465 (1910).

85 See 283 U.S. at 625. See also note 52, *supra.*

86 Davis v. Beason, 133 U.S. 333, 341–42 (1890) ; Church of Jesus Christ of Latter Day Saints v. United States, 136 U.S. 1, 49–50 (1890). Cf. Frohlickstein v. Mayor of Mobile, 40 Ala. 725, 727 (1867).

87 See Justice Jackson's dissent in United States v. Ballard, 322 U.S. 78, 92–93 (1944).

88 See Reynolds v. United States, 98 U.S. 145, 164 (1879) ; Ferriter v. Tyler, 48 Vt. 444, 465 (1876). Cf. a classic formulation by Roger Williams, quoted, MENDELSON, THE CONSTITUTION AND THE SUPREME COURT 432 (1959).

89 See, generally, Carter v. Carter Coal Co., 298 U.S. 238 (1936) ; Dobbins v. Commissioners of Erie County, 16 Pet. (U.S.) 435 (1842) ; Brown v. Maryland, 12 Wheat. (U.S.) 419 (1827).

90 249 U.S. 47 (1919).

91 *Id.* at 52.

92 268 U.S. 652 (1925).

93 *Id.* at 668.

94 Whitney v. California, 274 U.S. 357, 378–79 (1927) (concurring opinion).

95 Near v. Minnesota, 283 U.S. 698 (1931) ; DeJonge v. Oregon, 299 U.S. 353 (1937) ; Lovell v. Griffin, 303 U.S. 444 (1938) ; Hague v. CIO, 307 U.S. 496 (1939).

96 Herndon v. Lowry, 301 U.S. 242, 261 (1937).

97 308 U.S. 147 (1939).

98 *Id.* at 161.

99 Thornhill v. Alabama, 310 U.S. 88, 105–6 (1940) ; Carlson v. California, 310 U.S. 106, 113 (1940) ; Cantwell v. Connecticut, 310 U.S. 296, 311 (1940).

100 Bridges v. California, 314 U.S. 252, 263 (1941).

101 283 U.S. 359 (1931).

CHAPTER FOUR

[1] Civil Liberties Quarterly, June 1936, p. 1.

[2] Brief for Appellees, p. 49, Minersville School District v. Gobitis, 108 F(2d) 683 (3d Cir. 1939).

[3] Complainant's Brief on Motion To Dismiss, p. 4, Gobitis v. Minersville School District, 21 F. Supp. 581 (E.D. Pa. 1937).

[4] Boston Post, May 20, 1937.

[5] *Ibid.*, October 1, 1937.

[6] Brief for Appellees, pp. 5, 53–54, Minersville School District v. Gobitis, 108 F(2d) 683 (3d Cir. 1939).

[7] Letter, Olin R. Moyle to ACLU (New York office), November 1, 1937, ACLU Archives, vol. 958, "New York."

[8] ACLU Press Release, May 11, 1936, p. 1.

[9] Mass. Rept. Att'y Gen. 1935, at 108 (October 9, 1935). See also Mass. Rept. Att'y Gen. 1938, at 36 (January 21, 1938).

[10] Cf. Boston Post, April 18, 1939, giving a general figure of twenty-five.

[11] New York Times, October 24, 1935.

[12] Boston Post, October 1, 1937.

[13] *Ibid.*, May 20, 1937.

[14] ACLU Press Release, April 23, 1937.

[15] Commonwealth v. Johnson, 309 Mass. 476, 479, 35 N.E.(2d) 801, 803 (1941).

[16] New York Times, November 14, 1935; letter, James P. Roberts to Roger N. Baldwin, April 18, 1937, ACLU Archives, vol. 956, "Massachusetts."

[17] New York Times, March 11, 1940.

[18] Boston Post, October 1, 1937.

[19] *Ibid.*, May 20, 1937.

[20] Los Angeles Examiner, November 17, 1935.

[21] Letter, Roger N. Baldwin to Carleton Nicholls Sr., October 4, 1935, ACLU Archives, vol. 841, "Massachusetts."

[22] ACLU Minutes, October 28, 1935.

[23] Letters, A. Frank Reel to Olin R. Moyle, October 11, 1935; A. Frank Reel to Roger N. Baldwin, October 11, 1935; Roger N. Baldwin to Olin R. Moyle, November 18, 1935; all in ACLU Archives, vol. 841, "Massachusetts."

[24] Record, pp. 1–10, Nicholls v. Lynn, 297 Mass. 65, 7 N.E. (2d) 577 (1937).

[25] Letter, Roger N. Baldwin to Olin R. Moyle, November 18, 1935, ACLU Archives, vol. 841, "Massachusetts."

[26] *Ibid.*

[27] The brief is reproduced in ACLU Archives, vol. 841, "Massachusetts."

[28] Reproduced, *ibid.* See also letter, A. Frank Reel to Roger N. Baldwin, November 25, 1935, ACLU Archives, vol. 841, "Massachusetts."

[29] 297 Mass. 65, 7 N.E.(2d) 577 (1937).

[30] *Id.* at 68, 7 N.E. (2d) at 579.

[31] *Id.* at 70–71, 7 N.E.(2d) at 580.

[32] Letters, Roger N. Baldwin to Richard W. Hale, April 21, 1937; Roger N.

Baldwin to S. E. Angoff (of M.C.L.C.), April 7, 1937; both in ACLU Archives, vol. 956, "Massachusetts."

[33] Letters, Roger N. Baldwin to James P. Roberts, April 9, 1937; Roger N. Baldwin to S. E. Angoff, April 22, 1937; Roger N. Baldwin to Richard W. Hale, April 21, 1937; all in ACLU Archives, vol. 956, "Massachusetts."

[34] Letter, Richard W. Hale to Roger N. Baldwin, April 23, 1937, ACLU Archives, vol. 956, "Massachusetts."

[35] ACLU Press Release, April 23, 1936.

[36] Springfield Daily Republican (Mass.), April 18, 1936.

[37] Springfield Union (Mass.), April 2, 1937.

[38] Boston Post, April 23, 1936.

[39] *Ibid.*

[40] Springfield Union (Mass.), April 2, 1937.

[41] ACLU Press Release, April 23, 1936. See also letter, S. E. Angoff to Roger N. Baldwin, April 15, 1937, ACLU Archives, vol. 956, "Massachusetts."

[42] New Britain Herald, May 19, 1937.

[43] Springfield Evening Union (Mass.), September 24, 1938.

[44] See Boston Post, February 2, 1939; New York Times, October 31 and November 29, 1938.

[45] Commonwealth v. Johnson, 309 Mass. 476, 479, 35 N.E.(2d) 801, 803 (1941).

[46] Lipsig was secured by the ACLU, but received a small stipend from the Witnesses. See letter, Olin R. Moyle to A. L. Wirin, June 19, 1937, ACLU Archives, vol. 968, "Religious Freedom."

[47] Judicial Code, § 266, 28 U.S.C. § 380.

[48] New York Times, November 29, 1938.

[49] See the opinion in Johnson v. Deerfield, 25 F. Supp. 918, 918–19 (Mass. 1939).

[50] 25 F. Supp. 918 (Mass. 1939).

[51] Johnson v. Deerfield, 306 U.S. 621 (1939).

[52] Boston Post, February 2, 1939; New Haven Digest, February 3, 1939.

[53] Boston Post, February 3, 1939.

[54] Commonwealth v. Johnson, 309 Mass. 476, 479–80, 35 N.E.(2d) 801, 803 (1941).

[55] *Ibid.*

[56] North Adams Transcript (Mass.), July 21, 1939.

[57] *Ibid.*

[58] Letter, George K. Gardner to D.R.M., January 15, 1958.

[59] Letter, S. E. Angoff to Roger N. Baldwin, April 16, 1937, ACLU Archives, vol. 956, "Massachusetts."

[60] Boston Post, February 9, 1938.

[61] Springfield Union (Mass.), March 9, 1939.

[62] GA. CODE tit. 32, § 32-706 (1933); Leoles v. Landers, 184 Ga. 580, 582, 192 S.E. 218, 220 (1937).

[63] *Witness and Justices,* 30 TIME 34 (December 27, 1937).

[64] Atlanta Georgian, October 14, 1936.

⁶⁵ Atlanta Constitution, November 1, 1936.

⁶⁶ Atlanta Georgian, October 14 and October 17, 1936.

⁶⁷ Atlanta Constitution, November 1, 1936.

⁶⁸ Atlanta Georgian, October 17, 1936; *Witness and Justices,* 30 TIME 34 (December 27, 1937); Brief for Appellees, pp. 52–53, Minersville School District v. Gobitis, 108 F (2d) 683 (3d Cir. 1939).

⁶⁹ The petition, demurrer, and superior court decision are reproduced in ACLU Archives, vol. 955, "Georgia."

⁷⁰ 184 Ga. 580, 192 S.E. 218 (1937).

⁷¹ *Id.* at 585–86, 192 S.E. at 222.

⁷² Leoles v. Landers, 302 U.S. 656 (1937).

⁷³ Philadelphia Evening Bulletin, December 2, 1937.

⁷⁴ New York Times, November 14, 1935.

⁷⁵ *Ibid.,* December 1, 1939.

⁷⁶ *Ibid.,* November 2, 1935.

⁷⁷ Philadelphia Evening Bulletin, June 4, 1940.

⁷⁸ 17 GOLDEN AGE 307 (1935).

⁷⁹ New York Times, November 2, 1935.

⁸⁰ Brief for Appellees, p. 52, Minersville School District v. Gobitis, 108 F(2d) 683 (3d Cir. 1939); Stipulation of Facts between state attorneys and Isserman & Isserman, Hering v. State Board of Education, 117 N.J.L. 455, 189 Atl. 629 (1937).

⁸¹ ACLU Minutes, November 11, 1935. On Isserman's insistence, the Witnesses were required to support the cost of the suit. ACLU Minutes, November 18, 1935; letter, Abraham J. Isserman to Lucille B. Milner, April 16, 1937, ACLU Archives, vol. 957, "New Jersey."

⁸² Olin R. Moyle, personal interview, August 15, 1957. The brief is reproduced in ACLU Archives, vol. 957, "New Jersey."

⁸³ Reproduced in ACLU Archives, vol. 957, "New Jersey."

⁸⁴ *Ibid.*

⁸⁵ *Ibid.*

⁸⁶ 117 N.J.L. 455, 189 Atl. 629 (1937).

⁸⁷ *Ibid.*

⁸⁸ The original brief is reproduced in ACLU Archives, vol. 957, "New Jersey." The "Model Brief" is reproduced in ACLU Archives, vol. 872, "Flag Saluting: General." The two are substantially identical, save for the elimination of limiting proper nouns.

⁸⁹ See letters, dated May 13, 1937, Arthur Garfield Hays to A. H. Bissell, M. Chanalis, J. Gross and Judge A. A. Melnicker, ACLU Archives, vol. 957, "New Jersey."

⁹⁰ 118 N.J.L. 566, 194 Atl. 177 (1947).

⁹¹ Hering v. State Board of Education, 303 U.S. 624 (1938).

⁹² Jersey Journal, April 14, 1939; New York World-Telegram, April 14, 1939.

⁹³ N.J. Laws 1939, c. 65, § 1, at 108, N.J. REV. STAT. tit. 2, § 130–5 (Supp. 1940).

94 Oakland Tribune (Calif.), September 10, 1937.

95 Letter, F. A. Lee to Roger N. Baldwin, March 10, 1936, ACLU Archives, vol. 872, "Flag Saluting: General."

96 17 GOLDEN AGE 191 (1935).

97 Oakland Tribune (Calif.), September 10, 1937.

98 Los Angeles Examiner, November 25, 1938.

99 Fresno Bee (Calif.), January 25, 1936.

100 Letter, Olin R. Moyle to Lucille B. Milner, January 9, 1936, ACLU Archives, vol. 872, "Flag Saluting: General."

101 Olin R. Moyle, personal interview, August 15, 1957.

102 The opinion is unreported officially; an expanded version is contained in 32 LIBERTY no. 2. As to the date, see Complainant's Brief on Motion To Dismiss, p. 13, Gobitis v. Minersville School District, 21 F. Supp. 581 (E.D. Pa. 1937).

103 Gabrielli v. Knickerbocker, 74 Pac. (2d) 290 (Cal. App. 1937).

104 12 Cal. (2d) 85, 82 Pac. (2d) 391 (1938).

105 *Id.* at 91–92, 82 Pac. (2d) at 394–95.

106 Gabrielli v. Knickerbocker, 306 U.S. 621 (1939).

107 Million, *Validity of Compulsory Flag Salutes in Public Schools*, 28 KY. L. J. 306, 317 (1940).

108 Letters, Lucille B. Milner to L. D. Shinn, August 13, 1936; Lucille B. Milner to Fred Anderson, August 12, 1936; both in ACLU Archives, vol. 950, "Texas." See also Houston Post, January 5, 1937.

109 Note 108 *supra*; letters, Ellen K. Donahue to Arthur J. Mandell, September 26, 1936; Arthur J. Mandell to Ellen K. Donahue, October 7, 1936; both in ACLU Archives, vol. 950, "Texas."

110 Houston Post, January 5, 1937.

111 Letters, W. A. Combs to ACLU, January 18, 1937; Ellen K. Donahue to W. A. Combs, February 9, 1937; both in ACLU Archives, vol. 959, "Texas."

112 Letter, W. A. Combs to Olin R. Moyle, May 3, 1937, ACLU Archives, vol. 959, "Texas."

113 *Ibid.*; letter, W. A. Combs to Ellen K. Donahue, May 3, 1937, ACLU Archives, vol. 959, "Texas."

114 Note 112 *supra*; letter, H. A. Poth to W. A. Combs, October 19, 1937, ACLU Archives, vol. 959, "Texas."

115 121 S.W. (2d) 450 (Tex. Civ. App. 1938).

116 One justice emphasized that he concurred in the dismissal solely on the ground of mootness. *Id.* at 451. The case had been just as moot when the court denied a motion to dismiss in the preceding fall. Letter, W. A. Combs to A. L. Wirin, September 25, 1937, ACLU Archives, vol. 959, "Texas."

117 116 S.W. (2d) 836 (Tex. Civ. App. 1938).

118 *Id.* at 836–38.

119 *Id.* at 838–39.

120 279 N.Y. 523, 18 N.E. (2d) 840 (1939), *reversing*, 167 Misc. 436, 3 N.Y.S. (2d) 1006 (1938).

[121] Letter, Olin R. Moyle to ACLU, November 1, 1937, ACLU Archives, vol. 958, "New York."

[122] *Ibid.*

[123] Memo, Lucille B. Milner to Ellen K. Donahue, November 11, 1937, ACLU Archives, vol. 958, "New York." See also ACLU Minutes, November 1, 1937.

[124] New York Times, November 6, 1937. The full transcript of the trial is reproduced in ACLU Archives, vol. 958, "New York."

[125] Note 123 *supra;* The Flag and Grace, New York Times, November 14, 1937.

[126] *Ibid.,* November 6, 1937.

[127] *Ibid.,* December 4, 1937. This ruling provoked a bitter exchange between Hays and the State Superintendent's office. Letters, Arthur Garfield Hays to F. P. Graves (State Commissioner), December 7, 1937; E. E. Cole (Department Counsel) to Arthur Garfield Hays, December 10, 1937; Arthur Garfield Hays to E. E. Cole, December 17, 1937; all in ACLU Archives, vol. 958, "New York."

[128] 167 Misc. 436, 3 N.Y.S.(2d) 1006 (1938).

[129] 279 N.Y. 523, 18 N.E.(2d) 840 (1939).

[130] *Id.* at 529, 18 N.E.(2d) at 842.

[131] *Id.* at 531, 18 N.E.(2d) at 843.

[132] *Id.* at 536, 18 N.E.(2d) at 845.

[133] *Id.* at 538–39, 18 N.E.(2d) at 846–47.

[134] FLA. REPT. ATT'Y GEN. 1937–38, at 212 (April 13, 1937).

[135] Jacksonville Journal, November 26, 1937.

[136] Jacksonville American, December 3, 1937.

[137] Jacksonville Journal, November 26, 1937.

[138] Gobitis v. Minersville School District, 21 F. Supp. 581 (E.D.Pa. 1937).

[139] Jacksonville American, December 3, 1937.

[140] *Ibid.; Florida Times-Union,* December 3, 1937.

[141] Letter, Olin R. Moyle to ACLU, December 14, 1937, ACLU Archives, vol. 955, "Florida."

[142] See Letter, Frank McCallister to Lucille B. Milner, December 23, 1937, ACLU Archives, vol. 955, "Florida."

[143] 139 Fla. 43, 190 So. 815 (1939).

[144] *Id.* at 45–46, 190 So. at 816–17.

[145] *Id.* at 47, 190 So. at 817.

[146] *Id.* at 46–47, 190 So. at 817.

[147] Letter, Ellen K. Donahue to Helen P. Stokes, May 11, 1936, ACLU Archives, vol. 950, "Vermont."

[148] Letter, Rev. D. T. Yoder to Lucille B. Milner, February 18, 1936, ACLU Archives, vol. 950, "Vermont."

[149] Letter, Ellen K. Donahue to Helen P. Stokes, August 3, 1936, ACLU Archives, vol. 950, "Vermont."

[150] OHIO OPS. ATT'Y GEN. 1935–36, at 1650 (Opinion no. 5003, December 16, 1935).

[151] 17 GOLDEN AGE 266 (1936).

[152] Md. Rept. Att'y Gen. 1936, at 560 (September 15, 1936).

[153] Letter, F. A. Ballard (Ludke's attorney) to Lucille B. Milner, August 24, 1936, ACLU Archives, vol. 872, "Flag Saluting: General."

[154] Baltimore Evening Sun, January 5, 1938.

[155] Letter, Irving M. Clark (Seattle Civil Liberties Committee) to Roger N. Baldwin, April 21, 1936, ACLU Archives, vol. 950, "Washington." The children first learned of the flag-salute issue through a threatening speech by the school principal. Letter, L. C. Brown (Jehovah's Witnesses' Elma County Service Director) to Golden Age editor, April 19, 1936, ACLU Archives, vol. 950, "Washington."

[156] Letter, L. C. Brown to Golden Age editor, April 19, 1936, ACLU Archives, vol. 950, "Washington."

[157] Letter, Irving M. Clark to Roger N. Baldwin, April 21, 1936; undated, unsigned memo; both in ACLU Archives, vol. 950, "Washington."

[158] Letter, Irving M. Clark to Roger N. Baldwin, April 21, 1936; ACLU Bulletin, no. 714, May 15, 1936; both in ACLU Archives, vol. 950, "Washington."

[159] Undated, unsigned memo; letter, O. C. Pratt (Spokane school superintendent) to Ellen K. Donahue, October 29, 1936; both in ACLU Archives, vol. 950, "Washington."

[160] Letters, Ellen K. Donahue to W. C. Donovan, October 24, 1936; W. C. Donovan to Ellen K. Donahue, October 29, 1936; Ellen K. Donahue to Olin R. Moyle, November 7, 1936; all in ACLU Archives, vol. 950, "Washington."

[161] Letters, Olin R. Moyle to Ellen K. Donahue, September 30 and October 8, 1936, ACLU Archives, vol. 950, "Washington."

[162] Letters, Irving M. Clark to Ellen K. Donahue, November 6, 1936; Ellen K. Donahue to Mrs. Lillian Sylten, November 10, 1936; both in ACLU Archives, vol. 950, "Washington."

[163] Oklahoma News, February 18, 1938.

[164] New York Times, February 10, 1939.

[165] Spokane Spokesmen-Review, March 26, 1939.

[166] 17 Golden Age 307 (1936).

[167] Kansas City Star, September 8, 1938.

[168] Great Bend Tribune (Kan.), September 14, 1938.

[169] New York Times, November 1, 1935.

[170] Letter, Olin R. Moyle to Ellen K. Donahue, September 30, 1936, ACLU Archives, vol. 950, "Washington." The sentence was in lieu of a $200 fine. Brief for Appelleees, p. 53, Minersville School District v. Gobitis, 108 F(2d) 683 (3d Cir. 1939).

[171] Brief for Appellees, p. 53, Minersville School District v. Gobitis, 108 F(2d) 683 (3d Cir. 1939).

[172] Grand Rapids Herald, February 2, 1939.

[173] 17 Golden Age 138 (1935).

[174] 17 Golden Age 103 (1935).

[175] New York Times, October 20, 1935.

[176] Before 1937, the maximum age was sixteen. Pa. Stat. Ann. tit. 24,

§ 1421 (Purdon, 1936); Gobitis v. Minersville School District, 21 F. Supp. 581, 583 (E.D. Pa. 1937).

177 PA. STAT. ANN. tit. 24, § 1430 (Purdon, 1936).

178 *Id.*, § 1477.

179 *Id.*, §§ 1, 161, 331.

180 *Id.*, § 338.

181 *Id.*, § 1551. The reference to loyalty was added by Pa. Laws 1919, no. 263, at 544.

182 Complainant's Brief on Motion To Dismiss, p. 4, Gobitis v. Minersville School District, 21 F. Supp. 581 (E.D. Pa. 1937).

183 Walter Gobitis, personal interview, January 20, 1957; Pottsville Evening Journal, June 18, 1938.

184 Brief for Appellees, pp. 53–54, Minersville School District v. Gobitis, 108 F(2d) 683 (3d Cir. 1939).

185 *Id.* at 54–55.

186 In New Ringgold, a non-saluter was made to stand in a corner all day. *Id.* at 52.

187 Philadelphia Evening Bulletin, June 20, 1938.

188 Reading Eagle, December 1, 1935; Philadelphia Inquirer, December 5, 1937.

189 Wichita Eagle, December 10, 1935.

190 Lucille B. Milner, memorandum for files, January 31, 1936, ACLU Archives, vol. 872, "Flag Saluting: General"; *Fascism (Catholic Action— The Inquisition) in Pennsylvania,* 17 GOLDEN AGE 165 (1935); 2 PITT. L. REV. 206 (1936).

191 Letters, Lucille B. Milner to Olin R. Moyle, January 6, 1936; Olin R. Moyle to Lucille B. Milner, March 19, 1936, both in ACLU Archives, vol. 872, "Flag Saluting: General."

192 See Judge Gibson's opinion, Estep v. Borough of Canonsburg (Pa. C.P. 1937, unreported), reprinted in ACLU Archives, vol. 958, "Pennsylvania."

193 *Ibid.*

194 PA. OPS. ATT'Y GEN. 1935–36, at 100 (October 26, 1935).

195 Judge Gibson's opinion, note 192 *supra;* New York Times, November 8, 1935; Lucille B. Milner, memorandum for files, ACLU Archives, vol. 872, "Flag Saluting: General."

196 Letter, Olin R. Moyle to Lucille B. Milner, January 9, 1936, ACLU Archives, vol. 872 "Flag Saluting: General."

197 ACLU Press Release, May 11, 1936.

198 Pennsylvania Common Pleas, April 24, 1937, unreported. The decision is printed in full in ACLU Archives, vol. 958, "Pennsylvania."

199 Pittsburgh Sun-Telegraph, April 16, 1936; Monessen Daily Independent, April 17, 1936.

200 Pittsburgh Sun-Telegraph, April 16, 1936.

201 Monessen Daily Independent, April 17, 1936; unsigned, undated memorandum history of the Monessen affair, ACLU Archives, vol. 958, "Pennsylvania."

202 Unsigned, undated memorandum history of the Monessen affair, ACLU Archives, vol. 958, "Pennsylvania."

203 *Ibid.* See also the answer filed in the court by Gold *et al.*, reprinted in ACLU Archives, vol. 958, "Pennsylvania."

204 Letter, Olin R. Moyle to Ellen K. Donahue, January 14, 1937, ACLU Archives, vol. 958, "Pennsylvania." This two-pronged attack seems to have been a regular weapon in the Witness arsenal. See SCHNELL, THIRTY YEARS A WATCH TOWER SLAVE 164–65 (1956).

205 Letter, Olin R. Moyle to Ellen K. Donahue, January 14, 1937, ACLU Archives, vol. 958, "Pennsylvania"; Brief for Appellees, p. 54, Minersville School District v. Gobitis, 108 F(2d) 683 (3d Cir. 1939).

206 The most obvious explanation—inadequate data—is relatively unimportant here. The superb intelligence system maintained by the Witness national office makes its total estimates very reliable; if anything, they are too high.

207 Carleton Nicholls, Jr., Record, pp. 4, 7, Nicholls v. Lynn, 297 Mass. 65, 7 N.E.(2d) 577 (1937). Alma Hering, New York Times, October 30, 1935.

208 Letter, A. L. Wirin to W. A. Combs, May 11, 1937, ACLU Archives, vol. 959, "Texas."

209 One apparent exception is the *Bleich* case. Moyle denies taking any active part in this litigation, although his name appears on brief. Personal interview, August 15, 1957. It is not clear to what extent he was a free agent at this time, in view of his loss of face over the *Gabrielli* suit.

CHAPTER FIVE

1 POTTSVILLE SCHOOL DISTRICT, THE HISTORY OF SCHUYLKILL COUNTY 9 (1950).

2 Based on conversations with residents of the area.

3 Walter Gobitis, testimony (summary), Transcript of Record, p. 47, Minersville School District v. Gobitis, 310 U.S. 586 (1940) (cited hereafter in this chapter simply as "Record"). For the original examination on this point, see the original verbatim transcript of the trial (cited hereafter in this chapter as "Trial Record"), on file in the Federal Court Building, Philadelphia, Pennsylvania, at page 12. The proper name is *Gobitas*; for the purposes of simplicity, the name appearing in the court records is used throughout this study.

4 Walter Gobitis, personal interview, January 20, 1957.

5 Walter Gobitis, testimony, Record, p. 60; *God's in His Heaven ...*, 22 NEWSWEEK 81, 82 (July 5, 1943).

6 Walter Gobitis, personal interview, January 20, 1957.

7 Walter Gobitis, testimony, Record, p. 77; Trial Record, p. 13.

8 Charles E. Roudabush, testimony, Trial Record, p. 81.

9 KIRK, THE FLAG SALUTE CONTROVERSY IN THE SUPREME COURT (Unpublished Master's thesis in University of Wisconsin Library, 1957) 43. Kirk lists the other occupations represented on the board as piano tuner and teacher, textile executive, office clerk and brewery worker.

10 Letter, Charles E. Roudabush to John B. McGurl, January 27, 1938. Unless otherwise stated, all letters to, from and between Minersville school officials are to be found in Roudabush's personal file on the flag controversy, kept at Minersville High School.

11 Pottsville Evening Republican, November 11, 1935.

12 The refusals were already at least a week old when first mentioned in the press. Pottsville Evening Republican, October 16, 1935.

13 Walter Gobitis, personal interview, January 20, 1957. Gobitis still has nothing good to say about Roudabush.

14 Pottsville Evening Republican, October 20, 1935.

15 Walter Gobitis, personal interview, January 20, 1957.

16 Pottsville Evening Republican, October 16, 1935.

17 *Ibid.*, October 21, 1935.

18 Pottsville Evening Journal, October 22, 1935.

19 Minersville School Board Minutes, November 6, 1935. Gobitis remembers Roudabush's statement as a "one-hour harangue." Personal interview, January 20, 1957.

20 Note 19 *supra*; Claude L. Price (a member of the school board), phone conversation, January 21, 1957.

21 Pottsville Evening Republican, November 7, 1935. These short letters were addressed to Roudabush, and are preserved in his personal file on the controversy.

22 Minersville School Board Minutes, November 6, 1935.

23 Record, pp. 8, 32; Charles E. Roudabush, undated statement of facts regarding the controversy, preserved in his personal file.

24 Walter Gobitis, personal interview, January 20, 1957.

25 For a similar conclusion by a native of the area, see Kirk, *op. cit. supra* note 9, at 46–47.

26 Press reports of the November 6 meeting mention only the passage of the resolution. Pottsville Evening Republican, November 7, 1935.

27 Kirk, *op. cit. supra* note 9, at 42–43.

28 *Id.* at 40 n. 3.

29 Walter Gobitis, personal interview, January 20, 1957.

30 Walter Gobitis, testimony, Record, pp. 57, 74. The number of pupils enrolled in the school is based on Walter Gobitis, personal interview, January 20, 1957. See also Pottsville Evening Journal, June 18, 1938.

31 Walter Gobitis, testimony, Record, pp. 74, 78; Trial Record, pp. 20–21.

32 Walter Gobitis, personal interview, January 20, 1957. Apparently, he was able to buy legal advice, if not services. "... I spent a lot of time and money getting advice...." Record, pp. 52–53.

33 Printed, Record, p. 4.

34 Letters (identical), A. L. Wirin to Isidore Katz and Alexander H. Frey, April 28, 1937, ACLU Archives, vol. 958, "Pennsylvania."

35 Katz declined immediately. Letter, Isidore Katz to A. L. Wirin, April 29, 1937, ACLU Archives, vol. 958, "Pennsylvania." There is no record of Frey doing so, and his name was to crop up again later in the litigation.

[36] Olin R. Moyle, personal interview, August 15, 1957.

[37] Minersville School Board Minutes, May 12, 1937.

[38] Joseph W. Henderson, personal interview, January 25, 1957.

[39] Printed, Record, p. 13.

[40] Printed respectively, *id.* at 4–12, and 13–14.

[41] 28 U.S.C.A. § 41, sub-§§ 1, 14.

[42] Record, p. 11.

[43] *Id.* at 12.

[44] Defendants' Paper Book in Support of the Motion To Dismiss the Bill of Complaint, Gobitis v. Minersville School District, 21 F. Supp. 581 (E.D.Pa. 1937). Cited hereafter in this chapter as "Defendants' Paper Book." The only known copy of this document is in the personal files of Judge Maris, now of the United States Court of Appeals, Third Circuit.

[45] *Id.* at 7.

[46] *Id.* at 3–4.

[47] Barney v. City of New York, 193 U.S. 430 (1904) ; Memphis v. Cumberland Tel. & Tel. Co., 218 U.S. 624 (1910).

[48] See especially Marcus Brown Holding Co. v. Pollak, 272 Fed. 137 (S.D.N.Y. 1920).

[49] Defendants' Paper Book, p. 11.

[50] *Id.* at 13–14.

[51] Complainants' Brief on the Motion To Dismiss, Gobitis v. Minersville School District, 21 F. Supp. 581 (E.D.Pa. 1937). Cited hereafter simply as "Complainants' Brief." The only known copy of this document is in Judge Maris' personal files.

[52] *Id.* at 9–11.

[53] *Id.* at 17–18.

[54] See Terral v. Burke Construction Co., 257 U.S. 529 (1922) ; Frost v. Railroad Commission, 271 U.S. 583 (1926) ; Hanover Insurance Co. v. Harding, 272 U.S. 494 (1926). But cf. Packard v. Banton, 264 U.S. 140 (1924).

[55] Complainants' Brief, p. 34.

[56] *Ibid.*

[57] Gobitis v. Minersville School District, 21 F. Supp. 581 (E.D.Pa. 1937).

[58] 30 WHO'S WHO IN AMERICA 1772 (1958).

[59] Olin R. Moyle, personal interview, August 15, 1957.

[60] 21 F. Supp. at 584–85.

[61] The main reliance was on Home Tel. & Tel. Co. v. Los Angeles, 227 U.S. 278 (1912).

[62] Editorials, Philadelphia Record, December 3, 1937; Philadelphia Evening Bulletin, December 3, 1937.

[63] Philadelphia Inquirer, December 2, 1937.

[64] *Ibid.*, December 4, 1937.

[65] *Ibid.*, December 5, 1937.

[66] Philadelphia Evening Bulletin, December 2, 1937.

[67] *Ibid.*

[68] Letter, Albert Dammeyer (secretary) to Charles E. Roudabush, December 30, 1937.

69 Letter, Frank M. Heacock (county secretary) to Charles E. Roudabush, December 4, 1937.

70 Letter, Harry F. Koenig (Adjutant) to Charles E. Roudabush, December 9, 1937.

71 Letter, C. B. Helms (state secretary) to Charles E. Roudabush, December 17, 1937.

72 Letter, Maurice Rusener (secretary) to Charles E. Roudabush, January 3, 1938.

73 Letter, Charles E. Roudabush to C. B. Helms, December 20, 1937.

74 Certain key receipts are dated February 10 and 11, 1938. Record, pp. 64–67.

75 Letter, Joseph W. Henderson to John B. McGurl, January 21, 1938.

76 Letter, Charles E. Roudabush to Joseph W. Henderson, January 27, 1938.

77 Joint and Several Answers, Gobitis v. Minersville School District, 24 F. Supp. 271 (E.D.Pa. 1938), printed, Record, pp. 28–36. The title of this document refers to the fact that it served as the answer both of the school board, and of each individual defendant.

78 The allegation here referred specifically only to the possibility of education in some neighboring public school. This particular idea was dropped on Roudabush's advice that no such possibility existed in fact. Letter, Charles E. Roudabush to Joseph W. Henderson, January 27, 1938.

79 Record, p. 35.

80 Whenever one side's objection was overruled or an opposition objection was sustained, the losing side was granted an "exception"—in effect a notation in the record that timely objection had been made to the particular "error" committed by the court. This formality is not mentioned hereafter; it can be assumed in each instance.

81 Record, p. 50.

82 See Brief for Appellees, pp. 7–10, Minersville School District v. Gobitis, 108 F(2d) 683 (3d Cir. 1939).

83 *Ibid.*

84 *Ibid.*

85 Record, p. 79.

86 *Id.* at 80.

87 *Id.* at 92–93.

88 *Id.* at 94–95.

89 *Id.* at 94.

90 *Id.* at 97–98.

91 Defendants' Paper Book in Support of Requests for Findings of Fact and Conclusions of Law, Gobitis v. Minersville School District, 24 F. Supp. 271 (E.D.Pa. 1938). The only known copy of this document is in Judge Maris' personal files.

92 Brief in Behalf of Plaintiffs, Gobitis v. Minersville School District, 24 F. Supp. 271 (E.D.Pa. 1938). The only known copy of this document is in Judge Maris' personal files.

93 *Id.* at 15.

94 *Id.* at 16–17.

95 Reply Brief in Behalf of Plaintiffs, Gobitis v. Minersville School District, 24 F. Supp. 271 (E.D.Pa. 1938). The only known copy of this document is in Judge Maris' personal files.

96 *Id.* at 3–4.

97 Printed, Record, pp. 105–12.

98 Printed, *id.* at 113–20.

99 24 F. Supp. 271 (E.D.Pa. 1938).

100 *Id.* at 273.

101 *Id.* at 274.

102 *Ibid.*

103 *Ibid.*

104 *Id.* at 275.

105 Editorials, Philadelphia Evening Bulletin, June 21, 1938; Philadelphia Inquirer, June 20, 1938.

106 Philadelphia Evening Bulletin, June 20, 1938.

107 Editorial, Pottsville Evening Republican, June 21, 1938.

108 Pottsville Evening Republican, June 20, 1938.

109 Minersville School Board Minutes, June 29, 1938.

110 Letter, Claude L. Price (then board secretary) to Walter Gobitis, August 5, 1938.

111 Record, pp. 131, 132.

112 Charles E. Roudabush, undated statement of facts regarding the controversy, preserved in his personal file.

113 Minersville School Board Minutes, December 7, 1938; *id.*, February 1, 1939; letter, secretary (name illegible), Washington Camp P.O.S.A. to Charles E. Roudabush, October 17, 1938.

114 Note 112 *supra.*

115 Letter, Albert Dammeyer (secretary, New York office) to Charles E. Roudabush, August 30, 1938.

116 Printed, Record, pp. 132–49.

117 This document showed considerable sloppiness of drafting. For instance, Henderson objected to three totally nonexistent findings: that the flag-salute ceremony was not a long-standing Minersville custom, that there was jurisdiction under § 24(14), and that the Minersville regulation denied rights *secured* under the federal Constitution. Compare Record, pp. 144–46, with *id.* at 114–19.

118 Brief for Appellants, Minersville School District v. Gobitis, 108 F(2d) 683 (3d Cir. 1939).

119 *Id.* at 37.

120 Brief for Appellees, Minersville School District v. Gobitis, 108 F(2d) 683 (3d Cir. 1939).

121 *Id.* at 18.

122 *Id.* at 24–25.

123 *Id.* at 19.

124 See chapter iii, notes 11, 12, 13, 49.

125 Brief for Appellees, p. 35.

[126] 1 BLACKSTONE, COMMENTARIES ON THE LAWS OF ENGLAND *39, *41, *42, *43.

[127] This conclusion is confirmed by Moyle. Personal interview, August 15, 1957.

[128] Brief for Appellees, p. 40.

[129] Brief for American Civil Liberties Union, *Amicus Curiae*, Minersville School District v. Gobitis, 108 F(2d) 683 (3d Cir. 1939).

[130] Noted on the original docket entry for the case, 1938 term, no. 6862.

[131] 51 HARV. L. REV. 1418 (1938).

[132] United States v. Sprague, 44 F(2d) 967 (N.J. 1930).

[133] 25 F. Supp. 127 (N.J. 1938).

[134] 27 WHO'S WHO IN AMERICA 457 (1952).

[135] 30 *ibid.* 238 (1958).

[136] *Id.* at 467. Regarding Maris' appointment, see *id.* at 1772.

[137] Quoted, Kirk, *op. cit. supra* note 9, at 92.

[138] Minersville School District v. Gobitis, 108 F(2d) 683 (3d Cir. 1939).

[139] *Id.* at 685.

[140] 133 U.S. 333, 342, quoted, 108 F(2d) at 685.

[141] 108 F(2d) at 685.

[142] *Id.* at 689.

[143] *Id.* at 690.

[144] *Id.* at 691.

[145] *Ibid.* At this point, Clark cited several educational authorities—notably Ruediger—who had cast doubt on the efficacy of the flag ceremony.

[146] *Id.* at 692.

[147] Letter to the Religious Society Called Quakers, WASHINGTON, WRITINGS (Sparks ed.) 168–69.

[148] 108 F(2d) at 693.

[149] *Ibid.*

[150] *Ibid.*

[151] *Id.* at 694.

[152] *E.g., id.* at 691, 692.

[153] *Id.* at 692.

[154] Quoted, Kirk, *op. cit. supra* note 9, at 103–4.

[155] *Id.* at 103.

[156] Minersville School Board Minutes, December 4, 1939.

[157] Kirk, *op. cit. supra* note 9, at 105–8.

[158] Minersville School Board Minutes, January 8, 1940.

[159] Noted, *ibid.*

[160] Letter, Harry Koenig (adjutant) to Charles E. Roudabush, January 10, 1940.

[161] Kirk, *op. cit. supra* note 9, at 110–11.

[162] Brief in Support of Petition for Certiorari, Minersville School District v. Gobitis, 310 U.S. 586 (1940).

[163] 309 U.S. 645 (1940).

1 Brief for Petitioners, p. 5, Minersville School District v. Gobitis, 310 U.S. 586 (1940). Unless otherwise stated, all briefs and record entries cited in this chapter were filed in the Supreme Court in the *Gobitis* case.

2 307 U.S. 496 (1939). Three justices still on the Court had held that rights such as these were "secured" by the due process clause; four others had reserved judgment on this point while upholding jurisdiction under another rationale.

3 Brief for Petitioners, p. 19.

4 *Id.* at 21.

5 *Id.* at 19–20.

6 *Id.* at 21.

7 See Railroad Commission of Texas v. Pullman Co., 312 U.S. 496 (1941). Cf. Armstrong Paint & Varnish Works v. Nu-Enamel Corp., 305 U.S. 315 (1938).

8 Brief for Petitioners, p. 20.

9 I Peter 2:17 ("Honour the king.") comes close, but Romans 13:7, Matthew 22:21, Mark 12:17 and Luke 20:25 are noncommittal, while Matthew 10:12 is totally irrelevant.

10 Brief for Petitioners, p. 32.

11 STROUP, THE JEHOVAH'S WITNESSES 25–26 (1945).

12 Respondents' Brief, p. 9.

13 *Id.* at 12.

14 *Id.* at 13.

15 11 ENCYCLOPEDIA AMERICANA 316 (1927), quoted, Respondents' Brief, p. 16. Which edition Rutherford actually used is immaterial. See 11 ENCYCLOPEDIA AMERICANA 316 (1941).

16 Letter, George K. Gardner to D.R.M., January 15, 1958.

17 ACLU Minutes, March 25, 1940.

18 Letter, George K. Gardner to D.R.M., January 15, 1958.

19 Brief for the American Civil Liberties Union, *Amicus Curiae*, p. 11.

20 *Id.* at 15.

21 *Id.* at 18.

22 *Id.* at 22.

23 *Id.* at 26.

24 *Id.* at 27.

25 205 U.S. 34 (1907), upholding a state statute penalizing desecration or other improper use of the American flag.

26 *Proceedings of the House of Delegates, Chicago, Illinois, January 8–9, 1940,* 65 A.B.A. ANN. REP. 404, 417–18 (1940).

27 26 A.B.A.J. 120 (1940).

28 Participating were Clark, Zechariah Chafee, Jr. (Mass.), Douglas Arant (Ala.), Osmer C. Fitts (Vt.), Lloyd K. Garrison (Wis.), George I. Haight (Ill.), Monte M. Lemann (La.), Ross L. Malone, Jr. (N.M.), Burton W. Musser (Utah), Joseph A. Padway (Washington, D.C.) and Charles P. Taft (Ohio). Absent was John F. Neylan (Cal.). Brief for the Committee on the

Bill of Rights of the American Bar Association, as Friends of the Court, p. 1, n. 1. Cited hereafter as "Committee Brief."

[29] Letter, William G. Fennell to D.R.M., August 17, 1957. Fennell also mentions Professor Chafee as having been "vitally interested." Chafee, however, seems to have played a passive role at this stage of the proceedings. Letter, Grenville Clark to Roger N. Baldwin, March 25, 1940, ACLU Archives, vol. 2215, "Religious Freedom."

[30] MASON, HARLAN FISKE STONE: PILLAR OF THE LAW, 581, 853 n. 57 (1956).

[31] Letter, William G. Fennell to D.R.M., August 17, 1957.

[32] Committee Brief, p. 2.

[33] *Id.* at 15.

[34] *Id.* at 20.

[35] *Id.* at 31.

[36] This part of the brief substantially duplicated part of a previous speech by Clark on the issue. *The Limits of Free Expression*, 73 U.S.L. REV. 392, 402, 403 (1939).

[37] Committee Brief, p. 26.

[38] *Id.* at 27.

[39] *Id.* at 28.

[40] This line of argument also was lifted straight from Clark's 1939 speech. Clark, *supra* note 36, at 401–2.

[41] Joseph W. Henderson, personal interview, January 25, 1957. These were *general* impressions; Henderson had no clear recollection of his oral argument in *Gobitis*.

[42] Letter, John B. McGurl to Minersville Board of Education, April 26, 1940, quoted, KIRK, THE FLAG SALUTE CONTROVERSY 115 (1957).

[43] Rutherford's oral argument is one exception to the general lack of information; it is reprinted in full in CONSOLATION, May 29, 1940.

[44] Joseph W. Henderson, personal interview, January 25, 1957.

[45] Letter, George K. Gardner to D.R.M., January 15, 1958.

[46] Gardner specifically refused to give any details of the oral argument, while Frankfurter declined to discuss the case at all. *Ibid.*; letter, Felix Frankfurter to D.R.M., June 27, 1958.

[47] Hayden Covington, personal interview, February 1, 1957; Joseph W. Henderson, personal interview, January 25, 1957; letter, William G. Fennell to D.R.M., August 17, 1957.

[48] Covington was explicit on this point; the same implication was clear in the comments by Fennell and Gardner himself.

[49] FRANK, MARBLE PALACE: THE SUPREME COURT IN AMERICAN LIFE 105–6 (1958). For an extended discussion of this idiosyncracy, see THOMAS, FELIX FRANKFURTER: SCHOLAR ON THE BENCH 354–58 (1960). See also Mason, *op. cit. supra* note 30, at 603; McCUNE, THE NINE YOUNG MEN 100–101 (1947).

[50] See, for example, United States v. Lovett, 328 U.S. 303, 318 (1946) ; Adler v. Board of Education, 342 U.S. 485, 496 (1952).

[51] 310 U.S. 296 (1940).

[52] *Id.* at 303–4.

53 Pusey, Charles Evans Hughes 672–73 (1951) ; Schubert, Constitutional Politics 118 (1960).

54 Reed was Solicitor General at the time. As to Black, see Williams, Hugo L. Black: A Study in the Judicial Process 49–50, 63 (1950).

55 As Governor of Michigan, Murphy had refused to take drastic action against the sit-down strikers. As Attorney General, he established the Civil Liberties Unit (later the Civil Rights Section) in the Justice Department. As to Black, see Williams, *op. cit. supra*, at 39; Chambers v. Florida, 309 U.S. 227 (1940).

56 This paragraph is based on Pusey, *op. cit. supra* note 53, at 675–77; Mason, *op. cit. supra* note 30 at 789–90; Schubert, *op. cit supra* note 53, at 122, 124–25.

57 Pusey, *op. cit. supra* note 53, at 728–29. As to the uncertainty regarding the existence of a formal vote, compare Mason, *op. cit. supra* note 30, at 526.

58 310 U.S. 586 (1940).

59 Justice McReynolds concurred in the result only. There is no need to dwell on his possible reasons. On the personal side was his strong anti-semitism. Pusey, *op. cit. supra* note 53, at 670. More important, probably, were his growing estrangement from the rest of the Court and his resentment of Frankfurter's strong emphasis on judicial self-restraint.

60 Thomas, *op. cit. supra* note 49, at 11, 21.

61 Frankfurter & Greene, The Labor Injunction (1930). For an indirect assault, see Frankfurter & Landis, *Power To Regulate Contempts,* 37 Harv. L. Rev. 1010 (1924).

62 Josephson, *Profiles: Jurist* (Pt. II), 16 New Yorker 36, 42–46 (December 7, 1940) ; Thomas, *op. cit. supra* note 49, at 19–20. See also Frankfurter, The Case of Sacco and Vanzetti (1927).

63 Josephson, *Profiles: Jurist* (Pt. I), 16 New Yorker 24, 26–32 (November 30, 1940). Cf. Thomas, *op. cit. supra* note 49, at 22–25.

64 Note, Felix Frankfurter to Harlan F. Stone, April 27, 1940, quoted, Mason, Security through Freedom 217 (1955).

65 Frankfurter, *The Red Terror of Judicial Reform* (1924), in Law and Politics 10, 16 (1939).

66 Frankfurter, *Can the Supreme Court Guarantee Toleration?* (1925), in Law and Politics 195, 197 (1939).

67 Note, Felix Frankfurter to Harlan F. Stone, April 27, 1940, quoted, Mason, Security through Freedom 217, 218 (1955).

68 *Id.* at 220.

69 *Ibid.*

70 *Id.* at 219.

71 Minersville School District v. Gobitis, 310 U.S. 586, 599 (1940).

72 *Id.* at 594.

73 See Willard Hurst, *The Process of Constitutional Construction: The Role of History,* in Supreme Court and Supreme Law 55, 57 (Cahn ed. 1954).

74 Minersville School District v. Gobitis, 310 U.S. 586, 593 (1940).

[75] *Id.* at 594–95.

[76] *Id.* at 596.

[77] *Ibid.*

[78] *Ibid.*

[79] *Id.* at 598.

[80] *Id.* at 597–98.

[81] *Id.* at 599–600.

[82] *Id.* at 598.

[83] *Id.* at 600.

[84] *Id.* at 595.

[85] *Id.* at 599.

[86] *Id.* at 600.

[87] *Id.* at 599 n. 6.

[88] The phrase is by Justice Holmes, quoted, Mendelson, *Justices Black and Frankfurter: Supreme Court Majority and Minority Trends,* 12 JOURNAL OF POLITICS 66, 77 (1950).

[89] See *id.* at 77–78. In this regard, see Frankfurter's strong stand in disestablishment cases. McCollum v. Board of Education, 333 U.S. 203, 212 (1948); Zorach v. Clauson, 343 U.S. 306, 320 (1952). See also Everson v. Board of Education, 330 U.S. 1 (1947).

[90] See MASON, HARLAN FISKE STONE 262–89, 537, 705–6 (1956).

[91] See especially Perry v. United States, 294 U.S. 330, 358 (1935); MASON, HARLAN FISKE STONE 389–90 (1956).

[92] Quoted, MASON, HARLAN FISKE STONE 514 (1956). Italics are added.

[93] McCulloch v. Maryland, 4 Wheat. (U.S.) 316, 428–30 (1819); South Carolina State Highway Department v. Barnwell Brothers, 303 U.S. 177, 184 n. 2 (1938); Southern Pacific Co. v. Arizona, 325 U.S. 761, 767 n. 2 (1945); Burnet v. Coronado Oil and Gas Co., 285 U.S. 393, 406–8 (1932).

[94] See MASON, HARLAN FISKE STONE 103–7, 523 (1956).

[95] Quoted, *id.* at 107.

[96] This is the account given by Stone's law clerk, Allison Dunham, quoted, *id.* at 528 n. But cf. Frankfurter's version, *ibid.*

[97] *Id.* at 527–28. According to one source, Justice Murphy had last-minute doubts, but was persuaded by Hughes to stay with the majority. McCune, *op. cit. supra* note 49, at 214.

[98] MASON, HARLAN FISKE STONE 528 (1956). Apparently, Stone decided to read his opinion in full in the mistaken belief that Frankfurter intended to do so. By opinion time he was too worked up to change his plan. *Ibid.*

[99] Minersville School District v. Gobitis, 310 U.S. 586, 601 (1940).

[100] *Id.* at 602.

[101] *Id.* at 603–4.

[102] *Id.* at 604.

[103] *Id.* at 605.

[104] *Id.* at 606.

[105] *Id.* at 607.

[1] Gardner & Post, *The Constitutional Questions Raised by the Flag Salute and Teacher's Oath Acts in Massachusetts*, 16 B.U.L. REV. 803 (1936); Million, *Validity of Compulsory Flag Salutes in Public Schools*, 28 KY. L.J. 306 (1940); Booth, *Compulsory Flag Salutes*, 43 LAW NOTES 9 (April, 1939); Bloch, *Education for Citizenship and Commercial Law*, 7 L. SOC. J. 924 (1937); Hensley, *The Constitutional Aspects of Compulsory Pledges of Allegiance and Salutes to the American Flag*, 3 LAWYER 5 (November, 1939); Grinnell, *Children, the Bill of Rights and the American Flag*, 24 MASS. L.Q. 17 (April, 1939); Grinnell, *More about the Flag Salute Law*, 24 MASS. L.Q. 1 (July, 1939); Clark, *The Limits of Free Expression*, 73 U.S.L. REV. 392 (1939); Hart, *The Business of the Supreme Court at the October Terms 1937 and 1938*, 53 HARV. L. REV. 579 (1940); Kearney, *Digest of Church Law Decisions of 1939*, 15 NOTRE DAME LAW. 329 (1940).

[2] 44 LAW NOTES 5 (January, 1940).

[3] 20 B.U.L. REV. 356 (1940); 9 BROOKLYN L. REV. 205 (1940); 23 CORNELL L.Q. 582 (1938); 27 GEO. L.J. 231 (1938); 8 GEO. WASH. L. REV. 1094 (1940); 2 GEORGIA B.J. 74 (1940); 51 HARV. L. REV. 1418 (1938); 23 IOWA L. REV. 424 (1938); 6 KAN. CITY L. REV. 217 (1938); 41 LAW NOTES 45 (January, 1938); 36 MICH. L. REV. 485 (1938); 23 MINN. L. REV. 247 (1939); 74 N.Y.L. REV. 4 (1940); 2 OHIO ST. L.J. 151 (1936); 18 ORE. L. REV. 122 (1939); 12 ROCKY MT. L. REV. 202 (1939); 13 ST. JOHN'S L. REV. 144 (1938); 12 TEMP. L.Q. 513 (1938); 72 U.S.L. REV. 364 (1938); 14 U. CINC. L. REV. 444 (1940); 86 U. PA. L. REV. 431 (1938); 2 U. PITT. L. REV. 206 (1936); 4 U. PITT. L. REV. 243 (1938).

[4] Hart, *supra* note 1 at 604–5; Million, *supra* note 1; Kearney, *supra* note 1 at 308–10; 14 NOTRE DAME LAW. 115 (1938); 72 U.S.L. REV. 364 (1938).

[5] 8 GEO. WASH. L. REV. 1094 (1940); 6 KAN. CITY L. REV. 217 (1938).

[6] Booth, *supra* note 1 at 10; Hensley, *supra* note 1 at 6–8; Grinnell, *Children, the Bill of Rights and the American Flag*, 24 MASS. L.Q. 17 (April, 1939); Clark, *supra* note 1 at 399–403; 20 B.U.L. REV. 356 (1940); 9 BROOKLYN L. REV. 205 (1940); 23 CORNELL L.Q. 582 (1938); 27 GEO. L.J. 231 (1938); 2 GEORGIA B.J. 74 (1940); 51 HARV. L. REV. 1418 (1938); 23 IOWA L. REV. 424 (1938); 44 LAW NOTES 5 (January, 1940); 23 MINN. L. REV. 247 (1939); 74 N.Y.L. REV. 4 (1940); 18 ORE. L. REV. 122 (1939); 12 ROCKY MT. L. REV. 202 (1939); 12 TEMP. L.Q. 513 (1938); 14 U. CINC. L. REV. 444 (1940); 86 U. PA. L. REV. 431 (1938); 4 U. PITT. L. REV. 243 (1938).

[7] Gardner & Post, *supra* note 1; Bloch, *supra* note 1 at 929; Grinnell, *More about the Flag Salute Law*, 24 MASS. L.Q. 1 (July, 1939); 13 ST. JOHN'S L. REV. 144 (1938); 2 U. PITT. L. REV. 206 (1936).

[8] 36 MICH. L. REV. 485 (1938).

[9] 41 LAW NOTES 45 (January, 1938).

[10] Booth, *supra* note 1 at 10; Hensley, *supra* note 1 at 9, 10; 20 B.U.L. REV. 356, 359 (1940); 9 BROOKLYN L. REV. 205, 209 (1940); 27 GEO. L.J. 231, 231–32 (1938); 2 GEORGIA B.J. 74, 75–76 (1940); 51 HARV. L. REV. 1418, 1419–20 (1938); 23 IOWA L. REV. 424, 425 (1938); 23 MINN. L. REV. 247, 248–49 (1939); 74 N.Y.L. REV. 4, 4–5 (1940); 18 ORE. L. REV. 122, 127

(1939); 12 Rocky Mt. L. Rev. 202, 204 (1939); 12 Temp. L.Q. 513, 514 (1938); 14 U. Cinc. L. Rev. 444, 446–47 (1940).

[11] Booth, *supra* note 1 at 9; Hensley, *supra* note 1 at 10–11; Grinnell, *Children, the Bill of Rights and the American Flag*, 24 Mass. L.Q. 17 (April, 1939); 20 B.U.L. Rev. 356, 361–62 (1940); 9 Brooklyn L. Rev. 205, 208–9 (1940); 23 Cornell L.Q. 582, 584 (1938); 51 Harv. L. Rev. 1418, 1422–23 (1938); 74 N.Y.L. Rev. 4, 5–6 (1940).

[12] Hensley, *supra* note 1 at 9–10; 2 Georgia B.J. 74, 76 (1940); 18 Ore. L. Rev. 122, 126–27 (1939); 12 Rocky Mt. L. Rev. 202–7 (1939); 12 Temp. L.Q. 513, 514 (1938); 14 U. Cinc. L. Rev. 444, 445–46 (1940).

[13] 8 Geo. Wash. L. Rev. 1094, 1097 (1940); 36 Mich. L. Rev. 485, 487 (1938). The third favorable view was very mild, based mainly on the Bible reading precedents. 6 Kan. City L. Rev. 217 (1938).

[14] 8 Geo. Wash. L. Rev. 1094, 1097 (1940); 6 Kan. City L. Rev. 217, 219 (1938); 36 Mich. L. Rev. 485, 487 n. 14 (1938).

[15] Corwin, The Constitution and What It Means Today 199 (7th ed. 1941); Corwin, Constitutional Rev. Ltd. 111–12 (1941); Jackson, The Struggle for Judicial Supremacy 284–85 (1941); Wright, The Growth of American Constitutional Law 230 (1942).

[16] Cushman, *Constitutional Law in 1939–1940*, 35 Am. Pol. Sci. Rev. 250, 269–71 (1941); Rotnem & Folsom, *Recent Restrictions upon Religious Liberty*, 36 Am. Pol. Sci. Rev. 1053, 1060–61, 1063–64 (1942).

[17] Swisher, *Civil Liberties in War Time*, 55 Pol. Sci. Q. 321, 346 (1940).

[18] Butler, *Freedom of Religion Interpreted in Two Supreme Court Decisions*, 15 Cal. St. B.J. 161 (1940); Clark, *Reasoning of Mr. Justice Frankfurter in Interpreting the Constitution*, 16 Cal. St. B.J. 371 (1941); *The Compulsory Flag Salute in the Supreme Court*, 9 Int'l Jurid. Ass'n Mo. Bull. 1, 10 (1940); Fennell, *The Reconstructed Court and Religious Freedom: The Gobitis Case in Retrospect*, 19 N.Y.U.L.Q. Rev. 31 (1941); Beck, *Judicial Review under the Bill of Rights*, 12 Pa. B. Ass'n Q. 175 (1941).

[19] 40 Colum. L. Rev. 1068 (1940); 26 Cornell L.Q. 127 (1940); 29 Geo. L.J. 112 (1940); 3 Georgia B.J. 66 (1940); 11 J.B. Ass'n Kan. 172 (1942); 39 Mich. L. Rev. 149 (1940); 6 Mo. L. Rev. 106 (1941); 18 N.Y.U.L.Q. Rev. 124 (1940); 15 St. John's L. Rev. 95 (1940); 14 So. Calif. L. Rev. 73 (1940); 14 Temp. L.Q. 545 (1940); 14 U. Cinc. L. Rev. 570 (1940); 4 U. Det. L.J. 38 (1940); 15 Wash. L. Rev. 265 (1940).

[20] 1 Bill of Rights Rev. 267 (1941).

[21] Wechsler in Shulman, Wechsler, Biddle & Witmer, *Symposium on Civil Liberties*, 9 Am. L. Sch. Rev. 881 (1941); Galston, *Conscription of the Mind in Support of the Bill of Rights*, 1 Bill of Rights Rev. 269 (1941); Haight & Lerch, *Freedom of Religion*, 2 Bill of Rights Rev. 111 (1942); Harrison, *The New Chief Justice*, 29 Calif. L. Rev. 677 (1941); Cabaniss, *National Defense Raises Vital Civil Liberties Problem: Cases Reviewed*, 16 Cal. St. B.J. 18 (1941); O'Brien, *Restraints upon Individual Freedom in Times of National Emergency*, 26 Cornell L.Q. 523 (1941); Lowenstein, *Report of the Section on Civil Liberties: Civil Liberties and National Defense*, 9 Duke B. Ass'n J. 1

(1941) ; Wilkinson, *Some Aspects of the Constitutional Guarantees of Civil Liberty*, 11 FORDHAM L. REV. 50 (1942) ; White, *Certain Aspects of the Legal Status of the Church in the United States*, 1 JURIST 20 (1941) ; Clark, *Civil Liberties in Wartime*, 65 N.J.L.J. 1, 5 (1942) ; Kearney, *Digest of Church Law Decisions of 1940*, 16 NOTRE DAME LAW. 318 (1941) ; Wright, *Religious Liberty under the Constitution*, 27 VA. L. REV. 75 (1940) ; Lusky, *Minority Rights and the Public Interest*, 52 YALE L.J. 1 (1942).

22 47 DICK. L. REV. 117 (1941) ; 7 OHIO ST. L.J. 358 (1941) ; 90 U. PA. L. REV. 598 (1942).

23 1 BILL OF RIGHTS REV. 134 (1940).

24 Miner, *Religion and the Law*, 21 CHI.-KENT L. REV. 156 (1943) ; *Religious Immunity from Police Power*, 8 JOHN MARSHALL L.Q. 25 (1942). The latter entry is a straight reprint of Judge Miner's decision in Cook County Criminal Court in the case of City of Blue Island v. Kozul. His decision was reversed by the Illinois Supreme Court six months before the official date of the reprint. City of Blue Island v. Kozul, 379 Ill. 511, 41 N.E. (2d) 515 (1942). The first item listed is substantially the same opinion, slightly reworked by its author. These are treated as two comments mainly because they reflect the bias of two separate editors.

25 CORWIN, THE CONSTITUTION AND WHAT IT MEANS TODAY 199 (1941) ; CORWIN, CONSTITUTIONAL REVOLUTION LTD. 112 (1941) ; Wright, *op. cit. supra* note 15, at 230; CUSHMAN, *supra* note 16 at 270–71; Rotnem & Folsom, *supra* note 16 at 1063–64; Harrison, *supra* note 21 at 687; Butler, *supra* note 18, Clark, *supra* note 18; Wilkinson, *supra* note 21 at 57–59; White, *supra* note 21 at 32–39; Clark, *supra* note 21 at 5; Fennell, *supra* note 18; Kearney, *supra* note 21 at 318–19; Beck, *supra* note 18; Swisher, *supra* note 17 at 346; Wright, *supra* note 21 at 86–87; 1 BILL OF RIGHTS REV. 134 (1940) ; 1 BILL OF RIGHTS REV. 267 (1941) ; 40 COLUM. L. REV. 1068 (1940) ; 26 CORNELL L.Q. 127 (1940) ; 47 DICK. L. REV. 117 (1941) ; 29 GEO. L.J. 112 (1940) ; 3 GEORGIA B.J. 66 (1940) ; 39 MICH. L. REV. 149 (1940) ; 6 MO. L. REV. 106 (1941) ; 18 N.Y.U.L.Q. REV. 124 (1940) ; 15 ST. JOHN'S L. REV. 95 (1940) ; 14 SO. CALIF. L. REV. 73 (1940) ; 14 U. CINC. L. REV. 570 (1940) ; 4 U. DET. L.J. 38 (1940) ; 15 WASH. L. REV. 265 (1940).

26 Miner, *supra* note 24 at 163; *Religious Immunity from Police Power*, 8 JOHN MARSHALL L.Q. 25, 31–32 (1942) ; 11 J.B. ASS'N KAN. 172, 174 (1942) ; 14 TEMP. L.Q. 545 (1940).

27 Jackson, *op. cit. supra* note 15, at 284–85; Wechsler, *supra* note 21 at 887; Galston, *supra* note 21 at 275–77; Haight & Lerch, *supra* note 21 at 115; Cabaniss, *supra* note 21 at 25; O'Brien, *supra* note 21 at 533; Lowenstein, *supra* note 21 at 7; *The Compulsory Flag Salute in the Supreme Court*, 9 INT'L JURID. ASS'N MO. BULL. 1 (1940) ; Lusky, *supra* note 21 at 32–33; 7 OHIO ST. L.J. 358, 381 n.4 (1941) ; 90 U. PA. L. REV. 598, 598–99 (1942).

28 11 J.B. ASS'N KAN. 172, 174 (1942) ; 14 TEMP. L.Q. 545 (1940).

29 Miner, *supra* note 24 at 163; *Religious Immunity from Police Power*, 8 JOHN MARSHALL L.Q. 25, 31–32 (1942).

30 CORWIN, CONSTITUTIONAL REVOLUTION LTD. 112 (1941) ; Clark, *supra*

note 18; Fennell, *supra* note 18 at 33; Kearney, *supra* note 21 at 318–19; Beck, *supra* note 18; 47 Dick. L. Rev. 117, 121–22 (1941) ; 39 Mich. L. Rev. 149, 151–52 (1940) ; 6 Mo. L. Rev. 106, 107–10 (1941) ; 18 N.Y.U.L.Q. Rev. 124, 126 (1940) ; 15 St. John's L. Rev. 95, 96 (1940) ; 14 So. Calif. L. Rev. 73, 75 (1940) ; 14 U. Cinc. L. Rev. 570 (1940) ; 4 U. Det. L.J. 38, 39–40 (1940) ; 15 Wash. L. Rev. 265, 266 (1940).

[31] Corwin, The Constitution and What It Means Today 199 (1941) ; Cushman, *supra* note 16 at 269–71; Rotnem & Folsom, *supra* note 16 at 1060, 1063; Butler, *supra* note 18 at 162–63; Wilkinson, *supra* note 21 at 57; White, *supra* note 21 at 38; Fennell, *supra* note 18 at 38; 40 Colum. L. Rev. 1068, 1071 (1940) ; 26 Cornell L.Q. 127, 128 (1940) ; 39 Mich. L. Rev. 149, 151 (1940) ; 18 N.Y.U.L.Q. Rev. 124, 126 (1940) ; 14 U. Cinc. L. Rev. 570 (1940) ; 4 U. Det. L.J. 38, 40 (1940) ; 15 Wash. L. Rev. 265, 266 (1940).

[32] Wright, *op. cit. supra* note 15, at 230; Harrison, *supra* note 21 at 687; Clark, *supra* note 21 at 5; Swisher, *supra* note 17 at 346; Wright, *supra* note 21 at 86–87; 1 Bill of Rights Rev. 134, 135 (1940) ; 1 Bill of Rights Rev. 267, 268 (1941) ; 3 Georgia B.J. 66, 67 (1940).

[33] 1 Bill of Rights Rev. 134, 135 (1940).

[34] Clark, *supra* note 21 at 5.

[35] Cushman, *supra* note 16 at 271; Rotnem & Folsom, *supra* note 16 at 1061–63; 26 Cornell L.Q. 127, 128 (1940) ; 15 St. John's L. Rev. 95, 96, 97 (1940) ; 14 So. Calif. L. Rev. 73, 75–76 (1940) ; 14 U. Cinc. L. Rev. 570 (1940) ; 4 U. Det. L.J. 38, 40 (1940).

[36] Cushman, *supra* note 16 at 271.

[37] Rotnem & Folsom, *supra* note 16 at 1063.

[38] Fennell, *supra* note 18 at 38.

[39] Kearney, *supra* note 21 at 318–19.

[40] Corwin, Constitutional Revolution Ltd. 112 (1941).

[41] Corwin, The Constitution and What It Means Today 199 (1941) ; Wechsler, *supra* note 21 at 887; Cushman, *supra* note 16 at 269, 271; Rotnem & Folsom, *supra* note 16 at 1061, 1063; Butler, *supra* note 18 at 163–65; Cabaniss, *supra* note 21 at 25; Miner, *supra* note 24 at 163–64; O'Brien, *supra* note 21 at 533; Wilkinson, *supra* note 21 at 57–58; *The Compulsory Flag Salute in the Supreme Court*, 9 Int'l Jurid. Ass'n Mo. Bull. 1 (1940) ; *Religious Immunity from Police Power*, 8 John Marshall L.Q. 25, 31–32 (1942) ; White, *supra* note 21 at 37–38; Fennell, *supra* note 18 at 38; 40 Colum. L. Rev. 1068, 1071 (1940) ; 26 Cornell L.Q. 127, 128 (1940) ; 11 J.B. Ass'n Kan. 172, 174 (1942) ; 39 Mich. L. Rev. 149, 151 (1940) ; 18 N.Y.U.L.Q. Rev. 124, 126 (1940) ; 14 Temp. L.Q. 545, 546–47 (1940) ; 14 U. Cinc. L. Rev. 570 (1940) ; 7 U. Det. L.J. 38, 40 (1940) ; 90 U. Pa. L. Rev. 598, 599 (1942) ; 15 Wash. L. Rev. 265 (1940).

[42] *The Compulsory Flag Salute in the Supreme Court*, 9 Int'l Jurid. Ass'n Mo. Bull. 1 (1940).

[43] *Ibid.*

[44] Miner, *supra* note 24 at 163.

[45] 26 Cornell L.Q. 127, 128 (1940).

46 Cabaniss, *supra* note 21 at 25.

47 Butler, *supra* note 18 at 161–65.

48 Fennell, *supra* note 18 at 38.

49 White, *supra* note 21 at 38.

50 Cushman, *supra* note 16 at 269, 271; Rotnem & Folsom, *supra* at 1061, 1063; 40 COLUM. L. REV. 1068, 1071 (1940); 11 J.B. ASS'N KAN. 172, 174 (1942); 39 MICH. L. REV. 149, 151 (1940); 18 N.Y.U.L.Q. REV. 124, 126 (1940); 14 U. CINC. L. REV. 570 (1940); 90 U. PA. L. REV. 598, 599 (1942).

51 Rotnem & Folsom, *supra* note 16 at 1061.

52 90 U. PA. L. REV. 598, 598–99 (1942).

53 40 COLUM. L. REV. 1068, 1071 (1940).

54 CORWIN, THE CONSTITUTION AND WHAT IT MEANS TODAY 199 (1941); Wechsler, *supra* note 21 at 887; O'Brien, *supra* note 21 at 533; Wilkinson, *supra* note 21 at 57–58; 14 TEMP. L.Q. 545, 546–47 (1940); 4 U. DET. L.J. 38, 40 (1940); 15 WASH. L. REV. 265 (1940).

55 Wilkinson, *supra* note 21 at 57.

56 4 U. DET. L.J. 38, 40 (1940).

57 *Jehovah's Witnesses, Who Refuse To Salute the U.S. Flag, Hold Their National Convention*, 9 LIFE 20 (August 12, 1940).

58 Amidon, *Can We Afford Martyrs?* 29 SURVEY GRAPHIC 457 (1940).

59 Southworth, *Jehovah's 50,000 Witnesses*, 151 NATION 110, 111 (1940).

60 *High Court Finale*, 15 NEWSWEEK 36 (June 10, 1940).

61 *Radicals: Fifth Column*, 35 TIME 21 (June 10, 1940).

62 *Id.* at 22.

63 *Frankfurter vs. Stone*, 102 NEW REPUBLIC 843 (1940).

64 *Id.* at 843–44 (1940).

65 Hamilton & Braden, *The Supreme Court Today*, 103 NEW REPUBLIC 178 (1940).

66 *Id.* at 180.

67 *Unser Gott and Jehovah's Witnesses*, 103 NEW REPUBLIC 174 (1940).

68 *Id.* at 175.

69 *The Flag Salute Case*, 57 CHRISTIAN CENTURY 791 (1940).

70 *Ibid.*

71 *The Court Abdicates*, 57 CHRISTIAN CENTURY 845 (1940).

72 *Id.* at 846.

73 Holmes, *The Case of Jehovah's Witnesses*, 57 CHRISTIAN CENTURY 896, 898 (1940).

74 *Civil Liberty Endangered*, 59 CHRISTIAN CENTURY 798 (1942); Coe, *Our Waning Religious Liberties*, 59 CHRISTIAN CENTURY 806 (1942).

75 See notes 19, 21, *supra*.

76 38 CATHOLIC EDUCATION REVIEW 457 (1940).

77 Blakely, *The Flag Salute vs. Oregon Case*, 63 AMERICA 259 (1940); Blakely, *Omnipotent School Boards*, 63 AMERICA 286 (1940); *Comment*, 64 AMERICA 366 (1941).

78 Blakely, *Flag Salute vs. Oregon Case*, 63 AMERICA 259 (1940).

79 *Ibid.*

80 *Id.* at 259–60.

81 See FELIX, RUTHERFORD UNCOVERED (1937) ; McGinnis, *Witness Jehovah's Witnesses,* 5 CATHOLIC DIGEST 53 (September, 1941).

82 *Fighting Fire with Fire,* 61 AMERICA 421 (1939).

83 Katenkamp, *In Defense of California,* 19 BUSINESS EDUCATION WORLD 786 (1939).

84 Fuller, *Constitutional Liberties of Pupils and Teachers,* 11 HARVARD EDU-CATIONAL REVIEW 76, 81–82 (1941).

85 Commager, *Civil Liberties and Democracy,* 42 SCHOLASTIC 13 (March 22, 1943).

86 See COMMAGER, MAJORITY RULE AND MINORITY RIGHTS (1943).

87 Commager, *Civil Liberties and Democracy,* 42 SCHOLASTIC 13 (March 22, 1943).

88 Atlanta Constitution, Boston Post, Buffalo Evening News, Charleston Daily Mail, Chicago Daily News, Chicago Herald American, (Denver) Rocky Mountain News, Little Rock Gazette, Arkansas Gazette (Little Rock), Min-neapolis Star-Journal, New York Daily News, New York Daily Mirror, New York Journal-American, New York World-Telegram, Pottsville Evening Jour-nal.

89 Both editorials and bylined columns were counted. The discrepancy in number arises from the fact that the Cleveland Plain Dealer had one of each—tending in different directions.

90 Boston Globe, June 4, 1940; Detroit Free Press, June 4, 1940; Detroit News, June 4, 1940; Philadelphia Inquirer, June 4, 1940; Pittsburgh Post-Gazette, June 6, 1940; Pottsville Evening Republican, June 4, 1940; St. Paul Pioneer-Press, June 4, 1940; Washington Post, June 4, 1940.

91 Christian Science Monitor, June 6, 1940; Los Angeles Times, June 4, 1940; Gauss, Books, New York Herald-Tribune, July 21, 1940; New York Post, June 6, 1940; Denny, Freedom's Blows, Pittsburgh Press, June 4, 1940; St. Louis Post-Dispatch, June 6, 1940; Springfield Daily Republican, June 4, 1940.

92 Cleveland Plain Dealer, June 5, 1940; New York Sun, June 6, 1940.

93 Baltimore Evening Sun, June 6, 1940; Boston Transcript, June 4, 1940; Charleston Gazette, June 12, 1940; McDermott in Cleveland Plain Dealer, June 5, 1940; Kansas City Star, June 4, 1940; Louisville Courier-Journal, June 4, 1940; New York Times, June 5, 1940; Philadelphia Evening Bulletin, June 5, 1940; St. Louis Globe-Democrat, June 4, 1940; San Francisco Chroni-cle, June 4, 1940.

94 Washington Post, June 4, 1940.

95 Pittsburgh Post-Gazette, June 4, 1940.

96 St. Paul Pioneer-Press, June 4, 1940.

97 Boston Globe, June 4, 1940; Detroit Free Press, June 4, 1940; Detroit News, June 4, 1940; Philadelphia Inquirer, June 4, 1940; Pottsville Evening Republican, June 4, 1940.

98 Detroit Free Press, June 4, 1940; Detroit News, June 4, 1940.

99 Gauss, Books, New York Herald-Tribune, July 21, 1940; New York Post,

June 6, 1940; Denny, Freedom's Blows, Pittsburgh Press, June 4, 1940; Springfield Daily Republican, June 4, 1940.

[100] Los Angeles Times, June 4, 1940.

[101] St. Louis Post-Dispatch, June 6, 1940.

[102] Christian Science Monitor, June 6, 1940.

[103] Cleveland Plain Dealer, June 5, 1940.

[104] New York Sun, June 6, 1940.

[105] San Francisco Chronicle, June 4, 1940.

[106] Baltimore Evening Sun, June 6, 1940.

[107] Philadelphia Evening Bulletin, June 5, 1940.

[108] Philadelphia Evening Bulletin, June 18, 1938; Philadelphia Inquirer, June 20, 1938; Pottsville Evening Republican, June 21, 1938.

[109] Kansas City Star, June 15, 1943; Cleveland Plain Dealer, June 15, 1943; New York Times, June 19, 1943; San Francisco Chronicle, June 15, 1943.

[110] PFEFFER, CHURCH, STATE AND FREEDOM 523 (1953).

CHAPTER EIGHT

[1] PFEFFER, CHURCH, STATE AND FREEDOM 523 (1953); Rotnem & Folsom, *Recent Restrictions upon Religious Liberty*, 36 AM. POL. SCI. REV. 1053, 1061–63 (1942).

[2] ACLU Archives, vol. 2215, "Religious Freedom."

[3] Southworth, *Jehovah's 50,000 Witnesses*, 151 NATION 110, 111 (1940).

[4] Washington Post, June 3, 1940.

[5] Southworth, *supra* note 3 at 111.

[6] *Ibid.*

[7] Washington Post, June 3, 1940.

[8] New York Times, June 4, 1940.

[9] Southworth, *supra* note 3 at 111.

[10] Arkansas Democrat (Little Rock), June 2, 1940.

[11] Chicago Tribune, June 10, 1940; Holmes, *The Case of Jehovah's Witnesses*, 57 CHRISTIAN CENTURY 896, 896–97 (1940); *Jehovah's Witnesses—Victims or Front?* 57 CHRISTIAN CENTURY 813 (1940).

[12] New York Herald-Tribune, June 11, 1940; New York Times, June 11, 1940.

[13] New York Times, June 11, 1940.

[14] Chicago Tribune, June 10, 1940; *Jehovah's Witnesses—Victims or Front?* 57 CHRISTIAN CENTURY 813 (1940).

[15] New York Times, June 17, 1940; Charleston Gazette (W.Va.), June 30, 1940; Rotnem & Folsom, *supra* note 1 at 1061.

[16] Charleston Gazette (W.Va.), June 30, 1940.

[17] New York Times, June 20, 1940.

[18] Southworth, *supra* note 3 at 111.

[19] *Ibid.* See also Memorandum for files on telephone conversation, Roger N. Baldwin and Henry A. Schweinhaut, September 4, 1940, ACLU Archives, vol. 2215, "Religious Freedom."

[20] Kingdom News, October, 1940.

[21] New York Times, June 21, 1942; *Mob Action against Sect on the Increase,* 59 CHRISTIAN CENTURY 1204 (1942).

[22] New York Times, June 21, 1942.

[23] *Ibid.*

[24] Southworth, *supra* note 3 at 111.

[25] Rotnem & Folsom, *supra* note 1 at 1061; Washington News, July 23, 1940. This was one of the few such instances in which adequate remedial action was taken at the local level. The police chief was fired and the offending policemen were disciplined. Washington News, July 23, 1940.

[26] Catlette v. United States, 132 F(2d) 902, 903–4 (4th Cir. 1942).

[27] Beeler v. Smith, 40 F. Supp. 139, 141 (E.D.Ky. 1941).

[28] 10 INT'L JURID. ASS'N MO. BULL. 5, 6 n. 8 (1941).

[29] *Ibid.;* McKee v. State, 219 Ind. 247, 249, 37 N.E. (2d) 940, 941 (1941).

[30] Rotnem & Folsom, *supra* note 1 at 1061.

[31] See Woods County Enterprise (Okla.), June 6, 1940, referring to the ordinances of Waynoka, Oklahoma, and nearby towns.

[32] New York Times, June 29, 1940.

[33] New York Daily Worker, June 27, 1940.

[34] See Cox v. New Hampshire, 312 U.S. 569 (1941).

[35] *Witnesses Examined,* 36 TIME 40 (July 29, 1940).

[36] 57 CHRISTIAN CENTURY 1333 (1940).

[37] New York Times, June 7, 1940.

[38] Forster, *Jehovah's Witness Dismissals,* memorandum for files, ACLU Archives, vol. 2386, "Religious Freedom."

[39] *Ibid.*

[40] *Ibid.*

[41] *Witnesses To Be Rehired,* BUSINESS WEEK, April 10, 1943, p. 99.

[42] See letters, J. M. Britchey to Arthur B. Gaux, June 18, 1940; Watchtower Society to Francis Biddle, June 13, 1940; both in ACLU Archives, vol. 2215, "Religious Freedom." Both letters seem to refer to an *earlier* admonition to this effect.

[43] The complaints received after June 3 seem to give a pretty thorough *post hoc* report on incidents in May, but practically nothing on earlier months.

[44] While this designation of group-libel prosecutions may be debatable in view of the Witnesses' known capacity for vilification, it seems advisable in the circumstances. In practice, such prosecutions were directed at distribution of *any* Witness literature; some ordinances were enforced only against Jehovah's Witnesses.

[45] Computed by treating as a whole number the percentage of the population of the United States living in communities of a given size, and making that figure the denominator of a ratio, the numerator of which is the number of incidents in localities of that class. Thus, the index for cities of more than 100,000 population is 45/28.8.

[46] Rotnem & Folsom, *supra* note 1 at 1061.

[47] It must be admitted that the index tends to magnify the difference somewhat. A normal company of Witnesses might be able to contract and infuriate

the whole population of a town like Kutztown, Pennsylvania; it could hardly perform the same feat in Detroit or New York City, most inhabitants of which would not be aware of their presence. However, there is no really feasible way of computing an incident-per-unit-population-annoyed index.

[48] See Catlette v. United States, 132 F(2d) 902, 903 (4th Cir. 1942); Harrisburg Daily Register (Ill.), June 29, 1940.

[49] Letter, L. U. Stambaugh to Roger N. Baldwin, December 31, 1941, ACLU Archives, vol. 2386, "Religious Freedom."

[50] The national office exercises quite strict control over those aspects of local policy which interest it. See GELLERMAN, THE AMERICAN LEGION AS EDUCATOR 39–45 (1938).

[51] New Orleans Times-Picayune, June 30, 1940.

[52] The Witnesses' German printing plant was seized in 1933. Southworth, *supra* note 3 at 111. This sort of charge seems to appeal to Legion officials. Compare the incident described in Gellerman, *op. cit. supra* note 50, at 76.

[53] Southworth, *supra* note 3 at 112.

[54] Gary Post-Tribune (Ind.), March 10, 1942.

[55] Detroit Free Press, July 24, 1940.

[56] New Castle News (Pa.), August 10, 1942; letter, Roger N. Baldwin to Barney Yanofsky (of VFW national headquarters), May 16, 1941, ACLU Archives, vol. 2306, "Religious Freedom."

[57] Letter, Watchtower Society to ACLU, July 3, 1940, ACLU Archives, vol. 2215, "Religious Freedom." See also Southworth, *supra* note 3 at 111.

[58] Outside sources give just one such incident. Southworth, *supra* note 3 at 112.

[59] FELIX, RUTHERFORD UNCOVERED (1937); McGinnis, *Witness Jehovah's Witnesses,* 5 CATHOLIC DIGEST 53 (September, 1941).

[60] See ACLU Minutes, October 21, 1940; April 4, 1941; May 5, 1941; October 6, 1941.

[61] ACLU Minutes, June 10, 1940; New York Times, July 3, 1940; Raleigh Union-Herald (N.C.), October 31, 1940; letters, Arthur G. Hays to the mayor *et al.* of Erin, Tennessee, October 16, 1940, ACLU Archives, vol. 2259, "Religious Freedom."

[62] ACLU Minutes, September 9, 1940.

[63] Telegrams, Arthur G. Hays to the mayors of eighteen cities, July 23, 1940, ACLU Archives, vol. 2215, "Religious Freedom."

[64] ACLU Minutes, October 12, 1940.

[65] See, for example, telegrams, Roger N. Baldwin to Francis Biddle, July 23, August 7, September 19, 1940; letters, Roger N. Baldwin to J. H. Pratt (a Washington attorney), October 31, 1940, March 25, 1941, May 3, 1941. All in ACLU Archives, vols. 2215, 2306, "Religious Freedom." See also ACLU Minutes, August 12, 1940.

[66] 18 U.S.C. §§ 51, 52. Since 1948, these have been renumbered as 18 U.S.C. §§ 241, 242.

[67] The penalty listed is a maximum of one year's imprisonment and a fine of up to $1,000.

[68] Carr, Federal Protection of Civil Rights: Quest for a Sword chapter iii, *passim* (1947).

[69] While all cases under § 52 theoretically could be brought by information, thus avoiding this hurdle, the policy of the Department has been strongly in favor of seeking indictment in all civil rights cases. *Id.* at 135–36.

[70] *Id.* at 134–35.

[71] Memorandum for files on telephone conversation, Roger N. Baldwin and Henry A. Schweinhaut, September 4, 1940, ACLU Archives, vol. 2215, "Religious Freedom." Baldwin was sharply critical of this caution, taking the position that any prosecution, successful or not, would have a beneficial effect on the situation. Letter, Roger N. Baldwin to O. John Rogge, September 14, 1940, ACLU Archives, vol. 2215, "Religious Freedom."

[72] See Carr, *op. cit. supra* note 68, at 143–46.

[73] There clearly was a split in the Department as to the relative advisability of bringing prosecutions under § 20. See *Id.* at 156; letter, Roger N. Baldwin to J. H. Pratt, May 3, 1941, ACLU Archives, vol. 2306, "Religious Freedom." Berge supported the Section in the bringing of the prosecution in the Richwood "castor oil" case. Carr, *op. cit. supra*, at 156. He also supported the Section's requests for authorization to send out a special circular on Jehovah's Witnesses to the United States attorneys. Wendell Berge, Memorandum for the Acting Attorney General, July 30, 1941. A copy of this important statement was furnished the writer by the Civil Rights Section. It is cited hereafter as "Berge Memo, July 30, 1941."

[74] Jackson seems to have agreed only reluctantly to the prosecution in the landmark case of United States v. Classic, 313 U.S. 299 (1941). Carr, *op. cit. supra* note 68, at 86–87. He refused to authorize the prosecution of the Richwood "castor oil" assailants. It was only after Jackson left office that the prosecution was authorized. *Id.* at 156. It should be borne in mind that Jackson later voted to declare § 20 unconstitutional as applied to an essentially similar situation. Screws v. United States, 325 U.S. 91 (1945).

[75] Berge Memo, July 30, 1941, pp. 10–12.

[76] *Id.* at 10; Carr, *op. cit. supra* note 68, at 134–35.

[77] Catlette v. United States, 132 F(2d) 902 (4th Cir. 1942).

[78] Carr, *op. cit. supra* note 68, at 157 n. 9.

[79] Memorandum for files on telephone conversation, Roger N. Baldwin and Henry A. Schweinhaut, September 4, 1940, ACLU Archives, vol. 2215, "Religious Freedom."

[80] Letter, Francis Biddle to Roger N. Baldwin, July 25, 1940, ACLU Archives, vol. 2215, "Religious Freedom."

[81] *Ibid.*; Rotnem & Folsom, *supra* note 1 at 1061.

[82] Berge Memo, July 30, 1941, p. 12.

[83] *Ibid.*

[84] The speech is reprinted in full in ACLU Archives, vol. 2386, "Religious Freedom."

[85] Letter, Clifford Forster to Victor Rotnem, March 10, 1942, ACLU Archives, vol. 2386, "Religious Freedom."

86 Berge Memo, July 30, 1941. The issuance of the circular obviously had been expected since mid-1940. See telegrams, Roger N. Baldwin to Francis Biddle, August 8, 1940; Roger N. Baldwin to Henry A. Schweinhaut, September 19, 1940, ACLU Archives, vol. 2215, "Religious Freedom."

87 A copy of this memorandum was furnished the writer by the Civil Rights Section.

88 Zimmerman v. London, 38 F. Supp. 582 (S.D. Ohio 1941); Donley v. Colorado Springs, 40 F. Supp. 15 (Colo. 1941). Another such ordinance was interpreted by a state court so as not to apply to Jehovah's Witnesses' activities. Shreveport v. Teague, 200 La. 679, 8 So. (2d) 640 (1942).

89 39 F. Supp. 26 (Idaho 1941).

90 39 F. Supp. 30 (W.D. Pa. 1941).

91 42 F. Supp. 77 (N.D. Tex. 1941).

92 Hannan v. Haverhill, 120 F (2d) 87 (1st Cir. 1941); Manchester v. Leiby, 117 F (2d) 661 (1st Cir. 1941).

93 Hannan v. Haverhill, 314 U.S. 573 (1941); Leiby v. Manchester, 313 U.S. 562 (1941).

94 State *ex rel.* Wilson v. Russell, 146 Fla. 539, 1 So. (2d) 569 (1941); State *ex rel.* Hough v. Woodruff, 147 Fla. 299, 2 So. (2d) 577 (1941).

95 Tucker v. Randall, 18 N.J. Misc. 675, 15 Atl. (2d) 324 (Sup. Ct. 1940).

96 Village of South Holland v. Stein, 373 Ill. 472, 26 N.E. (2d) 868 (1940).

97 People v. Barber, 289 N.Y. 378, 46 N.E. (2d) 329 (1943).

98 Commonwealth v. Anderson, 308 Mass. 413, 32 N.E. (2d) 685 (1941).

99 Commonwealth v. Pascone, 308 Mass. 591, 33 N.E. (2d) 522 (1941).

100 Pascone v. Massachusetts, 314 U.S. 641 (1941).

101 State v. Cox, 91 N.H. 137, 16 Atl. (2d) 508 (1940).

102 312 U.S. 569 (1941).

103 *Id.* at 578.

104 40 F. Supp. 139 (E.D.Ky. 1941).

105 39 F. Supp. 373 (S.D.Ind. 1941).

106 Trent v. Hunt, 314 U.S. 573 (1941).

107 McKee v. State, 219 Ind. 247, 37 N.E. (2d) 940 (1941).

108 Lynch v. Muskogee, 47 F. Supp. 589 (E.D.Okla. 1942).

109 Oney v. Oklahoma City, 120 F (2d) 861 (10th Cir. 1941).

110 39 F. Supp. 708 (E.D.Ill. 1941).

111 Bevins v. Prindable, 314 U.S. 573 (1941).

112 City of Gaffney v. Putnam, 197 S.C. 237, 15 S.E. (2d) 130 (1941).

113 75 Okla. Crim. 390, 132 P (2d) 173 (1942).

114 10 Int'l Jurid. Ass'n Mo. Bull. 5, 7 n.13 (1941).

115 315 U.S. 568 (1942).

116 State v. Mead, 230 Iowa 1217, 300 N.W. 523 (1941).

117 State v. Richardson, 92 N.H. 178, 27 Atl. (2d) 94 (1942).

118 People v. Northum, 41 Cal. App. 284, 106 P (2d) 433 (1940).

119 Commonwealth v. Palms, 141 Pa. Super. 430, 15 Atl. (2d) 481 (1940).

120 320 U.S. 707 (1943).

121 The decision is unreported. See *ibid.*

[1] For reasons that will appear below, all of the complaints were received after July 18, 1942. It is often difficult, therefore, to date the original expulsion exactly.

[2] Zavilla v. School Board, 112 Colo. 183, 147 P(2d) 823 (1944) ; State v. Lefebvre, 91 N.H. 382, 20 Atl.(2d) 185 (1941) ; State v. Davis, 69 S.D. 328, 10 N.W.(2d) 288 (1943) ; N.H. REPT. ATT'Y GEN. 1938–40, at 40; N.M. REPT. ATT'Y GEN. 1941–42, at 137; N.C. REPT. ATT'Y GEN. 1942–44, 512. As to West Virginia, see chapter x *infra*.

[3] 11 U.S.L. WEEK 3279 (1943) ; New York World-Telegram, March 8, 1943. The figure of 20,000 given in the first source is clearly a misprint, in view of the Witnesses' limited numbers at that time.

[4] Quoted, N.H. REPT. ATT'Y GEN. 1938–40, at 40.

[5] See Zavilla v. School Board, 112 Colo. 183, 147 P(2d) 823 (1944) ; Brown v. Skustad (Minn. D.Ct. 1942, unreported).

[6] Miss. Laws 1942, c. 155, MISS. CODE ANN. § 6227 (1942).

[7] See Pendley v. State, 77 Okla. Crim. 259, 261, 141 P(2d) 118, 119 (1943).

[8] Boston Post, June 4, 1940.

[9] WASH. OPS. ATT'Y GEN. 1939–40, at 303.

[10] IDAHO REPT. ATT'Y GEN. 1939–40, at 13; ILL. OPS. ATT'Y GEN. 1941, at 16; MINN. REPT. ATT'Y GEN. 1939–40, at 93; NEB. REPT. ATT'Y GEN. 1939–42, at 401; N.H. REPT. ATT'Y GEN. 1938–40, at 40; N.M. REPT. ATT'Y GEN. 1941–42, at 137; N.C. REPT. ATT'Y GEN. 1942–44, at 512; VT. REPT. ATT'Y GEN. 1942–44, at 94.

[11] H.J.R. 303, 36 U.S.C. § 172 (Supp. 1942).

[12] AMERICAN LEGION, THE FLAG OF THE UNITED STATES: HOW TO RESPECT IT: HOW TO DISPLAY IT (1924).

[13] Wendell Berge, Memorandum to all United States attorneys, July 18, 1942. A copy of this memo, which contains the Rotnem memo in full, was furnished to the writer by the Civil Rights Section in 1957. A copy of the Rotnem memo is also attached as an appendix to Brief for Plaintiffs, Barnette v. West Virginia State Board of Education, 47 F. Supp. 251 (S.D.W.Va. 1942). For further elaboration of the CRS position, see Rotnem & Folsom, *Recent Restrictions upon Religious Liberty*, 36 AM. POL. SCI. REV. 1053, 1063–64 (1942).

[14] Quoted, West Virginia State Board of Education v. Barnette, 319 U.S. 624, 628 n.4 (1943).

[15] Undated, unsigned memorandum for files, ACLU Archives, vol. 2386, "Religious Freedom."

[16] Fla. Laws 1939, c. 22015, FLA. STAT. § 230.45 (Supp. 1945). This law was signed by the governor on June 11, 1943.

[17] 36 Luzern Leg. Reg. 247 (Pa. Q. Sess. 1942).

[18] NEB. REPT. ATT'Y GEN. 1939–42, at 401; N.M. REPT. ATT'Y GEN. 1941–42, at 137; WASH. OPS. ATT'Y GEN. 1941–42, at 249.

[19] See letters, Walter Gobitis to Gerald Gleeson (United States Attorney for the Eastern District of Pennsylvania), November 13, 1942; Gerald Gleeson to

Minersville School Board, December 30, 1942; John B. McGurl to Gerald Glee-son, January 5, 1943; all in Roudabush File.

20 One of these turned on the constitutionality of the compulsory salute and is discussed in section D *infra*. Bolling v. Superior Court 16 Wash.(2d) 373, 133 P(2d) 803 (1943).

21 309 Mass. 476, 35 N.E.(2d) 801 (1941).

22 91 N.H. 382, 20 Atl.(2d) 185 (1941).

23 *Id.* at 385, 20 Atl.(2d) at 187.

24 262 App. Div. 814, 28 N.Y.S.(2d) 92 (1941).

25 175 Misc. 451, 24 N.Y.S.(2d) 10 (Child. Ct. 1940).

26 *Id.* at 456, 24 N.Y.S.(2d) at 15.

27 16 Wash.(2d) 315, 133 P(2d) 526 (1943).

28 381 Ill. 214, 44 N.E.(2d) 888 (1942).

29 58 Ariz. 444, 120 P(2d) 808 (1942).

30 ARIZ. REPT. ATT'Y GEN. 1942–43 (Mimeo, on file, University of Michigan Law School Library). Under Arizona law, one who accepts a suspended sentence is estopped from appealing the conviction. Brooks v. State, 51 Ariz. 544, 78 P(2d) 498 (1938).

31 Davis v. Arizona, 319 U.S. 775 (1943).

32 Partain v. State, 77 Okla. Crim. 270, 141 P(2d) 124 (1943).

33 One of these cases turned on the constitutionality of the compulsory salute, and is discussed in Section D *infra*. State v. Smith, 155 Kan. 588, 127 P(2d) 518 (1942).

34 128 N.J.L. 472, 26 Atl.(2d) 881 (1942).

35 *Id.* at 476, 26 Atl.(2d) at 882. Jones v. Opelika, 316 U.S. 584 (1942), cited in the quoted passage, cast grave doubt on the continued vitality of the *Gobitis* precedent. See Section E *infra*.

36 Pa. Q. Sess. 1942 (unreported). A slip copy of this decision was furnished to the writer by Witness legal counsel Hayden Covington.

37 5 Monroe Leg. Rep. 24 (Pa. C.P. 1943).

38 Miss. Laws 1942 c. 178, MISS. CODE ANN. § 2402 (1942).

39 See Taylor v. Mississippi, 319 U.S. 583 (1943).

40 LA. CRIM. CODE § 1188 (1943).

41 OKLA. STAT. tit. 70, § 1092 (1941).

42 See Carter-Mort v. State, 77 Okla. Crim. 269, 141 P(2d) 122 (1943); Zimmerman v. State, 77 Okla. Crim. 266, 141 P(2d) 123 (1943); Pendley v. State, 77 Okla. Crim. 259, 141 P(2d) 118 (1943).

43 Minn. D.Ct. 1942 (unreported). A slip copy of this decision was furnished to the writer by Witness legal counsel Hayden Covington.

44 155 Kan. 588, 127 P(2d) 518 (1942).

45 16 Wash.(2d) 373, 133 P(2d) 803 (1943).

46 See Section E *infra*.

47 Cox v. New Hampshire; Chaplinsky v. New Hampshire; Hussock v. New York, 312 U.S. 659 (1941); Leiby v. Manchester, 313 U.S. 562 (1941); Bevins v. Prindable, 314 U.S. 573 (1941); Trent v. Hunt, 314 U.S. 573 (1941); Hannan v. City of Haverhill, 314 U.S. 641 (1941); Pascone v. Massachusetts, 314

U.S. 641 (1941). The last six cases above were per curiam memorandum dispositions.

48 316 U.S. 584 (1942). Included in this disposition were Bowden v. Fort Smith and Jobin v. Arizona, *ibid.* Unless otherwise indicated, all future references to the *Opelika* case should be read as applying to all three cases.

49 See, *e.g.*, State *ex rel.* Semansky v. Stark, 196 La. 307, 199 So. 129 (1940).

50 297 U.S. 233 (1936).

51 Giragi v. Moore, 301 U.S. 670 (1937), *affirming* 49 Ariz. 74, 64 P(2d) 819 (1937).

52 See Valentine v. Chrestensen, 316 U.S. 52, 55 (1942).

53 There may have been more. Courts did not always distinguish this sort of license requirement from others. See, *e.g.*, Douglas v. Jeannette, 39 F. Supp. 32 (W.D.Pa. 1941).

54 State v. Meredith, 197 S.C. 351, 15 S.E.(2d) 678 (1941); Thomas v. Atlanta, 59 Ga. App. 520, 1 S.E.(2d) 598 (1939); State *ex rel.* Semansky v. Stark, 196 La. 307, 199 So. 129 (1940); Cincinnati v. Mosier, 61 Ohio App. 81, 22 N.E.(2d) 418 (1939); People v. Gage, 179 Misc. 638, 38 N.Y.S.(2d) 817 (1942).

55 Cincinnati v. Mosier, People v. Gage, both *supra.*

56 City of Blue Island v. Kozul, 379 Ill. 511, 41 N.E.(2d) 515 (1942); State v. Greaves, 112 Vt. 222, 22 Atl.(2d) 497 (1941); McConkey v. City of Fredericksburg, 179 Va. 556, 19 S.E.(2d) 682 (1942); People *ex rel.* Mullaly v. Banks, 168 Misc. 515, 6 N.Y.S.(2d) 41 (Mag. Ct. 1938). In the last case mentioned, no religious element was present; the ruling was made specifically applicable to all forms of pamphleteering.

57 McConkey v. City of Fredericksburg, *supra.*

58 Commonwealth v. Stewart, 137 Pa. Super. 445, 9 Atl.(2d) 179 (1939), *app. permission den., id.* at XXXIII.

59 Commonwealth v. Reid, 144 Pa. Super. 569, 20 Atl.(2d) 841 (1941).

60 Cook v. City of Harrison, 180 Ark. 546, 21 S.W.(2d) 966 (1929).

61 Except as otherwise footnoted, all factual material in this paragraph is drawn from Jones v. Opelika, 316 U.S. at 585–91.

62 Jones v. Opelika, 242 Ala. 549, 7 So.(2d) 503 (1942); Bowden v. Fort Smith, 202 Ark. 614, 151 S.W.(2d) 1000 (1941); State v. Jobin, 58 Ariz. 144, 118 P(2d) 97 (1941).

63 316 U.S. 584 (1942).

64 *Ibid.*

65 Bowden v. Fort Smith, 315 U.S. 782 (1942), *vacating* 314 U.S. 651 (1941); Jones v. Opelika, 316 U.S. 584, 588, *vacating* 315 U.S. 782 (1942) *dismissing writ granted*, 314 U.S. 593 (1941).

66 316 U.S. at 592–93.

67 *Id.* at 596–97.

68 *Id.* at 598.

69 *Ibid.*

70 *Id.* at 608.

71 *Id.* at 621.

72 *Id.* at 598.

73 *Id.* at 623–24.

74 *In Memory of Mr. Justice Rutledge,* 341 U.S. V, VII–VIII.

75 129 F(2d) 24 (D.C. 1942).

76 *Id.* at 38.

77 318 U.S. 748, 796 (1943). These orders, prepared beforehand, were issued within a half-hour after Rutledge took his seat. New York Times, February 16, 1943.

78 319 U.S. 105 (1943).

79 Douglas v. Jeannette, 130 F(2d) 652, 654–55 (3d Cir. 1942).

80 319 U.S. 157 (1943).

81 Douglas v. Jeannette, 130 F(2d) 652 (3d Cir. 1942), *reversing* 39 F. Supp. 32 (W.D.Pa. 1941).

82 Press sources not ordinarily sympathetic to the Witnesses were openly hostile to *Opelika.* See, *e.g.,* Moley, *The Boot Is on the Other Leg,* 19 NEWS-WEEK 68 (June 29, 1942); *Ominous Decision,* 39 TIME 55 (June 22, 1942); Chicago Herald American, September 2, 1942; Michigan Catholic, September 17, 1942; Washington Times-Herald, February 17, 1943. See also Columbus Dispatch, May 5, 1943; Washington Star, May 7, 1943; Jackson Clarion Ledger (Miss.), May 6, 1943; Monessen Daily Independent (Pa.), May 14, 1943.

83 319 U.S. 103 (1943).

84 319 U.S. 141 (1943).

85 Busey v. District of Columbia, 319 U.S. 579 (1943).

86 Murdock v. Pennsylvania, 319 U.S. at 109–10.

87 *Id.* at 111.

88 319 U.S. at 150.

89 *Id.* at 151–52.

90 Justice Frankfurter, whose own dissenting opinion was merely an expansion of Reed's *Opelika* opinion, joined the general reasoning of Jackson's opinion—except, obviously, the part dissenting from *Struthers,* in which Frankfurter had concurred.

91 319 U.S. at 180.

92 *Id.* at 179.

93 *Id.* at 181–82.

CHAPTER TEN

1 W.VA. CODE § 1847 (1943).

2 *Id.,* § 904(4).

3 W.Va. Acts 1941, c. 32, W.VA. CODE § 1851(1) (1943).

4 W.Va. Acts 1923, c. 10, *re-enacted and streamlined,* W.Va. Acts 1941, c. 38, W.VA. CODE § 1734 (1943).

5 Quoted, West Virginia State Board of Education v. Barnette, 319 U.S. 624, 626 n. 1 (1943).

6 Quoted, *ibid.*

7 As an application of § 1734 of the code, this resolution might have been made mandatory on private schools as well. No attempt seems to have been

made to do so, although many private schools required the salute on their own.

[8] Brief for Plaintiffs, p. 6, Barnette v. West Virginia State Board of Education, 47 F. Supp. 251 (S.D.W.Va. 1942).

[9] Charleston Daily Mail, September 16, 1942.

[10] See State v. Mercante (W.Va., Hancock Cy. Cir. Ct. 1942, unreported). A slip copy of this decision was furnished the writer by Hayden Covington, Witness legal counsel.

[11] This incident also led to the firing of a too lenient principal. Letter, ———— (a teacher in the school involved) to W. W. Trent (State Superintendent), February 17, 1942. This letter is in the personal file of Ex-Superintendent Trent, cited hereafter as "Trent File." Names of correspondents have been withheld at Trent's request.

[12] Note 10, *supra.*

[13] State v. Slaughter (W.Va., Upshur Cy. Cir. Ct. 1942, unreported), cited in State v. Mercante, *supra.*

[14] Unless otherwise stated, all facts in this subsection are drawn from a continuing interview with Walter Barnette and Lucy, David and Loellen McClure cited hereafter as "Barnette-McClure interview." The correct spelling, by the way, seems to be *Barnett.* For simplicity, the spelling adopted in the court reports will be used throughout.

[15] Mr. McClure was not a Witness, and played no part in the events discussed here.

[16] David McClure reports that his principal tried, with the best of intentions, to jerk his hand up at the last instant during the ceremony to produce the necessary "compliance."

[17] Meldahl, a non-Witness and a member of the American Legion, proved a strong defender of the Witnesses' rights. It was Meldahl who brought the successful damage suit on behalf of the victims of the "castor oil" outrage at Richwood.

[18] State *ex rel.* Stull v. State Board of Education (W.Va. 1942, unreported), cited in State v. Mercante, *supra.* The number of attempts is drawn from Horace S. Meldahl, personal interview, January 7, 1957.

[19] Hayden Covington, personal interview, February 1, 1957.

[20] The documents mentioned in this paragraph are on file in the Federal Court Building in Charleston, West Virginia. Originally, Moore's order called for retired Circuit Judge Elliot Northcott. Parker's name was substituted when Northcott was unable to appear.

[21] Horace S. Meldahl, personal interview, January 7, 1957. On the spot reporting of these incidents is necessarily one-sided, as this writer was unable to get anything of use from the Attorney General's office. Aside from former Attorney General W. S. Wysong, who had nothing to offer, those who conducted the State Board's defense are either dead or at unknown out-of-state addresses.

[22] Charleston Gazette, September 16, 1942; Charleston Daily Mail, September 16, 1942.

[23] Charleston Gazette, September 16, 1942.

24 *Ibid.* See also Charleston Daily Mail, September 16, 1942.

25 Charleston Gazette, September 16, 1942.

26 Hayden Covington, personal interview, February 1, 1957.

27 Charleston Daily Mail, September 16, 1942.

28 Barnette v. West Virginia State Board of Education, 47 F. Supp. 251, 252 (S.D.W.Va. 1942).

29 Injunction on file in the Federal Court Building, Charleston, West Virginia.

30 A word seems to be in order regarding Judge Parker. Very active and influential in North Carolina Republican politics, he was appointed to the Fourth Circuit Court of Appeals in 1925. 30 WHO'S WHO IN AMERICA 1707 (1958). Parker may be remembered mainly for the fact that in 1930 the Senate refused by a single vote to confirm his appointment to the Supreme Court, because of his alleged ultraconservatism regarding the rights of Negroes and labor unions. See FRANK, MARBLE PALACE 48 (1958) ; PRITCHETT, THE AMERICAN CONSTITUTION 114 (1959).

31 Barnette v. West Virginia State Board of Education, 47 F. Supp. 251, 253 (S.D.W.Va. 1942).

32 *Id.* at 253–54.

33 *Id.* at 254.

34 *Id.* at 255.

35 Even the strongest Supreme Court statement of the rule at that time did not go so far as to demand a serious danger to the survival of the state itself. See Bridges v. California, 314 U.S. 252, 263 (1941).

36 Compare Barnette v. West Virginia State Board of Education, 47 F. Supp. 251, 254, 255 (S.D.W.Va. 1942), with Brief for Plaintiffs, pp. 38–39, 44, Barnette v. West Virginia State Board of Education, *supra.*

37 W. W. Trent, press release, October 7, 1942, Trent File. This action was later ratified by the State Board. State Board of Education Minutes, October 23, 1942.

38 Barnette-McClure interview, note 14, *supra.*

39 Horace S. Meldahl, personal interview, January 7, 1957.

40 Letter, W. W. Trent to Horace S. Meldahl, October 31, 1942, Trent File.

41 Letter, Horace S. Meldahl to —— (Ruddle, W.Va.), November 1, 1942, Trent File.

42 State Board of Education Minutes, October 23, 1942.

43 Horace S. Meldahl, personal interview, January 7, 1957.

44 Wysong denied that his successor could be both Attorney General and a soldier; he eventually had to be ousted by a writ of mandamus. State *ex rel.* Thomas v. Wysong, 125 W.Va. 369, 24 S.E.(2d) 463 (1943).

45 Horace S. Meldahl, personal interview, January 7, 1957.

46 First press mention of the completed appeal came the following morning. New York Times, January 5, 1943; New York Herald-Tribune, January 5, 1943.

47 Unless otherwise stated, all briefs cited in this section were filed in the

Supreme Court in West Virginia State Board of Education v. Barnette, 319 U.S. 624 (1943).

48 As has been stated, the brief filed in the District Court was substantially identical to the one filed in the Supreme Court. There were two differences: (a) the former brief quoted at much greater length from *Gobitis*, and (b) the second section of the Supreme Court brief had no counterpart in the brief filed in the court below.

49 Brief for Appellants, p. 12.

50 Minersville School District v. Gobitis, 310 U.S. 586, 600 (1940), quoted, Brief for Appellants, p. 12.

51 The Brief filed by Covington in the District Court differed radically from his Supreme Court brief in organization, but contained much the same material. The outstanding difference in content was that the District Court brief had a long section devoted to the legal effect of Public Law 623. Other differences will be noted in subsequent footnotes.

52 This appendix was not present in the District Court brief.

53 See Cummings v. Missouri, 71 U.S. (4 Wall.) 277 (1867) ; *Ex parte* Garland, 71 U.S. (4 Wall.) 333 (1867).

54 Brief for Appellees, p. 39.

55 *Id.* at 61.

56 *Id.* at 84.

57 Brief for the Committee on the Bill of Rights of the American Bar Association as Friends of the Court, cited hereafter as "Bill of Rights Committee Brief."

58 New York Times, March 9, 1943.

59 *Report of the Special Committee on the Bill of Rights: Minority Report of George L. Buist,* 68 A.B.A. REP. 258 (1943).

60 *Report of the Special Committee on the Bill of Rights,* 68 A.B.A. REP. 423 (1943) ; *Report of the Board of Governors, March 29, 1943,* 68 A.B.A. REP. 410 (1943).

61 Note 59 *supra.* Buist also objected strenuously to the haste with which the decision to file a brief was made. *Report of the Special Committee on the Bill of Rights: Minority Statement of George L. Buist,* 68 A.B.A. REP. 423, 424–25 (1943).

62 Chafee and Grenville Clark were asked to write the brief. Note 59 *supra.* Clark at that time was no longer a regular member of the Committee; subsequent correspondence confirms the impression that he took no very active part in the *Barnette* case.

63 Bill of Rights Committee Brief, p. 5.

64 *Id.* at 10.

65 261 U.S. 525 (1923).

66 Bill of Rights Committee Brief, p. 19.

67 *Id.* at 25.

68 Letter, William G. Fennell to D.R.M., August 17, 1957.

69 Letter, George K. Gardner to William G. Fennell, February 24, 1943. This

letter, and other correspondence on this point, are preserved in Mr. Fennell's personal file on the Jehovah's Witnesses cases in which he was involved.

[70] See FENNELL, COMPULSORY FLAG SALUTE IN SCHOOLS (1936); Fennell, *The Reconstructed Court and Religious Freedom: The Gobitis Case in Retrospect,* 19 N.Y.U.L.Q. REV. 31 (1941).

[71] Letter, William G. Fennell to D.R.M., August 17, 1957. Moyle eventually won his case, the verdict being affirmed in the amount of $15,000. Moyle v. Franz, 267 App. Div. 423, 46 N.Y.S.(2d) 667, *aff'd,* 293 N.Y. 842, 59 N.E.(2d) 437 (1944).

[72] Brief for American Civil Liberties Union, *Amicus Curiae,* p. 15.

[73] *Id.* at 17.

[74] *Id.* at 18–19.

[75] 312 U.S. 52 (1941).

[76] 11 U.S.L. WEEK 3279 (1943). All description and quotation of the oral argument itself is drawn from this source.

[77] See, *e.g.,* 21 NEWSWEEK 68, 70 (March 22, 1943). The general impression was strongly confirmed by the writer's meeting with Covington.

[78] Hayden Covington, personal interview, February 1, 1957.

[79] 319 U.S. 624 (1943). Unless otherwise stated, all quotations in this section are from the Supreme Court decision in *Barnette.*

[80] *Id.* at 630.

[81] For the sake of logical presentation, some liberties have been taken here with the chronological order of Jackson's arguments.

[82] 319 U.S. at 636.

[83] *Id.* at 637–38.

[84] *Id.* at 638.

[85] *Id.* at 640.

[86] *Id.* at 639.

[87] *Id.* at 640.

[88] *Id.* at 635.

[89] *Id.* at 634.

[90] *Id.* at 632.

[91] *Id.* at 633.

[92] *Ibid.*

[93] *Id.* at 640. See also *id.* at 633.

[94] Jackson's use of the Olander survey cut both ways; how could children be compelled to believe gibberish?

[95] 319 U.S. at 641.

[96] *Id.* at 642.

[97] *Id.* at 643–44.

[98] *Id.* at 644.

[99] *Ibid.*

[100] *Ibid.*

[101] *Id.* at 645.

[102] *Id.* at 645–46.

[103] *Id.* at 646.

104 As with Jackson's opinion, it has been necessary to take certain liberties with the chronological order of Frankfurter's points in the interest of logical presentation here.

105 319 U.S. at 662.

106 *Id.* at 647.

107 *Id.* at 651.

108 *Id.* at 665–66.

109 *Id.* at 648.

110 Subject, of course, to the limitations laid down in his *Gobitis* opinion: the integrity of the political process and the invalidity of state meddling in *religious* matters.

111 319 U.S. at 670. Cf. Frankfurter, *Can the Supreme Court Guarantee Toleration?* (1925), in LAW AND POLITICS 195, 197 (1939). Actually, the quoted passage from Frankfurter's opinion has been softened in the reports. As originally written it read, "It is self-delusive to believe that the liberal spirit can be enforced by judicial invalidation of illiberal legislation." Slip copy of the *Barnette* decision, furnished the writer by Hayden Covington.

112 319 U.S. at 656.

113 *Id.* at 664.

114 *Id.* at 653–54.

115 *Id.* at 652.

116 Jackson's free thought argument cited no cases, and bore little or no relation to Covington's freedom of silence argument.

117 See American Communications Association v. Douds, 339 U.S. 382, 435 (1950).

118 For more orthodox treatments, see, *e.g.*, Graves v. New York *ex rel.* O'Keefe, 306 U.S. 466 (1939); United States v. Darby, 312 U.S. 100 (1941); Smith v. Allwright, 321 U.S. 649 (1944).

119 MASON, HARLAN FISKE STONE 600–601 (1956).

120 *Id.* at 603–4, 606–7, 612–14.

CHAPTER ELEVEN

1 Berge, *Civil Liberties after a Year of War*, 15 OHIO B. ASS'N REPT. 625, 628 (1943); 43 COLUM. L. REV. 134 (1943); 31 GEO. L.J. 85 (1942); 11 GEO. WASH. L. REV. 112 (1942); 22 ORE. L. REV. 198 (1943); 17 TULANE L. REV. 497 (1943).

2 56 HARV. L. REV. 652 (1943).

3 43 COLUM. L. REV. 134 (1943); 11 GEO. WASH. L. REV. 112, 113–14 (1942); 22 ORE. L. REV. 198, 199–200, 202 (1943); 17 TULANE L. REV. 497, 499–500 (1943).

4 31 GEO. L.J. 85, 86–88 (1942); 56 HARV. L. REV. 652, 653–54 (1943).

5 Boudin, *Freedom of Thought and Religious Liberty under the Constitution*, 4 LAW. GUILD REV. 9 (June 1944); 43 COLUM. L. REV. 837 (1943); 32 GEO. L.J. 93 (1943); 42 MICH. L. REV. 319 (1943); 27 MINN. L. REV. 471 (1943); 22 NOTRE DAME LAW. 82 (1946); 17 TEMP. L.Q. 465 (1943); 22 TEX. L. REV. 230 (1944).

[6] 12 Geo. Wash. L. Rev. 72 (1943) ; 6 Georgia B.J. 249 (1944).

[7] 42 Mich. L. Rev. 186 (1943) ; 28 Minn. L. Rev. 133 (1944) ; 92 U. Pa. L. Rev. 103 (1943).

[8] 12 Geo. Wash. L. Rev. 72 (1943).

[9] 6 Georgia B.J. 249 (1944).

[10] Boudin, *supra* note 5; 43 Colum. L. Rev. 837 (1943).

[11] Boudin, *supra* note 5.

[12] 32 Geo. L.J. 93 (1943) ; 22 Tex. L. Rev. 230 (1944).

[13] 42 Mich. L. Rev. 319 (1943) ; 22 Notre Dame Law. 82 (1946) ; 17 Temp. L.Q. 465 (1943).

[14] 27 Minn. L. Rev. 471 (1943).

[15] 3 Jurist 503 (1943).

[16] 27 Minn. L. Rev. 471 (1943) ; 22 Notre Dame Law. 82 (1946) ; 17 Temp. L.Q. 465 (1943).

[17] *Blot Removed*, 41 Time 16 (June 21, 1943).

[18] Lawrence, *Revelations of a "Reconstructed Court,"* 14 United States News 26 (June 25, 1943). Lawrence went on roundly to condemn the Court for its cavalier attitude toward certain other constitutional provisions, notably the Tenth Amendment. *Id.* at 26–27.

[19] Powell, *The Flag-Salute Case*, 109 New Republic 16 (1943).

[20] *Court Upholds Freedom of Conscience*, 60 Christian Century 731 (1943).

[21] Reed, *Religion and the Supreme Court*, 25 Catholic Action 6, 21 (August 1943).

[22] *Comment on the Week*, 70 America 534 (1944).

[23] 32 Geo. L.J. 93 (1943).

[24] 3 Jurist 503 (1943).

[25] Rosenfeld, *Nobody* Has To *Salute United States Flag*, 32 Nations Schools 45 (August 1943).

[26] *Flag Salute Issue Finally Settled*, 107 American School Board Journal 40 (July 1943) ; *The Supreme Court Hands Down an Educationally Significant Decision*, 57 School and Society 696 (1943).

[27] Hodgdon, *School Law Review: Flag Salute Issue Settled*, 19 Clearing House 192 (1944) ; Hodgdon, *School Law Review: Patriotism and Compulsion*, 20 Clearing House 430 (1946) ; Hodgdon, *School Law Review: No More Compulsory Flag Salutes Allowed*, 21 Clearing House 499 (1947) ; *Education and the Flag Salute*, 2 Education for Victory 29 (November 15, 1943) ; *The Flag Salute*, 32 National Education Ass'n Journal 265 (1943).

[28] Hodgdon, *School Law Review: Flag Salute Issue Settled*, 19 Clearing House 192 (1944) ; *Education and the Flag Salute*, 2 Education for Victory 29 (November 15, 1943).

[29] Baltimore Evening Sun, Charleston Daily Mail (W.Va.), Charleston Gazette (W.Va.), Chicago Herald American, Minneapolis Star-Journal, New York Daily Mirror, New York Daily News, New York Post, New York World-Telegram, Philadelphia Inquirer, Pittsburgh Post-Gazette, Pottsville Evening Journal, Pottsville Evening Republican.

[30] Atlanta Constitution, June 15, 1943; Buffalo Evening News, June 16,

1943; Chicago Daily News, June 17, 1943; Christian Science Monitor, June 15, 1943; Cleveland Plain Dealer, June 15, 1943; Detroit Free Press, June 15, 1943; Kansas City Star, June 14, 1943; New York Sun, June 16, 1943; New York Times, June 19, 1943; Philadelphia Evening Bulletin, June 16, 1943; Pittsburgh Press, June 14, 1943; St. Louis Post-Dispatch, June 15, 1943; San Francisco Chronicle, June 15, 1943; Springfield Daily Republican, June 15, 1943.

[31] Brunswick News (Ga.), June 26, 1943; Hartford Courant, June 16, 1943; St. Louis Globe-Democrat, June 15, 1943; Washington Evening Star, June 14, 1943. The editorials in the first two papers were absolutely identical.

[32] Mallon in New York Journal-American, June 15, 1943.

[33] *Ibid.*

[34] Washington Evening Star, June 14, 1943.

[35] St. Louis Globe-Democrat, June 15, 1943.

[36] New York Times, June 19, 1943; Krock in New York Times, June 15, 1943; Lawrence in New York Times, June 20, 1943.

[37] Detroit Free Press, June 15, 1943.

[38] Atlanta Constitution, June 15, 1943; Buffalo Evening News, June 16, 1943; Christian Science Monitor, June 15, 1943; Philadelphia Evening Bulletin, June 16, 1943; San Francisco Chronicle, June 15, 1943.

[39] St. Louis Post-Dispatch, June 15, 1943.

[40] Cleveland Plain Dealer, June 15, 1943; Kansas City Star, June 14, 1943; New York Times, June 19, 1943, Springfield Daily Republican, June 15, 1943.

[41] Atlanta Constitution, June 15, 1943; Detroit Free Press, June 15, 1943; Lawrence in New York Times, June 20, 1943; San Francisco Chronicle, June 15, 1943.

[42] Krock in New York Times, June 15, 1943; Lawrence in New York Times, June 20, 1943; Pittsburgh Press, June 14, 1943.

[43] Lawrence in New York Times, June 20, 1943.

[44] Christian Science Monitor, June 15, 1943; Cleveland Plain Dealer, June 15, 1943.

[45] Chicago Daily News, June 17, 1943; New York Sun, June 16, 1943; St. Louis Post-Dispatch, June 15, 1943.

[46] Detroit Free Press.

[47] Cleveland Plain Dealer, New York Sun.

[48] Kansas City Star, New York Times, Philadelphia Evening Bulletin, San Francisco Chronicle.

[49] 320 U.S. 707 (1943).

[50] 319 U.S. 583 (1943). Discussed, Subsection 3, *infra.*

[51] Walter Gobitis, personal interview, January 20, 1957; Horace S. Meldahl, personal interview, January 7, 1957.

[52] Poulos v. New Hampshire, 345 U.S. 395 (1953). See also Niemotko v. Maryland, 340 U.S. 268 (1951); Saia v. New York, 334 U.S. 558 (1948).

[53] 319 U.S. 583 (1943).

[54] Pendley v. State, 77 Okla. Crim. 259, 141 P(2d) 118 (1943); Zimmerman v. State, 77 Okla. Crim. 266, 141 P(2d) 123 (1943); Carter-Mort v. State, 77

Okla. Crim. 269, 141 P(2d) 122 (1943). See also Partain v. State, 77 Okla. Crim. 270, 141 P(2d) 124 (1943).

55 State v. Davis, 69 S.D. 328, 19 N.W.(2d) 288 (1943).

56 Commonwealth v. Conte, 154 Pa. Super. 112, 35 Atl.(2d) 742 (1944); Commonwealth v. Crowley, 154 Pa. Super. 116, 35 Atl.(2d) 744 (1944). The original conviction in *Conte* had been handed down after the decision in *Barnette*. 154 Pa. Super. 112, 115, 35 Atl.(2d) 742, 743.

57 Morgan v. Civil Service Commission, 131 N.J.L. 441, 36 Atl.(2d) 898 (1944).

58 Zavilla v. School Board, 112 Colo. 183, 147 P(2d) 823 (1944).

59 Cory v. Cory, 70 Cal. App.(2d) 563, 161 P(2d) 385 (1945).

60 N.J. Laws 1944, c. 212, § 1, N.J. REV. STAT. tit. 18, § 14–80 (Supp. 1944).

61 There may be one other exception. A search of recent compilations of Oklahoma's statutes failed to turn up that state's earlier provision calling for flag exercises in the schools.

62 See Pendley v. State, 77 Okla. Crim. 259, 266, 141 P(2d) 118, 121 (1943).

63 MASS. REPT. ATT'Y GEN. 1942–44, at 64; COLO. REPT. ATT'Y GEN. 1945–46, at 130.

64 New York Journal American, June 16, 1943. This recalcitrance presumably was cut short by the statutory revision referred to above.

65 See STROUP, THE JEHOVAH'S WITNESSES 164 (1945). In spite of the copyright date, it is clear in context that this part of Stroup's book, at least, was written before June, 1943.

66 Walter Gobitis, personal interview, January 20, 1957; Dr. T. J. McGurl, telephone interview, January 21, 1957.

67 Department of Justice Circular No. 3356, Supp. No. 3, November 3, 1943. A copy of this circular was furnished the writer by the Civil Rights Section.

68 *Id.* at 2.

69 For a trivial dispute regarding the "under God" revision of the pledge, see Lewis v. Allen, 159 N.Y.S.(2d) 807 (1958).

70 339 U.S. 382 (1950). See also Osman v. Douds, 339 U.S. 846 (1950).

71 The last cases were Taylor v. Mississippi and Mathews v. West Virginia *ex rel.* Hamilton.

72 *Murdock* has had a curiously isolated impact as a precedent, because of its extreme preoccupation with the religious-commercial distinction. It has had no general doctrinal effect in religious freedom litigation, and is considered relevant only to very closely related factual situations. For example, cf. State v. King Colony Ranch, 350 P(2d) 841 (Montana, 1960).

73 321 U.S. 573 (1944).

74 322 U.S. 78 (1944).

75 325 U.S. 561 (1945).

76 The overruling of those precedents in Girouard v. United States, 328 U.S. 61 (1946) does not affect the issue; that decision cast no doubt on the *power* of Congress to exact the challenged condition.

77 321 U.S. 158 (1944).

78 In two cases, each decided by a four to four vote, it was unclear whether

the critical issue was freedom of speech or religion; the settings tend to suggest the former. To the extent that religion was at issue, however, it was religious *expression*, in the sense of *Cantwell*. Gara v. United States, 340 U.S. 857 (1950) ; Parker v. Illinois, 334 U.S. 816 (1948).

[79] Richter v. United States, 340 U.S. 892 (1950).

[80] Warren v. United States, 338 U.S. 947 (1950).

[81] Corporation of Presiding Bishop v. Porterville, 338 U.S. 805 (1949).

[82] Donner v. New York, 342 U.S. 884 (1951). Justices Black and Douglas dissented.

[83] Barlow v. Utah, 324 U.S. 829 (1945) ; Black v. Utah, 350 U.S. 923 (1955).

[84] Illinois *ex rel.* Wallace v. Labrenz, 344 U.S. 824 (1952).

[85] Ohio *ex rel.* Dunham v. Board of Education, 341 U.S. 915 (1951)

[86] Bunn v. North Carolina, 336 U.S. 942 (1949).

[87] Kut v. Board of Unemployment Compensation, 329 U.S. 669 (1946).

[88] Pilgrim Holiness Church Corp. v. Mitchell, 347 U.S. 1013 (1954).

[89] Gospel Army v. Los Angeles, 331 U.S. 543 (1947). Cf. Rescue Army v. Los Angeles, 331 U.S. 549 (1947). While both dismissals came on narrow technical grounds, they showed a marked disinclination to take up the issues involved.

[90] Gara v. United States, 178 F(2d) 38 (6th Cir. 1949) (incitement to resist draft) ; Richter v. United States, 181 F(2d) 591 (9th Cir. 1950) (refusal to register for draft) ; United States v. Kime, 188 F(2d) 677 (7th Cir. 1951) (same) ; Mitchell v. Pilgrim Holiness Church Corp., 210 F(2d) 879 (7th Cir. 1954) (F.L.S.A. and religious corporation) ; United States v. Kissinger, 250 F(2d) 940 (3d Cir. 1958) (crop limitation) ; Holdridge v. United States, 282 F(2d) 302 (8th Cir. 1960) (pacifist invasions of air base). Cf. Warren v. United States, 177 F(2d) 596 (10th Cir. 1949) (incitement to resist draft) ; United States v. Henderson, 180 F(2d) 711 (7th Cir. 1950) (refusal to register).

[91] United States v. Henderson, *supra.*

[92] State *ex rel.* Holcombe v. Armstrong, 39 Wash. (2d) 860, 239 P(2d) 545 (1952).

[93] State *ex rel.* Shoreline School District v. Superior Court, 55 Wash. (2d) 177, 346 P(2d) 999 (1960). The dangers involved in this survey of court rhetoric are well illustrated in the Washington cases. In *Shoreline*, the state court phrased its holding in uncompromising "secular regulation" terms—then cited *Holcombe* as controlling!

[94] People *ex rel.* Shapiro v. Dorin, 199 Misc. 643, 99 N.Y.S.(2d) 830 (Dom.Rel.Ct. 1948), aff'd *sub nom* People v. Donner, 302 N.Y. 857, 100 N.E. (2d) 48 (1948) ; Community Synagogue v. Bates, 1 N.Y.(2d) 445, 136 N.E. (2d) 488 (1956). Cf. People v. Parilli, 1 Misc.(2d) 201, 147 N.Y.S.(2d) 618 (Mag. Ct. 1955) ; People v. Peck, 7 N.Y.(2d) 76, 163 N.E. (2d) 866 (1959) ; Diocese of Rochester v. Planning Board, 1 N.Y.(2d) 508, 136 N.E.(2d) 827 (1956).

[95] Board of Zoning Appeals v. Decatur Company Jehovah's Witnesses, 233 Ind. 83, 117 N.E.(2d) 115 (1954).

96 Harden v. State, 188 Tenn. 17, 216 S.W.(2d) 708 (1948).

97 Congregational Committee (Jehovah's Witnesses) v. City Council, 287 S.W.(2d) 700 (Tex. Civ. App. 1956). But cf. Mitchell v. Davis, 205 S.W.(2d) 812 (1947).

98 Hill v. State, 38 Ala. App. 404, 88 So.(2d) 880, *cert. den.*, 264 Ala. 697, 88 So.(2d) 887 (1956).

99 Gospel Army v. Los Angeles, 27 Cal.(2d) 232, 163 P(2d) 704 (1945); Pencovic v. Pencovic, 45 Cal.(2d) 97, 287 P(2d) 501 (1955); Martin v. Industrial Accident Commission, 147 Cal. App.(2d) 137, 304 P(2d) 828 (1957). Cf. Corporation of Presiding Bishop v. Porterville, 90 Cal. App.(2d) 656, 203 P(2d) 823 (1949).

100 People *ex rel.* Wallace v. Labrenz, 411 Ill. 618, 104 N.E.(2d) 769 (1952); People v. Parker, 397 Ill. 305, 74 N.E.(2d) 523 (1947). Cf. Housing Authority v. Church of God, 401 Ill. 100, 81 N.E.(2d) 500 (1948).

101 Mosier v. Board of Health, 308 Ky. 829, 215 S.W.(2d) 467 (1948). Cf. Lawson v. Commonwealth, 291 Ky. 437, 164 S.W.(2d) 972 (1942).

102 Meyers v. Southwest Region Conference Assoc. Seventh Day Adventists, 230 La. 310, 88 So.(2d) 381 (1956).

103 Craig v. State, 220 Md. 590, 155 Atl.(2d) 684 (1959); Hopkins v. State, 193 Md. 489, 69 Atl.(2d) 456 (1949).

104 State v. Hershberger, 103 Ohio App. 188, 144 N.E.(2d) 693 (1955); State v. Hershberger, 150 N.E.(2d) 671 (Juv. Ct. 1958); State *ex rel.* Dunham v. Board of Education, 154 Ohio St. 469, 96 N.E.(2d) 413 (1951); Kut v. Albers Super Markets, 146 Ohio St. 522, 66 N.E.(2d) 643 (1946).

105 Rice v. Commonwealth, 188 Va. 224, 49 S.E.(2d) 342 (1948); Kirk v. Commonwealth, 186 Va. 839, 44 S.E.(2d) 409 (1947).

106 Commonwealth v. Renfrew, 332 Mass. 492, 126 N.E.(2d) 109 (1955).

107 *In re* State in Interest of Black, 3 Utah(2d) 315, 283 P(2d) 887 (1955); State v. Barlow, 107 Utah 292, 153 P(2d) 647 (1944).

108 State v. City of Tampa, 48 So.(2d) 78 (Fla. 1950).

109 Anderson v. State, 84 Ga. App. 259, 65 S.E.(2d) 848 (1951).

110 Morrison v. State, 252 S.W.(2d) 97 (Mo. 1952).

111 State v. Massey, 229 N.C. 734, 51 S.E.(2d) 179 (1949).

112 Allendale Congregation (Jehovah's Witnesses) v. Grosman, 30 N.J. 273, 152 Atl.(2d) 569 (1959); Sadlock v. Board of Education, 137 N.J.L. 85, 58 Atl.(2d) 218 (1948). But cf. Hoener v. Bertinato, 67 N.J. Super. 517, 171 Atl.(2d) 140 (1961); McBride v. McCorkle, 44 N.J. Super. 468, 130 Atl.(2d) 881 (1957).

113 Appeal of Trustees of Jehovah's Witnesses, 183 Pa. Super. 219, 130 Atl.(2d) 240 (1957); Commonwealth v. Bey, 166 Pa. Super. 136, 70 Atl.(2d) 693 (1950); Commonwealth v. Beiler, 168 Pa. Super. 462, 79 Atl.(2d) 134 (1951); Commonwealth v. Petersheim, 14 Som. 329 (Pa. Q. Sess. 1949).

114 Congregational Committee (Jehovah's Witnesses) v. City Council, 287 S.W.(2d) 700 (Tex. Civ. App. 1956) (city may not exclude churches from residential areas); Community Synagogue v. Bates, 1 N.Y.(2d) 445, 136 N.E.(2d) 488 (1956) (same); State v. City of Tampa, 48 So.(2d) 78 (Fla.

1950) (same); Board of Zoning Appeals v. Decatur Company Jehovah's Witnesses, 233 Ind. 83, 117 N.E.(2d) 115 (1954) (same; off-street parking requirement held excessive). But cf. Corporation of Presiding Bishop v. Porterville, 90 Cal. App.(2d) 656, 203 P(2d) 823 (1949) (residential exclusion upheld); Allendale Congregation (Jehovah's Witnesses) v. Grosman, 30 N.J. 273, 152 Atl.(2d) 569 (1959) (off-street parking requirement upheld); Appeal of Trustees of Jehovah's Witnesses, 183 Pa. Super. 219, 130 Atl.(2d) 240 (1957) (same).

[115] Commonwealth v. Petersheim, 14 Som. 429 (Pa. Q. Sess. 1949). But cf. Commonwealth v. Bey, 166 Pa. Super. 136, 70 Atl.(2d) 693 (1950); Commonwealth v. Beiler, 168 Pa. Super. 462, 79 Atl.(2d) 134 (1951).

[116] 366 U.S. 599 (1961).

[117] 366 U.S. 617 (1961). Companion cases not involving a religious freedom challenge were Two Guys From Harrison-Allentown v. McGinley, 366 U.S. 582 (1961); McGowan v. Maryland, 366 U.S. 420 (1961).

[118] Braunfeld v. Brown, 366 U.S. 599, 606 (1961).

[119] *Id.* at 608.

[120] *Id.* at 605.

[121] *Id.* at 606.

[122] *Id.* at 605.

[123] *Id.* at 614.

[124] McGowan v. Maryland, 366 U.S. 420, 462 (1961). Justice Frankfurter's concurring opinion applied to all four cases.

[125] This is at least in part a reflection of the general decline of that test in recent years. See Yates v. United States, 355 U.S. 66 (1957).

[126] See Vose, *Litigation as a Form of Pressure Group Activity*, 319 ANNALS OF THE ACADEMY OF POLITICAL AND SOCIAL SCIENCE 20 (Sept. 1958).

[127] *E.g.*, State v. Marble, 72 Ohio St. 21, 73 N.E. 1063 (1905). The fact that all states now make special provision for Christian Scientists and similar bona fide faith-healers in no way alters the basic constitutional issue.

INDEX

Ade, Lester K., 93
Adkins v. Children's Hospital, 221
American Bar Association Committee on the Bill of Rights. *See* Bill of Rights Committee, A.B.A.
American Civil Liberties Union: survey of flag laws, 5; early involvement in flag-salute controversy, 11–14 *passim;* participation in state flag-salute litigation, 57–61, 64, 66, 68–75 *passim;* legal strategy in flag cases, 79–80; brief in *Gobitis* (Cir. Ct.), 85, 111; brief in *Gobitis* (Sup. Ct.), 118, 123–26; efforts to stem anti-Witness persecution, 163–64, 177; and Justice Department, 177, 179; brief in license tax cases, 203; brief in *Barnette* (Sup. Ct.), 215, 222–24
American Communications Assoc. v. Douds, 243
American Legion: general promotion of flag respect, 6; and salute expulsions, 63, 64, 77; eventual support of Minersville school board stand, 84, 93, 116; involvement in anti-Witness persecution, 165, 166, 175–76, 184, 240; sponsorship of Public Law 623, 188; brief in *Barnette* (Sup. Ct.), 216–17, 220
American Legion Auxiliary, 7
American Newspaper Publishers Association, 203
Association of Patriotic Societies of Schuylkill County, 116

Baldwin, Roger N., 57, 59
Barnette v. West Virginia State Board of Education, 211–14, 236
Beeler v. Smith, 183
Belief, freedom of: treatment in *Cantwell,* 133; in *Gobitis* (Sup. Ct.),

145; in *Barnette* (Sup. Ct.), 228–29, 232; since *Barnette,* 244
Bellamy, Francis, 2
Berge, Wendell, 179, 188, 297 n. 3
Bevins v. Prindable, 184
Biggs, John, Jr., 111–12
Bill of Rights Committee, A.B.A.: brief in *Johnson v. Deerfield* (Sup. Ct.), 61; brief in *Gobitis* (Sup. Ct.), 118, 126–31, 140, 144, 145, 147, 217–21 *passim;* brief in *Barnette* (Sup. Ct.), 215, 220–22, 227, 234
Bird, Ira, 78
Black, Hugo L., 133, 134, 199–201, 206, 207, 225, 229, 244
Bodine, Judge (N.J. Sup. Ct.), 65, 192
Bolling v. Superior Court, 193–94, 195, 222
Bowden v. Fort Smith, 198
Brandeis, Louis D., 48, 53, 54
Braunfeld v. Brown, 246–47
Brennan, William, 246–47
Bricker, John W., 74
Brind, Charles A., 71
Britchey, Jerome M., 111, 123
Brodhead, George M., 87, 118
Brown, Justice (Fla. Sup. Ct.), 73
Brown v. Skustad, 193, 222
Bryan, A. C., Dr., 175–76
Buford, Justice (Fla. Sup. Ct.), 73
Buist, George L., 220
Busey v. District of Columbia, 202–3, 204
Butler, Pierce, 47
Byrnes, James F., 202

Campbell, Judge William (Wash. Juv. Ct.), 74
Cantwell v. Connecticut, 38–39, 132–33, 152, 159
Cardozo, Benjamin, 48

Chafee, Zechariah, 220–22
Chaillaux, Homer, 176
Chaplinsky v. New Hampshire, 184, 207, 252
Christian Science, 41
Church of God, 14–15
Church of Jesus Christ of Latter Day Saints, 45
Civil Rights Section, U.S. Justice Department: opposition to compulsory flag salute, 150, 181, 189; background, 177; prosecution of civil rights violations, 178–79, 180–81, 186, 297 nn. 71, 73, 74; difficulties within Justice Department, 178–80; mediation on behalf of Jehovah's Witnesses, 179–81, 186; memorandums to U.S. attorneys on religious freedom, 180–81, 189, 242–43
Clark, Grenville, 123, 126–31, 220
Clark, William S., 111–14, 213
"Clear and present danger" test: history, 52–54; relevance to religious freedom, 54–55, 115, 247, 252; invoked as religious freedom standard in *Barnette* litigation, 213, 218, 223, 229
Combs, W. A., 68–69
Committee on the Bill of Rights. *See* Bill of Rights Committee, A.B.A.
Committee for Industrial Organization v. Hague, 112
Commonwealth v. Bortlik, 192
Commonwealth v. Johnson, 61–62, 80, 123, 190, 222
Commonwealth v. Lesher, 43, 48–49, 49, 91, 108, 213
Commonwealth v. Merle, 192
Commonwealth v. Nemchik, 189, 192, 222
Consolation, 23
Covington, Hayden C.: Witness legal counsel, 121; participation in *Gobitis* (Sup. Ct.), 121; brief in license tax cases, 203; handling of Witness case in *Barnette* (D. Ct.), 211, 212, 214; brief and argument in *Barnette* (Sup. Ct.), 215, 217–20, 224
Cox v. New Hampshire, 183, 196
Crane, Judge (N.Y. Ct. App.), 71

Daughters of the American Revolution, 7, 60

Davis v. Beason, 113
Defenders of the Faith, 24, 25, 156
DeMolay, Order of, 56–57
Dever, Paul A., 56–57
Douglas, William O., 133, 199–201, 204–5, 225, 229, 243, 244, 247
Douglas v. Jeannette, 203, 204, 205–6
Dred Scott v. Sanford, 224
Due process of law, substantive: general, 35–36; right of parental control, 37–38

Eastus, Clyde, 180
Education laws: general, 1–2; flag respect, 3–4; Pennsylvania, 76; West Virginia, 208
Elijah Voice Society, 13
Elks, Massachusetts Society of, 8
Epworth League, 47
Estep v. Borough of Canonsburg, 77–78, 88, 117, 119

Felix, Father Richard, 156
Fennell, William G., 61, 66, 111, 123, 150–51, 152, 222
Ferriter v. Tyler, 44, 50, 252
First Amendment. *See* Belief, freedom of; Religion, freedom of; Speech, freedom of
Flag desecration, laws prohibiting, 8
Flag respect, required instruction in, 4
Flag-salute ceremony: history, 2–3; groups supporting, 2, 6–8, 93, 107, 116; similarity of salute to Nazi gesture, 3, 123; called for by statute, 3–6; general incidence, 5; alternative forms, 7, 77, 189; criticized as educational device, 9–10; school expulsions for refusal, 11–14 *passim*, 56–76 *passim*, 83, 187, 209, 210, 242; school law prosecutions arising out of refusal, 11–12, 60, 61, 64, 70, 77, 190, 209, 210, 241; delinquency prosecutions against parents of non-saluters, 13–14, 191–92, 241; lenient handling of refusals, 13, 15–16, 57, 64, 67, 75–76, 79, 93, 106, 189, 210; attempts to remove non-saluting children from parents, 13–14, 60, 61–62, 69–70, 74, 190–92, 241; dismissal of teachers for refusal, 15, 57, 77; state attorney general opinions on legality of com-

pulsion, 56–57, 72, 75, 77, 188, 189, 242; economic reprisals against non-saluters, 57, 62, 167, 241; miscellaneous legal action against non-saluters, 75, 192–93, 240–41; varying official attitudes in Pennsylvania toward refusals, 76–77, 93, 106; as pretext for persecution, 164, 166, 167, 172, 173, 176, 182; as condition of canvassing permit, 182; spread of compulsion after *Gobitis*, 187–88, 208–9; and Public Law 623, 188–90; decline of compulsion after *Barnette* decision, 241–43. *See also* Jehovah's Witnesses and flag salute

Follett v. McCormick, 244

Fourteenth Amendment. *See* Belief, freedom of; Due process of law; Religion, freedom of; Speech, freedom of

Fraenkel, Osmond K., 123, 203, 222

Frankfurter, Felix, 131–32, 136–43, 225, 230–33, 247

Franz, Frederick W., 97, 217

Frey, Alexander H., 85, 123

Gabrielli v. Knickerbocker, 67–68, 109, 110, 117, 119

Gallagher v. Crown Kosher Super Market, 246, 247

Gardner, George K., 62, 123–26, 131–32, 222

Gibson, Justice (Pa. Sup. Ct. ca. 1828), 48, 49

Gitlow v. New York, 53, 218

Gobitis, Lillian, 82, 83, 84, 97, 118, 242

Gobitis, Walter, 81–82, 83, 84, 94, 95–96, 118, 249

Gobitis, William, 82, 83, 84, 96–97, 118, 242

Gobitis v. Minersville School District: on motion to dismiss, 85–93, 148–49, 213, 215; final decision, 95–106, 148–49, 213, 215

Gold, James (Mayor, Monessen, Pa.), 78

Golden Age, The, 23, 25

Grand Army of the Republic Federation, 93

Graves, Frank P., 15

"Green River" ordinances, 182

Greer, J. P., 72

Gregg, Ralph B., 216

Grosjean v. American Press Co., 196, 197

Hague v. C.I.O., 118, 126, 128, 130, 145, 221

Hale, Richard W., 59

Halter v. Nebraska, 126

Hamilton v. Regents, 47–48, 64, 65, 66, 88, 90, 92, 102, 108, 110, 111, 114, 119, 124, 130, 134, 139, 225

Hardwicke v. Board of School Trustees, 44–45, 49, 51, 89, 110

Harlan, John M., 247

Hays, Arthur Garfield, 70–71, 111, 123, 177, 222, 275 n. 127

Henderson, Joseph W., 85, 87–88, 94–101 *passim*, 105–10 *passim*, 118–21, 131

Hering v. Board of Education, 64–66, 68, 69, 84, 101, 102, 108, 110, 114, 117, 119, 133, 192

Hessler, Charles E., 100

Hines v. Davidowicz, 224

Holmes, Oliver Wendell, Jr., 52, 53, 54

Holy Trinity Church v. U.S., 46, 110, 122, 218

Hughes, Charles Evans, 50, 134–35

Improved Order of Red Men, 93, 107

In re Jones, 191, 222

Isserman, Abraham J., 64, 65, 89, 90

Jackson, Robert H., 179, 205–6, 225–29, 243, 297 n. 74

Jehovah's Witnesses: origins, 17; doctrines, 17–20, 29, 32–33, 260 n. 10; influence of Rutherford on, 17, 19, 21–22; apocalyptic orientation, 18; influence of Russell on, 18–19, 21; missionary bent, 19–20; proselytization methods, 19–20, 22–26; organizational characteristics, 20–22; finances, 23; anti-Catholicism, 23, 25, 34; public relations before 1940, 25–26; and military service, 29–30; view of atonement, 260 n. 10

Jehovah's Witnesses and flag salute: first entry into flag-salute controversy, 30; doctrinal position, 32–33; Kingdom Schools for expelled children, 56, 70, 76, 78; deviations from official Witness line, 57, 79, 214;

legal strategy in flag-salute litigation, 67, 79, 84–85, 211. *See also* Flag-salute ceremony

Jehovah's Witnesses, legal troubles: license ordinances, 26–27, 166, 176, 182–83, 193–206, 244; group libel laws, 26, 28, 183–84; sabbath laws, 26, 184; breach of peace prosecutions, 26, 184–85; legal office strategy regarding, 27–28, 79; prohibition of pamphleteering, 27–28, 166, 185, 240; extra-legal Witness countermeasures, 28; sedition and related charges, 166–67, 183, 192–93, 240–41; "Green River" ordinances, 182; child labor laws, 184, 244. *See also* Persecution of Jehovah's Witnesses

Jehovites, 12–13, 16

Jobin v. Arizona, 198

Johnson, J. Harry, 75

Johnson v. Deerfield, 60–61, 114, 117, 119, 126, 133

Jones, Verna S., 84

Jones v. Opelika, 192, 195–202, 203, 204, 211, 212, 213, 215, 225

Junior Order United American Mechanics, 8

Justice, U.S. Department of: file on Jehovah's Witnesses, 168, 187, 242; split over anti-Witness persecution, 179, 180, 297 n. 73. *See also* Civil Rights Section, U.S. Justice Department

Kalodner, Harry E., 111, 112

Kelly, Raymond J., 176

Kennedy v. Moscow, 182, 207, 219, 232, 252

Kingdom Schools, 56, 70, 76, 78, 210

Knorr, Nathan Homer, 17

Ku Klux Klan, 7, 63

Landis, Cary D., 72

Lee, Howard B., 222

Lehman, Judge (N.Y. Ct. App.), 71–72, 192

Leoles v. Landers, 63–64, 66, 68, 84, 101, 102, 108, 110, 114, 117, 119, 133

Lipsig, James, 60

Lovell v. Griffin, 27, 28, 182, 195, 197

Lummus, Henry T., 32, 58

Lusky, Louis, 126

McCaughey, Harry M., 85, 89, 121

McClure, Lucy B., 210, 211, 214

McGurl, John B., 82, 83, 85, 87, 94, 118

McGurl, Dr. Thomas J., 82

McKee v. State, 184

McReynolds, James C., 37, 133, 134, 286 n. 59

Margiotti, Charles A., 77, 83

Maris, Albert B., 91–107 *passim*, 112, 213

Martin v. Struthers, 203–4, 204–5, 207, 247

Massachusetts Civil Liberties Committee, 57

Mathews v. West Virginia ex rel Hamilton, 185, 240

Matter of Latrecchia, 192, 222

Matter of Reed, 190–91

Meldahl, Horace S., 210–11, 214, 303 n. 17

Mennonites, 11–12

Methodist Episcopal Church, 47

Metzger, Erma, 84, 100

Minersville, Pa., 81

Minersville School Board, 82, 83, 85, 106–7, 116, 189–90, 242

Minersville School District v. Gobitis, Cir. Ct., 107–15, 144, 148–49, 213, 215, 218; Sup. Ct., 56, 118–46, 148–62 *passim*, 163, 165, 167, 168, 182, 187–95 *passim*, 201–7 *passim*, 208, 211–35 *passim*, 236–51 *passim*

Moore, Ben, 212

Morgan, Daniel, 66, 241

Morgan, Joy Elmer, 93

Mormons, 45

Morrill Act of 1862, 47

Mount, Thomas F., 118

Moyle, Olin R., Witness legal counsel, 27; participation in early flag-salute litigation, 32, 57, 60–61, 64, 69, 71, 73; co-operation with ACLU, 57–73 *passim*, 79–80, 85, 121, 131; opposition to suit in *Gabrielli* case, 67; legal strategy in flag-salute cases, 67, 79–80, 84; participation in *Gobitis* (D. Ct.), 84–85, 89–91, 94–102 *passim*; brief in *Gobitis* (Cir. Ct.), 109–11; dismissed as legal counsel, 121; libel suit against Watchtower Society, 222, 306 n. 71

Murdock v. Pennsylvania, 203, 204, 205, 207, 227, 237, 243, 244
Murphy, Frank: background, 134, 177, 286 n. 55; opinions in license tax cases, 199–202, 204–5, 206; change of heart on flag-salute issue, 201–2, 206–7, 287 n. 97; concurrence in *Barnette* (S. Ct.), 225, 229–30; votes in later religious freedom cases, 244.
Myers, Gary Cleveland, 10

Nagle, Mrs. Mildred, 75
National Flag Conferences, 1923 and 1924, 2
Nazism, 3, 30, 123, 154
Nicholls v. Lynn, 57–59, 61, 63, 84, 117
Northern California Civil Liberties Union, 67

O'Connor, Herbert, 74
Olson, Governor (Calif.), 68
Order of Independent Americans, 93, 107

Parental control, right of, 37–38
Parker, John J., 212, 213–14, 304 n. 30
Partlow, Ira J., 211, 212, 214
Patriotic Order of the Sons of America, 93, 107
Patriotic organizations: general indorsement of flag ceremony, 5–8; financial backing of Minersville school board in *Gobitis*, 93, 107, 116
Patriotism, 1–2
People v. Chiafreddo, 191
People ex rel Fish v. Sandstrom, 70–72, 117, 190, 192
"Persecution index," 173–75
Persecution of Jehovah's Witnesses: economic discrimination, 57, 62, 167; arbitrary arrest, 78, 164, 165, 168, 170–71; as response to *Gobitis*, 150, 153, 155, 163, 172; trends in, 163, 164, 168–73, 186; violence, 163, 164–66, 168–69, 184, 185; misapplication of penal statutes, 166, 168, 170–71, 183–85, 192–93, 240–41; statistics on, 163–64, 168, 169–71, 174; official involvement in, 164, 165, 166, 181, 183, 184, 185; Witness behavior as contributing to, 164, 167, 185; effect of World War II on, 164, 172; involvement of American Legion in, 165, 166, 175–76, 184; pre-eminence of Texas and Oklahoma, 173; a small-town phenomenon, 173–75; alleged involvement of Catholic Church, 176; involvement of Veterans of Foreign Wars in, 176; Civil Rights Section countermeasures against, 177–81, 186; after *Barnette*, 240–41. *See also* Jehovah's Witnesses and flag salute; Jehovah's Witnesses, legal troubles
Pierce v. Society of Sisters, 37, 38, 55, 58, 65, 90, 123, 136, 157, 219
Pledge of allegiance. *See* Flag-salute ceremony
Plummer, Judge (Cal. App.), 67
Pottsville Business College, 84, 101
Press comment: on *Gobitis* (D. Ct. and Cir. Ct.), 93, 106, 148–49; on state flag-salute decisions, 148–49; on *Gobitis* (Sup. Ct.), 149–62; on *Barnette* (D. Ct.), 236; on *Barnette* (Sup. Ct.), 236–40; on *Opelika*, 301 n. 82
Prince v. Massachusetts, 244, 247
Public Law 623, 188–89, 193, 211, 213, 223–24

Reed, Stanley, 133, 134, 198–99, 225
Reel, A. Frank, 57–59
Reid v. Brookville, 182, 203, 207, 219
Religion, freedom of: protected by Fourteenth Amendment, 38–39, 47; constitutional provisions, 39–41; precedents, 41–50; traditional standards governing, 48–52; present standards governing, 247–48
Religion, freedom of, interest-weighing: historical role misconceived, 48–49; rejected in old religious freedom decisions, 49–52; urged in Bill of Rights Committee brief in *Gobitis* (Sup. Ct.), 127–29; alternative ground in Stone's *Gobitis* dissent, 144–45, 146; treatment in press commentary, 150, 152–53, 156, 160–61, 236; treatment in license tax cases, 204–5; advanced in Witness and *amicus* briefs in *Barnette* (Sup. Ct.), 218, 220–21, 223; invoked in *Barnette* (Sup. Ct.), concurrence, 229–30, 233; post-*Bar-*

nette judicial treatment, 244, 245–47; present status, 247–48; evaluated, 252–53

Religion, freedom of, the "secular regulation" rule: long-established judicial rule of decision in religious freedom cases, 48–52, 55; defined, 51; evaluated, 51–52, 251–52; uneven treatment in early flag-salute decisions, 59, 63, 65, 68, 71–72, 73, 78; appeal to, rejected by lower courts in *Gobitis*, 93, 115; treatment in *Gobitis* (Sup. Ct.) briefs, 119, 126, 127–28; reaffirmed by *Gobitis* (Sup. Ct.), 139; treatment in press commentary, 149–52, 157, 158–59, 236, 237, 239; treatment in license tax cases, 197, 202–7 *passim*; reluctant application by state courts after *Gobitis*, 195; rejected in *Barnette* (D. Ct.), 213; treatment in *Barnette* (Sup. Ct.) briefs, 215, 218, 220–21; rejected by *Barnette* (Sup. Ct.) concurrences, 229–30; invoked in Frankfurter's *Barnette* dissent, 232; post-*Barnette* judicial treatment, 243–47, 311 n. 93; now defunct, 247

Re Summers, 244

Reynolds v. Rayborn, 69–70, 191

Reynolds v. U.S., 45, 50, 89, 119, 124, 139

Roberts, James P., 57–59

Roberts, Owen J., 133, 134, 225

Roman Catholic Church, 23–25, 176

Rotnem, Victor, 150, 177, 179, 189

Roudabush, Charles E.: identified, 82; role in Gobitis expulsions, 82–83; strong feelings on salute issue, 82, 83, 93, 97–99, 106–7; dealings with patriotic organizations, 93, 107, 116; reaction to adverse court proceedings, 93, 106–7, 112, 116; court testimony in *Gobitis* (D. Ct.), 97–99, 100

Rugg, Chief Justice (Mass. Sup. Ct.), 59

Russell, Chief Justice (Ga. Sup. Ct.), 63

Russell, Charles Taze, 13, 17, 18–19

Rutherford, Joseph F. ("Judge"): remolding of Witness movement under, 17, 19, 21–22; radio speech indorsing Witness flag-salute refusals, 31, 32–33, 56, 58, 82; influence on Moyle's flag-salute briefs, 64–65, 110; authorization of *Gabrielli* litigation, 67; brief in *Sandstrom*, 71; dismissal of Moyle, 121; non-co-operation with outside groups, 121; brief in *Gobitis* (Sup. Ct.), 121–23; oral argument in *Gobitis* (Sup. Ct.), 131

Rutledge, Wiley, 202–3, 204–5, 207, 215, 244

Salvation Army, 41

Schenck v. U.S., 52–53, 53

Schneider v. Irvington, 27–28, 53–54, 54, 128, 133, 141, 145, 195, 197, 221

Schweinhaut, Harry A., 177, 179

Seawell, Justice (Cal. Sup. Ct.), 67–68

Seventh Day Adventists, General Conference of, 203

Shields, Peter J., 67

Shinn v. Barrow, 68–69, 80

Sons of the American Revolution, 8

Speech, freedom of: history, 52–54; relevance to religious freedom issues, 54–55, 115, 213, 218, 223, 229; invoked as independent ground in flag-salute litigation, 89–90, 218–19; treatment in *Gobitis* (Sup. Ct.), 141

Spiritualist Church, 41

State ex rel Bleich v. Board of Education, 72–73

State v. Davis, 191

State v. DeLaney, 41, 49

State v. Lefebvre, 190, 222

State v. Mercante, 209

State v. Morris, 42, 49

State v. Smith, 193, 195, 222

Stewart, Potter, 246–47

Stone, Harlan F.: *Carolene Products* opinion, 36, 55, 128, 142, 143, 145–46; background, 143–44; dissent in *Gobitis* (Sup. Ct.), 144–46; dissent in *Opelika*, 199–201

Stone v. Stone, 191

Stromberg v. California, 54, 65, 90, 219

Strong, Dr. Sidney, 14

Stull, Paul, 210, 211, 214

Supreme Court, United States: direct appeal to, 60, 211; Justices, 133–34; internal proceedings, 134–35; "political" role, 249–51

Swift, John E., 62

Taylor v. Mississippi, 240–41

Terrell, Judge (Fla. Sup. Ct.), 73

Tremain, Russell, 13–14

Trent, W. W., 211–14

Trent v. Hunt, 183, 184, 207

United States attorneys, 178–81, 188–90, 242–43

United States v. Ballard, 244

United States v. Carolene Products Co., 36–37, 55, 128, 142, 145, 219, 223

United States v. Macintosh, 46–47, 48, 50, 51, 59, 88, 119, 134, 143, 244

United States v. Schwimmer, 46, 143, 244

Upham, James B., 2

Veterans of Foreign Wars, 6, 63, 176

Warren, Earl, 246

Wasliewski, Edmund, 82, 83

Watch Tower Bible and Tract Society, 21–22

Watchtower, 23, 25

Watchtower Bible and Tract Society, Inc., 21

Watkins, Harry E., 212

Watson v. Jones, 48, 110

West Virginia State Board of Education, 208–9, 211, 214, 235

West Virginia State Board of Education v. Barnette, 207, 215–35, 236–53 *passim*

Women's Patriotic Conference on National Defense, 7

Wooddell, W. Holt, 214, 215–16, 224

Woodworth, C. W., 25

Wysong, W. S., 211, 214

Youth's Companion, 2

Date

NOV 1 75

Lincoln Christian College

Demco 38-297